8 A-2	(a) Estimated uncollectible accounts, $38,880
8 A-3	(a) Estimated uncollectible accounts, $11,540
8 A-4	(b) Total estimated uncollectible accounts, $52,500
8 A-5	(a) Feb. 2, cash collected from note, $42,653
8 A-6	(c) Total current assets, $373,195
8 A-7	(c) One-year interest charge originally included in face amount, $25,500
8 B-1	(a) (2) Number of days' sales uncollected, Advantec, 81
8 B-2	(a) Estimated uncollectible accounts, $27,180
8 B-3	(b) Net accounts receivable, Jan. 31, $461,280
8 B-4	(a) Estimated uncollectible accounts, $6,740
8 B-5	(a) Feb. 2, cash collected from note, $30,688
8 B-6	(c) Total current assets, $741,232
8 B-7	(c) One-year interest charge originally included in face amount, $13,200
9-1	No key figure
9-2	(a) May 31 inventory, $280
9-3	(a) Sept. 30 inventory balance, $3,450
9-4	(b) (4) Jan. 15 LIFO inventory, $18,500
9-5	(a) (2) FIFO cost of goods sold, $18,100
9-6	(a) (3) LIFO cost of goods sold, $18,700
9-7	(a) (1) Average cost shrinkage loss, $567
9-8	(a) (2) LIFO cost of goods sold, $303,480
9-9	(b) (3) LIFO cost of goods sold, $7,420
9-10	(a) Gross profit rate, 1995, 43%
9-11	(b) (3) Gross profit, $264,144
9-12	(b) (1) Turnover rate, FIFO, 2.4 times
10 A-1	(c) Total cost of equipment, $91,200
10 A-2	Depreciation for 1997, (b) $36,000; (c) $33,750
10 A-3	(a) Depreciation for 1998, (3) $15,000
10 A-4	(c) Depreciation expense for 1996, $134,175
10 A-5	Gain on disposal of moving van, $4,000
10 A-6	No key figure
10 A-7	No key figure
10 A-8	(b) (1) Book value, $17,000
10 B-1	(a) Total cost of equipment, $220,720
10 B-2	Depreciation for 1997, (b) $65,600; (c) $64,800
10 B-3	Depreciation for 1995, (b) $15,000
10 B-4	(a) Accumulated depreciation: Machine C, $36,000
10 B-5	Gain on disposal of truck, $1,000
10 B-6	No key figure
10 B-7	No key figure
10 B-8	(b) (1) Book value, $6,800
CP-3	(a) Total assets: Alpine, $494,400; Nordic, $496,200; (b) revised net income: Alpine, $225,000
11-1	No key figure
11-2	No key figure
11-3	(a) Total current liabilities, $375,403

11-4	(b) Interest expense on Western Bank note, $3,200
11-5	(b) Interest expense on National Bank note, $4,704
11-6	(c) Total current liabilities, $337,186.50
11-7	(c) Unpaid balance, $8,331
11-8	(c) Jan. 1, 1997, unpaid balance, $539,370
11-9	(b) Total payroll cost, $27,538
11-10	(b) (4) Employer's total payroll costs, $251,854
11-11	(c) Total payroll cost, $15,089
12-1	No key figure
12-2	No key figure
12-3	No key figure
12-4	No key figure
12-5	No key figure
12-6	(a) Profit under percentage-of-completion, 1995, $3,000,000
12-7	(a) (1) Gross profit, $184,000
12-8	No key figure
12-9	No key figure
13 A-1	(b) Total assets, $220,800
13 A-2	(a) Net income, $54,000; (c) total assets, $217,720
13 A-3	(a) (4) Pascal's share, $28,000
13 A-4	(c) Stein's share, $26,100
13 A-5	(c) Bonus to Ritter, $30,000
13 A-6	(c) Bonus to Kim, $60,000
13 A-7	(a) Cash to Nix, $11,600
13 B-1	(b) Total assets, $277,800
13 B-2	(a) Net income, $54,500; (c) total assets, $175,500
13 B-3	(a) (2) Martin's share, $58,000
13 B-4	(a) Conrad's share, $102,600
13 B-5	(c) Bonus to Lee, $70,000
13 B-6	(d) Debit to Spence, Capital, $22,500
13 B-7	(b) Cash payment by Merit, $18,000
14 A-1	(b) Dec. 31, 1996, retained earnings, $1,937,000
14 A-2	(a) Total shareholders' equity, $15,370,000
14 A-3	Total shareholders' equity, $2,063,000
14 A-4	(b) Total shareholders' equity, $1,150,960
14 A-5	(b) Total assets, $1,512,100
14 A-6	(e) Total contributed capital, $11,800,000
14 B-1	(b) Dec. 31, 1996, retained earnings, $1,490,000
14 B-2	(a) Total shareholders' equity, $3,405,000
14 B-3	Total shareholders' equity, $2,112,000
14 B-4	(d) Total shareholders' equity, $890,200
14 B-5	(b) Total assets, $1,352,950
14 B-6	(f) Total contributed capital, $9,660,000
15 A-1	(a) Income before extraordinary items, $13,620,000
15 A-2	(a) Cumulative effect, $91,000

(continued on inside back cover)

EX LIBRIS

Name

Seventh Canadian Edition

ACCOUNTING:
The Basis for Business Decisions

Volume 2

Financial Accounting

Seventh Canadian Edition

ACCOUNTING:
The Basis for Business Decisions

Volume 2

Financial Accounting

ROBERT F. MEIGS, D.B.A.
San Diego State University

WALTER B. MEIGS, Ph.D., C.P.A.
University of Southern California

WAI P. LAM, Ph.D., F.C.A.
University of Windsor

McGraw-Hill Ryerson Limited

Toronto Montreal New York Auckland Bogotá
Caracas Lisbon London Madrid Mexico Milan
New Delhi Paris San Juan Singapore Sydney Tokyo

ACCOUNTING: THE BASIS FOR BUSINESS DECISIONS
Seventh Canadian Edition
Volume 2 / Financial Accounting

ISBN: 0-07-551795-7

1 2 3 4 5 6 7 8 9 0   RRD   4 3 2 1 0 9 8 7 6 5

Printed and bound in the United States of America by R. R. Donnelley (Canada) Limited

Care has been taken to trace ownership of copyright material contained in this text. The publishers will gladly take any information that will enable them to rectify any reference or credit in subsequent editions.

Sponsoring Editor: Kelly Smyth

Production Editor: Gail Marsden

Cover Design: Dianna Little

Cover Photograph: © G. K. and Vikki Hart/The Image Bank

Printing & Binding: R. R. Donnelley (Canada) Limited

Canadian Cataloguing in Publication Data

Meigs, Robert F.
    Accounting: the basis for business decisions

7th Canadian ed.
Includes index.
Contents: v. 1–2. Financial accounting—v. 3.
Managerial accounting.
ISBN 0-07-551660-8 (v. 1) ISBN 0-07-551795-7 (v. 2)
ISBN 0-07-551659-4 (v. 3)

1. Accounting. I. Meigs, Walter B., date–   .
II. Lam, Wai P., date–   .   III. Title.

HF5635.M45   1994   657'.044   C94-932029-3

Contents

Preface

These texts, Volumes 1, 2, and 3, are an introduction to the field of accounting and to the use of accounting information as a basis for business decisions. They are intended for use in the first university-level accounting course, which usually spans two semesters.

OUR GOALS IN THIS SEVENTH CANADIAN EDITION

We have tried to accomplish many things in this edition. Among our most important goals have been to:

1. Provide students with a better understanding of the environment in which accounting information is developed and used.
2. Shift emphasis from the preparation of accounting information to its interpretation and use.
3. Retain a course structure that meets the specific content requirements of most universities and colleges.

Providing Students with a Better Background

If students are to appreciate the nature of accounting, they first should have a basic understanding of the business environment. We find, however, that many introductory students lack this background. Often the introductory accounting course is also the students' first course in the business curriculum.

We give increased attention to explaining business practices before discussing accounting issues. Our focus is upon *current* business and accounting practices, not those of the past. For example, virtually every business with external reporting obligations now uses a perpetual inventory system. Yet many accounting textbooks continue to emphasize periodic systems. We emphasize *perpetual* inventory systems.

For purposes of illustration, textbooks traditionally assume the use of simple, manually maintained accounting records. Such records do not meet the needs of most modern businesses. We, too, find it convenient to use simple accounting records as the basis for many illustrations. However, we also explain how the information is processed in a computer-based environment.

Attention is given throughout the text to the role of *professional judgment* in both the development and interpretation of accounting information. We explain in some depth professional ethics for accountants in the field of public and private accounting. We also discuss audits, reviews, and the independent auditors' potential liability to the users of financial statements. Furthermore, we delineate the development and importance of international accounting standards in today's global business environment.

Shifting to a "User Orientation"

Today, relatively few introductory students will become professional preparers of accounting information. All, however, will become life-long information **users.** For this reason, we have shifted our emphasis significantly from the preparation of accounting information to its interpretation and use.

This shift in emphasis affects the text in several ways. For example, we have added new assignment material designed specifically to develop students' analytical, decision-making, and communication skills. Accordingly, a substantial number of stimulating and challenging problems/cases requiring the application of these critical skills have been incorporated in the final section of the assignment material entitled "Analytical and Decision Problems and Cases."

A user-oriented approach also affects topical content and emphasis. Topics relevant to basic business decisions now are addressed, even if these topics traditionally have been deferred to later accounting courses. Examples of such topics include accounting for postretirement costs, audits and reviews, "window dressing," and many of the disclosures that accompany financial statements.

Throughout the text, attention is given to analytical ratios and financial relationships. The chapter on analysis of financial statements now serves primarily as a review.

Increased attention also is given to the use of accounting information **by management.** No longer is this topic addressed only in a group of "managerial" chapters; it now is integrated throughout the text.

Some "traditional" accounting topics relate primarily to the preparation of accounting information and are of little significance to the information user. Examples include reversing entries, manual special journals, and alternative methods of recording accruals and deferrals. In our user-oriented approach, such topics are given less emphasis. Often they are presented in Supplemental Topic sections.

Preserving a Proven Course Structure

Some universities are experimenting with radically different approaches to the introductory accounting course. We have **not** embarked upon such a path. We have great respect for the existing structure of the introductory course, which has evolved from decades of experience and research. We recognize that many students transfer credit for this course from one institution to another. Some standardization of the curriculum is therefore essential.

We regard our changes in this seventh Canadian edition as **evolutionary,** not **revolutionary.** Faculty acquainted with our past editions will find much that is familiar.

ELEMENTS OF THE TEXTBOOK

This seventh Canadian edition introduces many new features and retains all of the time-honoured materials. Such a well-balanced blending makes this text uniquely suitable for today's business environment.

Chapter Introductions and Learning Objectives

Each chapter begins with a brief overview and a set of basic learning objectives. These learning objectives then are integrated with the text discussions.

Cases in Point

A distinctive feature of past editions has been the use of short **Cases in Point,** which are based upon actual events. Many new Cases in Point have been created for this edition as part of our increased focus on the contemporary business environment.

Supplemental Topics and Appendixes

A new feature in the structure of this edition is the inclusion of short **Supplemental Topic** sections at the end of several chapters. These Supplemental Topics are closely related to the content of the chapters in which they appear.

Students always should read the Supplemental Topic sections, as these discussions will enhance their overall understanding of the chapter. Instructors, however, may decide whether these topics are of sufficient general interest for inclusion in class discussions, homework assignments, and examinations. [Assignment material relating to Supplemental Topics are preceded by an asterisk (*).]

Chapter Reviews

Each chapter is followed by such learning aids as a **Glossary of Key Terms** and, in most chapters, a **Demonstration Problem** with a complete solution.

Assignment Material

One of the distinctive features of this seventh Canadian edition is the increase in the quantity and variety of the assignment material. Increased emphasis is placed upon the development of students' analytical abilities, decision-making skills, and communication skills. Much of the new assignment material is based upon the operations of well-known companies.

Six categories of assignments accompany the text. These are (1) Discussion Questions, (2) Multiple Choice Questions, (3) Exercises, (4) Problems, (5) Analytical and Decision Problems and Cases, and (6) Comprehensive Problems.

Discussion Questions are short and usually call for expository answers. In addition to developing writing and communication skills, these questions explore students' conceptual understanding of accounting.

Multiple Choice Questions focus on many of the most important concepts in the chapter. These questions are very useful in testing students' understanding of key aspects of the chapter material. They are both stimulating and challenging.

Exercises are short assignments, usually focusing upon a single concept. We have greatly increased the number and the variety of Exercises. By enabling instructors to cover basic concepts quickly, we hope to allow more time for discussing in class such assignments as our Analytical and Decision Problems and Cases.

Problems are longer than the Exercises and address several concepts at one time. Most chapters contain both an *A* and *B* problem series, each providing thorough coverage of the chapter. A few chapters contain a single—but longer—series of problems. The single series accommodates a greater variety of assignments.

Analytical and Decision Problems and Cases emphasize the development of analytical, decision-making, and communication skills. They also provide a wealth of assignment material well suited to in-class discussions.

To encourage the use of these assignments, we have developed a large number of Analytical and Decision Problems and Cases that cover a wide range of time requirements and difficulty levels. Many of our Exercises and Problems also call for analysis and the use of judgment.

We consider our six *Comprehensive Problems* to be among the most useful assignments in the text. Each of these problems ties together concepts presented over a span of chapters. Two of the Comprehensive Problems are similar in scope to a "practice set," and another involves the analysis of an actual annual report.

A *Checklist of Key Figures* for Problems and Comprehensive Problems appears on the front and back inside covers of the text. The purpose of these check figures is to aid students in verifying their problem solutions and in discovering their own errors.

The Flexibility of PRIMIS

The U.S. text, *Accounting: The Basis for Business Decisions,* Ninth Edition, by Meigs and Meigs, and selected supplementary materials are available on the McGraw-Hill/Primis custom publishing database. Any materials on the database can be configured and created to your specifications. The Primis database includes several McGraw-Hill accounting texts, selected Harvard business cases, and articles from various journals.

NEW AND EXTENSIVELY REVISED CHAPTERS

Many chapters in this seventh Canadian edition have been revised significantly. Almost every chapter contains greater emphasis upon the use of accounting information and more assignment material than ever before. Among the changes in topical content that will be noticed most readily are:

Chapter 1, "Accounting: The Language of Business," has been rewritten to provide a more comprehensive introduction to the process of financial reporting. We have added discussions of such topics as reporting requirements of publicly owned companies, auditing, and professional ethics. Also included is a new discussion of the nature and sources of generally accepted accounting principles. Moreover, the importance of a background in accounting as a "stepping stone" to positions in top management is illustrated. Career opportunities in accounting are discussed in a Supplemental Topic section at the end of the chapter.

In *Chapter 4,* we have revised the format of the work sheet. Our goal is to focus upon the **accounting processes** illustrated within the work sheet, not to present the document itself as a component of the accounting cycle.

Chapter 5, now entitled "Accounting for Merchandising Activities; Classified Financial Statements," exemplifies many of the changes in this edition. The opening pages of this chapter illustrate our concerted effort to explain business practices before discussing the accounting treatments accorded those practices.

In keeping with contemporary business practices, this chapter now emphasizes **perpetual inventory systems**—the type of system used in every large business organization. Periodic systems still receive thorough coverage; in fact, we have added an explanation of a "shortcut" periodic system that is used by many small businesses. Also, additional coverage on periodic inventory system is presented in a Supplemental Topic section at the end of the chapter.

The final portion of Chapter 5, "Introduction to Classified Financial Statements," typifies our increased emphasis upon the **use** of accounting information.

Chapter 6, "Accounting Systems, Internal Control, and Audits," emphasizes the capabilities of computer-based accounting systems, rather than the use of manual special journals. Among the new features of this chapter are examples of how data bases tailor information to meet the needs of different decision makers. New elements of this chapter also include discussions of financial and operational audits, and the related topics of employee fraud and management fraud. However, the coverage of manual special journals is not neglected; it is presented in a Supplemental Topic section at the end of the chapter.

Chapter 8, "Accounts Receivable and Notes Receivable," now includes discussions of the goals of credit management, accounts receivable turnover rates, strategies for quickly converting receivables into cash, and disclosure of concentrations of credit risk. These additions illustrate our increased emphasis on the use of accounting information by management, as well as by persons outside of the business organization.

Our coverage of notes receivable with interest included in the face amount has been moved to a Supplemental Topic section, as such notes are held primarily by financial institutions.

Chapter 9, "Inventories and the Cost of Goods Sold," has been revised extensively in light of our emphasis upon perpetual inventory systems. Also included are discussions of the just-in-time concept, inventory turnover rates, and the objectives of efficient inventory management.

Chapter 10, dealing with capital assets such as plant and equipment, includes extensively revised coverage of trade-ins.

Our coverage of liabilities, contained in **Chapters 11** and **16,** has been revised extensively. **Chapter 11** now focuses upon the types of liabilities **common to most business entities,** including long-term instalment debt. **Chapter 16,** in contrast, addresses those types of liabilities found primarily in the financial statements of large, publicly owned corporations. This format completes our coverage of accounting for the sole proprietorship type of unincorporated businesses in the first semester. It also heightens students' awareness of the differences in the business environments of small businesses and of large corporations.

Our coverage of liabilities also has been expanded in terms of topical content. Chapter 11 now includes long-term instalment debt, disclosure requirements relating to long-term debts, and increased emphasis on contingent losses and commitments. Extensively revised coverage of payroll liabilities now appears as a Supplemental Topic.

In Chapter 16, new or expanded coverage is given to topics that, because of their materiality, are relevant to the users of corporate financial statements. Examples include deferred income taxes and an employer's obligation for postretirement benefits.

Chapter 12, "Accounting Concepts, Professional Judgment, and Ethical Conduct," is new to this edition. One objective of this chapter is to review at one time many of the generally accepted accounting principles discussed throughout the text. Another objective is to look in some depth at key elements of a code of professional ethics.

Chapter 18, "Income Taxes and Business Decisions," has been substantially updated to include the most recent changes in tax legislation.

Chapter 20, "Analysis and Interpretation of Financial Statements," has been revised to reflect our emphasis of this topic throughout the textbook.

Chapter 22, "Cost Accounting Systems," contains new coverage of activity-based costing, just-in-time inventory systems, and total quality management.

SUPPLEMENTARY MATERIALS

This text is accompanied by a large number of supplementary learning and teaching aids. These supplements are listed below. A complete description of these materials is contained in the **Instructor's Guide.** If you would like information and costs on the supplemental materials, please contact your local McGraw-Hill Ryerson representative. We value both your interest and our supplements.

For the Student:

Study Guide to accompany Volume 1 by Meigs, Meigs, Meigs, and Lam
Study Guide to accompany Volume 2 and Volume 3 by Meigs, Meigs, Meigs, and Lam
Accounting Work Sheets, Chapters 1–12 by Meigs, Meigs, and Lam
Accounting Work Sheets, Chapters 13–26 by Meigs, Meigs, and Lam
Blank Forms for Problems and Cases

Accounting Information Manager: A General Ledger Program by John W. Wanlass

Accounting Information Manager: A Spreadsheet Program by John W. Wanlass

MicroGuide Computerized Accounting Tutorial by Jean Gutmann

Manual Simulations and Applications:

The Next Dimension: An Accounting Cycle Application by Mary A. Meigs and Wai P. Lam

Remington Restaurant Supply: An Accounting Cycle Application

Valley Building Materials Inc.; A Corporate Accounting Cycle Application

Adders 'n Keyes, 2/e by Brenda Mallouk

Deluxe Spa Products Incorporated: Using Management Accounting for Costing and Decision Making by Brenda Mallouk and Catherine Seguin

Premium Foods Corporation: A Financial Statement Analysis Case by Christie W. Johnson

Facts-by-FAX: An Accounting Cycle Application

Color Copy Co.: An Accounting Cycle Application

Echo Paint Co.: A Small Business Application with Forms by Richard A. Wright

Executive Woodcraft: A Managerial Accounting Application by Ronald W. Hilton

Printer Recharge, Inc.: A Corporate Practice Set by Phillip Ricci and Wanda G. Spruill

Computer-Based Simulations and Applications:

CYMA General Ledger Package: Shadow Mountain Hotel

CYMA General Ledger Package: Authenticity and Facts-by-FAX

Echo Paint Co.: A Small Business Application with Forms, by Richard A. Wright

Remington Restaurant Supply: A Computerized Accounting Cycle Application

Electronic Spreadsheet Application to Accompany the Premium Foods Corporation Financial Statement Analysis Case by Christie W. Johnson

For the Instructor:

Canadian:
Instructor's Manual
Solutions Manual
Overhead Transparencies
Test Bank (Manual and Computerized Versions)
Solutions to accompany The Next Dimension
Solutions to accompany Deluxe Spa Products Incorporated

American:
Lecture Video Series
Case Study Videos for Analysis and Critical Thinking
Instructor's Manual/Critical Thinking Guide to Accompany Case Study Videotapes by Mark S. Bettner
Electronic Classroom Presentations by Glenn Owen

Interactive Solutions Software
Teaching Transparencies
Report Card: Electronic Grading Software
Financial Statement Analysis Problem Set and Software
Solutions to Applications

Acknowledgements

This seventh Canadian edition has benefited from the perceptive inputs of the instructors and students who used the preceding edition. To those instructors and students, I express my sincere appreciation.

I am especially indebted to those reviewers who provided critical and constructive suggestions and to those who bestowed me with valuable advice. The suggestions and advice contributed greatly to the improvement in the text, supplementary, and assignment materials. Accordingly, I wish to thank all of the following individuals:

Mortimer Davis, Vanier College
Bruce W. Densmore, Mount Saint Vincent University
Randy Dickson, Red Deer College
Wendy Doyle, Mount Saint Vincent University
Gary Earle, Loyalist College
Adrian Feigelsohn, Royal Trust
Leo Gallant, St. Francis Xavier University
Peter Henderson, Douglas College
Tilly Jensen, Northern Alberta Institute of Technology
Ross Johnston, University of Windsor
Chris Kellman, Northwest College
Loris Macor, Coopers & Lybrand
Jim Macri, Ernst & Young
John Mitchell, Sault College
R. C. (Bob) Nichols, British Columbia Institute of Technology
Chris O'Neill, Algonquin College
Bill Ralston, Northwest College
Catherine Seguin, University of Toronto
Glen Sikorski, Niagara College
Ralph Sweet, Durham College

I greatly appreciate the expert attention, advice and assistance given to the seventh Canadian edition by the staff of McGraw-Hill Ryerson, especially Kelly Smyth, Susan Calvert, and Betty Tustin. Also, the excellent editing by Gail Marsden is much appreciated. My special thanks go to Sandy Berlasty for her assistance in typing part of the manuscript.

Finally, heartfelt appreciation is due to my family members—Jean, Angela, Lambert, and Gloria. Their patience and understanding have made this important academic endeavour more enjoyable. As well, they have done an outstanding job in typing, editing, and proofreading the manuscript of the text, solutions, and supplements.

Wai P. Lam

5 Partnerships and Corporations

*T*he next five chapters focus on accounting issues that affect partnerships and corporations. In Chapter 13, the specialized field of accounting for partnership is explored. In the other chapters, issues unique to corporations are discussed. Corporations play the dominant role in our economy. Corporations own more assets, earn more revenue, provide more jobs, and attract more capital than all other forms of business organizations combined.

Part 5 also contains Comprehensive Problem 4. This problem provides a review of much of the material of the first twelve chapters, as well as some corporate accounting issues.

13 Partnerships

In prior chapters we have used the sole proprietorship as a model in our study of basic accounting concepts. In this chapter we focus on the partnership and the accounting issues related to this form of business organization. Among these topics are the accounting for the formation of a partnership, the equitable division of partnership net income or net loss among the partners, the admission and the withdrawal of individual partners, and finally the liquidation of a partnership business.

Learning Objectives

After studying this chapter you should be able to:

1 *Describe the basic characteristics of a partnership.*
2 *Discuss the advantages and disadvantages of the partnership as a form of business organization.*
3 *Distinguish between a regular partnership and a limited partnership.*
4 *Account for the formation of a partnership.*
5 *Divide the net income of a partnership among the partners.*
6 *Account for the admission of a new partner and the withdrawal of a partner.*
7 *Account for the liquidation of a partnership.*

*T*hree types of business organization are common to Canadian business: the sole proprietorship, the partnership, and the corporation. Partnerships are a popular form of organization because they provide a convenient, inexpensive means of combining the capital and the special abilities of two or more persons. The partnership form of organization is widely used in all types of small business and also in the professions. A partnership is often referred to as a *firm;* the name of the firm often includes the word *company,* as, for example, "Adams, Barnes, and Company."

In Canada, each province has its own partnership legislation. The provincial partnership legislation may consist of one or more acts. All provincial partnership legislation covers essentially the same ground and provides essentially the same fundamental rules on the nature, organization, and operation of partnerships.

What constitutes a partnership? The answer can be found in the partnerships act. The legal definition of a partnership is essentially the same in all provincial legislation, except for minor differences in wording. The Ontario Partnerships Act, for example, has the following definition:

> Partnership is the relation that subsists between persons carrying on a business in common with a view to profit, but the relation between the members of a company or association that is incorporated by or under the authority of any special or general Act in force in Ontario or elsewhere, or registered as a corporation under any such Act, is not a partnership within the meaning of this Act.

In this chapter, we shall concentrate on the significant features of and the accounting problems peculiar to a partnership.

Significant Features of a Partnership

Before taking up the accounting problems peculiar to partnerships, it will be helpful to consider briefly some of the distinctive characteristics of the partnership form of organization. These characteristics (such as limited life and unlimited liability) all stem from the concept that a partnership is not a separate legal entity in itself but merely a voluntary association of individuals.

OBJECTIVE 1
Describe the
basic char-
acteristics of
a partner-
ship.

Ease of Formation   Generally, a partnership can be created with a minimum of formality. When two or more persons agree, orally or in writing, to carry on a business with a view to profit, such agreement constitutes a contract and a partnership is automatically created. The contract should be in writing in order to lessen the chances for misunderstanding and future disagreement. The voluntary aspect of a partnership agreement means that no one can be forced into a partnership or forced to continue as a partner.

CASE IN POINT   Richard and Mike were friends and employees of the same large corporation. They became interested in forming a partnership to acquire a nearby small business being offered for sale for a down payment of $50,000. They felt that they could manage the business (which had two employees) in their spare time. Richard and Mike agreed that each would deposit $25,000 in a partnership bank account. There was no written agreement of partnership. Richard made his deposit from his personal savings; Mike had only $10,000 of his own but was able to obtain the other $15,000 from his brother-in-law, Joe, to whom he described the business with great enthusiasm. Mike then deposited $25,000 in the partnership bank account and the business was purchased. Richard had never met Joe and was not aware of his $15,000 investment.

A few months later, Joe became annoyed because he had received no return on his investment. He appeared suddenly at the business while Richard was there, stating that he was a partner and demanding to see the accounting records and the bank statements. Richard refused, and after an angry argument, Joe was forcibly ejected. The question of whether Joe was a "silent partner" caused bitter disagreement among all three of the principals. During this dispute, the business was forced to shut down because of lack of working capital. Richard, Mike, and Joe each retained a lawyer to seek damages from the others.

Although a partnership may be at times a somewhat unstable form of organization, a written agreement of partnership might have avoided the problems encountered by Richard and Mike—and by Joe.

Limited Life A partnership may be ended at any time by the death or withdrawal of any member of the firm. Other factors that may bring an end to a partnership include the bankruptcy or incapacity of a partner, the expiration of the period specified in the partnership contract, or the completion of the project for which the partnership was formed. The admission of a new partner or the retirement of an existing member means an end to the old partnership, although the business may be and usually is continued by the formation of a new partnership.

Mutual Agency Each partner acts as an agent of the partnership, with authority to enter into contracts for the purchase and sale of goods and services. The partnership is bound by the acts of any partner as long as these acts are within the scope of normal operations. The factor of mutual agency suggests the need for exercising great caution in the selection of a partner. To be in partnership with an irresponsible person or one lacking in integrity is an intolerable situation.

Unlimited Liability Each partner is ***personally*** responsible for all the debts of the firm. The lack of any ceiling on the liability of a partner may deter a wealthy person from entering a partnership.

A new member joining an existing partnership may or may not assume liability for debts incurred by the firm prior to his or her admission. A partner withdrawing from membership must give adequate public notice of withdrawal; otherwise the former partner may be held liable for partnership debts incurred subsequent to his or her withdrawal. The retiring partner remains liable for partnership debts existing at the time of withdrawal unless the creditors agree to a release of this obligation.

Co-ownership of Partnership Property and Income When a partner invests a building, inventory, or other property in a partnership, he or she does not retain any personal right to the assets contributed. The property becomes jointly owned by all partners. Each member of a partnership also has an ownership right in the income of the partnership.

Advantages and Disadvantages of a Partnership

OBJECTIVE 2
Discuss the
advantages
and disad-
vantages of
the partner-
ship as a
form of busi-
ness organi-
zation.

Perhaps the most important advantage of most partnerships is the opportunity to bring together sufficient capital to carry on a business. The opportunity to combine special skills, as, for example, the specialized talents of an engineer and an accountant, may also induce individuals to join forces in a partnership. To form a partnership is much easier and less expensive than to organize a corporation. Members of a partnership enjoy more freedom from government regulation and more flexibility of action than do the owners of a corporation. The partners may withdraw funds and make business decisions of all types without the necessity of formal meetings or legalistic procedures.

Operating as a partnership **may** in some cases produce income tax advantages as compared with doing business as a corporation. The partnership itself is neither a legal entity nor a taxable entity. A partnership does not pay income taxes. However, the individual partners must pay income taxes on their respective shares of the partnership's net income.

Offsetting these advantages of a partnership are such serious disadvantages as limited life, unlimited liability (except for a limited partner in a limited partnership, as discussed in the following section), and mutual agency. Furthermore, if a business is to require a large amount of capital, the partnership is a less effective device for raising funds than is a corporation. Many persons who invest freely in common stocks of corporations are unwilling to enter a partnership because of the unlimited liability imposed on partners.

Limited Partnerships

OBJECTIVE 3
Distinguish
between a
regular
partnership
and a lim-
ited partner-
ship.

In past years a number of businesses have been organized as "limited partnerships." This form of organization is widely used for businesses that provide tax-sheltered income to investors, such as real estate syndications and mining ventures. However, limited partnerships are **not** appropriate for businesses in which the owners intend to be active managers. Recent tax legislation has also reduced greatly the income tax advantages formerly available to investors in limited partnerships.

A limited partnership must have at least one **general partner** as well as one or more **limited partners.** The general partners are partners in the traditional sense, with unlimited liability for the debts of the business and the right to make managerial decisions. The limited partners, however, are basically **investors** rather than traditional partners. They have the right to participate in the income of the business, but their liability for losses is limited to the amount of their investment. Also, limited partners do not actively participate in management of the business. Thus, the concepts of unlimited liability and mutual agency apply only to the general partners in a limited partnership.

In this chapter, we emphasize the characteristics and accounting practices of conventional partnerships rather than limited partnerships. Limited partnerships are discussed in depth in courses on business law and income taxes.

The Partnership Contract

Although a partnership can be formed by an oral agreement, it is highly desirable that a written partnership agreement be prepared, summarizing the partners' mutual understanding on such points as:

1 Names of the partners
2 The duties and rights of each partner, effective the specified date of formation of the partnership
3 Amount to be invested by each partner, including the procedure for valuing any noncash assets invested or withdrawn by partners
4 Methods of sharing net income and net losses
5 Withdrawals to be allowed each partner
6 Provision for liquidation, including the method for sharing a deficiency in a partner's capital account by other partners

Partnership Accounting

As mentioned earlier in this chapter, a partnership ***does not*** constitute a ***legal*** entity with an identity separate from its owners. However, from a record-keeping and reporting point of view, a partnership does constitute a ***separate and distinct accounting entity.***

An adequate accounting system and an accurate measurement of income are needed by every business, but they are especially important in a partnership because the net income is divided among two or more owners. Each partner needs current, accurate information on operations so that he or she can make intelligent decisions on such questions as additional investments, expansion of the business, or sale of an interest in the partnership.

CASE IN POINT Rowe and Davis were partners in an automobile dealership and auto repair shop. Rowe was the active manager of the business, but Davis had supplied nearly all the capital. Aware that the firm was quite profitable, Rowe devised a scheme to become the sole owner by buying out his partner. In order to persuade Davis to sell his interest at a bargain price, Rowe deliberately began falsifying the accounting records and financial statements in a manner to understate the earnings of the business. Much of the revenue from auto repair work was not recorded at all, depreciation expense was overstated, ending inventories were understated, and the cost of new items of plant and equipment were charged to expense. The result was a series of monthly income statements that showed the business operating at a larger loss each month. Faced with these discouraging financial statements, Davis became pessimistic over the prospects for the business and was on the verge of selling his interest to Rowe at a price far below the balance in his capital account.

However, a friend suggested that before selling out, Davis should insist upon an audit of the business by a public accounting firm. An audit was performed and revealed that the business was in fact highly profitable. When confronted by Davis with the auditors' findings, Rowe withdrew from the partnership and Davis became the sole owner.

Opening the Accounts of a New Partnership

OBJECTIVE 4
Account for
the forma-
tion of a
partnership.

When a partner contributes assets other than cash, a question always arises as to the value of such assets. The valuations assigned to noncash assets should be their ***current market values*** at the date of transfer to the partnership. The valuations assigned must be agreed to by all partners.

To illustrate the opening entries for a newly formed partnership, assume that on January 1, Joan Blair and Richard Cross, who operate competing retail stores, decide to form a partnership by consolidating their two businesses. A capital account will be opened for each partner and credited with the agreed valuation of the ***net assets*** (total assets less total liabilities) that the partner contributes. The journal entries to open the accounts of the partnership of Blair and Cross are as follows:

Entries for for-
mation of part-
nership.

Cash	*40,000*	
Accounts Receivable	*60,000*	
Inventory	*90,000*	
Accounts Payable		*30,000*
Joan Blair, Capital		*160,000*
To record the investment by Joan Blair in the partnership of Blair and Cross.		
Cash	*10,000*	
Inventory	*60,000*	
Land	*60,000*	
Building	*100,000*	
Accounts Payable		*70,000*
Richard Cross, Capital		*160,000*
To record the investment by Richard Cross in the partnership of Blair and Cross.		

Partnership accounting is similar to that in a sole proprietorship, except that separate capital and drawing accounts are maintained for each partner. These capital and drawing accounts show for each partner the amounts invested, the amounts withdrawn, and the appropriate share of partnership net income. In brief, each partner is provided with a history of his or her equity in the firm.

The values assigned to assets in the accounts of the new partnership may be quite different from the amounts at which these assets were carried in the accounts of their previous owners. For example, the land contributed by Cross and valued at $60,000 might have appeared in his accounting records at a cost of $20,000. The building that he contributed was valued at $100,000 by the partnership, but it might have cost Cross only $80,000 some years ago and might have been depreciated on his records to a net value of $60,000. Assuming that market values of land and buildings had risen sharply while Cross owned this property, it is only fair to recognize the ***current market value*** of these assets at the time he transfers them to the partnership and to credit his capital account accordingly. Depreciation of the building in the partnership accounts will be based on the assigned value of $100,000 at the date of acquisition by the partnership.

Additional Investments

Assume that after six months of operation the firm is in need of more cash, and the partners make an additional investment of $10,000 each on July 2. These additional investments are credited to the capital accounts as shown below:

Entry for additional investment	*Cash* *20,000*	
	Joan Blair, Capital	*10,000*
	Richard Cross, Capital	*10,000*
	To record additional investments.	

Drawing Accounts

The drawing account maintained for each partner serves the same purpose as the drawing account of the owner of a sole proprietorship. The transactions calling for debits to the drawing accounts of partners may be summarized as follows:

1 Cash or other assets withdrawn by a partner
2 Payments from partnership funds of the personal debts of a partner
3 Partnership cash collected on behalf of the firm by a partner but retained by the partner personally

Loans from Partners

Ordinarily any funds furnished to the firm by a partner are recorded by crediting that partner's capital account. Occasionally, however, a partnership may be in need of funds but the partners do not wish to increase their capital investment in the business, or perhaps one partner is willing to advance funds when the others are not. Under these circumstances, the advance of funds may be designated as a loan from the partner and credited to a liability account. However, partnership liabilities to outsiders always take precedence over liabilities to partners.

Closing the Accounts of a Partnership at Year-End

At the end of the accounting period, the balance in the Income Summary account is closed into the partners' capital accounts. The net income or losses of a partnership may be divided among the partners in *any manner agreed upon* by the partners. However, this agreement should be carefully stipulated in the partnership contract. In the event that the partners *do not* have a formal income-and-loss sharing agreement, the law requires all net income or losses to be *divided equally* among the partners.

In our illustration, let us assume that Blair and Cross have agreed to share net income equally. (We will discuss other income-and-loss sharing arrangements later in this chapter.) Assuming that the partnership earns net income of $60,000 in the first year of operations, the entry to close the Income Summary account is as follows:

<table>
<tr><td>**Closing income summary: net income shared equally**</td><td>Income Summary ....
    Joan Blair, Capital ....
    Richard Cross, Capital ....
To divide net income for the year in accordance with
partnership agreement to share it equally.</td><td>60,000</td><td>
30,000
30,000</td></tr>
</table>

The next step in closing the accounts is to transfer the balance of each partner's drawing account to his capital account. Assuming that withdrawals during the year amounted to $24,000 for Blair and $16,000 for Cross, the entry at December 31 to close the drawing accounts is as follows:

<table>
<tr><td>**Closing the drawing accounts to capital accounts**</td><td>Joan Blair, Capital...
Richard Cross, Capital......................................
    Joan Blair, Drawing ....
    Richard Cross, Drawing ....
To transfer debit balances in partners' drawing accounts to
their respective capital accounts.</td><td>24,000
16,000</td><td>

24,000
16,000</td></tr>
</table>

Income Statement for a Partnership The income statement for a partnership differs from that of a sole proprietorship in only one respect: a final section may be added to show the division of the net income between the partners, as illustrated below for the firm of Blair and Cross. The income statement of a partnership is consistent with that of a sole proprietorship in showing no income taxes expense and no salaries expense relating to services rendered by partners.

<table>
<tr><td colspan="3">**BLAIR AND CROSS**
Income Statement
For the Year Ended December 31, 19__</td></tr>
<tr><td>**Note division of net income**</td><td>Sales...</td><td></td><td>$600,000</td></tr>
<tr><td></td><td>Cost of goods sold ....</td><td></td><td>400,000</td></tr>
<tr><td></td><td>Gross profit ....</td><td></td><td>$200,000</td></tr>
<tr><td></td><td>Operating expenses:</td><td></td><td></td></tr>
<tr><td></td><td> Selling expenses.......................................</td><td>$100,000</td><td></td></tr>
<tr><td></td><td> General & administrative expenses ....</td><td>40,000</td><td>140,000</td></tr>
<tr><td></td><td>Net income ....</td><td></td><td>$ 60,000</td></tr>
<tr><td></td><td>Division of net income:</td><td></td><td></td></tr>
<tr><td></td><td> To Joan Blair (50%)....................................</td><td>$ 30,000</td><td></td></tr>
<tr><td></td><td> To Richard Cross (50%)................................</td><td>30,000</td><td>$ 60,000</td></tr>
</table>

Statement of Partners' Equity The partners will usually want an explanation of the change in their capital accounts from one year-end to the next. A supplementary schedule called a ***statement of partners' equity*** is prepared to show this information. A statement of partners' equity for Blair and Cross follows:

Changes in capital accounts during the year

	Blair	Cross	Total
BLAIR AND CROSS			
Statement of Partners' Equity			
For the Year Ended December 31, 19__			
Balances, Jan. 1, 19__	$160,000	$160,000	$320,000
Add: Additional investments	10,000	10,000	20,000
Net income for the year	30,000	30,000	60,000
Subtotals	$200,000	$200,000	$400,000
Less: Drawings	24,000	16,000	40,000
Balances, Dec. 31, 19__	$176,000	$184,000	$360,000

The balance sheet of Blair and Cross would show the capital balance for each partner, as well as the total capital of $360,000.

Partnership Income and Income Taxes

Partnerships Are Not Required to Pay Income Taxes Partners must include their shares of the partnership net income (after certain technical adjustments) on their individual income tax returns. Partnership net income is thus taxable to the partners individually in the year in which it is earned. The income tax rules applicable to investment in a partnership are covered in advanced accounting courses.

Note that partners report and pay tax on their respective shares of the net income earned by the partnership during the year and **not** on the amounts that they have drawn out of the business during the year. ***The net income of the partnership is taxable to the partners each year,*** even though there may have been no withdrawals. This treatment is consistent with that accorded a sole proprietorship.

The Nature of Partnership Net Income

The net income earned by partnerships, like those earned by sole proprietorships, compensate the owners for (1) personal services rendered to the business, (2) capital invested in the business, and (3) "entrepreneurial risk"—that is, taking the risk that the investments of personal services and of capital may be lost if the business is unsuccessful. Recognition of these three factors is helpful in developing an equitable plan for the division of partnership net income.

If one partner devotes full time to the business while another devotes little or no time, the difference in the partners' contributions of time and effort should be reflected in the income-sharing agreement. If one partner possesses special skills, the income-sharing agreement should reward this partner's talent. Also, partners may each provide different amounts of capital to the business entity. Again, the differences in the value of the partners' contributions to the business should be reflected in the income-and-loss sharing agreement.

To recognize the particular contributions of each partner to the business, partnership income-and-loss sharing agreements often include "salary allowances" to partners and "interest" on the balances of partners' capital accounts. These "salaries" and "interest" are **not expenses** of the business; rather, they are **steps in the computation made to divide partnership net income among the partners.**

In the preceding illustrations of the partnership of Blair and Cross, we assumed that the partners invested equal amounts of capital, rendered equal services, and divided net income equally. We are now ready to consider cases in which the partners invest **unequal** amounts of capital and services.

Dividing Partnership Net Income among the Partners

Partners can share net income or loss in any manner they decide upon; however, most income-sharing agreements fall under one of the following types:

OBJECTIVE 5
Divide the
net income
of a partner-
ship among
the part-
ners.

1 A fixed ratio. The fixed ratio method has already been illustrated in the example of the Blair and Cross partnership in which net income was shared equally, that is, 50% and 50%. Partners may agree upon any fixed ratio such as 60% and 40%, or 70% and 30%.

2 Salary allowances to the partners, with remaining net income or loss divided in a fixed ratio.

3 Interest allowances on partners' capital balances, with remaining net income or loss divided in a fixed ratio.

4 Salary allowances to the partners, interest allowances on partners' capital balances, and remaining net income or loss divided in a fixed ratio.

All these methods of sharing partnership net income are intended to recognize differences in the personal services rendered by partners and in the amounts of capital invested in the firm.

In the illustrations that follow, it is assumed that beginning balances in the partners' capital accounts were Brooke Adams, $160,000, and Ben Barnes, $40,000. At year-end, the Income Summary account showed a credit balance of $96,000, representing the net income for the year before any allowances for partners' salaries or interest on capital account balances.

Salaries to Partners, with Remainder in a Fixed Ratio

Because partners often contribute different amounts of personal services, partnership agreements often provide for partners' salaries as a factor in the division of net income.

For example, assume that Adams and Barnes agree to annual salary allowances of $24,000 for Adams and $48,000 for Barnes. These salaries, that total $72,000 per year, are agreed upon by the partners in advance. Of course, the net income of the business is not likely to be exactly $72,000 in a given year. Therefore, the income-and-loss sharing agreement should also specify a fixed ratio for dividing any income or loss remaining after giving consideration to the agreed-upon salary allowances. We will assume that Adams and Barnes agree to divide any remaining income or loss equally.

The division of the $96,000 in partnership net income between Adams and Barnes is illustrated in the following schedule. The first step is to allocate to each partner his or her agreed-upon salary allowance. This step allocates $72,000 of the partnership net income. The remaining $24,000 is then divided in the agreed-upon fixed ratio (50-50 in this example).

Division of Partnership Net Income

	Adams	Barnes	Net income
Net income to be divided			$96,000
Salary allowances to partners.......................	$24,000	$48,000	(72,000)
Remaining income after salary allowances...........			$24,000
Allocated in a fixed ratio:			
Adams (50%)....................................	12,000		
Barnes (50%).....................................		12,000	(24,000)
Total share to each partner	$36,000	$60,000	$ –0–

Income sharing; salary allowances and remainder in a fixed ratio

Under this agreement, Adams's share of the $96,000 net income amounts to $36,000 and Barnes's share amounts to $60,000. The entry to close the Income Summary account would be:

Income Summary...	96,000	
Brooke Adams, Capital		36,000
Ben Barnes, Capital		60,000

To close the Income Summary account by crediting each partner with agreed-upon salary allowance and dividing the remaining income equally.

The "salary allowances" used in dividing partnership net income are sometimes misinterpreted, even by the partners. These salary allowances are merely an agreed-upon device for dividing net income; they are **not expenses** of the business and are **not recorded in any ledger account.** A partner is considered an owner of the business, not an employee. Therefore, the services that a partner renders to the firm are assumed to be rendered in anticipation of earning a share of the net income, not a salary.

The amount of cash or other assets that a partner withdraws from the partnership may be greater than or less than the partner's salary allowance. Even if a partner decides to withdraw an amount of cash equal to his or her "salary allowance," the withdrawal should be recorded by debiting the partner's drawing account, **not by debiting an expense account.** Let us repeat the main point: **"salary allowances" to partners should not be recorded as expenses of the business.**[1]

Because of this treatment of salary allowances, the net income reported by a partnership will differ from the net income that would be reported if the business were organized as a corporation. Corporations do record as expenses any salaries paid to owners.[2]

[1] Some exceptions to this general rule will be discussed in advanced accounting courses.

[2] The net income reported by a corporation also differs from that reported by an unincorporated business because the corporation is subject to income taxes on its earnings. Accounting practices of corporations are discussed in later chapters.

Interest Allowances on Partners' Capital, with Remainder in a Fixed Ratio
Next we shall assume a business situation in which the partners spend very little time in the business and net income depends primarily on the amount of money invested. The income-sharing plan then might emphasize invested capital as a basis for the first step in allocating income.

For example, assume that Adams and Barnes agree that both partners are to be allowed interest at *15%* on their beginning capital balances, with any remaining income or loss to be divided equally. Net income to be divided is $96,000, and the beginning capital balances are Adams, *$160,000,* and Barnes, *$40,000.*

Division of Partnership Net Income

	Adams	Barnes	Net Income
Net income to be divided			$96,000
Interest allowances on beginning capital:			
Adams ($160,000 × 15%)..........................	$24,000		
Barnes ($40,000 × 15%)..........................		$ 6,000	
Total allocated as interest allowances			(30,000)
Remaining income after interest allowances			$66,000
Allocated in a fixed ratio:			
Adams (50%)....................................	33,000		
Barnes (50%)...................................		33,000	(66,000)
Total share to each partner	$57,000	$39,000	$ –0–

Income sharing; interest on capital and remainder in a fixed ratio

The entry to close the Income Summary account in this example would be:

Income Summary..	96,000	
Brooke Adams, Capital		57,000
Ben Barnes, Capital		39,000

To close the Income Summary account by crediting each partner with interest at 15% on beginning capital and dividing the remaining income equally.

Interest allowances on partners' capital, like partners' salary allowances, are computational devices used in dividing partnership net income. This "interest" is not recorded as an expense of the business.

Salary Allowances, Interest Allowances on Capital, and Remainder in a Fixed Ratio The preceding example took into consideration the difference in amounts of capital provided by Adams and Barnes but ignored any difference in personal services performed. In the next example, we shall assume that the partners agree to an income-sharing plan providing for salaries and for interest on beginning capitals. Salary allowances, as before, are authorized at $24,000 for Adams, $48,000 for Barnes. Beginning capital balances are $160,000 for Adams, $40,000 for Barnes. Partners are to be allowed interest at 10% on their beginning capital balances, and any income or loss remaining after authorized salary and interest allowances is to be divided equally.

Division of Partnership Net Income

	Adams	Barnes	Net Income
Net income to be divided			$96,000
Salary allowances to partners	$24,000	$48,000	(72,000)
Income after salary allowances			$24,000
Interest allowances on beginning capital:			
Adams ($160,000 × 10%)	16,000		
Barnes ($40,000 × 10%)		4,000	
Total allocated as interest allowances			(20,000)
Remaining income after salary and interest allowances			$ 4,000
Allocated in a fixed ratio:			
Adams (50%)	2,000		
Barnes (50%)		2,000	(4,000)
Total share to each partner	$42,000	$54,000	$ –0–

Margin note: Income sharing; salaries, interest, and remainder in a fixed ratio

The journal entry to close the Income Summary account in this case will be:

Income Summary	96,000	
Brooke Adams, Capital		42,000
Ben Barnes, Capital		54,000

To close the Income Summary account by crediting each partner with authorized salary, interest at 10% on beginning capital, and dividing the remaining income equally.

Authorized Salary and Interest Allowance in Excess of Net Income   In the preceding example the total of the authorized salaries and interest was $92,000 and the net income to be divided was $96,000. Suppose that the net income had been only *$80,000;* how should the division have been made?

If the partnership contract provides for salaries and interest on invested capital, these provisions are to be followed even though the net income for the year is *less* than the total of the authorized salaries and interest. If the net income of the firm of Adams and Barnes amounted to only $80,000, this amount would be allocated as follows:

Division of Partnership Net Income

	Adams	Barnes	Net Income
Net income to be divided			$ 80,000
Salary allowances to partners	$24,000	$48,000	(72,000)
Income after salary allowances			$ 8,000
Interest allowances on beginning capital:			
Adams ($160,000 × 10%)	16,000		
Barnes ($40,000 × 10%)		4,000	
Total allocated as interest allowances			(20,000)
Residual loss after salary and			
interest allowances			$(12,000)
Allocated in a fixed ratio:			
Adams (50%)	(6,000)		
Barnes (50%)		(6,000)	12,000
Total share to each partner	$34,000	$46,000	$ –0–

Margin note: Authorized salary and interest allowances in excess of net income

Notice that after deducting for the specified salary and interest allowances, there is a residual loss of $12,000 to be divided equally between Adams and Barnes. ***This does not mean that the partnership has generated a loss for the period.*** The partnership earned net income of $80,000. The residual loss allocation is simply a computational step in the process of dividing net income according to the partnership contract. The entry to close the Income Summary account will be as follows:

Income Summary	*80,000*	
Brooke Adams, Capital		*34,000*
Ben Barnes, Capital		*46,000*

To close the Income Summary account by crediting each
partner with authorized salary and with interest on invested
capital and by dividing the residual loss equally.

Admission of a New Partner

OBJECTIVE 6
Account for
the admis-
sion of a
new partner
and the
withdrawal
of a partner.

An individual may gain admission to an existing partnership in either of two ways: (1) by buying an equity interest from one or more of the present partners or (2) by making an investment in the partnership. When an incoming partner purchases an equity interest from a present member of the firm, the payment goes personally to the old partner, and there is no change in the assets or liabilities of the partnership. On the other hand, if the incoming partner acquires an equity interest by making an investment in the partnership, the assets of the firm are increased by the amount paid in by the new partner.

By Purchase of an Interest   When a new partner buys an equity interest from a present member of a partnership, the only change in the accounts will be a transfer from the capital account of the selling partner to the capital account of the incoming partner.

Assume, for example, that Pam Lee has an $80,000 equity interest in the partnership of Lee, Martin, and Nash. Lee arranges to sell her entire interest to Paul Trent for $100,000 cash. Partners Martin and Nash agree to the admission of Trent, and the transaction is recorded in the partnership accounts by the following entry:

Incoming partner buys interest from present partner

Pam Lee, Capital	*80,000*	
Paul Trent, Capital		*80,000*

To record the transfer of Pam Lee's equity interest to the
incoming partner, Paul Trent.

Note that the entry in the partnership accounts is for ***$80,000,*** the balance of Lee's capital account. The entry does ***not*** indicate the price paid by Trent to the retiring partner. The payment of $100,000 by Trent to Lee was a ***personal transaction*** between these two individuals; it does not affect the assets or liabilities of the partnership and, therefore, is ***not*** entered in the partnership accounting records.

As a separate but related example, assume that Trent is to gain admission to the firm of Lee, Martin, and Nash by purchasing one-fourth of the equity interest of each partner. The present capital accounts are as follows: Lee $80,000; Martin, $60,000; Nash, $100,000. Assume also that Trent makes payment directly to the old partners, ***not to the partnership.*** The amount paid to each existing partner for one-fourth of his or her equity interest is a privately negotiated matter, and the amounts of these payments are *not* recorded in the partnership records. The only entry required in the partnership accounting records is the following:

Pam Lee, Capital	20,000	
Pat Martin, Capital	15,000	
Tom Nash, Capital	25,000	
Paul Trent, Capital		60,000
To record purchase of 25% of each partner's equity by Paul Trent.		

This entry transfers to Paul Trent one-fourth of the balance formerly appearing in the capital accounts of each of the existing partners. The amounts actually paid to these partners by Trent are *not recorded* in the partnership accounts, because these payments did not flow into the partnership business entity. Thus, the transfer of ownership equity among the partners does not affect the assets, liabilities, or *total* partners' equity in the business.

By Investing in the Firm Now let us assume that an incoming partner acquires his or her equity interest by making an investment directly into the firm. In this case the payment by the new partner goes to the partnership and not to the partners as individuals; the investment therefore increases the partnership assets and also the total owners' equity of the firm. The portion of total equity granted to a new partner is based upon the terms negotiated by both existing and incoming partners. This equity interest (credited to the new partner's capital account) may be equal to, less than, or greater than the amount invested in the partnership by the incoming partner.

Assume that Ann Phillips and Judy Ryan are partners, each having a capital account of $100,000. They agree to admit Bart Smith and negotiate to grant him a one-half equity interest in the business upon his investment of $200,000 in cash. The recording of Smith's admission to the partnership is based on the following calculations:

Net assets (owners' equity) of old partnership	$200,000
Cash investment by Bart Smith	200,000
Net assets (owners' equity) of new partnership	$400,000
Smith's one-half interest	$200,000

To acquire an interest of $200,000 in the net assets of $400,000, Smith invested $200,000. In this situation, the amount of equity interest acquired is equal to the amount of Smith's investment. The entry to record the admission of Smith would be as follows:

Investment in business by new partner

Cash	200,000	
Bart Smith, Capital		200,000
To record the admission of Bart Smith to a one-half interest in the firm.		

Although Smith has a one-half equity interest in the net assets of the new firm of Phillips, Ryan, and Smith, he is not necessarily entitled to receive one-half of the net income. Income sharing is a matter for agreement among the partners; if the new partnership contract contains no mention of income sharing, the assumption is that the three partners intended to share net income and losses equally.

Allowing a Bonus to Former Partners If an existing partnership has exceptionally high earnings year after year, the present partners may demand a **bonus** as a condition of admission of a new partner. In other words, to acquire an equity interest of, say, $80,000, the incoming partner may be required to invest $120,000 in the partnership. The excess investment of $40,000 may be regarded as a bonus to the old partners and credited to their capital accounts in the established ratio for income sharing.

To illustrate the recording of a bonus to the old partners, let us assume that Jane Rogers and Richard Steel are members of a highly successful partnership. Their partnership agreement calls for net income and losses to be divided 60% to Rogers and 40% to Steel. As a result of profitable operations, the partners' capital accounts have doubled within a few years and presently stand at $100,000 each. David Taylor desires to join the firm and offers to invest $100,000 for a one-third equity interest. Rogers and Steel refuse this offer but extend a counteroffer to Taylor of $120,000 for a one-fourth equity interest in the capital of the firm and a one-fourth interest in net income. Taylor accepts these terms because of his desire to share in the unusually large net income of the business. The recording of Taylor's admission to the partnership is based on the following calculations:

Net assets (owners' equity) of old partnership	**$200,000**
Cash investment by David Taylor	120,000
Net assets (owners' equity) of new partnership	**$320,000**
Taylor's one-fourth equity interest	**$ 80,000**

Calculation of bonus to old partners

To acquire an interest of $80,000 in the net assets of $320,000, Taylor has invested $120,000. His **excess investment,** or **bonus,** of $40,000 will be allocated 60% to Rogers ($24,000) and 40% to Steel ($16,000), in accordance with the income-sharing arrangement in effect prior to Taylor's admission.

The entry to record Taylor's admission to the partnership follows:

Recording bonus to old partners

Cash	120,000	
David Taylor, Capital		80,000
Jane Rogers, Capital		24,000
Richard Steel, Capital		16,000
To record admission of David Taylor as a partner with a		
one-fourth interest in capital and net income.		

The total capital of the new partnership is now $320,000, in which Taylor has a one-fourth equity interest ($80,000). Rogers' capital account is $124,000 and Steel's capital account is $116,000 after admission of Taylor. Although in this case Taylor was also granted a one-fourth share of future partnership net income, **the equity interest and the income-sharing ratio of a partner are not necessarily the same.** Old partners Rogers and Steel will set a new income-sharing arrangement for the remaining 75% of net income to be divided between themselves.

Allowing a Bonus to New Partner An existing partnership may sometimes be very anxious to bring in a new partner who can bring needed cash to the firm. In other instances the new partner may possess special talents or may have advantageous business contacts that will add to the profitability of the partnership. Under either of these sets of circumstances, the present partners may offer the new member a bonus in the form of a capital account larger than the amount of the incoming partner's investment.

Assume, for example, that John Bryan and Merle Davis are partners in an existing partnership. Their partnership agreement calls for partnership net income and losses to be divided 70% to Bryan and 30% to Davis. Capital account balances are presently $120,000 for Bryan and $100,000 for Davis. Since the firm is in desperate need of cash, they offer to admit Kay Grant to a one-third equity interest in the firm upon her investment of only $80,000 in cash. The recording of Grant's admission to the partnership is based on the following calculations:

Net assets (owner's equity) of old partnership	*$220,000*
Cash invested by Kay Grant	*80,000*
Net assets (owners' equity) of new partnership	*$300,000*
Grant's one-third interest	*$100,000*

To acquire an equity interest of $100,000 in the new partnership's net assets of $300,000, Grant has invested only $80,000. The $20,000 excess allocated to Grant's capital account is a bonus to Grant from the existing partners, Bryan and Davis. A bonus granted to a new partner is charged to the existing partners' capital accounts according to the income-sharing arrangement in effect ***prior to*** admission of the new partner.

The following journal entry records the admission of Grant to a one-third equity interest in the business, with allowance of the $20,000 bonus to Grant from the two old partners:

Entry for bonus to new partner

Cash	*80,000*	
John Bryan, Capital	*14,000*	
Merle Davis, Capital	*6,000*	
Kay Grant, Capital		*100,000*

To record admission of Grant to a one-third interest, and the allowance of a $20,000 bonus to Grant: 70% from Bryan and 30% from Davis.

Withdrawal of a Partner

To illustrate the withdrawal or retirement of a partner, assume the following data for the partnership of Acres, Bundy, and Coe:

	Capital Account	Share of Net Income
Chris Acres	*$ 75,000*	*20%*
Brit Bundy	*125,000*	*30%*
John Coe	*100,000*	*50%*
Total partners' capital	*$300,000*	

We will use this data to illustrate the retirement of Coe and the treatment accorded the partners' capital accounts under several different assumptions.

Coe Sells His Interest to Someone Else   The simplest case is when Coe, with the consent of Acres and Bundy, sells his equity in the business to a new partner. In this case, the payment by the incoming partner goes directly to Coe, and there is *no change* in the assets or liabilities of the partnership. Regardless of the price received by Coe, the only entry required in the partnership accounts is to transfer the $100,000 balance in Coe's capital account into the capital account of the new partner. This transaction is virtually the same as the one described on page 632 for the admission of a new partner by purchase of an interest.

Now let us change this situation slightly and assume that Coe sells equal amounts of his equity in the business to his fellow partners, Acres and Bundy. If Acres and Bundy pay Coe from their *personal funds,* the assets and liabilities of the partnership are again unchanged. Regardless of the price Acres and Bundy pay to Coe, the transaction is recorded in the partnership accounting records merely by transferring the $100,000 in Coe's capital account into the capital accounts of the remaining two partners, as follows:

Notice there is no change in total capital	John Coe, Capital 100,000	
	Chris Acres, Capital	50,000
	Brit Bundy, Capital	50,000
	To record the sale of Coe's interest to Acres and Bundy.	

Coe's Interest Is Purchased by the Partnership   Now let us assume that the partnership pays Coe in cash for his equity in the business. (The distribution of assets other than cash to a retiring partner will be discussed in advanced accounting courses.) If the partnership pays Coe exactly $100,000 cash for his equity—an amount equal to the balance in his capital account—the entry is simple: debit Coe's capital account $100,000 and credit Cash $100,000. However, the payment to Coe may be greater or less than the balance in his capital account.

Partnership Pays Coe More Than the Balance in His Capital Account   A partner withdrawing from a partnership naturally expects to receive an amount for his or her equity that reflects the *current market value* of the partnership's net assets. Often, current market values exceed the book values appearing in the firm's balance sheet. For example, assets such as real estate may have appreciated greatly in value since they were acquired by the business. Also, if the business has been successful, it may have developed *unrecorded goodwill.*[3] Thus, the settlement paid to a retiring partner often is greater than the balance in the partner's capital account.

An amount paid to a retiring partner in excess of the balance in his or her capital account is treated as a *bonus to the withdrawing partner* and comes out of the capital accounts of the continuing partners. This bonus is charged against (debited to) the continuing partners' capital accounts in proportion to their *relative* income- and loss-sharing ratio.

---
[3]   As discussed in Chapter 10, goodwill is recorded only when it is purchased.

The term ***relative income-sharing ratio*** describes the relationship between the income- and loss-sharing ratios of the continuing partners, excluding the share formerly received by the retiring partner. The relative income- and loss-sharing ratio of each continuing partner is computed by the following formula:

$$\frac{\textbf{Percentage Formerly Received by This Partner}}{\textbf{Total Percentage Formerly Received by All Continuing Partners}}$$

Based upon this formula, the relative income- and loss-sharing ratios of Acres and Bundy are as follows:

Acres (20% ÷ 50%)	*40%*
Bundy (30% ÷ 50%)	*60%*

Assume now that Coe receives ***$140,000*** in cash from the partnership in full settlement of his equity in the firm. As Coe's capital account has a balance of only $100,000, he is receiving a ***$40,000 bonus*** from Acres and Bundy. This bonus is charged against the capital accounts of Acres and Bundy in relation to their relative income- and loss-sharing ratios (Acres, 40%; Bundy, 60%). Thus, Coe's withdrawal from the firm is recorded as follows:

Bonus paid to withdrawing partner

John Coe, Capital (retiring partner)	*100,000*	
Chris Acres, Capital	*16,000*	
Brit Bundy, Capital	*24,000*	
Cash		*140,000*

To record the withdrawal of partner Coe, and payment of his capital account plus a bonus of $40,000. Bonus charged 40% to Acres, 60% to Bundy.

Partnership Pays Coe Less Than the Balance in His Capital Account Now assume that Coe is willing to accept a cash payment of ***only $80,000*** in full settlement of his $100,000 capital account. This situation might arise if, for example, Coe has a pressing need for cash or the future of the firm is jeopardized by contingent losses not yet recorded in its balance sheet accounts. In our example, the continuing partners' equity in the firm will ***increase*** by a total of $20,000 as a result of Coe's withdrawal. Acres and Bundy should divide this ***"bonus to the continuing partners"*** in their relative income- and loss-sharing ratios. The entry is:

Payment to withdrawing partner of less than book equity

John Coe, Capital	*100,000*	
Cash		*80,000*
Chris Acres		*8,000*
Brit Bundy		*12,000*

To record the withdrawal of Coe, and settlement in full for $20,000 less than the balance of his capital account. Bonus to continuing partners allocated 40% to Acres, 60% to Bundy.

Death of a Partner

A partnership is dissolved by the death of any member. To determine the amount owing to the estate of the deceased partner, it is usually necessary to close the accounts and prepare financial statements. This serves to credit all partners with their individual shares of the net income earned during the fractional accounting period ending with the date of *dissolution.*

The partnership agreement may prescribe procedures for making settlement with the estate of a deceased partner. Such procedures often include an audit by public accountants, appraisal of assets, and computation of goodwill. If payment to the estate must be delayed, the amount owed should be carried in a liability account replacing the deceased partner's capital account.

Insurance on Lives of Partners Members of a partnership often obtain life insurance policies that name the partnership as the beneficiary. Upon the death of a partner, the cash collected from the insurance company is used to pay the estate of the deceased partner. In the absence of insurance on the lives of partners, there might be insufficient cash available to pay the deceased partner's estate without disrupting the operation of the business.

Liquidation of a Partnership

OBJECTIVE 7
Account for the liquidation of a partnership.

A partnership is terminated or dissolved whenever a new partner is added or an old partner withdraws. The termination or dissolution of a partnership, however, does not necessarily indicate that the business is to be discontinued. Often the business continues with scarcely any outward evidence of the change in membership of the firm. Termination of a partnership indicates a change in the membership of the firm, which may or may not be followed by liquidation.

The process of breaking up and discontinuing a partnership business is called *liquidation.* Liquidation of a partnership spells an end to the business. If the business is to be discontinued, the assets will be sold, the liabilities paid, and the remaining cash distributed to the partners.

Sale of the Business The partnership of Royal, Simms, and Tate sells its business to the North Corporation. The balance sheet appears as follows:

Partnership at time of sale

ROYAL, SIMMS, AND TATE
Balance Sheet
December 31, 19___

Assets		*Liabilities & Partners' Equity*	
Cash	$ 50,000	Accounts payable	$100,000
Inventory	200,000	Ann Royal, capital	140,000
Other assets	150,000	Ed Simms, capital	120,000
		Jon Tate, capital	40,000
Total	$400,000	Total	$400,000

The terms of sale provide that the inventory and other assets will be sold to the North Corporation for a consideration of $230,000, a price resulting in a loss of $120,000. The liabilities will not be transferred to North Corporation, but will be paid by the partnership out of existing cash plus the proceeds of the sale, prior to any distribution of cash to the partners.

The entry to record the sale of the inventory and other assets to North Corporation is:

Entry to record the sale of the business	*Cash*	*230,000*	
	Loss on Sale of Business	*120,000*	
	Inventory		*200,000*
	Other Assets		*150,000*
	To record the sale of all assets other than cash to North Corporation.		

Division of the Gain or Loss from Sale of the Business The gain or loss from the sale of the business must be divided among the partners in the agreed income- and loss-sharing ratio **before** any cash is distributed to them. The amount of cash to which each partner is entitled in liquidation cannot be determined until each capital account has been increased or decreased by the proper share of the gain or loss on disposal of the assets. Assuming that Royal, Simms, and Tate share net income and losses equally, the entry to allocate the $120,000 loss on the sale of the business will be as follows:

Entry to divide loss on sale	*Ann Royal, Capital*	*40,000*	
	Ed Simms, Capital	*40,000*	
	Jon Tate, Capital	*40,000*	
	Loss on Sale of Business		*120,000*
	To divide the loss on the sale of the business among the partners in the established ratio for sharing net income and losses.		

Distribution of Cash The balance sheet of Royal, Simms, and Tate appears as follows after the loss on the sale of the assets has been entered in the partners' capital accounts:

Balance sheet after sale of assets

ROYAL, SIMMS, AND TATE			
Balance Sheet			
(After the Sale of All Assets Except Cash)			
Assets		***Liabilities & Partners' Equity***	
Cash	*$280,000*	*Accounts payable*	*$100,000*
		Ann Royal, capital	*100,000*
		Ed Simms, capital	*80,000*
		Jon Tate, capital	*–0–*
Total	*$280,000*	*Total*	*$280,000*

The creditors must be paid in full before cash is distributed to the partners. The sequence of entries will be as follows:

(1) Pay creditors	*Accounts Payable*	*100,000*	
	Cash		*100,000*
	To pay the creditors in full.		
(2) Pay partners	*Ann Royal, Capital*	*100,000*	
	Ed Simms, Capital	*80,000*	
	Cash		*180,000*
	To complete liquidation of the business by distributing the remaining cash to the partners according to the balances in their capital accounts.		

Note that the equal division of the $120,000 loss on the sale of the business reduced the capital account of Jon Tate to zero; therefore, Tate received nothing when the cash was distributed to the partners. This action is consistent with the original agreement of the partners to share net income and losses equally. In working partnership liquidation problems, accounting students sometimes make the error of dividing the cash among the partners in the income- and loss-sharing ratio. An income- and loss-sharing ratio means just what the name indicates; it is a ratio for sharing net income and losses, *not a ratio for sharing cash or any other asset.* The amount of cash that a partner should receive in liquidation will be indicated by the balance in his or her capital account *after* the gain or loss from the disposal of assets has been divided among the partners in the agreed ratio for sharing net income and losses.

Treatment of Debit Balance in a Capital Account To illustrate this situation, let us change our assumptions concerning the sale of the assets by the firm of Royal, Simms, and Tate, and say that the partnership assets (except cash) are sold to North Corporation for $206,000. The amount of cash received by the partnership is $24,000 less than in the prior example, and the loss incurred on the sale of assets is ***$144,000*** rather than the ***$120,000*** previously illustrated. Tate's one-third share of a $144,000 loss would be $48,000, which would wipe out the $40,000 credit balance in his capital account and create an ***$8,000 debit balance.*** After the liabilities are paid, a balance sheet for the partnership would appear as follows:

Tate now owes $8,000 to the partnership

ROYAL, SIMMS, AND TATE
Balance Sheet
(After the Sale of All Assets Except Cash)

Assets		Partners' Equity	
Cash.........................	$156,000	Ann Royal, capital............	$ 92,000
		Ed Simms, capital	72,000
		Jon Tate, capital (deficiency)..	(8,000)
Total	$156,000	Total	$156,000

To eliminate the debit balance in his capital account, Tate should pay $8,000 to the partnership. If Tate makes this payment, the balance in his capital account will become zero, and the cash on hand will be increased to $164,000, which is just enough to pay Royal and Simms the balances shown in their capital accounts.

If Tate is unable to pay the $8,000 due to the firm, how should the $156,000 of cash on hand be divided between Royal and Simms, whose capital accounts stand at $92,000 and $72,000, respectively? Failure of Tate to pay in the debit balance means an additional loss to Royal and Simms. According to the original partnership agreement, Royal and Simms have equal income- and loss-sharing ratios. Since partnership agreements generally specify that such a debit balance or deficiency be shared in the net income and loss ratio, let us assume that this was included in the liquidation provisions of the partnership agreement. Therefore, each must absorb $4,000 additional loss caused by Tate's inability to pay the $8,000 due to the partnership. The $156,000 of cash on hand should be divided between Royal and Simms in such a manner that the capital account of each will be paid down to $4,000, their respective shares of the additional loss. The journal entry to record this distribution of cash to Royal and Simms is as follows:

Entry to record distribution of cash on hand

Ann Royal, Capital..	*88,000*	
Ed Simms, Capital..	*68,000*	
Cash		*156,000*

To divide the remaining cash by paying down the capital accounts of Royal and Simms to a balance of $4,000 each, representing the division of Tate's loss between them.

After this entry has been posted, the only accounts still open in the partnership records will be the capital accounts of the three partners. A trial balance of the ledger will appear as follows:

ROYAL, SIMMS, AND TATE
Trial Balance
(After Distribution of Cash)

Trial balance after cash distribution

Ann Royal, capital...		*$4,000*
Ed Simms, capital		*4,000*
Jon Tate, capital (deficiency).............................	*$8,000*	
	$8,000	*$8,000*

If Tate is able later to pay in the $8,000 debit balance, Royal and Simms will then receive the additional $4,000 each indicated by the credit balances in their accounts. However, if Tate is definitely unable to pay the $8,000, these accounts should be closed.

The sharing of a debit balance may become a rather difficult issue if the partnership agreement is silent or the partners fail to agree on how such a debit balance is to be shared. Even though there are provisions on this issue in the partnership legislation, they are potentially subject to different interpretations. One interpretation was provided in the English case *Garner v. Murray* (1904), where it was ruled that the debit balance was to be shared among the other partners in the ratio of their capital account balances as at the date of liquidation. The reason was that the debit balance was considered a personal debt of one partner to the other partners rather than a business or operating loss. As a practical matter, however, the issue of how the debit balance should be shared rarely arises, apparently because partnership agreements generally specify a method for such a situation.

In solving the problems on partnership liquidation in this text, it is assumed that the partnership agreement specifies the sharing of a debit balance of a partner's capital account by other partners in the net income and loss ratio.

CHAPTER REVIEW

KEY TERMS INTRODUCED OR EMPHASIZED IN CHAPTER 13

Dissolution (of a partnership)   Termination of an existing partnership by any change in the personnel of the partners or by liquidating the business.

General partner   A partner in a limited partnership who has the traditional rights and responsibilities of a partner, including mutual agency and unlimited personal liability for the debts of the business.

Limited partner   A partner in a limited partnership who has the right to participate in income, but whose liability for losses is limited to the amount he or she has invested and who does not have the right to participate in management of the business. A limited partner's role is that of an investor rather than that of a traditional partner.

Limited partnership   A partnership that has one or more *limited partners* as well as one or more *general partners.* Limited partnerships are used primarily to attract investment capital from the limited partners for such ventures as mining and real estate development.

Liquidation of a partnership   The process of breaking up and discontinuing a partnership, including the sale of assets, payment of creditors, and distribution of remaining assets to the partners.

Mutual agency   Authority of each partner to act as agent for the partnership within its normal scope of operations and to enter into contracts that bind the partnership.

Partnership contract   An agreement among partners on the formation and operation of the partnership. Usually includes such points as a plan for sharing net income, amounts to be invested, and provision for dissolution and liquidation.

Statement of partners' equity   A financial statement that shows for each partner and for the firm the amounts of beginning capitals, additional investments, net income, drawings, and ending capitals.

ASSIGNMENT MATERIAL

DISCUSSION QUESTIONS

1   Jane Miller is the proprietor of a small manufacturing business. She is considering the possibility of joining in partnership with Mary Bracken, whom she considers to be thoroughly competent and congenial. Prepare a brief statement outlining the advantages and disadvantages of the potential partnership to Miller.

2   Allen and Baker are considering forming a partnership. What do you think are the two most important factors for them to include in their partnership agreement?

3   What is meant by the term *mutual agency?*

4   A real estate development business is managed by two experienced developers and is financed by 50 investors from throughout the country. To allow maximum income tax benefits to the investors, the business is organized as a partnership. Explain why this type of business would probably be a limited partnership rather than a regular partnership.

5 What factors should be considered in drawing up an agreement as to the way in which net income shall be shared by two or more partners?

6 Scott has land having a book value of $50,000 and a current market value of $80,000 and a building having a book value of $70,000 and a current market value of $60,000. The land and building become Scott's sole capital contribution to a partnership. Assuming no bonus to any partner, what is Scott's capital balance in the new partnership? Why?

7 Is it possible that a partnership agreement containing interest and salary allowances as a step toward dividing net income could cause a partnership net loss to be distributed so that one partner's capital account would be decreased by **more** than the amount of the entire partnership net loss?

8 Partner John Young has a choice to make. He has been offered by his partners a choice between no salary allowance and a one-third share in the partnership net income or a salary of $16,000 per year and a one-quarter share of residual income. Write a brief memorandum explaining the factors he should consider in reaching a decision.

9 Helen Lee withdraws $25,000 from a partnership during the year. When the financial statements are prepared at the end of the year, Lee's share of the partnership net income is $45,000. Which amount must Lee report on her income tax return?

10 What factors should be considered when comparing the net income figure of a partnership to that of a corporation of similar size?

11 Explain the difference between being admitted to a partnership by buying an equity interest from an existing partner and by making an investment in the partnership.

12 If C is going to be admitted to the partnership of A and B, why is it first necessary to determine the current market value of the assets of the partnership of A and B?

13 Shirley Bray and Carl Carter are partners who share net income and losses equally. The current balances in their capital accounts are: Bray, $50,000; Carter, $35,000. If Carter sells his equity interest in the firm to Deacon for $70,000 and Bray consents to the sale, what entry should be made in the partnership accounting records?

14 Farley invests $80,000 cash in the partnership of Dale and Erskin, but is granted an equity interest of only $60,000 upon his admission to the partnership. What is the nature of the $20,000 difference between the amount invested by Farley and the equity interest he received? How is this $20,000 difference handled in the partnership accounting records?

15 Majors, who has a capital account balance of $90,000, received cash of $120,000 from the partnership of Linden, Majors, & Napp upon his retirement. Discuss the nature of the $30,000 paid to Majors in excess of his capital account balance and how this excess payment is handled in the partnership books upon Majors' withdrawal.

16 Describe how a **liquidation** of a partnership may differ from a **dissolution** of a partnership.

17 What measure can you suggest to prevent a partnership from having insufficient cash available to pay the estate of a deceased partner without disrupting the operation of the business?

18 Upon the death of Robert Bell, a partner in the firm of Bell, Cross, and Davis, Charles Bell, the son of Robert Bell, demanded that he replace his father as a member of the partnership. Can Charles Bell enforce this demand? Explain.

MULTIPLE CHOICE QUESTIONS

1 When a partnership is formed,

   a A written partnership agreement, signed by all partners, must be filed in the jurisdiction in which the partnership is formed.

   b Each partner may bind the business to contracts and may withdraw an unlimited amount of assets from the partnership, unless these rights are limited in the partnership contract.

   c Each member of the partnership is entitled to participate equally in the net income of and management of the partnership, unless the partnership is a limited partnership.

   d The partnership must file an income tax return and pay income taxes on its net income.

2 Carter and Dixie have capital account balances of $80,000 and $100,000, respectively, at the beginning of 1996. Their partnership agreement provides for interest on beginning capital account balances, 10%; salaries to Carter, $30,000, and to Dixie, $24,000; residual income or loss divided 60% to Carter and 40% to Dixie. Partnership net income for 1996 is $62,000. Neither partner made any additional investment in the partnership during 1996, but Carter withdrew $1,500 monthly and Dixie withdrew $1,000 monthly throughout 1996. The partnership balance sheet at December 31, 1996, should include:

   a Capital, Carter, $94,000

   b Capital, Carter, $100,000

   c Capital, Dixie, $30,000

   d Total partners' equity, $242,000

3 Quinn and Ryan are partners who divide net income and losses 30% to Quinn and 70% to Ryan. At the present time, Quinn's capital account balance is $80,000 and Ryan's capital account balance is $160,000. Stone is admitted to a one-third equity interest in the partnership for an investment of $60,000. Each of the following statements relating to the admission of Stone is true with the exception of:

   a Quinn has a capital account balance of $68,000 after recording Stone's admission.

   b Stone has a capital account balance of $60,000 upon his admission to the partnership.

   c Stone received a "bonus" of $40,000 from Quinn and Ryan.

   d Total capital (equity) of the new partnership is $300,000 after Stone's admission is recorded.

4 Link, Martin, and Nolan are partners dividing net income and losses 30% to Link, 40% to Martin, and 30% to Nolan. Their capital accounts are as follows: Link, $500,000; Martin, $100,000; Nolan, $400,000. Nolan decides to retire and receives $393,000 from the partnership in exchange for his equity interest. Recording Nolan's withdrawal involves:

   a A debit to Nolan's capital account for $393,000.

   b Debits to Link's and to Martin's capital accounts for $3,500 each.

    c A credit to Link's capital account for $3,000 and a credit to Martin's capital account for $4,000.

    d Credits to Link's and to Martin's capital accounts for $200,000 each.

5 When a partnership is liquidated:

    a Any cash distribution to partners is allocated according to the income- and loss-sharing ratios.

    b Cash is distributed to each partner in an amount equal to his or her capital account balance prior to the sale of partnership assets.

    c Any gain or loss on disposal of partnership assets is divided among the partners according to their relative capital account balances.

    d A partner who maintained a credit balance in his or her capital account prior to liquidation may end up owing cash to the partnership if partnership assets are sold at a loss.

EXERCISES

EXERCISE 13-1
Accounting Terminology

Listed below are nine technical terms introduced in this chapter:

Unlimited liability	*Partnership contract*	*Dissolution of partnership*
Liquidation	*Current market value*	*Interest on partners' capital*
General partner	*Limited partner*	*Partnership net income*

Each of the following statements may (or may not) describe one of these technical terms. For each statement, indicate the accounting term described, or answer "None" if the statement does not correctly describe any of the terms.

    a Serves to identify partners, specify capital contributions, and establish income-sharing formula.

    b The process of breaking up and discontinuing a partnership business.

    c Amounts to be entered in asset accounts of a partnership to record the investment of noncash assets by partners.

    d A method of dividing partnership net income to ensure that no partner's share of net income will be less than the prime rate of interest applied to his or her capital account.

    e A characteristic of the partnership type of organization that causes many wealthy investors to choose investments in limited partnerships or corporations rather than in regular partnerships.

    f Results from the retirement of a partner from the firm or the admission of a new partner.

    g A partner whose financial responsibility does not exceed the amount of his or her investment and who does not actively participate in management.

    h An income-sharing provision designed to compensate for differences in dollar amounts invested by different partners.

EXERCISE 13-2
Formation of a Partnership

A business owned by Fern Douglas was short of cash and Douglas therefore decided to form a partnership with Andy McKuen, who was able to contribute cash to the new partnership. The assets contributed by Douglas appeared as follows in the balance sheet of her business: cash, $600; accounts receivable, $34,900, with an allowance for doubtful accounts of $960; inventory, $45,600; and store equipment, $21,600. Douglas had recorded depreciation of $1,800 during her use of the store equipment in her sole proprietorship.

Douglas and McKuen agreed that the allowance for doubtful accounts was inadequate and should be $1,800. They also agreed that a current market value for the inventory was $54,000 and that the current market value of the store equipment was $19,000. You are to open the partnership accounts by making a general journal entry to record the investment by Douglas.

EXERCISE 13-3
Partners' Capital and Drawing Accounts

Explain briefly the effect of each of the transactions given below on a partner's capital and drawing accounts:

a Partner borrows funds from the business.

b Partner collects a partnership account receivable while on vacation and uses the funds for personal purposes.

c Partner receives in cash the salary allowance provided in the partnership agreement.

d Partner takes home merchandise (cost $80, selling price $120) for personal use.

e Partner has loaned money to the partnership. The principal together with interest at 15% is now repaid to the partner in cash.

EXERCISE 13-4
Dividing Partnership Income

Guenther and Firmin, both of whom are CAs, form a partnership, with Guenther investing $100,000 and Firmin, $80,000. They agree to share net income as follows:

1 Salary allowances of $80,000 to Guenther and $60,000 to Firmin.

2 Interest allowances at 15% of beginning capital account balances.

3 Any partnership net income in excess of the amount required to cover the interest and salary allowances to be divided 60% to Guenther and 40% to Firmin.

INSTRUCTIONS

The partnership net income for the first year of operations amounted to $247,000 before interest and salary allowances. Show how this $247,000 should be divided between the two partners. Use a three-column schedule of the type illustrated in this chapter. List on separate lines the amounts of interest, salaries, and the residual amount divided.

EXERCISE 13-5
Admission of a New Partner; Bonus to Old Partners

Abrams and Boling are partners with capital account balances of $102,000 and $63,000. They divide net income and losses one-third to Abrams and two-thirds to Boling. The partnership has been quite profitable and has an excellent reputation. Abrams and Boling agree to admit Cato to a one-third equity interest in the partnership for an investment of $105,000. The assets of the business are *not* to be revalued. Explain how the bonus to the old partners is computed and prepare a general journal entry to record the admission of Cato.

EXERCISE 13-6
Admission of a New Partner; Bonus Computation

Randall and Dirks are partners who divide net income and losses 60% to Randall and 40% to Dirks. At the present time, each partner's capital account balance is $140,000. Randall and Dirks agree to admit Foster to a one-fourth equity interest in the partnership for an investment of $80,000. Prepare a general journal entry to record the admission of Foster. Explain how any bonus (to existing partners *or* to the incoming partner) is computed.

EXERCISE 13-7
Withdrawal of a Partner

The capital accounts of the Triple D partnership are as follows: Drake, $90,000; Dunlap, $210,000; Dyson, $180,000. Net income and losses are allocated 25% to Drake, 50% to Dunlap, and 25% to Dyson. Dyson is withdrawing from the partnership and it is agreed that he shall be paid $240,000 for his interest because the earnings of the business are high in relation to the assets of the firm. Assuming that the excess of the settlement over the amount of Dyson's capital account is to be recorded as a bonus to Dyson, prepare a general journal entry to record Dyson's retirement from the firm.

EXERCISE 13-8
Liquidation of a Partnership

The CDE partnership is being liquidated. After all liabilities have been paid and all assets sold, the balances of the partners' capital accounts are as follows: Cooley, $42,000 credit balance; Dean, $16,000 *debit* balance; Emmett, $53,000 credit balance. The partners share net income and losses: Cooley, 10%; Dean, 60%; Emmet, 30%.

a How should the available cash (the only remaining asset) be distributed if it is impossible to determine at this date whether Dean will be able to pay the $16,000 he owes the firm? Draft the journal entry to record payment of all available cash at this time.

b Draft the journal entries to record a subsequent partial payment of $13,000 to the firm by Dean, and the distribution of this cash. Prepare a schedule (similar to the one prepared in part **a**) showing computation of amount to be distributed to each partner.

PROBLEMS

Group A

PROBLEM 13A-1
Formation of a Partnership; Closing the Income Summary Account

The partnership of Barton and Liu was formed on July 2, when Tina Barton and Sam Liu agreed to invest equal amounts and to share net income and losses equally. The investment by Barton consists of $40,000 cash and an inventory of merchandise valued at $56,000.

Liu also is to contribute a total of $96,000. However, it is agreed that his contribution will consist of the following assets of his business along with the transfer to the partnership of his business liabilities. The agreed values of the various items as well as their carrying values on Liu's records are listed below. Liu also contributes enough cash to bring his capital account to $96,000.

	Investment by Liu	
	Balances on Liu's Records	Agreed Value
Accounts receivable	$89,600	$89,600
Allowance for doubtful accounts	3,840	8,000
Inventory	9,600	12,800
Office equipment (net)	12,800	9,000
Accounts payable	28,800	28,800

INSTRUCTIONS

a Draft entries (in general journal form) to record the investments of Barton and Liu in the new partnership.

b Prepare the beginning balance sheet of the partnership (in report form) at the close of business July 2, reflecting the above transfers to the firm.

c On the following June 30 after one year of operation, the Income Summary account showed a credit balance of $78,000 and the Drawing account for each partner showed a debit balance of $32,000. Prepare journal entries to close the Income Summary account and the drawing accounts at June 30.

PROBLEM 13A-2
Dividing Partnership Income; Financial Statements

The adjusted trial balance of B & G Distributors indicates the following account balances at the end of the current year:

	Debit	Credit
Cash	$ 32,620	
Accounts receivable (net)	81,000	
Inventory	28,200	
Prepaid expenses	3,900	
Equipment	90,000	
Accumulated depreciation		$ 18,000
Notes payable		9,600
Accounts payable		38,520
Accrued expenses		2,880
Bolton, capital (beginning of year)		70,000
Bolton, drawing	10,080	
Gorman, capital (beginning of year)		60,000
Gorman, drawing	7,200	
Sales		648,960
Cost of goods sold	390,960	
Selling expenses	112,380	
Administrative expenses	91,620	
Totals	$847,960	$847,960

A perpetual inventory system is used by the company. The partnership agreement provided that partners are to be allowed 10% interest on invested capital as of the beginning of the year and that the residual net income is to be divided equally.

INSTRUCTIONS

a Prepare an income statement for the current year, using the appropriate accounts from the above list. At the bottom of the income statement, prepare a schedule showing the division of net income.

b Prepare a statement of partners' equity for the current year.

c Prepare a balance sheet at the end of the current year.

PROBLEM 13A-3
Various Methods for Dividing Partnership Net Income

Alicia Dunn and Roberto Pascal, both real estate appraisers, formed a partnership, with Dunn investing $40,000 and Pascal investing $60,000. During the first year, the net income of the partnership amounted to $45,000.

INSTRUCTIONS

a Determine how the $45,000 net income would be divided under each of the following four independent assumptions as to the agreement for sharing net income and losses. Using schedules of the types illustrated in this chapter, show all steps in the division of net income between the partners.

1 The partnership agreement does not mention income sharing.

2 Interest at 15% to be allowed on beginning capital investments and balance to be divided equally.

3 Salaries of $24,000 to Dunn and $20,000 to Pascal; balance to be divided equally.

4 Salaries of $18,000 to Dunn and $26,000 to Pascal; interest at 15% to be allowed on beginning capital investments; balance to be divided equally.

b Prepare the journal entry to close the Income Summary account, using the division of net income developed in part **4** above.

PROBLEM 13A-4
Dividing Part-nership Net Income and Loss

Financial Planners has three partners—Reed, Stein, and Trump. At the beginning their capital balances were: Reed, $140,000; Stein, $100,000; and Trump, $60,000. The partnership agreement provides that partners shall receive salary allowances as follows: Reed, none; Stein, $60,000; and Trump, $38,000. The partners shall also be allowed 12% interest annually on their beginning capital balances. Residual income or loss is to be divided: Reed, 50%; Stein, 30%; Trump, 20%.

INSTRUCTIONS

Prepare separate schedules showing how net income or loss will be divided among the three partners in each of the following cases. The figure given in each case is the annual partnership net income or loss to be allocated among the partners.

a Net income of $554,000

b Net income of $83,000

c Net loss of $19,000

PROBLEM 13A-5
Admission of a New Partner

Aspen Lodge is a partnership with a record of profitable operations. At the end of the current year the capital accounts of the three partners and the ratio for sharing net income and losses are as shown in the following schedule. At this date, it is agreed that a new partner, Wolfgang Ritter, is to be admitted to the firm.

	Capital	Income-Sharing Ratio
Olga Svenson	$300,000	60%
Jill Kidd	240,000	30%
Miles Kohl	180,000	10%

INSTRUCTIONS

For each of the following situations involving the admission of Ritter to the partnership, give the necessary journal entry to record his admission.

a Ritter purchases one-half of Kidd's equity interest in the firm, paying Kidd personally $150,000.

b Ritter buys a one-quarter equity interest in the firm for $200,000 by purchasing one-fourth of the present equity interest of each of the three partners. Ritter pays the three individuals directly.

c Ritter invests $200,000 in the firm and receives a one-fourth interest in the equity and net income of the business. In addition to the journal entry to record Ritter's admission, show computation of the equity interest received and bonus (if any) to either the old partners or to Ritter.

d Ritter invests $360,000 in the firm and receives a one-fourth interest in the equity and net income of the business. In addition to the journal entry to record Ritter's admission, show computation of the equity interest received and bonus (if any) to either the old partners or to Ritter.

PROBLEM 13A-6
Retirement of a Partner

In the partnership of World Travel Agency, the partners' capital accounts at the end of the current year were as follows: Roy Kim, $220,000; Susan John, $148,000; and Mark Ray, $60,000. The partnership agreement provides that net income will be shared 40% to Kim, 50% to John, and 10% to Ray. At this time Kim decides to retire from the firm.

INSTRUCTIONS Described below are a number of independent situations involving the retirement of Kim. In each case prepare the journal entries necessary to reflect the withdrawal of Kim from the firm.

a Kim sells three-fourths of his equity interest to Ray for $208,000 and the other one-fourth to John for $64,000. The payments to Kim are made from the personal funds of Ray and John, not from the partnership.

b Kim accepts $90,000 in cash and a patent having a book value of $100,000 in full payment for his equity interest in the firm. This payment consists of a transfer of partnership assets to the retiring partner. As the fair value of the patent is approximately $100,000, the continuing partners agree that a revaluation of assets is not needed. The excess of Kim's capital account over the payment to him for withdrawal should be credited to the continuing partners.

c Kim receives $100,000 in cash and a 10-year, 12% note for $180,000 in full payment for his equity interest. Assets are not to be revalued.

PROBLEM 13A-7
Liquidation of a Partnership

The partnership of Talent Scouts has ended its operations and is in the process of liquidation. All assets except for cash and accounts receivable have already been sold. The task of collecting the accounts receivable is now to be carried out as rapidly as possible. The general ledger balances are as follows:

	Debit	Credit
Cash..	$ 27,200	
Accounts receivable	116,800	
Allowance for doubtful accounts		$ 6,400
Liabilities		36,800
May, capital (income-loss share 30%)		43,200
Nix, capital (income-loss share 50%)		33,600
Peat, capital (income-loss share 20%)		24,000

INSTRUCTIONS For each of the two independent situations shown below, prepare journal entries to record the collection or sale of the receivables, the payment of liabilities, and the distribution of all remaining cash to the partners. Support all entries with adequate explanation; the entries for distribution of cash to the partners should have explanations showing how the amounts were determined.

a Collections of $66,400 are made on receivables, and the remainder are deemed uncollectible.

b Receivables are sold to a collection agency; the partnership receives in cash as a final settlement 30% of the gross amount of its receivables. The personal financial status of the partners is uncertain, but all available cash is to be distributed at this time.

Group B

PROBLEM 13B-1
Formation of a Partnership

The partnership of Silver and Hawk was formed on January 1, when Anna Silver and John Hawk agreed to invest equal amounts and to share net income equally. The investment by Silver consists of $44,000 cash and an inventory of merchandise valued at $76,000. Hawk is also to contribute a total of $120,000. However, it is agreed that his contribution will consist of the following assets of his business along with the transfer to the partnership of his business liabilities. The agreed value of the various items as well as their carrying values on Hawk's records are listed as follows:

	Investment by Hawk	
	Balances on Hawk's Records	Agreed Value
Accounts receivable...	$117,600	$117,600
Allowance for doubtful accounts	5,040	8,500
Inventory..	16,600	20,800
Office equipment (net)......................................	16,800	19,500
Accounts payable	37,800	37,800

Hawk also contributed enough cash to bring his capital account to $120,000.

INSTRUCTIONS **a** Draft general journal entries to record the investments of Silver and Hawk in the new partnership.

b Prepare the beginning balance sheet of the partnership (in report form) at the close of business January 1, reflecting the above transfers to the firm.

c On the following December 31 after one year of operations, the Income Summary account had a credit balance of $92,000 and the Drawing account for each partner showed a debit balance of $36,000. Prepare journal entries to close the Income Summary and the drawing accounts at December 31.

**PROBLEM 13B-2
Dividing Income; Financial Statement**

The adjusted trial balance of Design for Living indicates the following account balances at the end of the current year:

	Debit	Credit
Cash...	$ 17,800	
Accounts receivable	105,200	
Allowance for doubtful accounts		$ 2,000
Inventory..	28,500	
Showroom fixtures	32,400	
Accumulated depreciation		6,400
Notes payable		9,000
Accounts payable		38,000
Lloyd, capital..		70,000
Lloyd, drawing	32,000	
Johnson, capital...		60,000
Johnson, drawing	24,000	
Sales		648,000
Cost of goods sold...	391,000	
Selling expenses	110,000	
Administrative expenses...................................	92,500	
Totals..	$833,400	$833,400

There were no changes in partners' capital accounts during the year. Design for Living uses a perpetual inventory system. The partnership agreement provided that partners are to be allowed 15% interest on invested capital as of the beginning of the year and that the residual net income is to be divided equally.

INSTRUCTIONS **a** Prepare an income statement for the current year, using the appropriate accounts from the above list. At the bottom of the income statement, prepare a schedule showing the distribution of net income.

b Prepare a statement of partners' equity for the current year.

c Prepare a balance sheet at the end of the current year.

PROBLEM 13B-3
Sharing Partnership Net Income: Various Methods

A small nightclub called Comedy Tonight was organized as a partnership with Lewis investing $80,000 and Martin investing $120,000. During the first year, net income amounted to $110,000.

INSTRUCTIONS

a Determine how the $110,000 net income would be divided under each of the following three independent assumptions as to the agreement for sharing net income and losses. Use schedules of the type illustrated in this chapter to show all steps in the division of net income between the partners.

　1 Net income is to be divided in a fixed ratio: 40% to Lewis and 60% to Martin.

　2 Interest at 15% to be allowed on beginning capital investments and balance to be divided equally.

　3 Salaries of $36,000 to Lewis and $56,000 to Martin; interest at 15% to be allowed on beginning capital investments; balance to be divided equally.

b Prepare the journal entry to close the Income Summary account, using the division of net income developed in part **3** above.

PROBLEM 13B-4
Dividing Partnership Net Income and Loss

Research Consultants has three partners—Axle, Brandt, and Conrad. During the current year their capital balances were: Axle, $180,000; Brandt, $140,000; and Conrad, $80,000. The partnership agreement provides that partners shall receive salary allowances as follows: Axle, $10,000; Brandt, $50,000; Conrad, $28,000. The partners shall also be allowed 12% interest annually on their capital balances. Residual net income or loss is to be divided: Axle, one-half; Brandt, one-third; Conrad, one-sixth.

INSTRUCTIONS

Prepare separate schedules showing how net income will be divided among the three partners in each of the following cases.

a Net income of $526,000

b Net income of $67,000

c Net loss of $32,000

PROBLEM 13B-5
Admission of a New Partner

Art of Asia is a partnership organized by Howell and So. On this date the two partners agreed to admit a new partner, Lee. Howell and So have been dividing net income in a ratio of 3:2 (that is, 60% and 40%). The new partnership will have an income- and loss-sharing ratio of Lee, 50%; Howell, 25%; and So, 25%. The following is the condensed balance sheet at September 30.

ART OF ASIA
Balance Sheet
September 30

Assets		Liabilities & Partners' Equity		
Current assets	$180,000	Liabilities		$160,000
Plant & equipment (net)........	420,000	Partners' equity:		
		Howell, capital ...	$280,000	
		So, capital	160,000	440,000
Total	$600,000	Total		$600,000

INSTRUCTIONS   Described below are four different situations under which Lee might be admitted to partnership. Considering each independently, prepare the journal entries necessary to record the admission of Lee to the firm.

a   Lee purchases a one-half equity interest in the partnership from Howell for $260,000. Payment is made to Howell as an individual.

b   Lee purchases one-half of Howell's equity interest and one-half of So's equity interest, paying Howell $168,000 and So $96,000.

c   Lee invests $300,000 in the firm and receives a one-half interest in capital and net income. In addition to the journal entry to record Lee's admission, show computation of the equity interest received and bonus (if any) to either the old partners or to Lee.

d   Lee invests $560,000 in the firm and receives a one-half interest in the capital and net income of the business. In addition to the journal entry to record Lee's admission, show computation of the equity interest received and bonus (if any) to either the old partners or to Lee.

PROBLEM 13B-6
Withdrawal of
a Partner

Terra Management is a partnership of three individuals that specializes in the management of professional office buildings. The partnership owns and maintains offices in one such professional centre and provides management services for several other buildings owned by clients. At the end of the current year, the firm had the following balance sheet:

TERRA MANAGEMENT
Balance Sheet
December 31, 19__

Assets		*Liabilities & Partners' Equity*		
Cash.........................	$175,000	Liabilities		$198,000
Receivables	67,000	Partners' equity:		
Land........................	210,000	Spence, capital...	$264,000	
Building (net of accumulated		Carver, capital....	180,000	
depreciation)	260,000	Drake, capital	168,000	612,000
Furniture & fixtures (net of				
accumulated depreciation) ..	98,000			
Total	$810,000	Total		$810,000

The partners share net income and losses in the ratio of 50% to Spence, 30% to Carver, and 20% to Drake. It is agreed that Drake is to withdraw from the partnership on this date.

INSTRUCTIONS   Following are a number of different assumptions involving the withdrawal of Drake from the firm. Considering each case independently, prepare the general journal entry or entries needed to record Drake's withdrawal.

a   Drake, with the permission of the other partners, gives his equity to his brother-in-law, Holmes, who is accepted as a partner in the firm.

b   Drake sells one-fourth of his equity interest to Carver for $48,000 cash and sells the other three-fourths to Spence for $104,000 cash. The payments are made by Carver and Spence personally and not by the partnership.

c   Drake retries and agrees to accept as full settlement of his partnership interest $120,000 cash and accounts receivable having a book value of $36,000. These assets come from the firm. The partners agree that no revaluation of assets will be made.

d The partners agree that land is worth $390,000 at present market prices. They do not wish to write up this asset in the accounts but believe that Drake is entitled to a settlement that includes his 20% interest in the increase in value. Drake is paid $96,000 in cash and given a 2-year, 12% note for $108,000.

PROBLEM 13B-7
Liquidation; Insolvent Partners

The December 31 balance sheet of MRC Group, a partnership specializing in market research and consulting, appears below. In order to focus attention on the principles involved in liquidating a partnership, the balance sheet has been shortened by combining all assets other than cash under the caption of "Other assets."

Merit, Rush, and Carroll share net income in a ratio of 3 : 2 : 1, respectively. At the date of the balance sheet the partners decided to liquidate the business.

MRC GROUP
Balance Sheet
December 31, 19__

Assets		*Liabilities & Partners' Equity*		
Cash.........................	$ 90,000	Liabilities		$180,000
Other assets	450,000	Partners' equity:		
		Merit, capital	$135,000	
		Rush, capital	120,000	
		Carroll, capital ...	105,000	360,000
Total	$540,000	Total		$540,000

INSTRUCTIONS

For each of the three independent situations shown below, prepare journal entries to record the sale of the "other assets," payment of liabilities, division of the loss on the sale of "other assets" among the partners, and distribution of the available cash to the partners. Support all entries with adequate explanation; the entries for distribution of cash to the partners should have explanations showing how the amounts were determined.

a Other assets are sold for $378,000.

b Other assets are sold for $144,000. Each partner has personal assets and will contribute the amount necessary to cover any debit balance in his or her capital account that may arise in the liquidation process.

c Other assets are sold for $117,000. Rush has personal assets and will contribute any necessary amount. Merit and Carroll are both personally bankrupt; any deficiency in either capital account must be absorbed by remaining partners.

ANALYTICAL AND DECISION PROBLEMS AND CASES

A&D 13-1
Developing an Equitable Plan for Dividing Partnership Income

Juan Ramirez and Robert Cole are considering forming a partnership to engage in the business of aerial photography. Ramirez is a licensed pilot, is currently earning $48,000 a year, and has $50,000 to invest in the partnership. Cole is a professional photographer who is currently earning $30,000 a year. He has recently inherited $70,000 that he plans to invest in the partnership.

Both partners will work full-time in the business. After careful study, they have estimated that expenses are likely to exceed revenue by $10,000 during the first year of operations. In the second year, however, they expect the business to become profitable, with revenue exceeding expenses by an estimated $90,000. (Bear in mind that these estimates of expenses do not include any salaries or interest to the partners.) Under present market conditions, a fair rate of return on capital invested in this type of business is 20%.

INSTRUCTIONS

a On the basis of this information, prepare a brief description of the income-sharing agreement that you would recommend for Ramirez and Cole. Explain the basis for your proposal.

b Prepare a separate schedule for each of the next two years showing how the estimated amounts of net income would be divided between the two partners under your plan. (Assume that the original capital balances for both partners remain unchanged during the 2-year period. This simplifying assumption allows you to ignore the changes that would normally occur in capital accounts as a result of divisions of net income, or from drawings or additional investments.)

c Write a brief statement explaining the differences in allocation of income to the two partners and defending the results indicated by your income-sharing proposal.

**A&D 13-2
An Offer of
Partnership**

Upon graduation from university, Ray Bradshaw began work as a staff assistant for a national CA firm. During the next few years, Bradshaw received his CA certificate and was promoted to the level of senior on the firm's audit staff.

At this time, Bradshaw received an offer from a small local CA firm, Ames and Bolt, to join that firm as a third partner. Both Ames and Bolt have been working much overtime and they would expect a similar workload from Bradshaw. Ames and Bolt draw salaries of $60,000 each and share residual income equally. They offer Bradshaw a $60,000 salary plus one-third of residual income. The offer provides for Bradshaw to receive a one-third equity interest in the firm and requires him to make a cash investment of $120,000. Balance sheet data for the firm of Ames and Bolt are as follows:

Current assets	*$ 72,000*	*Current liabilities*	*$ 36,000*
Property & equipment	*288,000*	*Long-term liabilities*	*174,000*
		Ames, capital	*75,000*
		Bolt, capital	*75,000*
Total	*$360,000*	*Total*	*$360,000*

Projected net income of the local CA firm for the next four years is estimated below. These estimated earnings are before partners' salaries and are based on the assumption that Bradshaw joins the firm and makes possible an increased volume of business.

1st year	*$192,000*	*3rd year*	*$228,000*
2nd year	*$204,000*	*4th year*	*$240,000*

If Bradshaw decides to continue in his present position with the national CA firm rather than join the local firm, he estimates that his salary over the next four years will be as follows:

1st year	*$62,000*	*3rd year*	*$73,000*
2nd year	*$66,000*	*4th year*	*$80,000*

INSTRUCTIONS

a Assuming that Bradshaw accepts the offer from Ames and Bolt, determine the amount of his beginning capital and prepare the entry in the partnership accounts to record Bradshaw's admission to the firm.

b Compute the yearly amounts of Bradshaw's income from the partnership for the next four years. Compare these amounts with the salary that he will receive if he continues in his present employment and write a memo explaining the factors Bradshaw should consider in deciding whether to accept or decline the offer from Ames and Bolt.

c Assuming that Bradshaw declines the offer, suggest some alternatives that he might propose if he decides to present a counteroffer to Ames and Bolt.

14 Corporations: Organization and Shareholders' Equity

This chapter begins our study of businesses organized as corporations. First, we describe the nature of a corporation, explain the concept of a "separate legal entity," and discuss the advantages and disadvantages of the corporate form of organization. Next, we focus attention upon the shareholders' equity section of a corporate balance sheet. Contributed capital is distinguished from retained earnings, and preferred stock is contrasted with common stock. Distinctions are drawn among the concepts of no par value, par value, book value, and market value. Various shareholders' equity transactions are illustrated and explained, including the issuance of capital stock and the declaration and payment of cash dividends. Also covered are such topics as subscriptions to capital stock, accounting for donated capital, and the computation of book value per share.

Learning Objectives

After studying this chapter you should be able to:

1 *Discuss the advantages and disadvantages of organizing a business as a corporation.*

2 *Explain the rights of shareholders and the roles of corporate directors and officers.*

3 *Contrast the balance sheet presentation of the ownership equity in a corporation and in a sole proprietorship.*

4 *Account for the issuance of capital stock.*

5 *Discuss the features of preferred stock and common stock.*

6 *Discuss the factors affecting the market price of preferred stock and of common stock.*

7 *Explain the meaning and significance of book value and market value of capital stock.*

Who owns a corporation? The owners of a corporation are called ***shareholders.*** Shareholders in a large corporation such as Canadian Pacific or BCE, Inc. (Bell Canada Enterprises) include thousands of men and women, as well as many pension funds, mutual investment funds, labour unions, banks, universities, and other organizations. Because a corporation can be used to pool the savings of any number of investors, it is an ideal means of obtaining the capital necessary for large-scale business activities.

Nearly all large businesses and many small ones are organized as corporations. There are many more sole proprietorships and partnerships than corporations, but in dollar volume of business activity, corporations hold an impressive lead. Because of the dominant role of the corporation in our economy, it is important for everyone interested in business, economics, or politics to have an understanding of corporations and their accounting practices.

What Is a Corporation?

A corporation is a ***legal entity*** having an existence separate and distinct from that of its owners. In the eyes of the law a corporation is an "artificial person," having many of the rights and responsibilities of a real person.

A corporation, as a separate legal entity, may own property in its own name. Thus, the assets of a corporation belong to the corporation itself, ***not to the shareholders.*** A corporation has legal status in court—that is, it may sue and be sued as if it were a person. As a legal entity, a corporation may enter into contracts, is responsible for its own debts, and pays income taxes on its earnings.

Advantages of the Corporate Form of Organization

The corporation offers a number of advantages not available in other forms of organization. Among these advantages are the following:

OBJECTIVE 1
Discuss the advantages and disadvantages of organizing a business as a corporation.

1 **No personal liability for shareholders.** Creditors of a corporation have a claim against the assets of the corporation, not against the personal property of the shareholders. Thus, the amount of money that shareholders risk by investing in a corporation is ***limited to the amount of their investment.*** To many investors, this is the most important advantage of the corporate form.

2 **Ease of accumulating capital.** Ownership of a corporation is evidenced by transferable ***shares of capital stock.*** The sale of corporate ownership in units of one or more shares permits both large and small investors to participate in ownership of the business. Some corporations have half a million or more individual shareholders. A corporation whose ownership shares are offered for sale to the general public is said to be ***publicly owned.*** Of course not all corporations are large. Many small businesses are organized as corporations and restrict ownership to a limited group of shareholders. Such corporations are said to be ***closely held or privately owned.***

3 **Readily transferable ownership shares.** Shares of capital stock may be sold by one investor to another without dissolving or disrupting the business organization. The shares of most large corporations may be

bought or sold by investors in organized markets, such as the ***Toronto Stock Exchange.*** Investments in these shares have the advantage of ***liquidity,*** because investors may easily convert their corporate ownership into cash by selling their capital stock.

4 **Continuous existence.** A corporation is a separate legal entity with a perpetual existence. The continuous life of the corporation, despite changes in ownership, is made possible by the issuance of transferable shares of capital stock. By way of contrast, a partnership is a relatively unstable form of organization that is dissolved by the death or retirement of any of its members. The continuity of the corporate entity is essential to most large-scale business activities.

5 **Professional management.** The shareholders own the corporation, but they do not manage it on a daily basis. To administer the affairs of the corporation, the shareholders elect a ***board of directors.*** The directors, in turn, hire a president and other corporate officers to manage the business. There is no mutual agency in a corporation; thus, an individual shareholder has no right to participate in the management of the business unless he or she has been hired as a corporate officer.

Disadvantages of the Corporate Form of Organization

Among the disadvantages of the corporation are:

1 **Greater regulation.** A corporation comes into existence under the terms of federal or provincial laws and these same laws may provide for considerable regulation of the corporation's activities and disclosures. For example, the withdrawal of funds from a corporation is subject to certain limits set by law. Moreover, various securities acts administered by the provincial securities commissions require publicly owned corporations to make extensive disclosure of their affairs.

2 **Separation of ownership and control.** The separation of the functions of ownership and management may be an advantage in some cases but a disadvantage in others. On the whole, the excellent record of growth and earnings in most large corporations indicates that the separation of ownership and control has benefited rather than injured shareholders. In a few instances, however, a management group has chosen to operate a corporation for the benefit of insiders. The shareholders may find it difficult in such cases to take the concerted action necessary to oust the officers.

3 **Taxation.** The income of a partnership or a sole proprietorship is taxable only as personal income to the owners of the business. The income of a corporation, on the other hand, is subject to income taxes that must be paid by the corporation. Federal and provincial corporate income taxes take a share of a corporation's before-tax income. If a corporation distributes its earnings to shareholders, the shareholders must pay personal income taxes on the amounts they receive. This practice of first taxing corporate income to the corporation and then taxing distributions of that income to the shareholders is sometimes called ***double taxation.*** However, this double taxation is minimized by the federal dividend tax credit claimed by the shareholders.

Income Taxes in Corporate Financial Statements

As mentioned previously, a corporation is subject to income taxes on its earnings. Income taxes are levied as a percentage of *taxable income.* Taxable income is an amount developed in an income tax return, consisting of those revenues subject to income taxes, minus the expenses (deductions) allowed by income tax laws.

At the end of every accounting period, the estimated amount of a corporation's income taxes expense for the period is recorded in an adjusting entry. As illustrated in Chapter 11, this entry consists of a debit to *Income Taxes Expense* and a credit to the current liability *Income Taxes Payable.*[1]

Corporate income taxes expense cannot be determined with precision until several months after year-end, when the corporation completes the preparation of its annual income tax return. Thus, the end-of-period adjusting entries are based upon estimates.

The topic of corporate income taxes is discussed further in Chapter 18.

Formation of a Corporation

A corporation is created by obtaining *a certificate of incorporation* or *a corporate charter* from the federal or provincial government where the company is to be incorporated. To obtain a certificate of incorporation or a corporate charter, an application called the *articles of incorporation* is submitted to the federal or provincial government. Once the certificate or charter is obtained, the shareholders in the new corporation hold a meeting to elect *directors* and to pass *bylaws* as a guide to the company's affairs. The directors in turn hold a meeting at which officers of the corporation are appointed.

Organization Costs   The formation of a corporation is a much more costly step than the organization of a partnership. The necessary costs include the payment of an incorporation fee to the federal or provincial government, the payment of fees to lawyers for their services in drawing up the articles of incorporation, payments to promoters, and a variety of other outlays necessary to bring the corporation into existence. These costs are charged to an asset account called Organization Costs. In the balance sheet, organization costs appear under the "Other assets" caption, as illustrated on page 679.

The incurring of these organization costs leads to the existence of the corporate entity; consequently, the benefits derived from these costs may be regarded as extending over the entire life of the corporation. Since the life of a corporation may continue indefinitely, one might argue that organization costs are an asset with an unlimited life. However, such intangible assets as organization costs should be amortized over a maximum period of 40 years.[2] Income tax rules, on the other hand, permit three-quarters of the organization costs to be written off at an annual rate of 7% based on the

---

[1]   The recognition of income taxes expense may also involve "deferred" income taxes. This topic is addressed in Chapter 16.

[2]   CICA, *CICA Handbook* (Toronto), section 3060.32.

declining balance method. Consequently, most companies have elected to write off organization costs in this manner. Accountants have been willing to accept this practice, because organization costs are not material in dollar amount. The accounting principle of **materiality** permits departures from theoretical concepts on the grounds of convenience if the practice in question will not cause any material distortion of net income or financial position.

Rights of Shareholders   The ownership of capital stock in a corporation usually carries the following basic rights:

OBJECTIVE 2
Explain the
rights of
shareholders
and the roles
of corporate
directors
and officers.

1 To vote for directors, and thereby to be represented in the management of the business. The approval of a majority of shareholders may also be required for such important corporate actions as mergers and acquisitions, the selection of independent auditors, the incurring of long-term debts, the establishment of stock option plans, or the splitting of capital stock into a larger number of shares.

   When a corporation issues two classes of capital stock such as common stock and preferred stock, voting rights generally are granted only to the holders of common stock. These two different types of capital stock will be discussed in detail later in this chapter.

2 To share in income by receiving **dividends** declared by the board of directors. Shareholders in a corporation may not make withdrawals of company assets, as may an owner of an unincorporated business. However, the income of a profitable corporation may be distributed to shareholders in the form of cash dividends. The payment of a dividend always requires formal authorization by the board of directors.

3 To share in the distribution of assets if the corporation is liquidated. When a corporation ends its existence, the creditors of the corporation must first be paid in full; any remaining assets are divided among shareholders in proportion to the number of shares owned.

4 To subscribe for additional shares in the event that the corporation decides to increase the amount of capital stock outstanding. This **pre-emptive right** entitles shareholders to maintain their percentages of ownership in the company by subscribing, in proportion to their present shareholdings, to any additional shares issued. Under the Canada Business Corporations Act, a corporation may provide such a pre-emptive right in its articles of incorporation if it so wishes.

Shareholders' meetings usually are held once a year. Each share of capital stock generally is entitled to one vote. (Some corporations have shares with more than one vote, such as Norcen's "multiple voting ordinary shares" with five votes each and its "subordinate voting ordinary shares" with one vote each.) In large corporations, these annual meetings are usually attended by relatively few persons, often by less than 1% of the shareholders. Prior to the meeting, the management group will request shareholders who do not plan to attend in person to send in **proxy statements** assigning their votes to the existing management. Through this use of the proxy system, management may secure the right to vote as much as, perhaps, 80% or more of the total outstanding shares.

Functions of the Board of Directors The primary functions of the board of directors are to manage the corporation and to protect the interests of the shareholders. At this level, management may consist principally of formulating policies and reviewing acts of the officers. Specific duties of the directors include declaring dividends, setting the salaries of officers, reviewing the system of internal control with the internal auditors and with the company's independent auditors, and authorizing important contracts of various kinds.

In recent years increasing importance has been attached to the inclusion of outside directors on the boards of large corporations. The term ***outside directors*** refers to individuals who are not officers of the company and who thus have a view independent of that of the corporate officers. The influence of these outside directors on the corporation can be very significant. Also, the board of directors of large publicly owned corporations have recently become more aggressive and more responsive to the shareholders' interests.

CASE IN POINT In recent years, a number of chief executive officers of giant corporations have resigned or changed position or "retired" under the pressures of the corporations' boards of directors. These corporations include General Motors and IBM in the United States, and Petro-Canada in Canada.

Functions of Corporate Officers Corporate officers are the top level of the professional managers appointed by the board of directors to run the business. These officers usually include a president or chief executive officer (CEO), one or more vice presidents, a controller, a treasurer, and a secretary. A vice president is often made responsible for the sales function; other vice presidents may be given responsibility for such important functions as human resources, finance, and production.

The responsibilities of the controller, treasurer, and secretary are most directly related to the accounting phase of business operation. The ***controller,*** or chief accounting officer, is responsible for the maintenance of adequate internal control and for the preparation of accounting records and financial statements. Such specialized activities as budgeting, tax planning, and preparation of tax returns are usually placed under the controller's jurisdiction. The ***treasurer*** has custody of the company's funds and is generally responsible for planning and controlling the company's cash position. The ***secretary*** represents the corporation in many contractual and legal matters and maintains minutes of the meetings of directors and shareholders. Another responsibility of the secretary is to coordinate the preparation of the annual report, which includes the financial statements and other information relating to corporate activities. In small corporations, one officer frequently acts as both secretary and treasurer. The following organization chart indicates lines of authority extending from shareholders to the directors to the president and other officers.

**Typical corpo-
rate organiza-
tion**

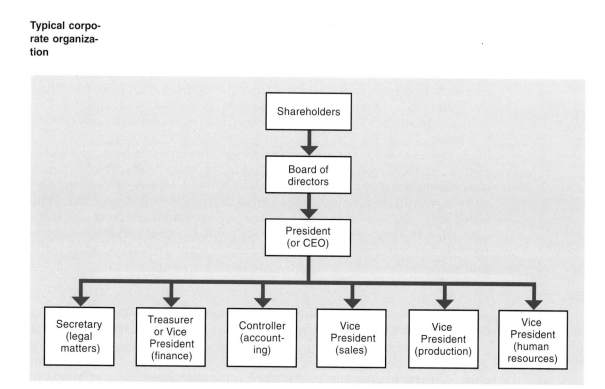

Shareholders' Equity[3]

The sections of the balance sheet showing assets and liabilities are much the same for a corporation as for a sole proprietorship. The owner's equity section is the principal point of contrast. In the balance sheet of a corporation, the term ***shareholders' equity*** is used instead of owners' equity.

*OBJECTIVE 3
Contrast the
balance
sheet pre-
sentation of
the owner-
ship equity
in a corpo-
ration and
in a sole
proprietor-
ship.*

The owners' equity in a corporation, as in other types of business organizations, is equal to the assets of the business minus the liabilities. However, corporation laws require that the shareholders' equity section of a corporate balance sheet clearly indicate the ***source*** of the owners' equity. The two basic sources of owners' equity are (1) investment by the shareholders ***(contributed capital),*** and (2) earnings from profitable operation of the business ***(retained earnings).***

When shareholders invest cash or other assets in the business, the corporation issues to them in exchange shares of capital stock as evidence of their ownership. In the simplest case, capital invested by the shareholders is recorded in the corporation's accounting records by a credit to an account entitled ***Capital Stock.*** The capital paid in by shareholders is regarded as permanent capital not ordinarily subject to withdrawal.

The increase in shareholders' equity arising from profitable operations is called ***retained earnings.*** At the end of the year the balance of the Income Summary account is closed into the Retained Earnings account.

---

3   According to the CICA's *Financial Reporting in Canada,* Twentieth Edition, 1993, pp. 135–136, the terms "shareholders' equity" and "capital stock" are most commonly used; thus, the first two terms are used in this book.

For example, if net income for the year is $70,000, the closing entry will be as follows:

Income Summary *70,000*
   Retained Earnings *70,000*
To close the Income Summary account by transferring the
year's net income into the Retained Earnings account.

If the company operates at a loss of, say, $25,000, the Income Summary account will have a debit balance. The account must then be credited to close it. The closing entry will be:

Retained Earnings *25,000*
   Income Summary *25,000*
To close the Income Summary account by transferring the
year's net loss into the Retained Earnings account.

If a corporation has sufficient cash, a distribution of income or earnings may be made to shareholders. Distributions of this nature are termed ***dividends*** and decrease both total assets and total shareholders' equity. Because dividends are regarded as distributions of earnings, the decrease in shareholders' equity is recorded in the Retained Earnings account. Thus, the amount of retained earnings at any balance sheet date represents the ***accumulated earnings of the company since the date of incorporation, minus any losses, and minus all dividends.***

Some people mistakenly believe that retained earnings represents a fund of cash available to a corporation. ***Retained earnings is not an asset; it is an element of shareholders' equity.*** Although the amount of retained earnings indicates the portion of total assets that are ***financed*** by the earnings retained by the corporation, it does ***not*** indicate the ***form*** in which these resources are currently held. The resources generated by retaining earnings may have been invested in land, buildings, equipment, or any other kind of asset. The total amount of cash owned by a corporation is shown by the balance of the Cash account, which appears in the asset section of the balance sheet.

Shareholders' Equity in the Balance Sheet For a corporation with $1,000,000 of capital stock and $600,000 of retained earnings, the shareholders' equity section of the balance sheet (omitting certain details) will appear as follows:

Contributed capital and retained earnings

Shareholders' equity:
 Capital stock *$1,000,000*
 Retained earnings *600,000* *$1,600,000*

If this same company had been unprofitable and had incurred losses totalling $300,000 since its incorporation, the shareholders' equity section of the balance sheet would be as follows:

Contributed capital less losses incurred

Shareholders' equity:
 Capital stock *$1,000,000*
 Less: Deficit *300,000* *$700,000*

This second illustration tells us that $300,000 of the original $1,000,000 invested by shareholders has been lost. Note that the capital stock in both illustrations remains at the fixed amount of $1,000,000, the shareholders' original investment. The accumulated income or losses since the organization of the corporation are shown as ***retained earnings*** or as a ***deficit*** and are not intermingled with the contributed capital. The term ***deficit*** indicates a negative amount of retained earnings.

Cash Dividends

The term ***dividend,*** when used by itself, is generally understood to mean a distribution of cash by a corporation to its shareholders. Dividends are stated as a specific amount per share of capital stock, as, for example, a dividend of $1 per share. The amount received by each shareholder is in proportion to the number of shares owned. Thus, a shareholder who owns 100 shares will receive $100.

Dividends are paid only through action by the board of directors. The board has full discretion to declare a dividend or to refrain from doing so. Once the declaration of a dividend has been announced, the obligation to pay the dividend is a current liability of the corporation and cannot be rescinded.

Because a dividend is declared on one date by the board of directors and paid at a later date, two separate journal entries are necessary. To illustrate the entries for declaration and payment of a cash dividend, assume that a corporation declares a dividend of $1 per share on 100,000 shares of outstanding capital stock. The dividend is declared on December 15 and is payable on January 25. The two entries would be as follows:

Dividends are first declared . . .	Dec. 15	*Retained Earnings*	*100,000*
		Dividends Payable..........................		*100,000*
		To record declaration by the board of directors of a cash dividend of $1 per share on the 100,000 shares of capital stock outstanding.	
. . . and then paid	Jan. 25	*Dividends Payable*	*100,000*
		Cash..		*100,000*
		To record payment of the $1 per share dividend declared Dec. 15 on the 100,000 shares of capital stock outstanding.	

The account ***Dividends Payable,*** which was credited at the date of declaring the dividend, is a current liability. If a company has more than one issue of capital stock (such as both common stock and preferred stock or class A and class B), it may use a separate Dividends Payable account for each issue.

Some companies in recording the declaration of a dividend will debit an account entitled Dividends instead of debiting the Retained Earnings account. Whenever a Dividends account is used, a closing entry will be required at the end of the year to transfer the debit balance in the Dividends account into the Retained Earnings account. Under either method the end result is a reduction in retained earnings for the amount of the dividends ***declared.*** (In our end-of-chapter material we will debit the Retained Earnings account, as illustrated above.)

What Is Capital Stock?

As previously mentioned, the caption ***capital stock*** in the balance sheet of a corporation represents the amount invested by the owners of the business. When the owners of a corporation invest cash or other assets in the business, the corporation issues capital stock as evidence of the investors' ownership equity.

The basic unit of capital stock is called a ***share,*** but a corporation may issue capital stock certificates in denominations of 1 share, 100 shares, or any other number. The total number of shares of capital stock outstanding at any given time represents 100% ownership of the corporation. ***Outstanding*** shares are those in the hands of shareholders. The number of shares owned by an individual investor determines the extent of his or her ownership of the corporation.

Assume, for example, that Star Corporation issues a total of 50,000 shares of capital stock to investors in exchange for cash. If you were to acquire 5,000 shares of the 50,000 shares, you would own a 10% interest in the corporation.

Authorization and Issuance of Capital Stock

OBJECTIVE 4 Account for the issuance of capital stock.

While the articles of incorporation ***may*** specify any maximum number of shares of capital stock that a corporation is authorized to issue, a corporation is ***not required*** to do so under the Canada Business Corporations Act. Thus, a corporation governed by the federal act does not have a limit on the maximum number of shares of capital stock it can issue unless it chooses to have one by stating such a limit in its articles of incorporation. The federal act does require, however, that the shares of capital stock of corporations be ***without par or nominal value.*** Provincial corporation legislation, such as the Ontario Business Corporations Act, parallels that of the federal act in these respects. On the other hand, certain provincial legislation (as well as legislation in the United States) still requires corporations to specify the maximum number of shares of capital stock they are authorized to issue and permits corporations to issue capital stock with a par value. Thus, some of the large corporations still have a maximum number of authorized capital stock and par value capital stock.

CASE IN POINT   Maritime Telegraph and Telephone has maximum authorized preferred and common stock, some with par value, and the premium on common stock (the excess of issue price over par value) is in excess of $38 million; Bow Valley Industries has 200 million shares of no-par common stock authorized, with only slightly over 54 million shares issued and outstanding.[4] In the United States, the common stock of Ford, AT&T, and Coca-Cola all have a par value of $1.

It should be noted that mere authorization of a capital stock issue (with or without a maximum limit) does not bring an asset into existence, nor

---

[4]   These corporations ranked among the 500 largest in Canada. See the annual Summer issue of *The Financial Post 500.*

does it give the corporation any capital. The obtaining of authorization from the federal or provincial government for a capital stock issue merely affords a legal opportunity to obtain assets through the sale of capital stock.

No-par Value Capital Stock

Federal and provincial corporation legislation clearly indicates that no-par value capital stock will become increasingly common in Canada. The following are some of the important reasons for the emergence of the concept of no-par value capital stock:

1 It avoids the assignment of an arbitrary amount as par value that is subject to misunderstanding by investors. For example, issued capital stock traded on stock exchanges at below its par value may sometimes be interpreted as a bargain even though the stock is at its fair market value. Thus, no-par stock eliminates such an opportunity for misunderstanding. Of course, the market value of any stock fluctuates according to the changes in the investors' perception about the value of the business, not according to the par value.

2 It provides a corporation with greater flexibility in the arrangement of its capital structure. For example, a corporation can split the existing no-par shares into a greater number of shares (as will be discussed in Chapter 15) without having to consider the effect on the par value. Also, no-par stock eliminates the problem of issuing stock at a discount, which generally is not allowed by law. Of course, since the par value is usually set at a very low amount, in reality the question of issuing stock at a discount seldom arises.

3 It eliminates the confusion and misunderstanding associated with the nature and meaning of such accounts as premium on capital stock, since no-par stock does not result in the establishment of these premium accounts.

Issuance of No-par Value Capital Stock   When no-par value capital stock is issued, the entire proceeds on the issue are credited to the Capital Stock account. Assuming that 60,000 shares of no-par value capital stock are issued at a price of $10 each, the entry to record the issue is as follows:

Entry for no-par capital stock

Cash	*600,000*	
Capital Stock		*600,000*
Issued 60,000 shares of no-par capital stock at a price of $10 a share.		

The amount credited to the Capital Stock account represents the ***legal capital*** or the ***stated capital***[5]—the amount that cannot be reduced except by (1) losses from business operations or (2) legal action taken by a majority vote of shareholders or permitted by the legislation governing the corporation.

---

[5]   "Stated capital" is the term used in the Canada Business Corporations Act and certain provincial corporations acts.

The shareholders' equity section of the balance sheet is illustrated as follows (assuming an unlimited number of authorized shares and the existence of $280,000 in retained earnings in order to have a complete illustration).

Shareholders' equity:

Capital stock, no-par value, authorized, an unlimited number	
of shares, issued and outstanding, 60,000 shares	*$600,000*
Retained earnings	*280,000*
Total shareholders' equity	*$880,000*

Par Value Capital Stock

The par value of capital stock represents the arbitrary amount assigned by a corporation as its legal capital per share. It merely indicates the amount per share to be entered in the Capital Stock account; it is *not* an indication of its market value. Par value may be $1, $2, $5, per share, or any amount decided upon by the corporation. Generally, the par values of most corporations are very small.

Issuance of Par Value Capital Stock   When par value capital stock is issued, the Capital Stock account is credited with the par value of the shares sold. Assuming that 80,000 shares of $2 par value capital stock are issued at a price of $2 each, the entry would be:

Entry for par value capital stock issued at par

Cash...	*160,000*	
Capital Stock		*160,000*
Issued 80,000 shares of $2 par value capital stock at their		
par value.		

When capital stock is sold for more than its par value, the Capital Stock account is credited with the par value of the shares issued, and a separate account, Premium on Capital Stock, is credited for the excess of selling price over par. If, for example, the issuance price is $3 rather than $2, as in the previous illustration, the entry for the 80,000 shares would be:

Capital stock issued in excess of par value

Cash...	*240,000*	
Capital Stock		*160,000*
Premium on Capital Stock		*80,000*
Issued 80,000 shares of $2 par value capital stock at a price		
of $3 a share.		

The premium (the amount in excess of par value) does not represent an income to the corporation. It is part of the invested capital, and it will be added to the capital stock on the balance sheet to show the total contributed capital.[6] The shareholders' equity section of the balance sheet is illustrated as follows. (An authorization for 1,800,000 shares and the existence of $70,000 in retained earnings are assumed in order to have a complete illustration.)

---

[6]   It is more appropriate to treat the premium on capital stock as part of the contributed capital than as part of contributed surplus, even though the latter is preferred by the *CICA Handbook*.

Corporation's
capital classi-
fied by source

Shareholders' equity:

Capital stock, $2 par value, authorized, 1,800,000 shares,	
issued and outstanding, 80,000 shares	*$160,000*
Premium on capital stock	*80,000*
Total contributed capital	*$240,000*
Retained earnings	*70,000*
Total shareholders' equity	*$310,000*

If capital stock is issued by a corporation for less than par, the account Discount on Capital Stock should be debited for the difference between the issuance price and the par value. The issuance of capital stock at a discount is not permitted under the federal and most provincial business corporations acts.

Preferred Stock and Common Stock

OBJECTIVE 5
Discuss the
features of
preferred
stock and
common
stock.

The account title **capital stock** is widely used when a corporation has issued **one class** of capital stock. In order to appeal to as many investors as possible, a corporation may issue more than one class of capital stock. Under the Canada Business Corporations Act, a corporation may have more than one class of capital stock, provided that the rights, privileges, restrictions, and conditions of each class are set forth in the articles of incorporation and that at least one class of capital stock has the rights typically associated with what is traditionally known as "common stock." These rights are identical with the first three rights mentioned earlier, namely, (1) to vote at any meeting of shareholders of the corporation, (2) to receive any dividend declared by the corporation, and (3) to receive the remaining property of the corporation on dissolution. The federal act does not use the terms "common" and "preferred" to distinguish the different classes of capital stock. However, since the terms "preferred stock" and "common stock" are still widely used in practice and have been proven useful in distinguishing classes of capital stock, they will be used throughout this book.

The basic type of capital stock issued by every corporation is generally called common stock. Common stock has the three basic rights previously mentioned. Whenever these rights are modified, the term preferred stock (or sometimes Class B Common) is used to describe this second type of capital stock. Some corporations issue two or more classes of preferred stock, each class having certain distinctive features designed to interest a particular type of investor. In summary, every business corporation has common stock; a good many corporations also issue preferred stock; and some companies have two or more types of preferred stock.

CASE IN POINT   The amount of preferred stock issued has been impressive. In recent years, the annual dollar amount of preferred stock issued ranged from around $400 million to over $3 billion. Many of these issues were cumulative preferred stock and the amount ranged from $50 million (Consumers' Gas) to $300 million (Canutilities Holdings) per issue.

Common stock may be regarded as the basic, residual element of ownership. It carries voting rights and, therefore, is the means of exercising control over the business. Common stock has unlimited possibilities of increase in value; during periods of business expansion, the market prices of common stocks of some leading corporations may rise to many times their former values. On the other hand, common stocks lose value more rapidly than other types of securities when corporations encounter periods of unprofitable business.

The following shareholders' equity section illustrates the balance sheet presentation for a corporation having both preferred and common stock; note that the item of retained earnings is not apportioned between the two groups of shareholders.

Balance sheet presentation of shareholders' equity

Shareholders' equity:

$12 cumulative preferred stock, no-par value, authorized, an unlimited number of shares, issued and outstanding, 200,000 shares	*$ 5,000,000*
Common stock, no-par value, authorized, an umlimited number of shares, issued and outstanding, 2,000,000 shares	*10,000,000*
Retained earnings	*3,500,000*
Total shareholders' equity	*$18,500,000*

Characteristics of Preferred Stock

The characteristics of preferred stocks vary from one issue to the next. The term ***preferred*** stems from the fact that these stocks almost always have "preference"—or priority—over the common stock in receiving dividends and in the event of liquidation. However, preferred shares usually ***lack*** significant advantages found in common stock. For example, the dividends paid to preferred shareholders normally ***do not increase*** if the company prospers. Also, preferred shareholders usually do ***not*** have voting rights and, therefore, have little say in management.

Among the features usually associated with preferred stock are the following:

1 Preferred as to dividends
2 Cumulative dividend rights
3 Preferred as to assets in event of the liquidation of the company
4 Callable or redeemable at the option of the corporation
5 No voting power

Another very important feature is a clause permitting the ***conversion*** of preferred stock into common at the option of the holder. Preferred stocks vary widely with respect to the special rights and privileges granted. Careful study of the terms of the individual preferred stock contract is a necessary step in the evaluation of any preferred stock.

Stock Preferred as to Dividends Stock preferred as to dividends is entitled to receive each year a dividend of specified amount before any dividend is paid on the common stock. The dividend is usually stated as a dollar amount per share. Some preferred stocks state the dividend preference as a ***percentage of par value.*** For example, a **9%** preferred stock with a par value of $100 per share would mean that $9 must be paid yearly on each share of preferred stock before any dividends are paid on the common. This dividend rate remains unchanged or fixed during the life of the preferred stock.

CASE IN POINT Bell Canada has a series of preferred stock at various dividend rates. For example, series 9 and 10 have dividend rates of $1.875 and $1.86 per share respectively; series 11, on the other hand, has a dividend rate of 7.64% per share.

In recent years, corporations also issued preferred stock with a ***floating rate*** of dividend rather than a fixed rate as discussed above. The floating rate is tied to the bank prime rate (an interest rate given to the most credit worthy customers). Thus, the amount of dividends the preferred shareholders receive changes as the bank prime rate changes. This means that these shareholders will receive and the corporations will pay a dividend rate that reflects the rate in the current market.

CASE IN POINT George Weston Limited has a number of "floating rate" preferred stock, among them: senior preferred stock-series A at 71% of average bank prime rate, junior preferred stock-series E at two-thirds average bank prime rate plus $\frac{3}{4}$%. Similarly, the "floating rate" preferred shares of Loblaw Companies Limited include: second preferred shares-first series at one-half of bank prime rate plus $\frac{7}{8}$%, second preferred shares-second series at one-half of bank prime rate plus $1\frac{1}{4}$%, and junior preferred shares-third series at two-thirds of average bank prime rate plus $\frac{3}{4}$%.

The holders of preferred stock have no assurance that they will always receive the indicated dividend. A corporation is obligated to pay dividends to shareholders only when the board of directors declares a dividend. Dividends must be paid on preferred stock before anything is paid to the common shareholders, but if the corporation is not prospering, it may decide not to pay dividends on either preferred or common stock. For a corporation to pay dividends, income must be earned and cash must be available. However, preferred stocks in general offer ***more assurance*** of regular dividend payments than do common stocks.

Cumulative Preferred Stock The dividend preference carried by most preferred stocks is a ***cumulative*** one. If all or any part of the regular dividend on the preferred stock is omitted in a given year, the amount omitted is said to be ***in arrears*** and must be paid in a subsequent year before any dividend can be paid on the common stock. Assume that a corporation was organized January 1, 1994, with 10,000 shares of $8 cumulative preferred stock and 50,000 shares of common stock. Dividends paid in 1994 were at the rate of $8 per share of preferred stock and $2 per share of common. In

1995, earnings declined sharply and the only dividend paid was $2 per share on the preferred stock. No dividends were paid in 1996. What is the status of the preferred stock at December 31, 1996? Dividends are in arrears in the amount of $14 per share ($6 omitted during 1995 and $8 omitted in 1996). On the entire issue of 10,000 shares of preferred stock, the dividends in arrears amount to $140,000.

Dividends in arrears *are not listed among the liabilities of a corporation, because no liability exists until a dividend is declared by the board of directors.* Nevertheless, the amount of any dividends in arrears on preferred stock is an important factor to investors and should always be *disclosed.* This disclosure is usually made by a note accompanying the balance sheet such as the following:

Footnote disclosure of dividends in arrears

Note 6: Dividends in arrears

As of December 31, 1996, dividends on the $8 cumulative preferred stock were in arrears to the extent of $14 per share and amounted in total to $140,000.

In 1997, we shall assume that the company earned a large income and wished to pay dividends on both the preferred and common stocks. Before paying a dividend on the common, the corporation must pay the $140,000 in arrears on the cumulative preferred stock *plus* the regular $8 per share applicable to the current year. The preferred shareholders would, therefore, receive a total of $220,000 in dividends in 1997; the board of directors would then be free to declare dividends on the common stock.

For a *noncumulative* preferred stock, any omitted dividend is lost forever. Because of this factor, investors view the noncumulative feature as an unfavourable element, even though noncumulative preferred stocks are still issued.

CASE IN POINT The investors' confidence that default on dividend obligations by large national financial institutions would be highly unlikely has enabled banks and trust companies to issue *noncumulative* preferred stocks. In a recent year, a number of banks and trust companies such as the Royal Bank, Toronto Dominion Bank, Bank of Montreal, Bank of Nova Scotia, and Royal Trustco issued over $1 billion of noncumulative preferred stock.

Stock Preferred as to Assets Most preferred stocks carry a preference as to assets in the event of liquidation of the corporation. If the business is terminated, the preferred stock is entitled to payment in full of its par value or a higher stated liquidation value before any payment is made on the common stock. This priority also includes any dividends in arrears.

Callable or Redeemable Preferred Stock Most preferred stocks include a *call* or *redemption provision.* This provision grants the issuing corporation the right to repurchase the stock from the shareholders at a stipulated *call (redemption) price.* The call price is usually slightly higher than the issued price or par value of the stock. For example, $100 par value preferred stock may be callable at $105 or $110 per share. In addition to paying the call price, a corporation that redeems its preferred stock must pay any dividends in arrears. A call provision gives a corporation flexibility in adjusting its financial structure, for example, by eliminating a preferred stock and replacing it with other securities if future growth of the company makes such change advantageous.

Convertible Preferred Stock   In order to add to the attractiveness of preferred stock as an investment, corporations sometimes offer a *conversion privilege* that entitles the preferred shareholders to exchange their shares for common stock in a stipulated ratio. If the corporation prospers, its common stock will probably rise in market value, and dividends on the common stock will probably increase. The investor who buys a convertible preferred stock rather than common stock has greater assurance of regular dividends. In addition, through the conversion privilege, the investor is assured of sharing in any substantial increase in value of the company's common stock.

As an example, assume that Remington Corporation issued a $9, no-par, convertible preferred stock on January 2, at a price of $100 per share. Each share was convertible into four shares of the company's no-par value common stock at any time. The common stock had a market price of $20 per share on January 2, and an annual dividend of $1 per share was being paid. During the next few years, Remington Corporation's earnings increased, the dividend on the common stock was raised to an annual rate of $3, and the market price of the common stock rose to $40 per share. At this point the preferred stock would have a market value of *at least $160,* since it could be converted at any time into four shares of common stock with a market value of $40 each. In other words, the market value of a convertible preferred stock will tend to move in accordance with the price of the common.

When the dividend rate is increased on the common stock, some holders of the preferred stock may convert their holdings into common stock in order to obtain a higher cash return on their investments. If the holder of 100 shares of the preferred stock presented these shares for conversion, Remington Corporation would make the following journal entry:

Conversion of
preferred stock
into common

$9 Convertible Preferred Stock	*10,000*	
Common Stock		*10,000*
To record the conversion of 100 shares of no-par preferred		
stock into 400 shares of no-par value common stock.		

Note that the issue price recorded for the 400 shares of common stock is based upon the *carrying value* of the preferred stock in the accounting records, not upon market prices at the date of conversion.

Participating Preferred Stock   On rare occasions, a corporation may issue a participating preferred stock. A *participating* preferred stock is one that, in addition to the regular specified dividend, is entitled to participate (or share) in some manner in additional dividends declared by the board of directors.

For example, assume a corporation has outstanding both common stock and $8 *fully participating,* no-par value preferred stock issued at $100 each. Any dividends declared are first allocated (at $8 per share or 8%) to the preferred shareholders. After the common shareholders are allocated an equivalent dividend (8% of the amount of the common stock issued and outstanding), the preferred and common shareholder groups share proportionally the residual amount, if any. ***Partially participating*** preferred stock is subject to limits on amounts received in excess of the stated preferred dividend.

Market Price of Preferred Stock

OBJECTIVE 6
Discuss the factors affecting the market price of preferred stock and of common stock.

Investors buy preferred stocks primarily to receive the dividends that these shares pay. Thus, the dividend rate is one important factor in determining the market price of a preferred stock.

But what happens to the market price of an $8 preferred stock, originally issued at $100, if government policies and other factors cause long-term interest rates to rise to, say, 15% or 16%? If investments offering a return of 16% are readily available, investors will no longer pay $100 for a share of preferred stock that provides a dividend of only $8 per year. Thus, the market price of the preferred stock will fall to about half of its original issue price, or about $50 per share. At this market price, the stock offers a 16% return (called the ***dividend yield***) to an investor purchasing the stock ($8 per year ÷ $50 = 16%). However, if the prevailing long-term interest rates decline to the 8% range, the market price of this $8 preferred stock should rise quickly to approximately the original issued price of $100.[7]

In conclusion, the market price of preferred stock ***varies inversely with interest rates.*** As interest rates rise, preferred stock prices decline; as interest rates fall, preferred stock prices rise.

Market Price of Common Stock

Interest rates also have a significant effect upon the market prices of common stocks. However, common stock dividends are not fixed in amount. If the company prospers, these dividends are likely to increase—perhaps every year. Therefore, ***investors' expectations*** as to the profitability of ***future operations*** greatly affect the market value of common shares.

In addition, many large corporations grow by acquiring smaller companies with excellent future prospects. This generally is accomplished by offering to buy all (or most) of the smaller company's common stock at a price that will induce the existing shareholders to sell. As preferred shareholders usually have no voting rights, an investor seeking control of a business entity need not acquire these shares.

Bear in mind that after shares have been issued they belong to the ***shareholders,*** not to the issuing corporation. Therefore, changes in the market price of the shares ***do not affect the financial statements of the corporation,*** and these changes are not recorded in the corporation's accounting records. The contributed capital shown in a corporate balance sheet represents the amount ***received when the stock was issued,*** not the current market value of shares.

Issuing Capital Stock: The Role of an Underwriter

When a large amount of capital stock is to be issued, most corporations use the services of an investment dealer, frequently referred to as an ***under-***

---

[7] To simplify the discussion, the effect of dividend tax credit is ignored.

writer. The underwriter guarantees the issuing corporation a specific price for the stock and makes a profit by selling the shares to the investing public at a slightly higher price. The corporation records the issuance of the stock at the net amount received from the underwriter. The use of an underwriter assures the corporation that the entire capital stock issue will be sold without delay and that the entire amount of funds to be raised will be available on a specific date.

The price that a corporation will ask for a new issue of capital stock is based upon such factors as (1) expected future earnings and dividends, (2) the financial strength of the company, and (3) the current state of the investment markets. However, if the corporation asks too much, it simply will not find an underwriter or other buyers willing to purchase the shares.

Stock Issued for Assets Other Than Cash

Corporations generally sell their capital stock for cash and use the cash to buy the various types of assets needed in the business. Sometimes, however, a corporation may issue shares of its capital stock in a direct exchange for land, buildings, or other assets. Capital stock may also be issued in payment for services rendered by lawyers and promoters in the formation of the corporation.

When a corporation issues capital stock in exchange for services or for assets other than cash, the transaction should be recorded at the current *market value* of the goods or services received. For some types of assets such as land or buildings, the services of a firm of professional appraisers may be useful in establishing current market value. Often, the best evidence as to the market value of these goods or services is the market value of the shares issued in exchange. For example, assume that a company issues 10,000 shares of its no-par value common stock in exchange for land. Competent appraisers may have differing opinions as to the market value of the land. But let us assume that the company's stock is currently selling on a stock exchange for $90 per share. It is logical to say that the cost of the land to the company is $900,000, the market value of the shares issued in exchange.

Once the valuation has been decided, the entry to record the issuance of the stock in exchange for the land is as follows:

Notice the use of current market values

Land	*900,000*	
Common Stock		*900,000*
To record the issuance of 10,000 shares of no-par value		
common stock in exchange for land. Current market value of		
stock ($90 per share) used as basis for valuing the land.		

Similarly, if 100 shares of the no-par value common stock with a market value of $90 per share are issued to lawyers and promoters for their services of $9,000 in the formation of the corporation, the entry to record the exchange is:

Organization costs	*9,000*	
Common Stock		*9,000*
To record the issuance of 100 shares of no-par value common		
stock in exchange for organization costs of $9,000.		

As mentioned earlier, the fair market value of the assets such as land and building may also be used as a basis of valuation if it is proven to be more objective and reliable than the market value of the shares used in the exchange. The responsibility for the determination of market value rests with the board of directors of the corporation. Thus, the board must assess all available evidence to ensure that the most objective and reliable basis of valuation is used.

Subscriptions to Capital Stock

Small, newly formed corporations sometimes offer investors an opportunity to **subscribe** to shares of the company's capital stock. Under a subscription plan, the investors agree to purchase specified numbers of shares at a stated price *at a future date,* often by making a series of instalment payments. The stock is issued after the entire subscription price has been collected.

In summary, selling stock through subscriptions is similar to selling merchandise on a "layaway" plan. One reason for this procedure is to attract small investors. Another reason is to appeal to investors who prefer not to invest cash until the corporation is ready to start business operations.

When stock is subscribed, the company debits Stock Subscriptions Receivable for the subscription price and credits Capital Stock Subscribed for the subscription price of the shares. Later, as instalments are collected, the entry is a debit to Cash and a credit to Stock Subscriptions Receivable. When the entire subscription price has been collected, the stock certificates are issued. The issuance of the stock is recorded by debiting Capital Stock Subscribed and crediting Capital Stock. The following illustration demonstrates the accounting procedures for stock subscriptions.

In this example, 10,000 shares of no-par value common stock are subscribed at a price of $15. Subscriptions for 6,000 of these shares are then collected in full from one subscriber. A partial payment is received from another subscriber on the other 4,000 shares.

Entry for subscription of common stock	Stock Subscriptions Receivable *150,000*	
	Common Stock Subscribed	*150,000*
	Received subscriptions for 10,000 shares of no-par value common stock at price of $15 a share.	

When the subscriptions for 6,000 shares are collected in full, certificates for 6,000 shares will be issued. The following entries are made:

Cash *90,000*		
Stock Subscriptions Receivable	*90,000*
Collected subscriptions in full for 6,000 shares at $15 each.	

Entries for subscriptions collected in full	Capital Stock Subscribed *90,000*	
	Common Stock	*90,000*
	Issued certificates for 6,000 fully paid shares of no-par common stock at $15 a share.	

The subscriber to the remaining 4,000 shares paid only half of the amount of the subscription but promised to pay the remainder within a month. Stock certificates will not be issued until the subscription is collected in full, but the partial collection is recorded by the following entry:

Entry for partial collection of subscription

Cash	*30,000*	
Stock Subscriptions Receivable		*30,000*
Collected partial payment on subscription for 4,000 shares.		

From the corporation's point of view, Stock Subscriptions Receivable is a current asset, which ordinarily will be collected within a short time. If financial statements are prepared between the date of obtaining subscriptions and the date of issuing the stock, the Capital Stock Subscribed account is regarded as legal capital and will appear in the shareholders' equity section of the balance sheet.

Donated Capital

On occasion, a corporation may receive assets as a gift. To increase local employment, for example, some cities have given corporations the land upon which to build factories. When a corporation receives such a gift, both total assets and total shareholders' equity increase by the market value of the assets received. ***No income is recognized when a gift is received;*** the increase in shareholders' equity is regarded as contributed capital. The receipt of a gift is recorded by debiting the appropriate asset accounts and crediting an account entitled ***Donated Capital.***

For example, the entry to record the donation of land with a market value of $390,000 is as follows:

Land	*390,000*	
Donated Capital		*390,000*
To record the donation of land with a market value		
of $390,000.		

Donated capital appears in the shareholders' equity section of the balance sheet, as illustrated on page 680.

Shareholder Records in a Corporation

A large corporation with shares listed on the Toronto Stock Exchange or other exchanges usually has millions of shares outstanding and hundreds of thousands of shareholders. Each day many shareholders sell their shares; the buyers of these shares become new members of the company's family of shareholders. An investor purchasing capital stock in a corporation receives a ***stock certificate*** from the company indicating the number of shares acquired. If the investor later sells these shares, this stock certificate must be surrendered to the corporation for cancellation before a new certificate is issued to the new owner of the shares.

A corporation must have an up-to-date record of the names and addresses of this constantly changing army of shareholders so that it can send dividend cheques, financial statements, and voting forms to the right people. Also, the corporation must make sure that old stock certificates are cancelled as new ones are issued so that no excess certificates become outstanding.

Shareholders Subsidiary Ledger   When there are numerous shareholders, it is not practical to include a separate account for each shareholder in the general ledger. Instead, a single controlling account entitled Capital Stock appears in the general ledger, and a ***shareholders subsidiary ledger*** is maintained. This ledger contains an account for each individual share-holder. Entries in the shareholders subsidiary ledger are made in number of shares rather than in dollars. Thus, each shareholder's account shows the number of shares owned and the dates of acquisitions and sales. This record enables the corporation to send each shareholder a single dividend cheque, even though the shareholder may have acquired several stock cer-tificates at different dates.

A corporation that has one or more issues of preferred stock outstand-ing, as well as common stock, will maintain a separate set of shareholders subsidiary records for each issue.

Stock Transfer Agent and Stock Registrar   Large, publicly owned corpora-tions use an independent stock transfer agent and a stock registrar to maintain their shareholder records and to establish strong internal control over the issuance of stock certificates. These transfer agents and registrars usually are large banks or trust companies. When stock certificates are to be transferred from one owner to another, the old certificates are sent to the transfer agent, who cancels them, makes the necessary entries in the shareholders subsidiary ledger, and prepares a new certificate for the new owner of the shares. This new certificate then must be registered with the stock registrar before it represents valid and transferable ownership of stock in the corporation.

Small, closely held corporations generally do not use the services of independent registrars and transfer agents. In these companies, the share-holder records usually are maintained by a corporate officer. To prevent the accidental or fraudulent issuance of an excessive number of stock cer-tificates, even a small corporation should require that each certificate be signed by at least two designated corporate officers.

Book Value per Share of Common Stock

OBJECTIVE 7
Explain the meaning and signifi-cance of book value and market value of capital stock.

Because the equity of each shareholder in a corporation is determined by the number of shares he or she owns, an accounting measurement of inter-est to many shareholders is book value per share of common stock. Book value per share is equal to the ***net assets*** represented by one share of common stock. The term ***net assets*** means total assets minus total liabili-ties; in other words, net assets are equal to total shareholders' equity. Thus in a corporation that has issued common stock only, the book value per share is computed by dividing total shareholders' equity by the number of shares outstanding (or subscribed).

For example, assume that a corporation has 4,000 shares of common stock outstanding and the shareholders' equity section of the balance sheet is as follows:

How much is book value per share?

Common stock, no-par value (4,000 shares outstanding)	*$ 44,000*
Retained earnings	*76,000*
Total shareholders' equity	*$120,000*

The book value per share is $30; it is computed by dividing the share-holders' equity of $120,000 by the 4,000 shares of outstanding stock. In computing book value, we are not concerned with the number of authorized shares but merely with the **outstanding** shares, because the total of the outstanding shares represents 100% of the shareholders' equity.

CASE IN POINT   Book value per share is regularly reported in such financial news media as *The Financial Post* and in the annual reports of such large corporations as Dofasco Inc., George Weston Limited, Bombardier, Ivaco, and United Dominion. For example, Dofasco's book value in a recent year was $12.98.

Book Value When a Company Has Both Preferred and Common Stock
Book value is usually computed only for common stock. If a company has both preferred and common stock outstanding, the computation of book value per share of common stock requires two steps. First, the ***redemption value*** or ***call price*** of the entire preferred stock issue and any dividends in arrears are deducted from total shareholders' equity. Second, the remaining amount of shareholders' equity is divided by the number of common shares outstanding to determine book value per common share. This procedure reflects the fact that the common shareholders are the residual owners of the corporate entity.

To illustrate, assume that the shareholders' equity of Video Corporation at December 31 is as follows:

Two classes of stock

$8 preferred stock, no-par, callable at $110, issued and outstanding, 10,000 shares	$1,000,000
Common stock, no-par, issued and outstanding, 50,000 shares	1,250,000
Retained earnings	130,000
Total shareholders' equity	$2,380,000

Because of a weak cash position, Video Corporation has paid no dividends during the current year. As of December 31, dividends in arrears on the cumulative preferred stock total **$80,000.**

All the equity belongs to the common shareholders, except the $1.1 million call price ($110 × 10,000 shares) applicable to the preferred stock and the $80,000 of dividends in arrears on preferred stock. The calculation of book value per share of common stock is shown below:

Total shareholders' equity		$2,380,000
Less: Equity of preferred shareholders:		
Call price of preferred stock	$1,100,000	
Dividends in arrears	80,000	1,180,000
Equity of common shareholders		$1,200,000
Number of common shares outstanding		50,000
Book value per share of common stock		
($1,200,000 ÷ 50,000 shares)		$24

Book Value and Market Price To some extent, book value may be used in evaluating the reasonableness of the market price of a stock. However, it must be used with great caution; the fact that a stock is selling at less than book value does not necessarily indicate a bargain.

Book value is a historical concept, representing the amounts invested by shareholders plus the amounts earned and retained by the corporation. If a stock is selling at a price well ***above*** book value, investors believe that management has created a business worth substantially more than the historical cost of the resources entrusted to its care. This, in essence, is the sign of a successful corporation. If the excess of market price over book value becomes very great, however, investors should consider whether the company's prospects really justify a market price so much above the underlying book value of the company's resources.

On the other hand, if the market price of a stock is ***less than*** book value, investors believe that the company's resources are worth less than their cost while under the control of current management. Thus, the relationship between book value and market price is one measure of investors' confidence in a company's management.

Balance Sheet for a Corporation Illustrated

A fairly complete balance sheet for a corporation is illustrated below and on the following page. Note the inclusion in this balance sheet of liabilities for income taxes payable and dividends payable. These liabilities do not appear in the balance sheet of an unincorporated business. Note also that the caption for each capital stock account indicates the type of capital stock and the number of shares authorized and issued. The caption for preferred stock also indicates the dividend rate, call price, and other important features.

Bear in mind that current practice includes many alternatives in the choice of terminology and the arrangement of items in financial statements.

DEL MAR CORPORATION
Balance Sheet
December 31, 1996

Assets

Current assets:

Cash and cash equivalents		$ 305,600
Accounts receivable (net)		1,215,200
Inventories (lower of FIFO and net realizable value)		1,300,800
Short-term prepayments		125,900
Total current assets		$2,947,500
Plant and equipment:		
Land—at cost		900,000
Buildings and equipment—at cost	$5,283,000	
Less: Accumulated depreciation	1,250,000	4,033,000
Other assets: Organization costs		14,000
Total assets		$7,894,500

Liabilities & Shareholders' Equity

Current liabilities:	
Accounts payable	$ 998,100
Income taxes payable	324,300
Dividends payable	109,700
Interest payable	20,000
Total current liabilities	$1,452,100
Long-term liabilities: Bonds payable, 12%, due Oct. 1, 2006	1,000,000
Total liabilities...	$2,452,100
Shareholders' equity:	
Cumulative $8 preferred stock, no-par, callable	
at $104, authorized, an unlimited number of	
shares, issued and outstanding, 10,000 shares	$1,000,000
Common stock, no-par, authorized, an unlimited	
number of shares, issued and outstanding,	
600,000 shares	2,670,000
Common stock subscribed, 2,500 shares	20,000
Donated capital	210,000
Total contributed capital	$3,900,000
Retained earnings	1,542,400
Total shareholders' equity	$5,442,400
Total liabilities & shareholders' equity	$7,894,500

CHAPTER REVIEW

KEY TERMS INTRODUCED OR EMPHASIZED IN CHAPTER 14

Board of directors Persons elected by common shareholders to direct the affairs of a corporation.

Book value per share The shareholders' equity represented by each share of common stock, computed by dividing common shareholders' equity by the number of common shares outstanding.

Call (redemption) price The price to be paid by a corporation for each share of callable (redeemable) preferred stock if the corporation decides to call (redeem) the preferred stock.

Capital stock Transferable units of ownership in a corporation. A broad term that may refer to common stock, preferred stock, or both.

Closely held corporation A corporation owned by a limited group of shareholders, usually a small corporation.

Common stock A type of capital stock that possesses the basic rights of ownership including the right to vote. Represents the residual element of ownership in a corporation.

Contributed capital The amounts invested in a corporation by its shareholders (also includes donated capital).

Cumulative preferred stock A class of preferred stock with a provision that if dividends are reduced or omitted in any year, this amount of dividends accumulates and must be paid prior to payment of dividends on common stock.

Deficit   Accumulated losses incurred by a corporation. A negative amount of retained earnings.

Dividend   A distribution of cash by a corporation to its shareholders.

Floating rate   A dividend rate for preferred stock that is tied to the bank prime interest rate.

Legal capital   Equal to the ***proceeds of no-par value*** or the ***par value*** of capital stock issued. This amount represents a "permanent commitment" of capital by the owners of a corporation and cannot be removed without special legal action. Of course, it may be eroded by losses.

Non-cumulative preferred stock   A class of preferred stock with a provision that any dividends omitted in any year are lost forever.

No-par value   Capital stock without nominal or par value.

Organization costs   Costs incurred to form a corporation.

Par value   The ***legal capital*** of a corporation. Represents the minimum amount per share to be invested in the corporation by its owners and cannot be withdrawn except by special legal action.

Preferred stock   A class of capital stock usually having preferences as to dividends and in the distribution of assets in event of liquidation.

Premium on capital stock   The amount paid in by shareholders for the capital stock in excess of its par value.

Publicly owned corporation   A corporation whose ownership shares are offered for sale to the general public.

Retained earnings   That portion of shareholders' equity resulting from income earned and retained in the business. Retained earnings is increased by the earning of net income and is decreased by the incurring of net losses and by the declaration of dividends.

Shareholder   Someone with an ownership interest in a corporation. The percentage of this ownership interest is determined by the percentage of the outstanding shares owned.

Shareholders' equity   The excess of assets over liabilities. The two main sources are investments by the shareholders and earnings from profitable operations.

Shareholders subsidiary ledger   A record showing the number of shares owned by each shareholder.

Stock certificate   A document issued by a corporation (or its transfer agent) as evidence of the ownership of the number of shares stated on the certificate.

Stock registrar   An independent agent retained by a corporation to provide assurance against overissuance of stock certificates.

Stock transfer agent   A bank or trust company retained by a corporation to maintain its records of capital stock ownership and to make transfers from one investor to another.

Underwriter   An investment dealer who handles the sale of a corporation's capital stock to the public.

DEMONSTRATION PROBLEM FOR YOUR REVIEW

At the close of the current year, the shareholders' equity section of Rockhurst Corporation's balance sheet was as follows:

Shareholders' equity:

$8 preferred stock, no-par value, authorized, an unlimited number of shares, callable at $102 per share, issued and outstanding, 120,000 shares		$12,360,000
Common stock, no-par value, authorized, an unlimited number of shares:		
Issued and outstanding 2,000,000	$32,000,000	
Subscribed, 800,000 shares	12,800,000	44,800,000
Retained earnings		2,680,000
Total shareholders' equity		$59,840,000

Assets of the corporation include **subscriptions receivable, $7,200,000.**

INSTRUCTIONS   On the basis of this information, answer the following questions and show any necessary supporting computations.

a   What is the total annual dividend requirement on the outstanding preferred stock?

b   What was the average price per share received by the corporation for its common stock, including shares subscribed?

c   What is the average amount per share that subscribers to common stock have yet to pay on their subscriptions?

d   What is the total amount of legal capital, including shares subscribed?

e   What is the book value per share of common stock? (Assume no dividends in arrears.)

SOLUTION TO DEMONSTRATION PROBLEM

a $960,000 (120,000 shares × $8 per share)

b	*Total issue price of common shares (including subscribed)..............*	*$44,800,000*
	Shares issued and subscribed (2,000,000 + 800,000)....................	*2,800,000*
	Average issue price per share ($44,800,000 ÷ 2,800,000 shares)..........	*$16*
c	*Subscriptions receivable ....*	*$ 7,200,000*
	Shares subscribed	*800,000*
	Average amount due per share ($7,200,000 ÷ 800,000 shares)...........	*$9*
d	*$57,160,000 ($12,360,000 preferred, $44,800,000 common)*	
e	*Total shareholders' equity...*	*$59,840,000*
	Less: Claims of preferred shareholders (120,000 shares	
	× $102 call price)	*12,240,000*
	Equity of common shareholders.......................................	*$47,600,000*
	Common shares outstanding or subscribed	
	(2,000,000 + 800,000)...	*2,800,000*
	Book value per share ($47,600,000 ÷ 2,800,000 shares)	*$17*

ASSIGNMENT MATERIAL

DISCUSSION QUESTIONS

1   Why are large corporations often said to be **publicly owned?**

2   Distinguish between corporations and partnerships in terms of the following characteristics:

    a Owners' liability for debts of the business

    b Transferability of ownership interest

    c Continuity of existence

    d Taxation on income

3 What are the basic rights of the owner of a share of corporate stock? In what way are these basic rights commonly modified with respect to the owner of a share of preferred stock?

4 Distinguish between ***contributed capital*** and ***retained earnings*** of a corporation. Why is such a distinction useful?

5 If the Retained Earnings account has a debit balance, how is it presented in the balance sheet and what is it called?

6 Explain the reasons for the emergence of the concept of no-par value capital stock in federal and provincial corporation legislation.

7 Explain the significance of ***par value.*** Does par value indicate the reasonable market price for a share of capital stock? Explain.

8 Describe the usual nature of the following features as they apply to a share of preferred stock: (a) cumulative, (b) convertible, and (c) callable (redeemable).

9 Why is noncumulative preferred stock considered a very unattractive form of investment?

10 When capital stock is issued by a corporation in exchange for assets other than cash, accountants face the problem of determining the dollar amount at which to record the transaction. Discuss the factors to be considered and explain their significance.

11 State the classification (asset, liability, shareholders' equity, revenue, or expense) of each of the following accounts:

    a Subscriptions receivable

    b Organization costs

    c Preferred stock

    d Retained earnings

    e Capital stock subscribed

    f Premium on common stock

    g Income taxes payable

12 A professional baseball team received as a gift from the city the land upon which to build a stadium. What effect, if any, will the receipt of this gift have upon the baseball team's balance sheet and income statement? Explain.

13 Explain the following terms:

    a Stock transfer agent

    b Shareholders subsidiary ledger

    c Underwriter

    d Stock registrar

14 What does ***book value per share*** of common stock represent? Does it represent the amount common shareholders would receive in the event of liquidation of the corporation? Explain briefly.

15 How is book value per share of common stock computed when a company has both preferred and common stock outstanding?

16 What would be the effect, if any, on book value per share of common stock as a result of each of the following independent events: (a) a corporation obtains a bank loan; (b) a dividend is declared (to be paid in the next accounting period).

17 In the great stock market crash of October 19, 1987, the market price of **IBM's** capital stock fell by over $31 per share. Explain the effects, if any, of this decline in share price on IBM's balance sheet.

MULTIPLE CHOICE QUESTIONS

1 When a business is organized as a corporation:

 a Shareholders are liable for the debts of the business only in proportion to their percentage ownership of capital stock.

 b Shareholders do *not* have to pay personal income taxes on dividends received, because the corporation is subject to income taxes on its earnings.

 c Fluctuations in the market value of outstanding shares of capital stock do *not* affect the amount of shareholders' equity shown in the balance sheet.

 d Each shareholder has the right to bind the corporation to contracts and to make other managerial decisions.

2 Great Plains Corporation was organized with authorization to issue 100,000 shares of no-par value common stock. Forty thousand shares were issued to Tom Morgan, the company's founder, at a price of $5 per share. No other shares have yet been issued.

 a Morgan owns *40*% of the shareholders' equity of the corporation.

 b The corporation should recognize a $200,000 gain on the issuance of these shares.

 c If the balance sheet includes retained earnings of $50,000, total *contributed* capital amounts to $250,000.

 d In the balance sheet, the Common Stock account will have a $200,000 balance, regardless of the income earned or losses incurred since the corporation was organized.

3 Which of the following is *not* a characteristic of the *common stock* of a large, publicly owned corporation?

 a The shares may be transferred from one investor to another without disrupting the continuity of business operations.

 b Voting rights in the election of the board of directors.

 c A cumulative right to receive dividends.

 d After issuance, the market value of the stock is unrelated to its issued price or par value.

4 Tri-County Electric is a profitable utility company that has increased its dividend to *common* shareholders every year for 62 consecutive years. Which of the following is *least* likely to affect the market price of the company's *preferred* stock?

 a The company's earnings are expected to increase significantly over the next several years.

 b An increase in long-term interest rates.

 c The annual dividend paid to preferred shareholders.

 d Whether or not the preferred stock carries a conversion privilege.

5 The following information is taken from the balance sheet and related disclosures of Blue Oyster Corporation:

Total contributed capital	*$5,400,000*
Outstanding shares:	
Common stock, no-par value.....................................	*100,000 shares*
$6 preferred stock, no-par value, callable at $108 per share,	
issued at $100 per share.......................................	*10,000 shares*
Preferred dividends in arrears......................................	*2 years*
Total shareholders' equity..	*$4,700,000*

Which of the following statements is true? (More than one answer may be correct.)

a The preferred dividends in arrears amount to $120,000 and should appear as a liability in the corporate balance sheet.

b The book value per share of common stock is $35.

c The shareholders' equity section of the balance sheet should include a deficit of $700,000.

d The company has paid no dividend on its ***common*** stock during the past two years.

EXERCISES

EXERCISE 14-1
Accounting Terminology

Listed below are nine technical accounting terms introduced or emphasized in this chapter:

Retained earnings	*Preferred stock*	*No-par value*
Deficit	*Common stock*	*Book value*
Dividend in arrears	*Contributed capital*	*Market value*

Each of the following statements may (or may not) describe one of these technical terms. For each statement, indicate the term described, or answer "None" if the statement does not correctly describe any of the terms.

a That portion of shareholders' equity arising from the issuance of capital stock.

b The type of capital stock most likely to increase in value as a corporation becomes increasingly profitable.

c The net assets represented by one share of common stock.

d A distribution of cash by a corporation to its owners.

e The type of capital stock for which the dividend usually is fixed in amount.

f Cash provided by profitable operations that is available for distribution to shareholders as dividends.

g The per-share value of common stock that reflects investors' expectations of future profitability.

h A dividend paid to common shareholders that is smaller than the dividend paid in the prior year.

EXERCISE 14-2
Computing Retained Earnings

Johnson Pump, Inc., began operations in 1995. In that year, the corporation earned net income of $195,000 and paid dividends of $2.25 per share on its 40,000 outstanding shares of capital stock. In 1996, the corporation incurred a net loss of $127,000 and paid no dividends.

INSTRUCTIONS

a Prepare the journal entry to close the Income Summary account at December 31, 1996 (the year of the $127,000 net loss).

b Compute the amount of retained earnings or deficit that will appear in the company's balance sheet at December 31, 1996.

EXERCISE 14-3
Recording Dividends

Westfall Corporation has outstanding 60,000 shares of no-par value common stock, which were issued for $22 per share. The net income in the first year of operations was $235,000. On December 31, the board of directors declared a dividend of $1.50 per share, payable on January 31 of the following year.

INSTRUCTIONS

a Prepare the journal entries at December 31 of the first year (1) to close the Income Summary account and (2) to record declaration of the dividend.

b Prepare the journal entry to record payment of the dividend on January 31 of the second year.

c Compute the amount of retained earnings reported in Westfall's balance sheet at *December 31,* the end of the first year of operations.

d Assume that the board of directors of Westfall did not meet on December 31 as above but waited until January 15 of the second year because the chairperson was on vacation. On January 15, they declared the dividend of $1.50 per share payable on February 15. Compute the amount of retained earnings that would have been reported in Westfall's balance sheet at *December 31,* the end of the first year of operations in this situation.

EXERCISE 14-4
Shareholders' Equity Section of a Balance Sheet

When Enviro Systems, Inc., was formed, the company was authorized to issue an unlimited number of shares of no-par value, $8 cumulative preferred stock, and an unlimited number of no-par value common stock. The preferred stock is callable at $106.

Then 2,500 shares of the preferred stock were issued at a price of $103 per share, and 70,000 shares of the common stock were sold for $13 per share. At the end of the current year, Enviro Systems, Inc., has retained earnings of $297,000. Prepare the shareholders' equity section of the company's balance sheet at the end of the current year.

EXERCISE 14-5
Dividends: Preferred and Common

The shareholders' equity at December 31, 1996, of Palermo Corporation appears below:

Shareholders' equity:

Preferred stock, $4.50 cumulative, no-par, 40,000 shares issued and outstanding	$2,000,000
Preferred stock, $12, noncumulative, no-par, 8,000 shares issued	800,000
Common stock, no-par, 400,000 shares issued and outstanding	4,800,000
Retained earnings	890,000
Total shareholders' equity	$8,490,000

INSTRUCTIONS

Assume that all the stock was issued on January 1, 1994, and that no dividends were paid during the first two years of operations. During 1996 Palermo Corporation declared and paid total cash dividends of $736,000.

a Compute the amount of cash dividends paid during 1996 to each of the three classes of stock.

b Compute the dividends paid *per share* during 1996 for each of the three classes of stock.

c Palermo Corporation generated a net loss of $190,000 in 1994 and earned net income of $627,000 in 1995. Compute the amount of net income (or net loss) generated by Palermo during 1996.

CHAPTER

15 Corporations: Operations and Additional Shareholders' Equity Transactions

In this chapter we explore special topics relating primarily to the financial statements of large corporations. The chapter is divided into two major parts. In the first part, we show how an income statement is organized to present certain "unusual" items separately from the income or loss from normal business activities. Also, we illustrate and explain the presentation of earnings per share, with emphasis upon the interpretation of the different per-share amounts. In the second part, we look at various shareholders' equity transactions, including cash dividends, stock dividends, stock splits, prior period adjustments, and treasury stock transactions. Also, we explain the presentation of the statement of retained earnings.

Learning Objectives

After studying this chapter you should be able to:

1 *Explain predictive information and its relation to the presentation of discontinued operations, extraordinary items, and accounting changes in the income and other financial statements.*

2 *Compute earnings per share.*

3 *Distinguish between basic and fully diluted earnings per share.*

4 *Account for stock dividends and stock splits, and explain the probable effect of these transactions upon market price.*

5 *Describe and prepare a statement of retained earnings.*

6 *Define prior period adjustments and explain how they are presented in financial statements.*

7 *Account for treasury stock transactions.*

REPORTING THE RESULTS OF OPERATIONS

The most important aspect of corporate financial reporting, in the view of most shareholders, is the determination of periodic net income. Both the market price of common stock and the amount of cash dividends per share depend to a considerable extent on the current level of earnings (net income). Even more important than the absolute amount of net income is the *trend* of earnings over time.

Developing Predictive Information in the Income Statement

OBJECTIVE 1 Explain predictive information and its relation to the presentation of discontinued operations, extraordinary items, and accounting changes in the income and other financial statements.

An income statement tells us a great deal about the performance of a company over the past year. For example, study of the income statement makes clear the types and amounts of revenue earned and expenses incurred as well as the amounts of gross profit and net income. But can we expect this year's income statement to predict *next year's* performance? If the transactions summarized in the income statement for the year just completed were of a normal recurring nature, such as selling merchandise, paying employees, and incurring other normal expenses, we can reasonably assume that the operating results were typical and that somewhat similar results can be expected in the following year. However, in any business, unusual and nonrecurring events may occur that cause the current year's net income to be quite different from the net income we should expect the company to earn in the future. For example, the company may have sustained large losses in the current year from an earthquake or some other event that is not likely to recur in the near future.

Ideally, the results of unusual and nonrecurring events should be shown in a separate section of the income statement *after* the income or loss from normal business activities has been determined. Income from *normal and recurring* activities presumably should be a more useful figure for *predicting future earnings* than is a net income figure that includes the results of nonrecurring events. The problem in creating such an income statement, however, is in determining which events are so unlikely to recur that they should be excluded from the results of "normal" operations. The categories of events that require special treatment in the income statement are (1) the results of discontinued operations and (2) extraordinary items. An income statement with such separate disclosure can serve as a basis for evaluating past performance and for predicting future performance.

Reporting Unusual Events—An Illustration

To illustrate the presentation of these events, assume that Ross Corporation operates both a small chain of retail stores and two motels. Near the end of the current year, the company sells both motels to a national hotel chain. In addition, Ross Corporation reports two "extraordinary items." An income statement illustrating the correct format for reporting these events appears as follows:

INSTRUCTIONS   From this information, compute answers to the following questions:

a   What was the average issuance price of a share of preferred stock?

b   What is the total dollar amount of the annual dividend requirement on preferred stock?

c   What was the average issuance price of a share of common stock?

d   What is the current book value per share of common stock?

e   What is the total contributed capital?

f   Total dividends of $1,012,000 were declared on the preferred and common stock during the year, and the balance of retained earnings at the beginning of the year was $5,184,000. What was the amount of net income for the year?

Group B

PROBLEM 14B-1
Journal Entries for Corporate Transactions

Shown below are selected transactions of St. Claire Vineyards for the year ended December 31, 1996:

Jan. 19   Issued capital stock to Martin DiBello in exchange for land. Two firms hired to appraise the land have differing opinions as to the fair market value of the real estate. DiBello, however, agrees to accept 10,000 shares of no-par value capital stock as a fair exchange. St. Claire's stock is widely traded and is quoted at $19 per share on a stock exchange on this date.

June 10   At their June meeting, the board of directors declared a dividend of 20 cents per share, payable on July 15, to owners of the corporation's 200,000 outstanding shares of capital stock.

July 15   Paid the dividend declared on June 10.

Dec. 10   At their December meeting, the board of directors declared a dividend of 25 cents per share, payable on January 15 of the following year. No capital stock has been issued since the January 19 transaction.

Dec. 31   Recorded income tax expense for the three months ended December 31, 1996, $34,900. These taxes will be paid in early 1997. (Income taxes for the first nine months of 1996 have already been recorded and paid.)

Dec. 31   Closed the Income Summary account at the end of a profitable period. Net income, $365,000.

INSTRUCTIONS   a   Prepare journal entries to record the above transactions.

b   Assume the balance sheet of St. Claire Vineyards at December 31, 1995, reported retained earnings of $1,215,000. Compute the amount of retained earnings to be reported in the corporation's balance sheet at December 31, *1996.* Show computation.

PROBLEM 14B-2
Shareholders' Equity in a Balance Sheet

Early in 1992, Sinclair Press was organized with authorization to issue an unlimited number of shares of no-par value preferred stock and of no-par value common stock. Ten thousand shares of the preferred stock were issued at $100 each, and 170,000 shares of common stock were sold for $15 per share. The preferred stock pays an $8 cumulative dividend and is callable at $105.

During the first four years of operations (1992 through 1995), the corporation earned a total of $1,025,000 and paid dividends of 75 cents per share each year on the common stock. In 1996, however, the corporation reported a net loss of $340,000 and paid no dividends.

INSTRUCTIONS

a　Prepare the shareholders' equity section of the balance sheet at December 31, 1996. Include a supporting schedule showing your computation of the amount of retained earnings or deficit.

b　Draft a footnote to accompany the financial statements disclosing any dividends in arrears at the end of 1996.

**PROBLEM 14B-3
Shareholders' Equity Section—A More Challenging Problem**

Maria Martinez organized Manhattan Transport Limited in January 1993. The corporation immediately issued at $7.50 per share 100,000 of its unlimited authorized shares of no-par common stock. On January 2, **1994,** the corporation sold at $110 per share the entire 5,000 authorized shares of 8%, $100 par value, cumulative preferred stock. On January 2, **1995,** the company again needed money and issued 5,000 shares of its unlimited authorized shares of $9, no-par, cumulative preferred stock for a total of $512,000.

　　The company suffered losses in its first two years reporting a deficit of $170,000 at the end of 1994. During 1995 and 1996 combined, the company earned a total of $890,000. Dividends of 50 cents per share were paid on common stock in 1995 and $1.60 per share in 1996.

INSTRUCTIONS

Prepare the shareholders' equity section of the balance sheet at December 31, 1996. Include a supporting schedule showing your computation of retained earnings or deficit at the balance sheet date.

**PROBLEM 14B-4
Dividends, Closing Entries, and Shareholders' Equity**

Hua Lai organized Pacific Rim Corporation early in 1995. On January 9, the corporation issued to Hua Lai and other investors 100,000 of its unlimited authorized shares of no-par value common stock at a price of $9 per share.

　　After the revenue and expense accounts (except income taxes expense) were closed into the Income Summary account at the end of the year, that account showed a before-tax income of $288,000. Income taxes were determined to be $64,000. No dividends were paid during 1995.

　　On January 15, 1996, the board of directors declared a cash dividend of 75 cents per share, payable February 15.

INSTRUCTIONS

a　Prepare the journal entries for 1995 to (1) record the issuance of the common stock, (2) record the income tax liability at December 31, (3) close the Income Taxes Expense account into the Income Summary account, and (4) close the Income Summary account.

b　Prepare the journal entries in 1996 for the declaration of the dividend on January 15 and payment of the dividend on February 15.

c　Operations in 1996 resulted in a $158,800 net loss. Prepare the journal entry to close the Income Summary account at December 31, 1996.

d　Prepare the shareholders' equity section of the balance sheet at December 31, 1996. Include a separate supporting schedule showing your determination of retained earnings or deficit at that date. Disregard the possibility of an income tax refund.

**PROBLEM 14B-5
Issuance of Capital Stock and Stock Subscriptions**

For several years, Kathryn Mead has operated a successful business organized as a sole proprietorship. In order to raise the capital to operate on a larger scale, she decided to organize a new corporation to continue in the same line of business. In January, Mead organized Down Home, Inc., which was authorized to issue unlimited shares of no-par value common stock. During January, Down Home, Inc., completed the following transactions:

Jan.　9　Issued 8,000 shares of common stock to various investors for cash at $32 per share.

Jan. 12 Issued 27,000 shares of common stock to Mead in exchange for assets with a current market value as follows:

Inventory	$198,000
Land	235,000
Building	124,000
Equipment	307,000

Jan. 14 Received an invoice from a lawyer for $8,950 for services relating to the formation of Down Home, Inc. The invoice will be paid in 30 days.

Jan. 15 Received subscriptions for 7,000 shares of common stock at $32 per share; 2,000 of the shares were subscribed by Mead and 5,000 were subscribed by other investors.

Jan. 31 Collected from Mead the full amount of her subscription to 2,000 shares of common stock and issued a stock certificate for these shares. (No collection has yet been made from the subscribers to the other 5,000 shares.)

The corporation will begin operations in February; no revenue was earned and no expenses were incurred during January. No depreciation of plant assets and no amortization of organization cost will be recognized until February, when operations get under way.

INSTRUCTIONS **a** Prepare journal entries to record the transactions for January in the accounting records for Down Home, Inc.

b Prepare a classified balance sheet for the corporation at January 31.

PROBLEM 14B-6
Analysis of Shareholders' Equity

The year-end balance sheet of LaserTech, Inc., includes the following shareholders' equity section (with certain details omitted):

Shareholders' equity:

$8.80 cumulative preferred stock, $100 par value, callable at $110,	
authorized 30,000 shares	$ 1,200,000
Common stock, no-par value, authorized unlimited shares,	
issued and outstanding, 310,000 shares	7,440,000
Premium on preferred stock	60,000
Donated capital	960,000
Retained earnings	4,680,000
Total shareholders' equity	$14,340,000

INSTRUCTIONS On the basis of this information, answer the following questions and show any necessary supporting computations:

a How many shares of preferred stock are outstanding?

b What is the amount of the annual dividend requirement on preferred stock?

c What was the average issuance price of a share of common stock?

d What was the average issuance price of a share of preferred stock?

e What is the current book value per share of common stock?

f What is the total contributed capital?

g Assume that net income for the year was $2,100,000 and the balance of retained earnings at the beginning of the year was $3,302,000. What was the amount of dividend declared during the year for the preferred and common stock?

ANALYTICAL AND DECISION PROBLEMS AND CASES

A&D 14-1
Par, Book, and Market Values. An Open-Ended Discussion

Microsoft Corp. is the producer of such software products as *Windows, Excel,* and *Word.* In mid-1990, an investment service published the following per-share amounts relating to Microsoft's only class of capital stock:

Par value	$ 0.001
Book value (estimated)	6.50
Market value	73.00

INSTRUCTIONS

a Without reference to dollar amounts, explain the nature and significance of *par value, book value,* and *market value.*

b Comment upon the *interrelationships,* if any, among the per-share amounts shown for Microsoft Corp. What do these amounts imply about the company and its operations? Also comment upon what these amounts imply about the security of *creditors'* claims against the company.

A&D 14-2
Issuing Stock for Assets Other Than Cash

The following independent cases involve the issuance of capital stock in exchange for assets other than cash.

1 DuPar Corporation, a successful, family-owned company, is in the process of acquiring a tract of land suitable for the construction of a factory. The DuPar Corporation has agreed to offer 26,000 shares of common stock in exchange for the land, which has an agreed fair market value of $650,000, based on two independent appraisals. DuPar Corporation stock is not traded on any stock exchange.

INSTRUCTIONS

Give the journal entry that should be made to record this transaction under each of the following assumptions:

a The stock has a $2 par value.

b The stock has *no* par value.

2 Irwin Products, a well-established company, issued 3,800 shares of its $5 par value common stock in exchange for certain patents. The patents were entered in the accounts at $19,000. At this time, Irwin Products common stock was quoted on the over-the-counter market at "25 bid and 27 asked"; that is, sellers were offering stock at $27 per share, and buyers were offering to buy at $25 per share.

INSTRUCTIONS

a Comment on the company's treatment of this transaction. Write a brief statement explaining whether you agree or disagree, and why.

b What is the essential difference between the evidence available to the accountant as a basis for the record of DuPar Corporation and the evidence available for Irwin Products?

A&D 14-3
Factors Affecting the Market Prices of Preferred and Common Stocks

ADM Labs is a publicly owned company with several issues of capital stock outstanding. Over the past decade, the company has consistently earned modest income and has increased its common stock dividend annually by 5 or 10 cents per share. Recently the company introduced several new products that you believe will cause future sales and income to increase dramatically. You also expect a gradual increase in long-term interest rates from their present level of about 9% to, perhaps, 10% or 10½%. Based upon these forecasts, explain whether you would expect to see the market prices of the following issues of ADM capital stock increase or decrease. Explain your reasoning in each answer.

a   8%, $100 par value, preferred stock (currently selling at $90 per share)

b   No-par value common stock (currently paying an annual dividend of $1.20 and selling at $40 per share)

c $5, no-par value, convertible preferred stock (currently selling at $119 per share)

A&D 14-4
Whether or Not
To Incorporate

Mario Valenti owns Valenti Ford, a successful automobile dealership. For 25 years, Valenti has operated the business as a sole proprietorship and has acted as both owner and manager. Now, he is 70 years old and is planning on retiring from active management. However, he wants the dealership to stay in the family; his long-term goal is to leave the business to his two children and five grandchildren.

Valenti is wondering whether or not he should incorporate his business. If he were to reorganize Valenti Ford as a corporation, he could then leave an appropriate number of shares of capital stock to each of his heirs. Otherwise, he could leave the entire business to his heirs to be operated as a partnership. In selecting the appropriate form of business entity, Valenti has formulated the following objectives:

1   **Ownership:** Valenti wants each of his two children to own 25% of the business and each of his five grandchildren to own 10%.

2   **Continuity of existence:** Valenti wants the business to continue indefinitely, even if one or more of the heirs should die or should no longer want to participate in ownership.

3   **Management:** When Valenti retires, he plans to give Joe Heinz, a long-time employee, responsibility for managing the business. Although Valenti wants to keep the ownership of the business in the family, he does not believe that any of his family members have the time or experience to manage the business on a daily basis. In fact, Valenti believes that two of his grandchildren simply have no "business sense," and he does not want them to participate in management.

4   **Income taxes:** Valenti wants to organize the business in a manner that will minimize the income taxes to be paid by his heirs. He expects that all the earnings of the business normally will be distributed to its owners on an annual basis.

5   **Owners' liability:** Valenti recognizes that an automobile dealership might become liable for vast amounts of money, if, for example, improper repairs caused a customer's car to be involved in an accident. Although the business carries insurance, he wants to be sure that his heirs' equity in the business does not place their personal assets at risk in the event of business losses.

INSTRUCTIONS

a   For each of the five numbered paragraphs above, explain how the choice of business organization (partnership or corporation) relates to Valenti's stated objective.

b   In light of your analysis in part **a**, above, would you recommend that Valenti reorganize Valenti Ford as a corporation, or leave the business unincorporated so that his heirs may operate it as a partnership?

A&D 14-5
Dividend Distribution and Policy

Sarkis Corporation has been in business for a number of years. Even though it has been profitable, Sarkis Corporation's performance has been erratic: 1995, net loss of $182,000; 1996, net income of $212,000; and 1997, net income of $298,000. The shareholders' equity of Sarkis at December 31, 1994 showed, among other items, the following:

Capital stock issued and outstanding:

$8 noncumulative preferred, 5,000 shares	*$ 500,000*
$6 cumulative preferred, 6,000 shares	*600,000*
$5 cumulative fully-participating preferred, 10,000 shares	*1,000,000*
Common, 100,000 shares	*2,000,000*
Retained earnings	*810,000*

There were no capital stock transactions for the years 1995 to 1997.

INSTRUCTIONS **a** Compute the amount of dividends for each of the four classes of capital stock for the years 1995, 1996 and 1997, based on the following dividend policies:
   1 Distribute an amount that is the greater of the regular dividends or the net income for the year.
   2 Distribute an amount that is equal to the net income for the year.

b Based on the answers in **a** above, which dividend policy is more beneficial to the common shareholders? Explain.

15 Corporations: Operations and Additional Shareholders' Equity Transactions

In this chapter we explore special topics relating primarily to the financial statements of large corporations. The chapter is divided into two major parts. In the first part, we show how an income statement is organized to present certain "unusual" items separately from the income or loss from normal business activities. Also, we illustrate and explain the presentation of earnings per share, with emphasis upon the interpretation of the different per-share amounts. In the second part, we look at various shareholders' equity transactions, including cash dividends, stock dividends, stock splits, prior period adjustments, and treasury stock transactions. Also, we explain the presentation of the statement of retained earnings.

Learning Objectives

After studying this chapter you should be able to:

1 *Explain predictive information and its relation to the presentation of discontinued operations, extraordinary items, and accounting changes in the income and other financial statements.*

2 *Compute earnings per share.*

3 *Distinguish between basic and fully diluted earnings per share.*

4 *Account for stock dividends and stock splits, and explain the probable effect of these transactions upon market price.*

5 *Describe and prepare a statement of retained earnings.*

6 *Define prior period adjustments and explain how they are presented in financial statements.*

7 *Account for treasury stock transactions.*

REPORTING THE RESULTS OF OPERATIONS

The most important aspect of corporate financial reporting, in the view of most shareholders, is the determination of periodic net income. Both the market price of common stock and the amount of cash dividends per share depend to a considerable extent on the current level of earnings (net income). Even more important than the absolute amount of net income is the **trend** of earnings over time.

Developing Predictive Information in the Income Statement

OBJECTIVE 1 Explain predictive information and its relation to the presentation of discontinued operations, extraordinary items, and accounting changes in the income and other financial statements.

An income statement tells us a great deal about the performance of a company over the past year. For example, study of the income statement makes clear the types and amounts of revenue earned and expenses incurred as well as the amounts of gross profit and net income. But can we expect this year's income statement to predict **next year's** performance? If the transactions summarized in the income statement for the year just completed were of a normal recurring nature, such as selling merchandise, paying employees, and incurring other normal expenses, we can reasonably assume that the operating results were typical and that somewhat similar results can be expected in the following year. However, in any business, unusual and nonrecurring events may occur that cause the current year's net income to be quite different from the net income we should expect the company to earn in the future. For example, the company may have sustained large losses in the current year from an earthquake or some other event that is not likely to recur in the near future.

Ideally, the results of unusual and nonrecurring events should be shown in a separate section of the income statement **after** the income or loss from normal business activities has been determined. Income from **normal and recurring** activities presumably should be a more useful figure for **predicting future earnings** than is a net income figure that includes the results of nonrecurring events. The problem in creating such an income statement, however, is in determining which events are so unlikely to recur that they should be excluded from the results of "normal" operations. The categories of events that require special treatment in the income statement are (1) the results of discontinued operations and (2) extraordinary items. An income statement with such separate disclosure can serve as a basis for evaluating past performance and for predicting future performance.

Reporting Unusual Events—An Illustration

To illustrate the presentation of these events, assume that Ross Corporation operates both a small chain of retail stores and two motels. Near the end of the current year, the company sells both motels to a national hotel chain. In addition, Ross Corporation reports two "extraordinary items." An income statement illustrating the correct format for reporting these events appears as follows:

ROSS CORPORATION
Income Statement
For the Year Ended December 31, 1996

Net sales		$8,000,000
Cost and expenses:		
Cost of goods sold	$4,580,000	
Selling expenses..	1,500,000	
General and administrative expenses	920,000	
Income taxes (on continuing operations).................	300,000	7,300,000
Income from continuing operations		$ 700,000
Discontinued operations:		
Operating loss on motels (net of $90,000 income tax benefit)	$ (210,000)	
Gain on sale of motels (net of $195,000 income taxes)	455,000	245,000
Income before extraordinary items........................		$ 945,000
Extraordinary items:		
Gain on expropriation of land for a highway (net of $45,000 income taxes)	$ 105,000	
Loss from earthquake damage to a retail store (net of $75,000 income tax benefit)................	(175,000)	(70,000)
Net income		$ 875,000

Notice the order in which the "special items" are reported

This income statement is designed to illustrate the presentation of various "unusual events." Rarely, if ever, will all these types of events appear in the income statement of one company within a single year.

Continuing Operations

The first section of the income statement contains only the results of **continuing business activities**—that is, the retail stores. Notice that the income taxes expense shown in this section relates **only to continuing operations.** The income taxes relating to the "unusual events" are shown separately in the income statement as adjustments to the amounts of these items.

Income from Continuing Operations   The subtotal **income from continuing operations** measures the profitability of the ongoing operations. This subtotal should be helpful in making predictions of the company's future earnings. For example, if we predict no significant change in the profitability of its retail stores, we would expect Ross Corporation to earn a net income of approximately $700,000 next year.

Discontinued Operations

If management has sold or discontinued a **segment** of the business, or enters into a formal plan to sell or discontinue a **segment** of the business, the results of that segment's operations are shown separately in the income statement. This enables users of the financial statements to better evaluate the performance of the company's ongoing (continuing) operations and to better predict the company's future performance.

Two items are included in the "discontinued operations" section of the income statement: (1) the income or loss from *operating* the segment prior to its disposal, net of applicable income taxes and (2) the gain or loss on *disposal* of the segment, net of applicable income taxes. Notice also that the income taxes relating to the discontinued operations are *shown separately* from the income taxes expense relating to continuing business operations.

Discontinued Operations Must Be a "Segment" of the Business To qualify for separate presentation in the income statement, the discontinued operations must represent an *entire segment* of the business. A "segment" of a business is a separate line of business activity or an operation that services a particular class of customers. For example, the sale of an oil and gas operation by a real estate company or the sale of the wholesale division selling food to retail stores by a company whose other operations consist of selling food through its restaurants would constitute a disposal of a segment of business.[1]

CASE IN POINT Large corporations usually have many segments of business. Imasco has four segments, one of which is the Shoppers Drug Mart. If Imasco closes an individual Shoppers Drug Mart store, such a closure does not qualify as "discontinued operations" because Imasco remains in the drug store business. However, if Imasco were to sell the entire Shoppers Drug Mart operation, the drug store activities would be shown in Imasco's income statement as "discontinued operations."

Discontinued Operations Are Not Really "Unusual" In recent years, a characteristic of the Canadian economy has been the "restructuring" of many large corporations. As part of this restructuring, corporations often sell one or more segments of the business. Thus, the presence of "discontinued operations" is not uncommon in the income statements of large corporations.

CASE IN POINT Some time ago, George Weston Limited (the fourth largest company in Canada) disposed of its Canadian InterBake biscuit business, its Peter J. Schmitt wholesale operation in the U.S., and its White Swan consumer and industrial tissue product business for a total price tag of more than $389 million. Similarly, Placer Dome, a giant mining company, agreed to sell its U.S. oil and gas operation at about $336 million U.S. so that it could concentrate on mining activities.

---

[1]   CICA, *CICA Handbook* (Toronto), section 3475.05.

Extraordinary Items

The second category of events requiring disclosure in a separate section of the income statement is extraordinary items. Extraordinary items are those items resulting from events or transactions that have met all of the following three characteristics or criteria:

1 not expected to occur frequently over several years

2 not typical of the normal business activities of the entity

3 not dependent primarily on decisions or determinations by management or owners[2]

To clarify the application of these characteristics, the Accounting Standards Board of the CICA has provided some explanations and examples. First, the determination of whether an event is expected to occur frequently over several years requires the determination of the frequency of the occurrence of such events in the recent past and in the foreseeable future. Accordingly, a farmer's crop loss from drought does not meet this first criterion if drought conditions in the area are normally experienced every three or four years.[3]

Second, the factors that determine whether a transaction or event typifies the normal business activities of the entity should include: "type and scope of operations, characteristics of the industry, operating policies, nature of products and services, and the environment in which the entity operates."[4] Thus, the following, regardless of size, do not qualify because they are from normal business activities: (1) losses and provisions for losses with respect to bad debts and inventories, (2) gains and losses from fluctuations in foreign exchange rates, (3) adjustments with respect to contract prices, (4) gains and losses from write-down or sale of property, plant, equipment or other investments, (5) income tax reductions on utilization of prior period losses or reversal of previously recorded tax benefits.[5]

Third, a transaction or event would not depend primarily on decisions or determinations by management or owners "if their decisions or determinations would not normally influence the transactions or events."[6] Therefore, sale of land originally intended for plant expansion, but later held for appreciation, would not meet this criterion.

Because the criteria for extraordinary items are very restrictive, extraordinary items are quite rare. The following are examples that are likely to meet the three criteria recommended in the *CICA Handbook:*

1 The expropriation of a corporation's land and buildings for a highway.

2 The destruction of a large portion of a wheat crop by a tornado.

---

[2]   CICA, *CICA Handbook* (Toronto), section 3480.02.

[3]   Ibid., section 3480.03.

[4]   Ibid., section 3480.04.

[5]   Ibid.

[6]   Ibid., section 3480.05.

3 An explosion in a nuclear reactor resulting in high-level radioactive emission.

4 The destruction of an airplane of a major airline by a terrorist attack.[7]

When a gain or loss resulting from a transaction or an event qualifies as an extraordinary item, it appears under a *separate heading* called *extraordinary items,* following the sub-heading "income before extraordinary items," net of applicable income taxes. The nature of the gain or loss should be adequately and clearly described. Such a separate and distinct presentation, as illustrated in the income statement of Ross Corporation, enables users of the financial statements to better evaluate and predict the performance of the company's on-going (continuing) operations.

Accounting Changes

Other matters having an effect on the evaluation and prediction of the trend of earnings include: (1) a change in an accounting policy, (2) a change in an accounting estimate, and (3) a correction of an error in prior period financial statements. These matters are covered by Section 1506, *"Accounting Changes,"* of the *CICA Handbook.* The recommendations of the *CICA Handbook* are highlighted in the following paragraphs.

Changes in Accounting Policy encompass changes in accounting principles as well as accounting methods used in the preparation of financial statements. As stated in Chapter 12 and other chapters, the consistent application of accounting principles and methods from one accounting period to another enhances the usefulness of financial statements on a comparative basis. Also, management may justify a change to another acceptable accounting principle on the grounds that it is more appropriate. For example, a change in determining inventory cost from a weighted-average to a first-in first-out method or a change in recognizing depreciation expense from a straight-line to a declining-balance method constitutes a change in accounting policy, when such a change is *not* the result of changed circumstances, experience, or new information.[8]

Since a change in accounting policy affects two or more accounting periods, Section 1506 of the *CICA Handbook* recommends that the effect of an accounting policy change be reflected on a *retroactive* basis with a *restatement* of those prior period financial statements affected by the change. Thus, each of those prior period financial statements presented on a comparative basis is to be restated to reflect the new accounting policy. In addition, the cumulative effect of the change on the periods preceding the earliest period included in the comparative financial statements is treated as an adjustment to the beginning balance of retained earnings of the earliest period. If comparative statements are not prepared, an adjustment

---

[7] Ibid., section 3480.05 and .06.

[8] Ibid., section 1506.03.

should be made to the current period's beginning retained earnings for the cumulative effect of the change on prior periods.

Changes in Accounting Estimates include such items as a revision of the estimate of the amount of allowance for doubtful accounts or a revision of the estimate of a nine-year useful life of a depreciable asset to a six-year life. A change in an estimate is a result of ***new*** information. For example, a change in the method of depreciation of a plant asset that results from changed circumstances, experience, or new information would be treated as a change in accounting estimate. Section 1506 of the *CICA Handbook* recommends that the effect of such a change be accounted for in the period of change or in the period of change and the applicable future periods, depending on whether the change affects one or more periods. Thus, this differs from the treatment of a change in accounting policy in that a re-statement of prior periods or a cumulative adjustment is ***not*** required.

Corrections of Errors are required when errors are discovered in prior period financial statements. Errors may result from a mistake in computation, a misinterpretation or misrepresentation of information, an oversight of available information, or a misappropriation of assets.[9] Examples of corrections of errors include the discovery that inventories were materially overstated and depreciation expenses were substantially understated in prior period financial statements. Section 1506 of the *CICA Handbook* recommends that a correction of an error be accounted for ***retroactively*** and that the prior period financial statements presented for comparative purposes be ***restated.*** In addition, it requires disclosure in the current period regarding: (1) a description of the error, (2) the effect of the correction of the error on the financial statements of the current and prior periods, and (3) the fact that the prior period financial statements presented for comparative purposes have been restated. The disclosure of the effect of the correction on such significant items as net income, earnings per share, and working capital also may be appropriate. These requirements for a correction of an error are logical because they make comparisons of performance of a business enterprise over a number of periods more meaningful and not misleading.

The chart at the top of page 704 summarizes the accounting and reporting requirements of Section 1506 of the *CICA Handbook*. It is interesting to note that both a change in an accounting policy and a correction of an error in prior period financial statements receive the same treatment— retroactive application and restatement. Such a treatment is also accorded to prior period adjustments as discussed later in this chapter. Thus, although these two types of accounting changes do not have the four characteristics of a prior period adjustment, both of them are required to have the same retroactive application and restatement of prior period financial statements.

---

9   Ibid., section 1506.26.

Type of Accounting Change	Financial Statements Affected		Accounting and Reporting Requirements
	Income	Retained Earnings	
1. Change in accounting policy	Prior period	Current and prior periods	Retroactive application and restatement
2. Change in accounting estimate	Current or current and future periods	Not applicable	Current or current and prospective application
3. Correction of error in prior period	Prior period	Current and prior periods	Retroactive application and restatement

The in-depth coverage of the topic of accounting changes is more appropriately covered in the intermediate accounting course.

Earnings per Share (EPS)

*OBJECTIVE 2
Compute
earnings per
share.*

Perhaps the most widely used of all accounting statistics is ***earnings per share*** of common stock. Everyone who buys or sells stock in a corporation needs to know the annual earnings per share. Stock market prices are quoted on a per-share basis. If you are considering investing in Canadian Pacific stock at a price of, say, $20 per share, you need to know the earnings per share and the annual dividend per share in order to decide whether this price is reasonable. In other words, how much earning power and how much dividend income would you be getting for each share you buy?

To compute earnings per share, the annual net income applicable to the common shareholders is divided by the average number of common shares outstanding. The concept of earnings per share applies ***only to common stock;*** preferred stock has no claim to earnings beyond the stipulated preferred stock dividends.

Many financial analysts express the relationship between earnings per share and market price per share as a ***price-earnings ratio*** (p/e ratio). This ratio is computed by dividing the market price per share of common stock by the annual earnings per share.

Weighted-Average Number of Shares Outstanding The simplest example of computing earnings per share is found when a company has issued only common stock and the number of shares outstanding has not changed during the year. In this situation, the net income for the year divided by the number of shares outstanding at year-end equals earnings per share.

In many companies, however, the number of shares of stock outstanding changes one or more times during the year. When additional shares are issued in exchange for assets during the year, the computation of earnings per share is based upon the ***weighted-average*** number of shares outstanding.[10]

The weighted-average number of shares for the year is determined by multiplying the number of shares outstanding by the fraction of the year that said number of shares outstanding remained unchanged. For example, assume that 100,000 shares of common stock were outstanding during the first nine months of 1996 and 140,000 shares during the last three months. Assume also that the increase in shares outstanding resulted from the sale of 40,000 shares for cash. The weighted-average number of shares outstanding during 1996 would be ***110,000*** determined as follows:

100,000 shares × $\frac{9}{12}$ of a year	*75,000*
140,000 shares × $\frac{3}{12}$ of a year	*35,000*
Weighted-average number of common shares outstanding	*110,000*

This procedure gives more meaningful earnings per share data than if the total number of shares outstanding at the end of the year were used in the calculations. By using the weighted-average number of shares, we recognize that the proceeds from the sale of the 40,000 shares were available to generate earnings only during the last three months of the year. Although the weighted-average number of shares outstanding must be used in earnings-per-share computations, this figure does not appear in the shareholders' equity section of the balance sheet. A balance sheet prepared at year-end reports the ***actual*** number of shares outstanding at that date, regardless of when the shares were issued during the year.

Preferred Dividends and Earnings per Share   When a company has preferred stock outstanding, the preferred shareholders participate in net income to the extent of the preferred stock dividends. To determine the earnings ***applicable to the common stock,*** we first deduct from net income the amount of current year preferred stock dividends. The annual dividend on ***cumulative*** preferred stock is ***always*** deducted, even if not declared by the board of directors for the current year. Noncumulative preferred stock dividends are deducted only if declared.

To illustrate, let us assume that Tanner Corporation has 200,000 shares of common stock and 10,000 shares of $6 cumulative preferred stock outstanding throughout the year. Net income for the year 1996 totals $560,000. Earnings per share of common stock would be computed as follows:

Net income	*$560,000*
Less: Dividends on preferred stock (10,000 shares × $6)	*60,000*
Earnings applicable to common stock	*$500,000*
Weighted-average number of common shares outstanding	*200,000*
Earnings per share of common stock ($500,000 ÷ 200,000 shares)	*$2.50*

---

[10]   When the number of shares outstanding changes as a result of a stock split or a stock dividend (discussed later in this chapter), the computation of the weighted-average number of shares outstanding should be adjusted ***retroactively*** to the beginning of the period, as if the shares had been outstanding for the whole period. Earnings per share data for prior years thus will be consistently stated in terms of the current capital structure.

Even when there are dividends in arrears, only the **current year's** cumulative preferred stock dividend is deducted in the earnings per share computation. Dividends in arrears from previous years have already been deducted in the prior years' earnings per share computations.

Presentation of Earnings per Share in the Income Statement   All publicly owned corporations are **required** to present earnings per share data in their **income statements.**[11] If an income statement includes subtotals for income from continuing operations, or for income before extraordinary items, per-share figures are shown for income before discontinued operations and extraordinary items as well as for net income. Also, it is desirable to show the earnings per share for discontinued operations and extraordinary items to stress their effect on the final earnings per share.[12] This additional per-share amount is computed by substituting the amount of the appropriate subtotal for the net income figure in the preceding calculation.

To illustrate all of the potential per-share computations, we will expand our Tanner Corporation example to include income from continuing operations and income before extraordinary items. We should point out, however, that all of these figures seldom appear in the same income statement. Very few companies have both discontinued operations and an extraordinary item to report in the same year. The following condensed income statement is intended to illustrate the proper format for presenting earnings per share figures and to provide a review of the calculations.

TANNER CORPORATION
Condensed Income Statement
For the Year Ended December 31, 1996

Net sales	$9,000,000
Costs and expenses (including income taxes on continuing operations)...	8,310,000
Income from continuing operations	$ 690,000
Loss from discontinued operations (net of income tax benefits)...........	(90,000)
Income before extraordinary items.......................................	$ 600,000
Extraordinary loss (net of income tax benefit)	(40,000)
Net income	$ 560,000
Earnings per share of common stock:	
Earnings from continuing operations	$3.15[a]
Loss from discontinued operations	(.45)
Earnings before extraordinary items	$2.70[b]
Extraordinary loss	(.20)
Net earnings...	$2.50[c]

Earnings per share figures are required in the income statement

[a]   ($690,000 − $60,000 preferred dividends) ÷ 200,000 shares
[b]   ($600,000 − $60,000) ÷ 200,000 shares
[c]   ($560,000 − $60,000) ÷ 200,000 shares

---

[11]   CICA, *CICA Handbook* (Toronto), section 3500.06.

[12]   Ibid., section 3500.12.

Interpreting the Different Per-Share Amounts To knowledgeable users of financial statements, each of these figures has a different significance. Earnings per share from continuing operations represents the results of continuing and ordinary business activity. This figure is the most useful one for evaluating current operating results and for predicting future operating results. ***Net earnings*** per share, on the other hand, shows the overall operating results of the current year, including any discontinued operations and extraordinary items.

Unfortunately the term ***earnings per share*** often is used without qualification in referring to various types of per-share data. When using per-share information, it is important to know exactly which per-share statistic is being presented. For example, the price-earnings ratios (market price divided by earnings per share) for common stocks listed on major stock exchanges are reported daily in ***The Financial Post*** and many other newspapers. Which earnings per share figures are used in computing these ratios? If a company reports an extraordinary gain or loss, the price-earnings ratio is computed using the per-share ***earnings before the extraordinary item.*** Otherwise, the ratio is based upon ***net earnings*** (net income) per share.

Basic and Fully Diluted Earnings per Share

OBJECTIVE 3
Distinguish between basic and fully diluted earnings per share.

Let us assume that a company has an outstanding issue of preferred stock that is convertible into shares of common stock at a rate of, say, two shares of common for each share of preferred. The conversion of this preferred stock would increase the number of common shares outstanding and might ***dilute*** (reduce) earnings per share. Any common shareholder interested in the trend of earnings per share will want to know what effect the conversion of the preferred stock would have upon this statistic.

To inform investors of the potential dilution that might occur, two figures are presented for each earnings per share statistic. The first figure, called ***basic*** earnings per share, is based upon the weighted-average number of common shares actually outstanding during the year. Thus, this figure ignores the potential dilution represented by the convertible preferred stock.[13] The second figure, called ***fully diluted*** earnings per share, shows the impact that conversion of the preferred stock would have upon basic earnings per share.

Basic earnings per share are computed in the same manner illustrated in our preceding example of Tanner Corporation. Fully diluted earnings per share, on the other hand, are computed on the assumption that all the preferred stock ***had been converted into common stock at the beginning of the current year.***[14] (The mechanics of computing fully diluted earnings per share are covered in the intermediate accounting course.)

---

[13] If certain criteria are met, preferred shares are treated, for example, as ***"common stock"*** and are entered into the computation of basic earnings per share. This and other complex issues relating to earnings per share are discussed in section 3500 of the *CICA Handbook* and in intermediate accounting texts.

[14] If the preferred stock had been issued during the current year, we would assume that it was converted into common stock on the date it was issued.

It is important to remember that fully diluted earnings per share represent a ***hypothetical case.*** This statistic is computed even though the preferred stock actually was ***not*** converted during the year. The purpose of showing fully diluted earnings per share is to warn common shareholders what ***could*** have happened. When the difference between basic and fully diluted earnings per share becomes significant, investors should recognize the ***risk*** that future earnings per share may be reduced by conversions of other securities into common stock.

When a company reports both basic and fully diluted earnings per share, the price-earnings ratio shown in newspapers is based upon the ***basic*** figure (and before discontinued operations and extraordinary items).

OTHER SHAREHOLDERS' EQUITY TRANSACTIONS

Cash Dividends

The prospect of receiving cash dividends is a principal reason for investing in the capital stocks of corporations. An increase or a decrease in the established rate of dividends will usually cause an immediate rise or fall in the market price of the company's capital stock. Shareholders are keenly interested in prospects for future dividends and as a group are strongly in favour of more generous dividend payments. The board of directors, on the other hand, is primarily concerned with the long-run growth and financial strength of the corporation; it may prefer to restrict dividends to a minimum in order to conserve cash for the purchase of plant and equipment or for other needs of the company. Many of the so-called "growth companies" plow back into the business most of their earnings and pay only very small cash dividends.

The preceding discussion suggests three requirements for the payment of a cash dividend. These are:

1 **Retained earnings.**   Since dividends represent a distribution of earnings to shareholders, the theoretical maximum for dividends is the total undistributed net income of the company, represented by the credit balance of the Retained Earnings account. As a practical matter, many corporations limit dividends to somewhere near 40% of annual net income, in the belief that a major portion of the net income must be retained in the business if the company is to grow and to keep pace with its competitors.

2 **An adequate cash position.**   The fact that the company reports large earnings does not mean that it has a large amount of cash on hand. Cash generated from earnings may have been invested in such assets as inventory, new plant and equipment, or used in paying off debts. There is no necessary relationship between the balance in the Retained Earnings account and the balance in the Cash account. The traditional expression of "paying dividends out of retained earnings" is misleading. Cash dividends can be paid only "out of" cash.

3 **Dividend action by the board of directors.**   Even though a company's net income is substantial and its cash position seemingly satisfactory, dividends are not paid automatically. A formal action by the board of directors is necessary to declare a dividend.

Dividend Dates

Four significant dates are involved in the distribution of a dividend. These dates are:

1 **Date of declaration.** On the day on which the dividend is declared by the board of directors, a liability to make the payment comes into existence.

2 **Date of record.** The date of record always follows the date of declaration, usually by a period of two to four weeks, and is always stated in the dividend declaration. In order to be eligible to receive the dividend, a person must be listed as the owner of the stock on the date of record.

3 **Ex-dividend date.** The ex-dividend date is significant for investors in companies with stocks traded on the stock exchanges. To permit the compilation of the list of shareholders as of the record date, it is customary for the stock to go *ex-dividend* four business days before the date of record. A stock is said to be selling ex-dividend on the day that it loses the right to receive the latest declared dividend. A person who buys the stock before the ex-dividend date is entitled to receive the dividend; conversely, a shareholder who sells shares before the ex-dividend date does not receive the dividend.

4 **Date of payment.** The declaration of a dividend always includes announcement of the date of payment as well as the date of record. Usually the date of payment comes from two to four weeks after the date of record.

The journal entries to record the declaration and payment of a cash dividend were illustrated in Chapter 14 but are repeated here with emphasis on the date of declaration and date of payment.

Entries made on declaration date and . . .	June 1	Retained Earnings....................................	100,000	
		Dividends Payable		100,000
		To record declaration of a cash dividend of $1 per share on the 100,000 shares of common stock outstanding. Payable July 10 to shareholders of record on June 20.		
. . . on payment date	July 10	Dividends Payable	100,000	
		Cash..		100,000
		To record payment of $1 per share dividend declared June 1 to shareholders of record on June 20.		

As mentioned in Chapter 14, some companies record the declaration of a dividend by debiting a Dividends account instead of debiting Retained Earnings. In this case, a closing entry is required at the end of the year to transfer the debit balance of the Dividends account into the Retained Earnings account. Under either method, the balance of the Retained Earnings account ultimately is reduced by the amount of all dividends *declared* during the period.

Most dividends are paid in cash, but occasionally a dividend declaration calls for payment in assets other than cash. A large distillery once paid a dividend consisting of a bottle of whiskey for each share of stock. When a corporation goes out of existence (particularly a small corporation with only a few shareholders), it may choose to distribute noncash assets to its owners rather than to convert all its assets into cash.

In some cases, a cash dividend may be "paid" in common stock through an "automatic dividend reinvestment plan" whereby the cash dividends may be **automatically** reinvested. Thus, those shareholders who have chosen this plan will receive the cash dividends in common stock and the entry would debit retained earnings and credit common stock. To make such a plan attractive to the shareholders, the price for these new shares is usually below the current market price. Such a plan is beneficial to the company as it can conserve the cash needed for operations and expansion.

CASE IN POINT   MacLean Hunter has an automatic dividend reinvestment plan, which offers its shareholders the opportunity to reinvest their cash dividends for new common stock at 95% of the current market price. In a recent year, $6 million of the $45 million of cash dividends were reinvested.

Liquidating Dividends

A **liquidating dividend** occurs when a corporation pays a dividend that **exceeds the balance in the Retained Earnings account.** Thus, the dividend returns to shareholders all or part of their paid-in capital investment. Liquidating dividends usually are paid only when a corporation is going out of existence or is making a permanent reduction in the size of its operations. Normally dividends are paid as a result of profitable operations; shareholders may assume that a dividend represents a distribution of earnings unless they are notified by the corporation that the dividend is a return of invested capital.

Stock Dividends

OBJECTIVE 4
Account for stock dividends and stock splits, and explain the probable effect of these transactions upon market price.

Stock dividend is a term used to describe a distribution of **additional shares of stock** to a company's shareholders in proportion to their present holdings. In brief, the dividend is payable in **additional shares of stock** rather than in cash. Most stock dividends consist of additional shares of common stock distributed to holders of common stock, and our discussion will be limited to this type of stock dividend.

An important distinction must be drawn between a cash dividend and a stock dividend. In a **cash dividend,** assets are distributed by the corporation to the shareholders. Thus, a cash dividend reduces both assets and shareholders' equity. In a **stock dividend,** however, **no assets are distributed.** Thus, a stock dividend causes **no change** in assets or in total shareholders' equity. Each shareholder receives additional shares, but his or her total ownership in the corporation is **no larger than before.**

To illustrate this point, assume that a corporation with 2,000 shares of stock is owned equally by James Davis and Susan Miller, each owning 1,000 shares of stock. The corporation declares a stock dividend of 10% and distributes 200 additional shares (10% of 2,000 shares), with 100 shares going to each of the two shareholders. Davis and Miller now hold 1,100 shares apiece, but each *still owns one-half of the business.* Furthermore, the corporation has not changed in size; its assets and liabilities and its total shareholders' equity are exactly the same as before the stock dividend.

Now let us consider the logical effect of this stock dividend upon the *market price* of the company's stock. Assume that before the stock dividend, the outstanding 2,000 shares in our example had a market price of $110 per share. This price indicates a total market value for the corporation of $220,000 (2,000 shares × $110 per share). As the stock dividend does not change total assets or total shareholders' equity, the total market value of the corporation *should remain $220,000* after the stock dividend. As 2,200 shares are now outstanding, the market price of each share *should fall* to $100 ($220,000 ÷ 2,200 shares). In short, the market value of the stock *should fall in proportion* to the number of new shares issued. Whether the market price per share *will* fall in proportion to a small increase in number of outstanding shares is another matter. The market prices of common stocks are influenced by many different factors.

Reasons for Issuing Stock Dividends   Although stock dividends cause no change in total assets or total shareholders' equity, they are popular both with management and with shareholders. Management likes stock dividends because they do not cost anything (other than administrative costs)—the corporation does not have to surrender any assets. Shareholders enjoy stock dividends because often the market price of the stock *does not fall enough* to reflect fully the increased number of shares. While this failure of the stock price to fall proportionately is not logical, it is nonetheless a common phenomenon. In such cases, the stock dividend actually does increase the total market value of the corporation and of each shareholder's investment.

Entries to Record a Stock Dividend   In accounting for *small* stock dividends (say, less than 20%), the *market value* of the new shares is transferred from the Retained Earnings accounts to the contributed capital accounts. This process sometimes is called *capitalizing* retained earnings. The overall effect is the same as if the dividend had been paid in cash, and the shareholders had immediately reinvested the cash in the business in exchange for additional shares of stock. Of course, no cash actually changes hands—the new shares of stock are sent directly to the shareholders.

To illustrate, Aspen Corporation, on June 1, has outstanding 100,000 shares of no-par value common stock with a market value of $22 per share. On this date, the company declares a 10% stock dividend, distributable on July 15 to shareholders of record on June 20. The entry at June 1 to record the *declaration* of this dividend is:

Stock dividend declared; note use of market price of stock

Retained Earnings *220,000*
    Stock Dividend to Be Distributed *220,000*
Declared a 10% stock dividend consisting of 10,000 shares (100,000 shares × 10%) of no-par value common stock, market price $22 per share. Distributable July 15 to shareholders' of record on June 20.

The Stock Dividend to Be Distributed account is **not a liability,** because there is no obligation to distribute cash or any other asset. If a balance sheet is prepared between the date of declaration of a stock dividend and the date of distribution of the shares, this account should be presented in the shareholders' equity section of the balance sheet.

Notice that the Retained Earnings account was debited for the **market value** of the shares to be issued (10,000 shares × $22 per share = $220,000). Notice also that **no change** occurs in the total amount of shareholders' equity. The amount removed from the Retained Earnings account was simply transferred into another shareholders' equity account.

On July 15, the entry to record the **distribution** of the dividend shares is:

Stock dividend distributed

Stock Dividend to Be Distributed   220,000
       Common Stock   220,000
Distributed 10,000 share stock dividend declared June 1.

Large stock dividends (for example, those in excess of 20 to 25%), on the other hand, generally have the effect of proportionately reducing the market price of the stock. For example, a 100% stock dividend would reduce the market price by about 50%, because twice as many shares would be outstanding. A 100% stock dividend is very similar to the 2-for-1 **stock split** discussed in the following section of this chapter.

Stock Splits

A corporation may split its stock by increasing the number of outstanding shares of common stock. The purpose of the split is to reduce substantially the market price of the common stock, with the intent of making the stock more attractive to investors.

For example, assume that Pelican Corporation has outstanding 1 million shares of no-par value stock. The market price is $90 per share. The corporation now increases the number of shares from 1 million to 2 million. This action would be called a 2-for-1 stock split. A shareholder who owned 100 shares of the stock before the split would own 200 shares after the split. Since the number of outstanding shares has been doubled without any change in total assets or total shareholders' equity, the market price of the stock should drop from $90 to approximately $45 a share.

A stock split does not change the balance of any ledger account; consequently, the transaction may be recorded merely by **a memorandum entry** in the general journal and in the Common Stock account. For Pelican Corporation, this memorandum entry might read:

Memorandum entry to record a stock split

Sept. 30   Memorandum: Issued additional 1 million shares of common stock in a 2-for-1 stock split.

The description of common stock also is changed in the balance sheet to reflect the greater number of shares outstanding.

Stock may be split in any desired ratio. Among the more common ratios are 2 for 1, 3 for 2, and 3 for 1. The determining factor is the number of shares needed to bring the price of the stock into the desired trading range.

For example, assume that a stock is selling at a price of $150 per share and that management wants to reduce the price to approximately $30 per share. This objective may be accomplished with a **5-for-1** stock split ($150 ÷ 5 = $30).

Distinction between Stock Splits and Large Stock Dividends What is the difference between a 2-for-1 stock split and a 100% stock dividend? There is very little difference; both will double the number of outstanding shares without changing total shareholders' equity, and both should serve to cut the market price of the stock approximately in half. The stock dividend, however, will cause a transfer from the Retained Earnings account to the Common Stock account equal to the declared dollar amount for no-par value or to the par value of the dividend shares. A 2-for-1 stock split will reduce the par value per share by one-half, but it will not change the dollar balance of any account.

After an increase in the number of shares as a result of a stock split or stock dividend, earnings per share are computed in terms of the increased number of shares. In presenting 5- or 10-year summaries, the earnings per share for earlier years are ***retroactively restated*** to reflect the increased number of shares currently outstanding and thus make the trend of earnings per share from year to year a valid comparison.

Statement of Retained Earnings

OBJECTIVE 5
Describe
and prepare
a statement
of retained
earnings.

The term ***retained earnings*** refers to the portion of shareholders' equity derived from profitable operations. Retained earnings is increased by earning net income and is reduced by incurring net losses and by the declaration of dividends.

In addition to a balance sheet and an income statement, a complete set of financial statements includes a statement of retained earnings and a statement of changes in financial position. The statement of changes in financial position will be discussed in Chapter 19; a statement of retained earnings is illustrated below:

SHORE LINE CORPORATION
Statement of Retained Earnings
For the Year Ended December 31, 1996

Retained earnings, December 31, 1995		$600,000
Net income for 1996		180,000
Subtotal		$780,000
Less: Cash dividends:		
Preferred stock ($5 per share)	$ 17,500	
Common stock ($2 per share)	55,300	
10% stock dividend	140,000	212,800
Retained earnings, December 31, 1996		$567,200

Appropriations and Restrictions of Retained Earnings A few corporations transfer a portion of their retained earnings into separate accounts called ***appropriations*** or ***reserves.*** The purpose of such appropriations or reserves is to indicate to users of financial statements that a portion of retained earnings is not available for the declaration of cash dividends. The limitation on cash dividends may be established voluntarily by the board of directors or it may be required by law or contract.

Most corporations disclose restrictions on the declaration of cash dividends in notes accompanying the financial statements. For example, a company with total retained earnings of $10,000,000 might include the following note in its financial statements:

Footnote disclosure of restrictions placed on retained earnings

Note 7: Restriction of retained earnings

As of December 31, 1996, certain long-term debt agreements prohibited the declaration of cash dividends that would reduce the amount of retained earnings below $5,200,000. Retained earnings not so restricted amounted to $4,800,000.

Prior Period Adjustments

Prior period adjustments are those gains or losses that have **all four** of the following characteristics:

OBJECTIVE 6 Define prior period adjustments and explain how they are presented in financial statements.

1 are specifically identified with and directly related to the business activities of particular prior periods

2 are not attributable to economic events occurring subsequent to the date of the financial statements for such prior periods

3 depend primarily on decisions or determinations by persons other than management or owners

4 could not be reasonably estimated prior to such decisions or determinations[15]

Because of the restrictiveness of these characteristics, prior period adjustments are rare. The *CICA Handbook* provides only two examples:

1 nonrecurring adjustments or settlements of income taxes

2 settlements of claims resulting from litigation[16]

In contrast to extraordinary items described earlier in the chapter, **prior period adjustments** are excluded from the determination of net income for the current accounting period and are applied retroactively to the income of the related prior periods.[17] The financial statements affected by such an adjustment, when presented for comparative purposes, are to be **restated,** together with any related income tax effect. In the period where a prior period adjustment occurs, the following disclosures are required:

1 a description of the adjustment

2 its effects on the financial statements of the current and prior periods

---

[15] CICA, *CICA Handbook,* section 3600.03.

[16] Ibid., section 3600.02.

[17] Ibid., section 3600.06.

3 the fact regarding the restatement of the financial statements of prior periods that are presented.[18]

Also, the beginning balance of retained earnings for the periods subsequent to the period to which the adjustment relates should be ***restated.***

To illustrate, assume that in 1996 Jilin Corporation settled with the tax authority the assessment of additional income taxes of $60,000 for 1992. This prior period adjustment is presented in the comparative statements of earnings for 1996 and 1995 as follows:

Statement of retained earnings shows prior period adjustments, net income, and dividends

JILIN CORPORATION
Statement of Retained Earnings
For Years Ended December 31

	1996	*1995*
Retained earnings at beginning of year:		
As originally reported	*$860,000*	*$820,000*
Prior period adjustment—additional income taxes for 1992	*(60,000)*	*(60,000)*
As restated	*$800,000*	*$760,000*
Net income...	*160,000*	*110,000*
Subtotal..	*$960,000*	*$870,000*
Less: Cash dividends on common stock	*80,000*	*70,000*
Retained earnings at end of year..............................	*$880,000*	*$800,000*

The additional income taxes for 1992 are shown as an adjustment to the beginning balance of retained earnings for both 1996 and 1995 because these beginning amounts were overstated by $60,000. Also, this presentation serves to explain all changes in retained earnings during the accounting period.

Treasury Stock

Corporations sometimes acquire shares of their own capital stock by purchase in the open market. Paying out cash to acquire shares will reduce the assets of the corporation and reduce the shareholders' equity by the same amount. One reason for such purchases is to have stock available to reissue to officers and employees under bonus plans. Other reasons may include a desire to increase the reported earnings per share or to support the current market price of the stock.

Treasury stock may be defined as shares of a corporation's own capital stock that have been issued and later ***acquired by the issuing company,*** but that have not been cancelled or permanently retired. Treasury shares may be held indefinitely or may be issued again at any time. Shares of capital stock held in the treasury are not entitled to receive dividends, to vote, or to share in assets upon dissolution of the company. In the computation of earnings per share, shares held in the treasury are not regarded as outstanding shares.

A corporation may, under certain provincial legislation, acquire its own capital stock for the purpose of reissuing or cancelling it in the future.

---

[18]   Ibid., section 3600.08.

However, other legislation such as the Canada Business Corporations Act and the Ontario Business Corporations Act require that such acquired capital stock be cancelled or restored to the authorized but unissued status. Thus, corporations under such legislation are prohibited from having treasury stock. Also, corporation legislation does not permit a corporation to acquire its own capital stock when it is insolvent or if such an acquisition would render it insolvent.

Recording Purchases of Treasury Stock

OBJECTIVE 7
Account for treasury stock transactions.

Purchases of treasury stock should be recorded by debiting the Treasury Stock account with the cost of the stock. For example, if Torrey Corporation acquires 1,500 shares of its own no-par stock at a price of $100 per share, the entry is as follows:

Treasury Stock	150,000	
Cash		150,000
Purchased 1,500 shares of no-par treasury stock at $100 per share.		

Treasury Stock Is Not an Asset When treasury stock is purchased, the corporation is eliminating part of its shareholders' equity by a payment to one or more shareholders. The purchase of treasury stock should be regarded as a *reduction of shareholders' equity,* not as the acquisition of an asset. For this reason, the Treasury Stock account should appear in the balance sheet *as a deduction in the shareholders' equity section.* The presentation of treasury stock in a corporate balance sheet is illustrated on page 718.

Reissuance of Treasury Stock

When treasury shares are reissued, the Treasury Stock account is credited for the cost of the shares reissued and Contributed Capital from Treasury Stock Transactions account is debited or credited for any difference between *cost* and the reissue price. To illustrate, assume that 1,000 of the treasury shares acquired by Torrey Corporation at a cost of $100 per share are now reissued at a price of $115 per share. The entry to record the reissuance of these shares at a price above cost would be:

Treasury stock reissued at a price above cost

Cash..	115,000	
Treasury Stock.......................................		100,000
Contributed Capital from Treasury Stock Transactions .		15,000
Sold 1,000 shares of treasury stock, which cost $100,000, at a price of $115 per share.		

If treasury stock is reissued at a price below cost, contributed capital from previous treasury stock transactions of the same class is reduced (debited) by the excess of cost over the reissue price.[19] To illustrate, assume that Torrey Corporation reissues its remaining 500 shares of treasury stock (cost $100 per share) at a price of $90 per share. The entry would be:

---

[19] CICA, *CICA Handbook* (Toronto), section 3240.20.

Reissued at a price below cost	*Cash...*	*45,000*	
	Contributed Capital from Treasury Stock Transactions	*5,000*	
	* Treasury Stock...*		*50,000*
	Sold 500 shares of treasury stock, which cost $50,000, at a price of $90 each.		

If there is insufficient or no contributed capital from previous treasury stock transactions to cover the excess, the balance or the entire excess of the cost of the treasury shares over the reissue price may be recorded as a debit to Retained Earnings.[20]

No Income or Loss on Treasury Stock Transactions   Notice that ***no income or loss is recognized on treasury stock transactions,*** even when the shares are reissued at a price above or below cost. A corporation earns income by selling goods and services to outsiders, not by issuing or reissuing shares of its own capital stock. When treasury shares are reissued at a price above cost the corporation receives from the new shareholder an amount of contributed capital larger than the reduction in shareholders' equity when the corporation acquired the treasury shares. Conversely, if treasury shares are reissued at a price below cost, the corporation ends up with less contributed capital as a result of the purchase and reissuance of the shares. Thus, any changes in shareholders' equity resulting from treasury stock transactions are regarded as changes in ***contributed capital*** and are ***not*** included in the measurement of net income.

Restriction of Retained Earnings for Treasury Stock Owned   Purchases of treasury stock, like cash dividends, are distributions of assets to the shareholders in the corporation. Corporate laws generally require that distributions to shareholders (including purchases of treasury stock) cannot exceed the balance in the Retained Earnings account. Therefore, retained earnings usually are restricted by an amount equal to the ***cost*** of any shares held in the treasury.

Stock "Buyback" Programs

In past years, most treasury stock transactions involved relatively small dollar amounts. Hence, the topic was not of much importance to investors or other users of financial statements. Late in 1987, however, many corporations in the United States initiated large "buyback" programs, in which they repurchased huge amounts of their own common stock.[21] As a result of these programs, treasury stock has become a very material item in the balance sheets of many corporations.

---

[20]   Ibid.

[21]   On October 19, 1987, a date known as ***Black Monday,*** stock prices around the world suffered the largest one-day decline in history. Many economists and investors believed that this stock market "crash" would trigger a worldwide economic depression. Within hours of the market's close on Black Monday, many large corporations announced their intention to enter the market and spend hundreds of millions of dollars repurchasing their own shares. In the opinions of the authors, the announcement of these buyback programs did much to stabilize the world's financial markets, restore investors' confidence, and possibly avoid a depression.

CASE IN POINT   Shown below is the cost of the treasury stock listed in the balance sheets of several publicly owned corporations in the United States at the end of a recent year.

	Treasury Stock	
Company	At Cost (in Thousands)	As a % of Other Elements of Shareholders' Equity*
Coca-Cola	$ 3,235,963	48
Exxon	16,224,000	35
Lotus	194,937	41
King World	159,587	72

*   To place these holdings in perspective, we have shown the cost of the treasury stock as a percentage of total shareholders' equity **before** deducting the cost of the repurchased shares.

These large buyback programs serve several purposes. First, by creating demand for the company's stock in the marketplace, these programs tend to increase the market value of the shares. Also, reducing the number of shares outstanding usually increases earnings per share. When stock prices are low, some companies find that they can increase earnings per share by a greater amount through repurchasing shares than through expanding business operations.

Illustration of a Shareholders' Equity Section

The following shareholders' equity section of a balance sheet illustrates the various items discussed in this chapter. You should be able to explain the nature and origin of each account and disclosure.

The published financial statements of leading corporations indicate that there is no one standard arrangement for the various items making up the shareholders' equity section. Variations occur in the selection of titles, in the sequence of items, and in the extent of detailed classification.

Shareholders' equity:
   Capital stock:
      $9 preferred stock, no-par value, unlimited authorized shares,
         1,000 shares issued and outstanding $260,000
      Common stock, no-par value, unlimited authorized shares,
         issued 60,000 shares, of which 1,000 are held in treasury 543,000
      Common stock subscribed, 6,000 shares 30,000
      Contributed capital from treasury stock transactions 5,000
         Total contributed capital $838,000
   Retained earnings (of which $12,000, an amount equal to the
      cost of treasury stock purchased, is unavailable for dividends) 162,000
                                                                              $1,000,000
      Less: Treasury stock, common, 1,000 shares at cost 12,000
   Total shareholders' equity $988,000

CHAPTER REVIEW

KEY TERMS INTRODUCED OR EMPHASIZED IN CHAPTER 15

Basic earnings per share   Net income applicable to the common stock divided by weighted-average number of common shares outstanding during the year (or some other accounting period).

Book value   The shareholders' equity represented by each share of common stock. Book value is computed by dividing the common shareholders' equity by the number of common shares outstanding during the year.

Changes in accounting estimates   Include such items as a revision of the estimate of the amount of allowance for doubtful accounts or a revision of the estimate of a nine-year useful life of a depreciable asset to a six-year life.

Changes in accounting policy   Encompass changes in accounting principles as well as accounting methods used in the preparation of financial statements.

Comparative financial statements   Financial statements of the current year and the preceding year that are presented together to facilitate comparison.

Corrections of errors   Required when errors are discovered in prior period financial statements. Such errors may result from a mistake in computation, a misinterpretation or misrepresentation of information, an oversight of available information, and a misappropriation of assets.

Date of record   The date on which a person must be listed as a shareholder in order to be eligible to receive a dividend. Follows the date of declaration of a dividend by two to four weeks.

Discontinued operations   The net operating results (revenue and expenses) of a segment of a company that has been or is being sold.

Earnings per share   Net income applicable to the common stock divided by the weighted-average number of common shares outstanding during the year.

Ex-dividend date   A date generally four days prior to the date of record specified in a dividend declaration. A person buying a stock prior to the ex-dividend date also acquires the right to receive the dividend. The four-day interval permits the compilation of a list of shareholders as of the date of record.

Extraordinary items   Transactions and events that are not dependent on decisions by management or owners, unusual in nature, and occur infrequently—for example, a large earthquake loss. Such items are shown separately in the income statement after the determination of Income before Extraordinary Items.

Fully diluted earnings per share   Earnings per share computed under the assumption that all convertible securities had been converted into additional common shares at the beginning of the current year. The purpose of this hypothetical computation is to warn common shareholders of the risk that future earnings per share might be diluted by the conversion of other securities into common stock.

Price-earnings (p/e) ratio   Market price of a share of common stock divided by annual earnings per share.

Prior period adjustment   An adjustment to the earnings reported in the financial statements of a prior year. Prior period adjustments are recorded directly in the Retained Earnings account and are not included in the income statement of the current period; examples, settlement of income taxes and litigations.

Segment of a business   Those elements of a business that represent a separate and distinct line of business activity or that service a particular class of customers.

Statement of retained earnings   A basic financial statement explaining the change during the year in the amount of retained earnings.

Stock dividend A distribution of additional shares to common shareholders in proportion to their holdings.

Stock split An increase in the number of shares outstanding. The additional shares are distributed proportionately to all common shareholders. Purpose is to reduce market price per share and encourage wider public ownership of the company's stock. A 2-for-1 stock split will give each shareholder twice as many shares as previously owned.

Treasury stock Shares of a corporation's stock that have been issued and then acquired, but not cancelled by the corporation.

DEMONSTRATION PROBLEM FOR YOUR REVIEW

The shareholders' equity of Sutton Corporation at December 31, 1995, is shown below:

Shareholders' equity:

Common stock, no-par, unlimited shares authorized, 40,000 shares issued and outstanding	*$ 600,000*
Retained earnings	*1,500,000*
Total shareholders' equity	*$2,100,000*

Transactions affecting shareholders' equity during 1996 are as follows:

Mar. 31 A 5-for-4 stock split proposed by the board of directors was approved by vote of the shareholders. The 10,000 new shares were distributed to shareholders.

Apr. 1 The company purchased 2,000 shares of its common stock on the open market at $37 per share.

July 1 The company reissued 1,000 shares of treasury stock at $45 per share.

July 1 Issued for cash 20,000 shares of previously unissued no-par value common stock at a price of $45 per share.

Dec. 1 A cash dividend of $1 per share was declared, payable on December 30, to shareholders of record at December 14.

Dec. 22 A 10% stock dividend was declared; the dividend shares are to be distributed on January 15 of the following year. The market price of the stock on December 22 was $48 per share.

The net income for the year ended December 31, 1996, amounted to $177,000, after an extraordinary loss of $35,400 (net of $17,600 income tax benefits).

INSTRUCTIONS **a** Prepare journal entries (in general journal form) to record the transactions relating to shareholders' equity that took place during the year.

b Prepare the lower section of the income statement for 1996, beginning with the *income before extraordinary items* and showing the extraordinary loss and the net income. Also illustrate the presentation of earnings per share in the income statement, assuming that earnings per share is determined on the basis of the *weighted-average* number of shares outstanding during the year.

c Prepare a statement of retained earnings for the year ending December 31, 1996.

SOLUTION TO DEMONSTRATION PROBLEM

a   *General Journal*

Mar. 31	*Memorandum: Shareholders approved a 5-for-4 stock split. This action increased the number of shares of common stock outstanding from 40,000 to 50,000. The 10,000 new shares were distributed.*		
Apr. 1	*Treasury Stock*	*74,000*	
	Cash		*74,000*
	Acquired 2,000 shares of treasury stock at $37 per share.		
July 1	*Cash*	*45,000*	
	Treasury Stock		*37,000*
	Contributed Capital from Treasury Stock		
	Transactions		*8,000*
	Sold 1,000 shares of treasury stock at $45 per share.		
1	*Cash*	*900,000*	
	Common Stock		*900,000*
	Issued 20,000 shares of previously unissued no-par value common stock for cash of $45 per share.		
Dec. 1	*Retained Earnings*	*69,000*	
	Dividends Payable		*69,000*
	To record declaration of cash dividend of $1 per share on 69,000 shares of common stock outstanding (1,000 shares in treasury are not entitled to receive dividends).		

Note: Entry to record the payment of the cash dividend is not shown here since the action does not affect the shareholders' equity.

22	*Retained Earnings*	*331,200*	
	Stock Dividends to Be Distributed		*331,200*
	To record declaration of 10% stock dividend consisting of 6,900 shares of no-par value common stock to be distributed on Jan. 15 of next year.		
31	*Income Summary*	*177,000*	
	Retained Earnings		*177,000*
	To close Income Summary account.		

b   **SUTTON CORPORATION**
                         Partial Income Statement
                     For Year Ended December 31, 1996

Income before extraordinary items	*$212,400*
Extraordinary loss (net of $17,600 income tax benefits)	*(35,400)*
Net income	*$177,000*

Earnings per share:*	
Income before extraordinary items	*$3.60*
Extraordinary loss	*(0.60)*
Net income	*$3.00*

*   On 59,000 weighted-average number of shares of common stock outstanding during 19__, determined as follows:

Jan. 1–Mar. 31: (40,000 + 10,000 shares issued pursuant to a 5 for 4 split) $\times \frac{1}{4}$ of year...........	12,500
Apr. 1–June 30: (50,000 − 2,000 shares of treasury stock) $\times \frac{1}{4}$ of year	12,000
July 1–Dec. 31: (50,000 + 20,000 shares of new stock − 1,000 shares of treasury stock) $\times$	
$\frac{1}{2}$ of year	34,500
Weighted-average number of shares outstanding	59,000

c

SUTTON CORPORATION
Statement of Retained Earnings
For Year Ended December 31, 1996

Retained earnings, December 31, 1995		$1,500,000
Add: Net income for 1996		177,000
Subtotal		$1,677,000
Less: Cash dividends ($1 per share)	$ 69,000	
10% stock dividend	331,200	400,200
Retained earnings, December 31, 1996		$1,276,800

ASSIGNMENT MATERIAL

DISCUSSION QUESTIONS

1 What is the purpose of arranging an income statement to show subtotals for *Income from Continuing Operations* and for *Income before Extraordinary Items?*

2 Pappa Joe's owns 30 pizza parlors and a minor league baseball team. During the current year, the company sold three of its pizza parlors and closed another when the lease on the building expired. Should any of these events be classified as "discontinued operations" in the company's income statement? Explain.

3 Define *extraordinary items.* Give three examples of losses that qualify as extraordinary items and three examples of losses that would *not* be classified as extraordinary.

4 Briefly describe the nature and accounting treatment of each of the following:
   a A change in an accounting policy
   b A change in an accounting estimate
   c A correction of an error in prior period financial statements

5 In past years, the management of St. Thomas Medical Supply had consistently estimated the allowance for doubtful accounts at 2% of total accounts receivable. At the end of the current year, management estimated that uncollectible accounts would equal 4% of accounts receivable. Should the uncollectible accounts expense of prior years be recomputed in order to show in the comparative income statements of previous years the effect of this change in accounting estimate?

6 Even though *a change in accounting principle* and *prior period adjustment* affect the income of past accounting periods, their natures are different. Explain how they are reported in the financial statements.

7 In the current year, Garden Products decided to switch from use of an accelerated method of depreciation to the straight-line method. Will the cumulative effect of this change in accounting principle increase or decrease the amount of retained earnings reported at the beginning of the preceding year (assume a two-year comparative statement is presented)? Explain.

8 *Earnings per share* and *book value per share* are statistics that relate to common stock. When both preferred and common stock are outstanding, explain the computation involved in determining the following:
   a Earnings allocable to the common shareholders
   b Aggregate book value allocable to the common shareholders

9 Assume a corporation has only common stock outstanding. Is the number of common shares used in the computation of earnings per share *always* the same as the number of common shares used in computing book value per share for this corporation? Is the number of common shares used in computing these two statistics *ever* the same? Explain.

10 Explain how each of the following is computed:

a Price-earnings ratio

b Basic earnings per share

c Fully diluted earnings per share

11 Throughout the year, Gold Seal Nineteen Limited had 4 million shares of common stock and 120,000 shares of convertible preferred stock outstanding. Each share of preferred is convertible into four shares of common. What number of shares should be used in the computation of (a) basic earnings per share and (b) fully diluted earnings per share?

12 A financial analyst notes that Baxter Corporation's earnings per share have been rising steadily for the last five years. The analyst expects the company's net income to continue to increase at the same rate as in the past. In forecasting future basic earnings per share, what special risk should the analyst consider if Baxter's basic earnings are significantly larger than its fully diluted earnings?

13 Explain the significance of the following dates relating to dividends: date of declaration, date of record, date of payment, ex-dividend date.

14 What is the purpose of a *stock split?*

15 Distinguish between a *stock split* and a *stock dividend.* Is there any reason for the difference in accounting treatment of these two events?

16 What are *prior period adjustments?* How are they presented in financial statements?

17 Identify three items that may appear in a statement of retained earnings as changes in the amount of retained earnings.

18 What is *treasury stock?* Why do corporations purchase their own shares? Is treasury stock an asset? How should it be reported in the balance sheet?

19 Corporation laws generally require that retained earnings be restricted for dividend purposes to the extent of the cost of treasury shares. What is the reason for this legal rule?

MULTIPLE CHOICE QUESTIONS

1 The primary purpose of showing unusual types of events separately in the income statement is to:

a Increase earnings per share.

b Assist users of the income statement in evaluating and predicting the profitability of normal, ongoing operations.

c Minimize the income taxes paid on the results of ongoing operations.

d Prevent unusual losses from recurring.

2 Which of the following situations would be presented in a separate section of the current year's income statement of Marlow Corporation? During the current year:

a Marlow's Vancouver headquarters are destroyed by a tornado.

    b Marlow sells its entire juvenile furniture operations and concentrates upon its remaining children's clothing segment.

    c Marlow changes from the straight-line method of depreciation to the declining-balance method.

    d Marlow's accountant discovers that the entire price paid several years ago to purchase company offices in Winnipeg had been charged to a Land account; consequently, no depreciation has ever been taken on these buildings.

3 When a corporation has outstanding both common and preferred stock:

    a Basic and fully diluted earnings per share are reported only if the preferred stock is cumulative.

    b Earnings per share are reported for each type of stock outstanding.

    c Earnings per share may be computed without regard to the amount of dividends declared on common stock.

    d Earnings per share may be computed without regard to the amount of the annual preferred dividends.

4 The statement of retained earnings:

    a Is a basic financial statement that shows such items as prior period adjustments, net income, and dividends declared.

    b Indicates the amount of cash available for the payment of dividends.

    c Includes prior period adjustments and cash dividends, but not stock dividends.

    d Shows revenue, expenses, and dividends for the accounting period.

5 On December 10, 1995, Totem Corporation acquired 2,000 of its own no-par stock at a price of $60 per share. In 1996, 500 of the treasury shares are reissued at a price of $70 per share. Which of the following statements is correct?

    a The treasury stock purchased is recorded at cost and is shown in Totem's December 31, 1995, balance sheet as an asset.

    b The two treasury stock transactions result in an overall reduction in Totem's shareholders' equity of $85,000.

    c Totem recognizes a gain of $10 per share on the reissuance of the 500 treasury shares in 1996.

    d Totem's shareholders' equity was increased by $110,000 when the treasury stock was acquired.

EXERCISES

EXERCISE 15-1
Accounting Terminology

Listed below are nine technical accounting terms introduced or emphasized in this chapter:

p/e ratio	*Treasury stock*	*Discontinued operations*
Stock dividend	*Extraordinary item*	*Prior period adjustment*
Basic earnings per share	*Change in accounting policy*	*Fully diluted earnings per share*

Each of the following statements may (or may not) describe one of these technical terms. For each statement, indicate the term described, or answer "None" if the statement does not correctly describe any of the terms.

a A gain or loss that is beyond management's control, unusual in nature, and not expected to recur in the foreseeable future.

b The asset represented by shares of capital stock that have not yet been issued.

c A distribution of additional shares of stock that reduces retained earnings but causes no change in total shareholders' equity.

d The inventory costing method has been changed from weighted average to first-in, first-out.

e An adjustment to the beginning balance of retained earnings to correct an error previously made in the measurement of net income.

f A statistic expressing a relationship between the current market value of a share of common stock and the underlying earnings per share.

g A separate section sometimes included in an income statement as a step in helping investors to evaluate and predict the profitability of ongoing business activities.

h A hypothetical figure indicating what earnings per share would have been if all securities convertible into common stock had been converted at the beginning of the current year.

EXERCISE 15-2
Discontinued
Operations

During the current year, SunSports, Inc., operated two business segments: a chain of surf and dive shops and a small chain of tennis shops. The tennis shops were not profitable and were sold near year-end to another corporation. SunSports' operations for the current year are summarized below. The first two captions, "Net sales" and "Costs and expenses," relate only to the company's continuing operations.

Net sales...	*$9,800,000*
Costs and expenses (including applicable income taxes).....................	*8,600,000*
Operating loss from tennis shops (net of $76,800 income tax benefit).........	*192,000*
Loss on sale of tennis shops (net of $129,200 income tax benefit)............	*348,000*

The company had 150,000 shares of a single class of capital stock outstanding throughout the year.

INSTRUCTIONS

Prepare a condensed income statement for the year. At the bottom of the statement, show any appropriate earnings-per-share figures.

EXERCISE 15-3
Extraordinary
Items, Ac-
counting
Changes, and
Prior Period
Adjustments

Select the ***best*** answer for each of the following multiple-choice questions:

1 Accounting changes include

   a A change in accounting policy and in accounting estimate

   b A correction of error in a prior period

   c A prior period adjustment

   d a and b

   e a, b, and c

2 An extraordinary item reflects an event that is

   a Unusual, material, and beyond management's control

   b Not reasonably estimated, not related to economic events, but within management's control

   c Not typical, infrequent, and beyond management's control

   d Not typical, irregular, but a recurring factor for ordinary operation evaluation

   e An element of an accounting change

3 Changes in accounting policy encompass

   a Changes in the statement of changes in financial position

    b Changes in accounting principles and methods

    c Changes in accounting estimates

    d Corrections of errors in prior period financial statements

    e Extraordinary items and prior period adjustments

4 Changes in accounting estimates include

    a Revision of the amount of allowance for doubtful accounts

    b Revision of the useful life of a depreciable asset

    c Revision of the residual value of a depreciable asset

    d A change of depreciation method

    e **a**, **b**, and **c**

5 Retroactive application and restatement are required by

    a A change in accounting policy

    b A change in accounting estimate

    c A correction of an error in a prior period

    d **a** and **c**

    e **a** and **c** and a prior period adjustment.

6 An accounting change requiring a current or current and prospective application is

    a A change in accounting estimate

    b A change in accounting policy and accounting estimate

    c A change in accounting policy and accounting estimate as well as a correction of a prior period error

    d An extraordinary item

    e A prior period adjustment

**EXERCISE 15-4
Reporting an
Extraordinary
Item**

For the year ended December 31, Union Chemical had net sales of $8,000,000, costs and other expenses (including income taxes) of $7,060,000, and an extraordinary gain (net of $200,000 income taxes) of $400,000. Prepare a condensed income statement (including earnings per share), assuming that 500,000 shares of common stock were outstanding throughout the year.

**EXERCISE 15-5
Computing
Earnings Per
Share:
Changes in
Number of
Shares Out-
standing**

In the year just ended, Sunshine Citrus earned net income of $6,300,000. The company has issued only one class of no-par value capital stock, of which 1 million shares were outstanding at January 1. Compute the company's earnings per share under each of the following *independent* assumptions:

a No change occurred during the year in the number of shares outstanding.

b On October 1, the company issued an additional 200,000 shares of capital stock in exchange for cash of $1,500,000.

c On July 1, the company distributed an additional 200,000 shares of capital stock as a 20% stock dividend. On July 1, Sunshine's stock had a market value of $7.25 per share.

**EXERCISE 15-6
Computing
Earnings Per
Share: Effect
of Preferred
Stock**

The net income of Carriage Trade Clothiers amounted to $2,550,000 for the current year. Compute the amount of earnings per share assuming that the shares of capital stock outstanding throughout the year consisted of:

a 300,000 shares of no-par value common stock and no preferred stock.

b 200,000 shares of $9, no-par value preferred stock and 300,000 shares of no-par value common stock.

EXERCISE 15-7
Restating Earnings per Share After a Stock Dividend

The 1994 annual report of **R&W Ko Corporation** included the following comparative summary of earnings per share over the last three years:

	1994	1993	1992
Earnings per share	$3.03	$2.22	$1.30

Early in 1995, the company declared and distributed a 100% stock dividend. Following this stock dividend, the company reported earnings per share of $2.35 for 1995.

INSTRUCTIONS

a Prepare a three-year schedule similar to the one above, but compare earnings per share during the years 1995, 1994, and 1993.

b In preparing your schedule, which figure (or figures) did you have to restate? Why? Explain the logic behind your computation.

EXERCISE 15-8
Restating Earnings per Share After a Stock Split

The 1994 annual report of **Nathan Corporation** included the following comparative summary of earnings per share over the last three years:

	1994	1993	1992
Earnings per share	$6.69	$4.86	$3.78

During 1995, the company split its common stock 3 for 1. Following this stock split, the company reported earnings per share of $3.05 in 1995 and $3.78 in 1996.

INSTRUCTIONS

a Prepare a three-year schedule similar to the one above, but compare earnings per share during the years 1996, 1995, and 1994.

b In preparing your schedule, which figure (or figures) did you have to restate? Why? Explain the logic behind your computation.

EXERCISE 15-9
Cash Dividends, Stock Dividends and Stock Splits

Global Technology Corporation has 500,000 shares of no-par value capital stock outstanding on January 1. The following equity transactions occurred during the current year:

Apr. 30 Distributed additional shares of capital stock in a 2-for-1 stock split. Market price of stock was $35 per share.

June 1 Declared a cash dividend of 60 cents per share.

July 2 Paid the 60-cent cash dividend to shareholders.

Aug. 1 Declared a 5% stock dividend. Market price of stock was $19 per share.

Sept. 10 Issued shares pursuant to the 5% stock dividend declared on August 1.

INSTRUCTIONS

a Prepare journal entries to record the above transactions.

b Compute the number of shares of capital stock outstanding at year-end.

EXERCISE 15-10
Effect of Stock Dividends on Stock Price

Tarreytown Corporation has a total of 80,000 shares of common stock outstanding and no preferred stock. Total shareholders' equity at the end of the current year amounts to $5 million and the market value of the stock is $66 per share. At year-end, the company declares a 10% stock dividend—one share for each ten shares held. If all parties concerned clearly recognize the nature of the stock dividend, what should you expect the market price per share of the common stock to be on the ex-dividend date?

**EXERCISE 15-11
Recording
Treasury Stock
Transactions**

Cachet, Inc., engaged in the following transactions involving treasury stock:

Feb. 10   Purchased for cash 14,500 shares of treasury stock at a price of $30 per share.

June 4   Reissued 6,000 shares of treasury stock at a price of $33 per share.

Dec. 22   Reissued 4,000 shares of treasury stock at a price of $28 per share.

INSTRUCTIONS

a Prepare general journal entries to record these transactions.

b Compute the amount of retained earnings that should be restricted because of the treasury stock still owned at December 31.

**EXERCISE 15-12
Effects of Various Transactions upon Earnings per Share**

Explain the immediate effects, if any, of each of the following transactions upon a company's net earnings per share:

a Split the common stock 3 for 1.

b Realized a gain from the sale of a discontinued operation.

c Declared and paid a cash dividend on common stock.

d Declared and distributed a stock dividend on common stock.

e Acquired several thousand shares of treasury stock.

**EXERCISE 15-13
Where to Find
Financial Information**

You have now been exposed to the following financial statements issued by corporations: balance sheet, income statement and statement of retained earnings. Listed below are various items frequently of interest to a corporation's owners, potential investors, and creditors, among others. You are to specify which of the above corporate financial statements, if any, reports the desired information. If the listed item is not reported in any formal financial statement issued by a corporation, indicate an appropriate source for the desired information.

a Number of shares of stock outstanding as of year-end

b Total dollar amount of cash dividends declared during the current year

c Market value per share at balance sheet date

d Cumulative dollar effect of an accounting error made in a previous year

e The disposal of a segment of the business.

f Loss from an earthquake

g Earnings per share of common stock

h Book value per share

i Price/earnings (p/e) ratio

j The total amount the corporation paid to buy back shares of its own stock that it now holds

PROBLEMS

Group A

**PROBLEM 15A-1
Reporting Unusual Events;
Using Predictive Subtotals**

Gulf Coast Airlines operated both an airline and several motels located near airports. During the year just ended, all motel operations were discontinued and the following operating results were reported:

Continuing operations (airlines):

Net sales..	$51,120,000
Costs and expenses (including income taxes on continuing operations) ...	43,320,000

Other data:

Operating income from motels (net of $388,000 income taxes).............	864,000
Gain on sale of motels (net of $2,230,000 income taxes)	4,956,000
Extraordinary loss (net of $1,512,000 income tax benefit)..................	3,360,000

The extraordinary loss resulted from the destruction of an airliner by terrorists. Gulf Coast Airlines had 1,200,000 shares of capital stock outstanding throughout the year.

INSTRUCTIONS

a Prepare a condensed income statement including proper presentation of the discontinued motel operations and the extraordinary loss. Include all appropriate earnings per share figures.

b Assume that you expect the profitability of Gulf Coast's airlines operations to **decline by** 6% next year, and the profitability of the motels to decline by 10%. What is your estimate of the company's net earnings per share next year?

PROBLEM 15A-2
Accounting Changes

The following comparative statement of retained earnings relates to Waterloo Corporation, which began operations in 1993.

	December 31	
	1995	1994
Retained earnings at beginning of year...........................	$ 900,000	$680,000
Net income..	260,000	220,000
Retained earnings at end of year................................	$1,160,000	$900,000

Waterloo decided on January 1, 1996, to change its depreciation method from declining-balance to straight-line. The information for the depreciation expense is as follows:

Year	Declining-Balance	Straight-Line
1993	$100,000	$42,000
1994	75,000	42,000
1995	56,250	42,000

INSTRUCTIONS

a Compute the amount of cumulative effect on the beginning balance of retained earnings for 1995, as a result of the change in depreciation method and indicate whether the effect is an increase or a decrease. (Disregard income tax considerations.)

b How would the income statements for 1994 and 1995 be affected by the change in depreciation method? (Disregard income tax considerations.)

c Assuming that after the 1996 net income of $188,000 was recorded, the company discovered that it should have changed the useful life of the assets in 1996. This change would have increased the depreciation expense by $12,000 for each of 1995, 1996, and 1997. Explain how this change would affect the net income and retained earnings for these three years. (Disregard income tax considerations.)

PROBLEM 15A-3
Format of an Income Statement and a Statement of Retained Earnings

The following data are relating to the operations of Academic Testing Services, Inc., during 1996:

Continuing operations:

Net sales..	$15,750,000
Costs and expenses (including applicable income taxes).................	12,800,000

Other data:

Operating income during 1996 on segment of the business discontinued near year-end (net of $112,500 income taxes)...........................	225,000
Loss on disposal of discontinued segment (net of $337,500 income tax benefit)	675,000
Extraordinary loss (net of $390,000 income tax benefit)	780,000
Cumulative effect of change in accounting principle for a three-year period to December 31, 1995, resulted in an increase in total net income..	135,000
Settlement of income tax assessment for 1992...........................	150,000
Cash dividends declared...	925,000

INSTRUCTIONS

a Prepare a condensed income statement for 1996, including earnings per share statistics. Academic Testing Services, Inc., had 300,000 shares of no-par value common stock and 40,000 shares of $6.25, no-par value preferred stock outstanding throughout the year.

b Prepare a statement of retained earnings for the year ended December 31, 1996. As originally reported, retained earnings at December 31, 1995 amounted to $6,450,000.

c Compute the amount of cash dividend *per share* of *common stock* declared by the board of directors for 1996. Assume no dividends in arrears on the preferred stock.

PROBLEM 15A-4
Reporting Unusual Events: A Comprehensive Problem

The following income statement was prepared by a new and inexperienced employee in the accounting department of Keller Interiors, a business organized as a corporation.

KELLER INTERIORS
Income Statement
For the Year Ended December 31, 1996

Net sales...		$10,800,000
Gain on sale of treasury stock		54,000
Premium on capital stock...		510,000
Prior period adjustment (net of $30,000 income taxes)		60,000
Extraordinary gain (net of $18,000 income taxes)		36,000
Total revenue		$11,460,000
Less:		
Cost of goods sold..	$6,000,000	
Selling expenses	1,128,000	
General and administrative expenses......................................	1,896,000	
Income taxes (on continuing operations)	720,000	
Operating loss on discontinued operations (net of $126,000 income tax benefit)..	252,000	
Loss on disposal of discontinued operations (net of $210,000 income tax benefit)...	420,000	
Cumulative effect of change in accounting principle	84,000	
Dividends declared on capital stock..	350,000	
Total costs and expenses...		10,850,000
Net income..		$ 610,000

INSTRUCTIONS **a** Prepare a corrected income statement for the year ended December 31, 1996. Include at the bottom of your income statement all appropriate earnings per share figures. Assume that throughout the year, the company had outstanding a weighted average of 200,000 shares of a single class of capital stock.

      b Prepare a statement of retained earnings for 1996. (As originally reported, retained earnings at December 31, 1995 amounted to $1,400,000.)

PROBLEM 15A-5
Effects of
Stock Divi-
dends, Stock
Splits, and
Treasury Stock
Transactions

At the beginning of the year, Recovery Sciences, Inc., has total shareholders' equity of $660,000 and 20,000 outstanding shares of a single class of capital stock. During the year, the corporation completes the following transactions affecting its shareholders' equity accounts:

Jan. 10   A 10% stock dividend is declared and distributed. (Market price, $40 per share.)

Mar. 15   The corporation acquires 1,000 shares of its own capital stock at a cost of $40.50 per share.

May 30   All 1,000 shares of the treasury stock are reissued at a price of $44.90 per share.

July 31   The capital stock is split 2 for 1.

Dec. 15   The board of directors declares a cash dividend of $1.10 per share, payable on January 15.

Dec. 31   Net income of $127,600 (equal to $2.90 per share) is reported for the year ended December 31.

INSTRUCTIONS Compute the amount of total shareholders' equity, the number of shares of capital stock outstanding, and the book value per share following each successive transaction. Organize your solution as a three-column schedule with these separate column headings: (1) Total Shareholders' Equity, (2) Number of Shares Outstanding, and (3) Book Value per Share.

PROBLEM 15A-6
Recording
Stock Divi-
dends and
Treasury Stock
Transactions

At the beginning of 1996, OverNight Letter showed the following amounts in the shareholders' equity section of its balance sheet:

Shareholders' equity:

Capital stock, no-par value, unlimited shares authorized, issued	
and outstanding, 382,000 shares	*$4,584,000*
Retained earnings	*2,704,600*
Total shareholders' equity	*$7,288,600*

    The transactions relating to shareholders' equity accounts during the year are as follows:

Jan. 3   Declared a dividend of $1 per share to shareholders of record on January 31, payable on February 15.

Feb. 15   Paid the cash dividend declared on January 3.

Apr. 12   The corporation purchased 6,000 shares of its own capital stock at a price of $40 per share.

May 9   Reissued 4,000 shares of the treasury stock at a price of $44 per share.

June 1   Declared a 5% stock dividend to shareholders of record at June 15, to be distributed on June 30. The market price of the stock at June 1 was $42 per share.

June 30   Distributed the stock dividend declared on June 1.

Aug. 4 Reissued 600 of the 2,000 remaining shares of treasury stock at a price of $37 per share.

Dec. 31 The Income Summary account, showing net income for the year of $1,928,000 was closed into the Retained Earnings account.

INSTRUCTIONS

a Prepare in general journal form the entries to record the above transactions.

b Prepare the shareholders' equity section of the balance sheet at December 31, 1996. Use the format illustrated in this chapter. Include a supporting schedule showing your computation of retained earnings at that date.

c Compute the maximum cash dividend per share that legally could be declared at December 31, 1996 without impairing the contributed capital of OverNight Letter.

PROBLEM 15A-7
Preparing the Shareholders' Equity Section: A Challenging Case

The Mandella family decided early in 1995 to incorporate their family-owned vineyards under the name Mandella Corporation. The corporation was authorized to issue unlimited shares of a single class of no-par value capital stock. Presented below is the information necessary to prepare the shareholders' equity section of the company's balance sheet at the end of 1995 and at the end of 1996.

1995. In January the corporation issued to members of the Mandella family 150,000 shares of capital stock in exchange for cash and other assets used in the operation of the vineyards. The fair market value of these assets indicated an issue price of $30 per share. In December, Joe Mandella died, and the corporation purchased 10,000 shares of its own capital stock from his estate at $34 per share. Because of the large cash outlay to acquire this treasury stock, the directors decided not to declare cash dividends in 1995 and instead declared a 10% stock dividend to be distributed in January of 1996. The stock price at the declaration date was $35 per share. Net income for 1995 was $940,000.

1996. In January the corporation distributed the stock dividend declared in 1995, and in February, the 10,000 treasury shares were sold to Maria Mandella at $39 per share. In June, the capital stock was split 2 for 1. On December 15, the directors declared a cash dividend of $2 per share, payable in January of 1997. Net income for 1996 was $1,080,000.

INSTRUCTIONS

Using the format illustrated in this chapter, prepare the shareholders' equity section of the balance sheet at:

a December 31, 1995

b December 31, 1996

Show any necessary computations in supporting schedules.

Group B

PROBLEM 15B-1
Reporting Unusual Events; Using Predictive Subtotals

Sea Quest Corporation operated both a fleet of commercial fishing vessels and a chain of six seafood restaurants. The restaurants continuously lost money and were sold to a large restaurant chain near year-end. The operating results of Sea Quest Corporation for the year ended December 31, 1996, are shown below:

Continuing operations (fishing fleet):	
Net sales..	$23,000,000
Costs and expenses (including applicable income taxes)..................	20,100,000
Other data:	
Operating loss from restaurants (net of $770,000 income tax benefit)......	1,540,000
Gain on sale of restaurant properties (net of $230,000 income taxes)......	460,000
Extraordinary loss (net of $360,000 income tax benefit)....................	720,000

The extraordinary loss resulted from the expropriation of a fishing vessel by a foreign government.

Sea Quest Corporation had 500,000 shares of capital stock outstanding throughout the year.

INSTRUCTIONS

a Prepare a condensed income statement including proper presentation of the discontinued restaurant operations and the extraordinary loss. Include all appropriate earnings per share figures.

b Assume that you expect the profitability of Sea Quest's fishing operations to *increase by 5%* in the next year and the profitability of the restaurants to remain unchanged. What is your estimate of the company's net earnings per share for 1997?

PROBLEM 15B-2
Accounting Changes

The following is a comparative statement of retained earnings for Fudan Limited for the last two years.

| | December 31 | |
	1996	1995
Retained earnings at beginning of year...........................	$480,000	$300,000
Net income..	200,000	180,000
Retained earnings at end of year.................................	$680,000	$480,000

Fudan Limited was incorporated on January 2, 1994, and used a straight-line method of depreciation for its depreciable assets until January 1, 1997. At that time, Fudan changed its depreciation method from straight-line to double-declining. The net income for 1997, based on the new depreciation method, is $286,000. The information for depreciation expense is as follows:

Year	Straight-Line	Declining-Balance
1994	$54,000	$120,000
1995	54,000	72,000
1996	54,000	43,200

INSTRUCTIONS

a Prepare a comparative statement of retained earnings for 1996 and 1997. (Disregard income tax considerations.)

b How would the income statement for 1995 be affected by the change in depreciation method? Explain. (Disregard income tax considerations.)

c Assuming that after the net income of $286,000 for 1997 was recorded, an engineering report showed that the company should have changed the useful life of its depreciable assets in 1997. Such a change would have decreased the depreciation expense by $14,600 for 1996 and by $8,620 for 1997. Explain how this change would affect the net income and retained earnings for 1996, 1997, and 1998. (Disregard income tax considerations.)

PROBLEM 15B-3
Format of an Income Statement and a Statement of Retained Earnings

Shown on the next page are data relating to the operations of Synthetic Genetics, Inc., during 1996:

Continuing operations:

Net sales...	$21,000,000
Costs and expenses (including applicable income taxes).................	18,300,000

Other data:

Operating loss during 1996 on segment of the business discontinued near year-end (net of $150,000 income tax benefit)....................	300,000
Loss on disposal of discontinued segment (net of $450,000 income tax benefit)...	900,000
Extraordinary gain (net of $310,000 income taxes)	620,000
Cumulative effect of change in accounting principle from 1992 to 1995 resulted in an increase in total net income	140,000
Settlement of lawsuit against the company related to 1990, net of $120,000 income tax benefit...	240,000
Cash dividends declared...	1,200,000

INSTRUCTIONS

a Prepare a condensed income statement for 1996, including earnings per share statistics. Synthetic Genetics had 400,000 shares of no-par value common stock as well as 50,000 shares of $8, no-par value preferred stock outstanding throughout 1996.

b Prepare a statement of retained earnings for the year ended December 31, 1996. As originally reported, retained earnings at December 31, 1995, amounted to $7,400,000.

c What was the cash dividend *per share* of *common stock* declared by Synthetic Genetics' board of directors for 1996? Assume there were no dividends in arrears on the preferred stock.

PROBLEM 15B-4
Reporting the Results of Operations—A Comprehensive Problem

Katherine McCall, the accountant for Alternative Energy Systems, was injured in a skiing accident, and the following income statement was prepared by a temporary employee with little knowledge of accounting:

ALTERNATIVE ENERGY SYSTEMS
Income Statement
For the Year Ended December 31, 1996

Net sales..		$5,400,000
Gain on sale of treasury stock		30,000
Premium on capital stock...		120,000
Operating income from segment of business discontinued during the year (net of $100,000 income taxes)...		200,000
Cumulative effect of change in accounting principle		75,000
Total revenue		$5,825,000
Less:		
Prior period adjustment (net of $125,000 income tax benefit) ...	$ 250,000	
Cost of goods sold...	2,480,000	
Selling expenses	1,160,000	
General and administrative expenses...........................	820,000	
Income taxes on continuing operations.......................	270,000	
Extraordinary loss (net of $115,000 income tax benefit)	230,000	
Loss on sale of discontinued segment (net of $225,000 income tax benefit)..	450,000	
Dividends declared on capital stock...........................	300,000	5,960,000
Net loss...		$ 135,000

INSTRUCTIONS   **a** Prepare a corrected income statement for the year ended December 31, 1996. Include at the bottom of your income statement all appropriate earnings per share figures. Assume that throughout the year the company had outstanding a weighted average of 50,000 shares of a single class of capital stock.

b Prepare a statement of retained earnings for 1996. Assume that retained earnings at December 31, 1995, were originally reported at $2,300,000.

PROBLEM 15B-5
Effects of Stock Dividends, Stock Splits, and Treasury Stock Transactions

On January 1, Alton Pump & Compressor Corporation has total shareholders' equity of $4,400,000 and 50,000 outstanding shares of a single class of capital stock. During the year, the corporation completes the following transactions affecting its shareholders' equity accounts:

Jan. 10 The board of directors declares a cash dividend of $4.20 per share, payable on February 15.

Apr. 30 The capital stock is split 2 for 1.

June 11 The corporation acquires 2,000 shares of its own capital stock at a cost of $56.60 per share.

July 21 All 2,000 shares of the treasury stock are reissued at a price of $61.60 per share.

Nov. 10 A 5% stock dividend is declared and distributed (market value $60 per share).

Dec. 31 Net income of $378,000 (equal to $3.60 per share) is reported for the year.

INSTRUCTIONS Compute the amount of total shareholders' equity, the number of shares of capital stock outstanding, and the book value per share following each successive transaction. Organize your solution as a three-column schedule with these separate column headings: (1) Total Shareholders' Equity, (2) Number of Shares Outstanding, and (3) Book Value per Share.

PROBLEM 15B-6
Recording Stock Dividends and Treasury Stock Transactions

The shareholders' equity of Cornish Productions, Inc., at January 1, 1996, is as follows:

Shareholders' equity:

Common stock, no-par value, authorized, unlimited shares, issued	
and outstanding, 260,000 shares	*$5,365,000*
Retained earnings	*2,810,000*
Total shareholders' equity	*$8,175,000*

During the year the following transactions relating to shareholders' equity occurred:

Jan. 15 Paid a $1.50 per share cash dividend declared in December of the preceding year. This dividend was properly recorded at the declaration date and was the only dividend declared during the preceding year.

June 10 Declared a 10% stock dividend to shareholders of record on June 30, to be distributed on July 15. At June 10, the market price of the stock was $35 per share.

July 15 Distributed the stock dividend declared on June 10.

Aug. 4 Purchased 10,000 shares of treasury stock at a price of $30 per share.

Oct. 15 Reissued 6,000 shares of treasury stock at a price of $32 per share.

Dec. 10 Reissued 2,000 shares of treasury stock at a price of $28.50 per share.

Dec. 15   Declared a cash dividend of $1.50 per share to be paid on January 15 to shareholders of record on December 31.

Dec. 31   The Income Summary account, showing net income of $1,620,000, was closed into the Retained Earnings account.

INSTRUCTIONS

a Prepare in general journal form the entries necessary to record these transactions.

b Prepare the shareholders' equity section of the balance sheet at December 31, 1996, following the format illustrated in this chapter. Include a note following your shareholders' equity section indicating any portion of retained earnings that is not available for dividends. Also include a supporting schedule showing your computation of the balance of retained earnings at year-end.

c Comment on whether Cornish Productions, Inc., increased or decreased the total amount of cash dividends declared during the year in comparison with dividends declared in the preceding year.

PROBLEM 15B-7
Preparing the Shareholders' Equity Section of a Balance Sheet

David Klein was a free-lance engineer who developed and patented a highly efficient turbocharger for automotive engines. In 1995, Klein and Scott Harris organized Performance, Inc., to manufacture the turbocharger. The corporation was authorized to issue unlimited shares of no-par value capital stock. Presented below is the information necessary to prepare the shareholders' equity section of the company's balance sheet at the end of 1995 and at the end of 1996.

1995. On January 20, the corporation issued 80,000 shares of common stock to Harris and other investors for cash at $34 per share. In addition, 10,000 shares of common stock were issued on that date to Klein in exchange for his patents. In November, Klein was killed while auto racing in Europe. At the request of Klein's heirs, Performance, Inc., purchased the 10,000 shares of its stock from Klein's estate at $45 per share. Because of the unexpected cash outlay to acquire treasury stock, the directors decided against declaring any cash dividends in 1995. Instead, they declared a 5% stock dividend that was distributed on December 31. The stock price at the declaration date was $42 per share. Net income for the year was $415,000.

1996. In March, the 10,000 treasury shares were reissued at a price of $52 per share. In August, the stock was split 4 for 1. On December 20, the directors declared a cash dividend of 70 cents per share, payable in January of 1997. Net income for the year was $486,000.

INSTRUCTIONS   Prepare the shareholders' equity section of the balance sheet at:

a December 31, 1995

b December 31, 1996

Use the format illustrated in this chapter and show any necessary supporting computations.

ANALYTICAL AND DECISION PROBLEMS AND CASES

A&D 15-1
What's This?

The following events have been reported in the financial statements of large corporations.

a **TransCanada PipeLines** sold all of its United States oil and gas properties held by its wholly owned subsidiary for approximately $150 million. In the year of disposal, the U.S. operation had an operating income of $2.4 million. Also, the loss on disposal of the U.S. operation amounted to $52.7 million.

b **Banister Continental Ltd.** reduced the remaining useful lives of certain older pieces of construction equipment. This change increased depreciation expense and decreased net income for the year by $1,030,000.

c **Union Carbide Corp.** sustained a large loss as a result of the explosion of a chemical plant.

d **Algoma Central Railway** received $951,000 in settlement of a claim relating to a fire aboard one of its vessels a few years ago. Income taxes applicable to the settlement amounted to $422,000.

e **Derlan Industries Limited** changed its policy of accounting for capital stock issue costs by charging these costs to retained earnings rather than capitalizing them as an asset. The cumulative effect of this change affecting the beginning balance of retained earnings for the preceding year was $2,370,000. Also, the effect of this change for the preceding year was $2,734,000.

INSTRUCTIONS Indicate how each of these items should be accounted for or presented in the financial statements. Briefly explain the reasons for your answers.

A&D 15-2
The Case of the Extraordinarily Ordinary Loss

In 1994, a large corporation recognized a $68 million loss from the write-off of certain foreign-based assets due to "escalating war, social upheaval, the weakening economies of oil-producing nations, and growing political instability." (The operations in these foreign countries were not discontinued.) The company originally classified this loss as an extraordinary item. Upon reviewing the company's financial statements, however, the securities commission requested that the company reclassify this item as a normal operating loss. In 1995, the company revised its 1994 income statement to comply with the commission's request.

INSTRUCTIONS Indicate the effect of the reclassification of this loss upon the company's:

a Net income for 1994.

b Income before extraordinary items for 1994.

c Income from continuing operations in 1994.

d Price-earnings ratio as shown in financial newspapers such as *The Financial Post.*

e 1995 financial statements.

f Ability to pay cash dividends.

Explain the reasoning behind your answers.

A&D 15-3
Is There Life without Baseball?

Midwestern Publishing, Inc., publishes two newspapers and until recently owned a professional baseball team. The baseball team had been losing money for several years and was sold at the end of 1995 to a group of investors who plan to move it to a larger city. Also in 1995, Midwestern suffered an extraordinary loss when its Raytown printing plant was damaged by a tornado. The damage has since been repaired. A condensed income statement follows:

MIDWESTERN PUBLISHING, INC.
Income Statement
For the Year Ended December 31, 1995

Net revenue		$41,000,000
Costs and expenses		36,500,000
Income from continuing operations		$ 4,500,000
Discontinued operations:		
Operating loss on baseball team	$(1,300,000)	
Gain on sale of baseball team	4,700,000	3,400,000
Income before extraordinary items		$ 7,900,000
Extraordinary loss:		
Tornado damage to Raytown printing plant		(600,000)
Net income		$ 7,300,000

INSTRUCTIONS On the basis of this information, answer the following questions. Show any necessary computations and explain your reasoning.

a What would Midwestern's net income have been for 1995 if it **had not** sold the baseball team?

b Assume that for 1996, you expect a 7% increase in the profitability of Midwestern's newspaper business but had projected a $2,000,000 operating loss for the baseball team if Midwestern had continued to operate the team in 1996. What amount would you forecast as Midwestern's 1996 net income *if the company had continued to own and operate the baseball team?*

c Given your assumptions in part **b,** but given that Midwestern *did* sell the baseball team in 1995, what would you forecast as the company's estimated net income for 1996?

d Assume that the expenses of operating the baseball team in 1995 amounted to $32,200,000, net of any applicable income tax effects. What was the team's *net revenue* for the year?

A&D 15-4
Using Earnings per Share Statistics

For many years Canadian Studios has produced television shows and operated several FM radio stations. Late in the current year, the radio stations were sold to Times Publishing, Inc. Also during the current year, Canadian Studios sustained an extraordinary loss when one of its camera trucks caused an accident in a grand prix auto race. Throughout the current year, the company had 3 million shares of common stock and a large quantity of convertible preferred stock outstanding. Earnings per share reported for the current year were as follows:

	Basic	Fully Diluted
Earnings from continuing operations	$8.20	$6.80
Earnings before extraordinary items	$6.90	$5.50
Net earnings	$3.80	$2.40

INSTRUCTIONS a Briefly explain why Canadian Studios reports fully diluted earnings per share amounts as well as earnings per share computed on a basic basis. What is the purpose of showing investors the fully diluted figures?

b What was the total dollar amount of the extraordinary loss sustained by Canadian Studios during the current year?

c Assume that the price-earnings ratio shown in the morning newspaper for Canadian Studios' common stock indicates that the stock is selling at a price equal to 10 times the reported earnings per share. What is the approximate market price of the stock?

d Assume that you expect both the revenue and expenses involved in producing television shows to increase by 10% during the coming year. What would you forecast as the company's net earnings per share (basic basis) for the coming year under each of the following independent assumptions? (Show your computations and explain your reasoning.)

1 *None* of the convertible preferred stock is converted into common stock during the coming year.

2 *All* of the convertible preferred stock is converted into common stock at the beginning of the coming year.

16 Special Types of Liabilities

"Routine" types of business liabilities were discussed in Chapter 11. In this second chapter about liabilities we explore many special types of liabilities. We will consider such questions as: How can a corporation borrow a huge amount of money on a long-term basis from many small, short-term investors? Why are some long-term lease agreements viewed as liabilities, whereas others are not? How can the balance sheet of a large corporation that has promised millions of dollars of retirement benefits to its employees include no liability for this obligation? And just what are deferred taxes, anyway?

The liabilities discussed in this chapter appear primarily in the financial statements of large, publicly owned corporations. Some, however, also affect the financial statements of smaller organizations.

Learning Objectives:

After studying this chapter you should be able to:

1 *Describe the typical characteristics of corporate bonds.*

2 *Explain the tax advantage of raising capital by issuing bonds instead of stock.*

3 *Account for the issuance of bonds, accrual and payment of interest, and retirement of bonds.*

4 *Describe the relationship between interest rates and bond prices.*

5 *Explain the effects of amortizing bond discount and premium upon bond interest expense.*

6 *Amortize bond discount and premium by the straight-line and the effective interest methods.*

7 *Explain the accounting treatment of operating leases and of capital leases.*

8 *Account for the costs of pensions and other postretirement benefits.*

9 *Explain the nature of deferred income taxes.*

*10 *Explain the accounting treatment of convertible bonds payable.*

---

* *Supplemental Topic, "Convertible Bonds Payable"*

BONDS PAYABLE

Financially sound corporations may arrange limited amounts of long-term financing by issuing notes payable to banks or to insurance companies. But to finance a large project, such as developing an oil field or purchasing a controlling interest in the capital stock of another company, a corporation may need more capital than any single lender can supply. When a corporation needs to raise large amounts of long-term capital—perhaps 50, 100, or 500 million dollars (or more)—it generally sells additional shares of capital stock or issues **bonds payable.**

What Are Bonds?

OBJECTIVE 1 Describe the typical characteristics of corporate bonds.

The issuance of bonds payable is a technique for splitting a very large loan into a great many transferable units, called bonds. Each bond represents a **long-term, interest-bearing note payable,** usually in the face amount (or par value) of $1,000, or some multiple of $1,000. The bonds are sold to the investing public, enabling many different investors (bondholders) to participate in the loan.

Bonds usually are very long-term notes, maturing in perhaps 15 or 20 years. The bonds are transferable, however, so individual bondholders may sell their bonds to other investors at any time. Most bonds call for semiannual interest payments to the bondholders, with interest computed at a specified **contract rate** (the interest rate printed on the bonds) throughout the life of the bond. Thus, investors often describe bonds as "fixed income" investments. An example of a corporate bond issue is the 10.25% bonds payable of Maritime Telegraph & Telephone, which were issued some years ago and are due August 1, 2006. With this bond issue, Maritime Telegraph & Telephone borrowed $50 million by issuing 50,000 bonds of $1,000 each, at an annual contract interest rate of 10.25%. Each bondholder is issued a single **bond certificate** indicating the number of bonds purchased. Investors such as mutual funds, banks, and insurance companies often buy thousands of bonds at one time.

Bonds payable differ from capital stock in several ways. First, bonds payable are a liability; thus, bondholders are **creditors** of the corporation, not owners. Bondholders generally do not have voting rights and do not participate in the earnings of the corporation beyond receiving contractual interest payments. Next, bond interest payments are **contractual obligations** of the corporation. Dividends, on the other hand, do not become legal obligations of the corporation until they have been formally declared by the board of directors. Finally, bonds have a specified **maturity date,** upon which the corporation must redeem the bonds at their face amount. Capital stock, on the other hand, does not have a maturity date and may remain outstanding indefinitely.

Authorization of a Bond Issue Formal approval of the board of directors and the shareholders may be required before bonds can be issued. If the bonds are to be sold to the general public, certain requirements of the provincial securities commissions must be met, just as for an issue of capital stock that is offered to the public.

When bonds are issued, the corporation usually utilizes the services of an investment dealer, called an **underwriter.** The underwriter guarantees the issuing corporation a specific price for the entire bond issue and makes a profit by selling the bonds to the investing public at a higher price. The corporation records the issuance of the bonds at the net amount received from the underwriter. The use of an underwriter assures the corporation that the entire bond issue will be sold without delay, and the entire amount of the proceeds will be available at a specific date.

Transferability of Bonds   Corporate bonds, like capital stocks, are traded daily on organized securities exchanges, such as the **Toronto Stock Exchange.** The holders of a 20-year bond issue need not wait 20 years to convert their investments into cash. By placing a telephone call to a broker, an investor may sell bonds within a matter of minutes at the going market price. This quality of **liquidity** is one of the most attractive features of an investment in corporate bonds.

Quoted Market Prices   Bond prices are quoted as a **percentage** of their face value or **maturity** value, which is usually $1,000. The maturity value is the amount the issuing company must pay to redeem the bond at the date it matures (becomes due). A $1,000 bond quoted at **102** would therefore have a market price of $1,020 (102% of $1,000). The following line from *The Financial Post* summarizes certain information on one of Bell Canada's bonds:

What is the market value of this bond?	Bonds	Interest Rate	Maturity date	Bid	Yield
	Bell Can.	12.650%	Nov. 15, 03	$122.50	7.38%

This line of condensed information indicates that Bell Canada's 12.650% (contract interest rate) bonds will be matured on November 15, 2003, the buyers were willing to pay $122.50 or $1,225 for a bond of $1,000 face value, and the yield rate (the effective interest rate) on the bid price is 7.38%.

The primary factors that determine the market value of a bond are (1) the relationship of the bond's interest rate to other investment opportunities, (2) the length of time until the bond matures, and (3) investors' confidence that the issuing company has the financial strength to make all future interest and principal payments promptly. Thus, a bond with a 10% interest rate will command a higher market price than an 8% bond with the same maturity date if the two companies issuing the bonds are of equal financial strength.

A bond selling at a market price greater than its maturity value is said to be selling at a **premium;** a bond selling at a price below its maturity value is selling at a **discount.** As a bond nears its maturity date, the market price of the bond moves toward the maturity value. At the maturity date the market value of the bond will be exactly equal to its maturity value, because the issuing corporation will redeem the bond for that amount.

Types of Bonds Bonds secured by the pledge of specific assets are called ***mortgage bonds.*** An unsecured bond is called a ***debenture bond;*** its value rests upon the general credit of the corporation. A debenture bond issued by a very large and strong corporation may have a higher investment rating than a secured bond issued by a corporation in less satisfactory financial condition.

Bond interest is usually paid semiannually by mailing to each bondholder a cheque for six months' interest on the bonds he or she owns.[1] Almost all bonds are ***callable (redeemable),*** which means that the corporation has the right to redeem the bonds ***in advance*** of the maturity date by paying a specified ***call (redemption) price.*** To compensate bondholders for being forced to give up their investments, the call price usually is somewhat higher than the face value of the bonds.

Corporations must maintain a ***bondholders subsidiary ledger,*** showing each bondholder's name and address and the face value of bonds owned. This record provides the information necessary for determining the amount of interest payable to each bondholder and for notifying bondholders if their bonds are called.

Traditionally, bonds have appealed to conservative investors, interested primarily in a reliable income stream and in the safety of the principal that they have invested. To make a bond issue more attractive to these investors, some corporations create a bond ***sinking fund,*** designated for repaying the bonds at maturity. At regular intervals, the corporation deposits cash into this sinking fund. A bond sinking fund is not classified as a current asset, because it is not available for the payment of current liabilities. Such funds are shown in the balance sheet under the caption "Long-term Investments," which appears just below the current asset section.

As an additional attraction to investors, corporations sometimes include a conversion privilege in the bond indenture. A ***convertible bond*** is one that may be exchanged at the option of the bondholder for a specified number of shares of common stock. Thus, the market value of a convertible bond tends to fluctuate with the market value of an equivalent number of shares of common stock.

"Junk Bonds" In recent years, some corporations have issued securities that have come to be known as ***junk bonds.*** This term describes a bond issue that involves a substantially greater risk of default than normal. A company issuing junk bonds usually has so much long-term debt that its ability to meet interest and principal repayment obligations has become questionable. To compensate bondholders for this unusual level of risk, junk bonds promise a substantially higher rate of interest than do more "highly rated" bonds.

---

[1] In recent years, corporations have issued only ***registered*** bonds, for which interest is paid by mailing a cheque to the registered owners of the bonds. In past decades, some companies issued ***coupon bonds*** or ***bearer bonds,*** which had a series of redeemable coupons attached. At each interest date, the bondholder was to "clip" the coupon and present it to a bank to collect the interest. These bonds posed a considerable hazard to investors—if the investor lost the coupon, or forgot about an interest date, he or she received no interest.

Tax Advantage of Bond Financing

OBJECTIVE 2
Explain the
tax advan-
tage of rais-
ing capital
by issuing
bonds in-
stead of
stock.

A principal advantage of raising money by issuing bonds instead of stock is that interest payments are **deductible** in determining income subject to corporate income taxes. Dividends paid to shareholders, however, are **not deductible** in computing taxable income.

To illustrate, assume that a corporation pays income taxes at a rate of **30%** on its taxable income. If this corporation issues $10 million of 10% bonds payable, it will incur interest expense of $1 million per year. This interest expense, however, will reduce taxable income by $1 million, thus reducing the corporation's annual income taxes by $300,000. As a result, the **after-tax** cost of borrowing the $10 million is only **$700,000,** as shown below:

Interest expense ($10,000,000 × 10%)	**$1,000,000**
Less: Income tax savings ($1,000,000 deduction × 30%)	**300,000**
After-tax cost of borrowing	**$700,000**

A short-cut approach to computing the after-tax cost of borrowing is simply multiplying the interest expense by **1 minus the company's tax rate,** as follows: $1,000,000 × (1 − .30) = $700,000.

Accounting for Bonds Payable

OBJECTIVE 3
Account for
the issuance
of bonds,
accrual and
payment of
interest, and
retirement
of bonds.

Accounting for bonds payable closely parallels accounting for notes payable. The "accountable events" in the life of a bond issue usually are (1) issuance of the bonds, (2) semiannual interest payments, (3) accrual of interest payable at the end of each accounting period,[2] and (4) retirement of the bonds at maturity.

To illustrate these events, assume that on March 1, 1995, Wells Corporation issues $1 million of 12%, 20-year bonds payable.[3] These bonds are dated March 1, 1995, and interest is computed from this date. Interest on the bonds is payable semiannually, each September 1 and March 1. If all of the bonds are sold at par value (face amount), the issuance of the bonds on March 1 will be recorded by the following entry:

Cash	1,000,000	
Bonds Payable		1,000,000
Issued 12%, 20-year bonds payable at a price of 100.		

Every September 1 during the life of the bond issue, Wells Corporation must pay $60,000 to the bondholders ($1,000,000 × .12 × ½ = $60,000). This semiannual interest payment will be recorded as shown below:

Bond Interest Expense	60,000	
Cash		60,000
Semiannual payment of bond interest.		

---

[2] To simplify our illustrations, we assume in all of our examples and assignment material that adjusting entries for accrued bond interest payable are made **only at year-end.** In practice, these adjustments usually are made on a monthly basis.

[3] The amount of $1 million is used only for purposes of illustration. As explained earlier, actual bond issues are for many millions of dollars.

Every December 31 (the year-end date), Wells Corporation must make an adjusting entry to record the four months' interest that has accrued since September 1:

Bond Interest Expense...............................	*40,000*	
Bond Interest Payable		*40,000*

To accrue bond interest payable for four months ended Dec. 31 ($1,000,000 × .12 × $\frac{4}{12}$ = $40,000).

The accrued liability for bond interest payable will be paid within a few months and, therefore, is classified as a current liability.

Two months later, on March 1, a semiannual interest payment is made to bondholders. This transaction represents payment of the four months' interest accrued at December 31, and of two months' interest that has accrued since year-end. If we assume that the company does not use reversing entries, the entry to record the semiannual payments every March 1 will be:

Bond Interest Expense...............................	*20,000*	
Bond Interest Payable	*40,000*	
Cash		*60,000*

To record semiannual interest payment to bondholders, and to recognize two months' interest expense accrued since year-end ($1,000,000 × .12 × $\frac{2}{12}$ = $20,000).

When the bonds mature 20 years later on March 1, 2015, two entries are required: one entry to record the regular semiannual interest payment (which is the same as the above entry on March 1) and a second entry to record the retirement of the bonds. The entry to record retirement of the bond issue is:

Bonds Payable	*1,000,000*	
Cash		*1,000,000*

Paid face amount of bonds at maturity.

Bonds Issued between Interest Dates The semiannual interest dates (such as January 1 and July 1, or April 1 and October 1) are printed on the bond certificates. However, bonds are often issued between the specified interest dates. The ***investor*** is then required to pay the interest accrued to the date of issuance ***in addition*** to the stated price of the bond. This practice enables the corporation to pay a full six months' interest on all bonds outstanding at the semiannual interest payment date. The accrued interest collected from investors purchasing bonds between interest payment dates is thus returned to them on the next interest payment date.

To illustrate, let us modify our illustration to assume that Wells Corporation issues $1 million of 12% bonds at a price of 100 on ***May 1***—two months ***after*** the date printed on the bonds. The amount received from the bond purchasers now will include two months' accrued interest, as follows:

Bonds issued between interest dates

Cash......................................	*1,020,000*	
Bonds Payable......................................		*1,000,000*
Bond Interest Payable		*20,000*

Issued $1,000,000 face value of 12%, 20-year bonds at 100 plus accrued interest for two months ($1,000,000 × 12% × $\frac{2}{12}$ = $20,000).

Four months later on the regular semiannual interest payment date, a full six months' interest ($60 per each $1,000 bond) will be paid to all bondholders, ***regardless of when they purchased their bonds.*** The entry for the semiannual interest payment is illustrated below:

<table>
<tr><td>Notice only
part of the in-
terest payment
is charged to
expense</td><td>*Bond Interest Payable* ....
Bond Interest Expense.................................
    Cash ....
Paid semiannual interest on $1,000,000 face value of 12%
bonds.</td><td>*20,000*
40,000</td><td>

60,000</td></tr>
</table>

Now consider these interest transactions from the standpoint of the ***investors.*** They paid for two months' accrued interest at the time of purchasing the bonds, and then received cheques for six months' interest after holding the bonds for only four months. They have, therefore, been compensated properly for the use of their money for four months.

When bonds are subsequently sold by one investor to another, they sell at the quoted market price ***plus accrued interest*** since the last interest payment date. This practice enables the issuing corporation to pay all the interest for an interest period to the investor owning the bond at the interest date. Otherwise, the corporation would have to make partial payments to every investor who bought or sold the bond during the interest period. This would be costly and impractical.

The amount that investors will pay for bonds is the ***present value*** of the principal and interest payments they will receive. Before going further in our discussion of bonds payable, it will be helpful to review the concepts of present value and effective interest rate.

The Concept of Present Value

The concept of present value is based upon the "time value" of money—the idea that receiving money today is preferable to receiving money at some later date. Assume, for example, that a bond will have a maturity value of $1,000 five years from today but will pay no interest in the meantime. Investors would not pay $1,000 for this bond today, because they would receive no return on their investment over the next five years. There are prices less than $1,000, however, at which investors would buy the bond. For example, if the bond could be purchased for $600, the investor could expect a return (interest) of $400 from the investment over the five-year period.

The ***present value*** of a future cash receipt is the amount that a knowledgeable investor will pay ***today*** for the right to receive that future payment. The exact amount of the present value depends upon (1) the amount of the future payment, (2) the length of time until the payment will be received, and (3) the rate of return required by the investor. However, the present value will always be ***less*** than the future amount. This is because money received today can be invested to earn interest and thereby becomes equivalent to a larger amount in the future.

The rate of interest that will cause a given present value to grow to a given future amount is called the ***discount rate*** or ***effective interest rate.*** The effective interest rate required by investors at any given time is regarded as the going ***market rate*** of interest. (The procedures for computing the present value of a future amount are illustrated in Appendix A at the end of this chapter.)

The Present Value Concept and Bond Prices The price at which bonds will sell is the present value to investors of the future principal and interest payments. If the bonds sell at par, the market interest rate is equal to the *contract interest rate* (or nominal rate) printed on the bonds. The *higher* the effective interest rate that investors require, the *less* they will pay for bonds with a given contract rate of interest. For example, if investors insist upon a 10% return, they will pay less than $1,000 for a 9%, $1,000 bond. Thus, if investors require an effective interest rate *greater* than the contract rate of interest for the bonds, the bonds will sell at a *discount* (price less than face value). On the other hand, if investors require an effective interest rate of *less* than the contract interest rate, the bonds will sell at a *premium* (price above face value).

OBJECTIVE 4 Describe the relationship between interest rates and bond prices.

A corporation wishing to borrow money by issuing bonds must pay the going market rate of interest. Since market rates of interest are fluctuating constantly, it must be expected that the contract rate of interest may vary somewhat from the market interest rate at the date the bonds are issued. Thus, bonds may be issued at either a discount or a premium.

Bonds Issued at a Discount

To illustrate the sale of bonds at a discount, assume that SCUBA TECH plans to issue $1 million face value of 9%, 10-year bonds, interest payable semiannually. At the issuance date of January 1, the going market rate of interest is slightly above 9% and the bonds sell at a price of only **98** ($980 for each $1,000 bond). The issuance of the bonds will be recorded by the following entry:

Issuance of bonds at a discount

Cash...	*980,000*	
Discount on Bonds Payable.............................	*20,000*	
Bonds Payable......................................		*1,000,000*
Issued $1,000,000 face value of 9%, 10-year bonds at 98.		

If a balance sheet is prepared immediately after the issuance of the bonds, the liability for bonds payable will be shown as follows:

Reporting the net liability

Long-term liabilities:		
9% bonds payable, due in 10 years	*$1,000,000*	
Less: Discount on bonds payable.............................	*20,000*	*$980,000*

The amount of the discount is deducted from the face value of the bonds payable to show the *carrying value* or book value of the liability. At the date of issuance, the carrying value of bonds payable is equal to the amount for which the bonds were sold. In other words, the amount of the company's liability at the date of issuing the bonds is equal to the *amount of money borrowed.* Over the life of the bonds, however, we shall see that this carrying value gradually increases until it reaches the face value of the bonds at the maturity date.

Bond Discount as Part of the Cost of Borrowing In Chapter 11, we illustrated two ways in which interest charges can be specified in a note payable: the interest may be stated as an annual percentage rate of the face amount of the note, or it may be included in the face amount. Bonds issued at a discount include *both* types of interest charge. The $1 million bond issue in our SCUBA TECH example calls for cash interest payments of $90,000 per year ($1,000,000 × 9% contract interest rate), payable semiannually. In addition to making the semiannual interest payments, the corporation must redeem the bond issue for $1 million on the maturity date. This maturity value is *$20,000 more* than the $980,000 received when the bonds were issued. Thus, the $20,000 discount in the issue price may be regarded as an *interest charge included in the maturity value of the bonds.*

Although the interest charge represented by the discount will not be paid to bondholders until the bonds mature, SCUBA TECH benefits from this cost during the entire period that it has the use of the bondholders' money (that is, from the date of issue, which is not necessarily the date of the bonds, to the maturity date of the bonds). Therefore, the cost represented by the discount should be allocated over the life of the bond issue. The process of allocating bond discount to interest expense is termed *amortization* of the discount.

Bonds are sometimes issued between interest dates. In this situation the bonds are outstanding for a shorter time; therefore, the amortization period is shorter. For example, if a 10-year bond issue dated January 1, 1996, is issued on March 1, 1996, the bonds will be outstanding for 9 years and 10 months, or a total of *118 months.* Under the straight-line method of amortization, the discount amortized per month will be $\frac{1}{118}$ of the total discount.

Whenever bonds are issued at a discount, the total interest cost over the life of the bonds is equal to the total of the regular cash interest payments *plus the amount of the discount.* For the $1 million bond issue in our example, the total interest cost over the 10-year life of the bonds is *$920,000* of which $900,000 represents the 20 semiannual cash interest payments and $20,000 represents the discount. The average annual interest expense, therefore, is *$92,000* ($920,000 ÷ 10 years), consisting of $90,000 paid in cash and $2,000 amortization of the bond discount (which will be paid in one lump sum of $20,000 when the bonds mature). This analysis is illustrated below:

OBJECTIVE 5 Explain the effects of amortizing bond discount and premium upon bond interest expense.

OBJECTIVE 6 Amortize bond discount and premium by the straight-line and the effective interest methods.

Total cash interest payments to bondholders		
($1,000,000 × 9% × 10 years)...		$900,000
Add: Interest charge included in face amount of bonds:		
Maturity value of bonds...	$1,000,000	
Amount borrowed	980,000	20,000
Total cost of borrowing over life of bond issue		$920,000
Average annual interest expense ($920,000 ÷ 10 years).........................		$ 92,000

Similarly, bond premium reduces the interest cost, as explained later.

Amortization of Bond Discount The simplest method of amortizing bond discount is the *straight-line method,* which allocates an equal portion of the discount to Bond Interest Expense in each period.[4] In our example, the Discount on Bonds Payable account has a beginning debit balance of

[4] An alternative method of amortization, called the *effective interest method,* is illustrated later in this chapter. Although the effective interest method is theoretically preferable to the straight-line method, the resulting differences generally are not material in dollar amount.

$20,000; each year $\frac{1}{10}$ of this amount, or $2,000, will be amortized into Bond Interest Expense. Assuming that the interest payment dates are June 30 and December 31, the entries to be made each six months to record bond interest expense are as follows:

Payment of bond interest and straight-line amortization of bond discount

Bond Interest Expense..	*45,000*	
Cash		*45,000*
Paid semiannual interest on $1,000,000 of 9%, 10-year bonds.		
Bond Interest Expense..	*1,000*	
Discount on Bonds Payable		*1,000*
Amortized discount for six months on 10-year bond issue		
($20,000 discount × $\frac{1}{20}$).		

The two entries shown above to record the cash payment of bond interest and to record the amortization of bond discount can conveniently be combined into one compound entry, as follows:

Bond Interest Expense..	*46,000*	
Cash		*45,000*
Discount on Bonds Payable		*1,000*
To record payment of semiannual interest on $1,000,000 of 9%,		
10-year bonds ($1,000,000 × 9% × $\frac{1}{2}$) and to amortize $\frac{1}{20}$ of the		
$20,000 discount on the 10-year bond issue.		

Regardless of whether the cash payment of interest and the amortization of bond discount are recorded in separate entries or combined in one entry, the amount recognized as Bond Interest Expense is the same—$46,000 each six months, or a total of $92,000 a year. An alternative accounting procedure that will produce the same results is to amortize the bond discount only at year-end rather than at each interest-payment date.

Note that the additional interest expense resulting from amortization of the discount does not require any additional cash payment. The credit portion of the entry is to the contra-liability account, Discount on Bonds Payable, rather than to the Cash account. Crediting this contra-liability account increases the carrying value of bonds, which is a long-term liability. The original $20,000 discount will be completely amortized by the end of the tenth year, and the net liability (carrying value) will be the full face value of the bonds.

In this example, the bonds were outstanding for the full term of 10 years or 120 months. If the bonds had been issued between interest dates, say, March 1, rather than January 1, the amortization period would have been the shortened life of 118 months.

Zero Coupon Bonds Some companies have issued bonds that pay *no interest* over the life of the bond. Thus, the entire interest charge is included in the face amount of the bonds and is represented by a **very large discount** at the issuance date. Such bonds, called **zero coupon** (or **zeros**), usually are issued at a price of less than 20% of their maturity value.

The discount on zero coupon bonds is so material that the straight-line method of amortization produces misleading results. Therefore, generally accepted accounting principles require that the discount on such bonds be amortized by the **effective interest method,** which is discussed later in this chapter.

Further discussion of zero coupon bonds is deferred to the intermediate accounting course and to courses in corporate finance.

Bonds Issued at a Premium

Bonds will sell **above** par if the contract rate of interest specified on the bonds is **higher** than the current market rate for bonds of this grade. Let us now change our basic illustration by assuming that the $1 million issue of 9%, 10-year bonds is sold at a price of 102 ($1,020 for each $1,000 bond). The entry is as follows:

Issuance of bonds at a premium

Cash	*1,020,000*	
Bonds Payable		*1,000,000*
Premium on Bonds Payable		*20,000*
Issued $1,000,000 face value of 9%, 10-year bonds at price of 102.		

If a balance sheet is prepared immediately following the sale of the bonds, the liability will be shown as follows:

Reporting the carrying value of the liability

Long-term liabilities:		
9% bonds payable, due in 10 years	*$1,000,000*	
Add: Premium on bonds payable	*20,000*	*$1,020,000*

The amount of any unamortized premium is **added** to the maturity value of the bonds payable to show the current carrying value of the liability. Over the life of the bond issue, this carrying value will be **reduced** toward the maturity value of $1 million.

Bond Premium as Reduction in the Cost of Borrowing We have illustrated how issuing bonds at a discount increases the cost of borrowing above the amount of the regular cash interest payments. Issuing bonds at a premium, on the other hand, **reduces the cost of borrowing below the amount of the regular cash interest payments.**

The amount received from issuance of the bonds is $20,000 greater than the amount that must be repaid at maturity. This $20,000 premium is not a gain but is to be offset against the periodic interest payments in determining the net cost of borrowing.

Whenever bonds are issued at a premium, the total interest cost over the life of the bonds is equal to the regular cash interest payments **minus the amount of the premium.** In our example, the total interest cost over the life of the bonds is computed as $900,000 of cash interest payments, minus $20,000 of premium amortized (which is not paid back to the bondholders), or a net borrowing cost of **$880,000.** The average annual interest expense will be **$88,000,** consisting of $90,000 paid in cash each year, less an offsetting $2,000 reduction in the net liability for bonds payable that results from amortization of the premium.

The semiannual entries on June 30 and December 31 to record the payment of bond interest and amortization of bond premium (by the straight-line method) are as follows:

Payment of bond interest and straight-line amortization of bond premium

Bond Interest Expense	*45,000*	
Cash		*45,000*
Paid semiannual interest on $1,000,000 of 9%, 10-year bonds.		
Premium on Bonds Payable	*1,000*	
Bond Interest Expense		*1,000*
Amortized premium for six months on 10-year bond issue ($20,000 premium × $\frac{1}{20}$).		

In our prior discussion of bond discount, we stated that if bonds are issued between interest dates, the amortization period will be shortened. This concept also applies to bonds issued at a premium. In brief, the period for amortization of either bond discount or premium is determined by the number of years and months the bonds are actually outstanding (that is, from the date the bonds are sold to the maturity date).

Year-End Adjustments for Bond Interest Expense

In the preceding illustration, it was assumed that one of the semiannual dates for payment of bond interest coincided with the end of the company's accounting year. In many cases, however, the semiannual interest payment dates will fall during an accounting period rather than on the last day of the year.

For purposes of illustration, assume that $1 million of 12%, 10-year bonds are issued at a price of 97 on **October 1,** 1996. Interest payment dates are April 1, and October 1. The total discount to be amortized amounts to $30,000, or $1,500 in each six-month interest period. (Notice that the discount is amortized at a rate of $250 per month, using a straight-line method of amortization.) Now also assume that the corporation closes its accounts at the end of each calendar year. At December 31, an **adjusting entry** will be needed to (1) record accrued interest at the 12% contract rate for the three months since October 1 and (2) amortize the bond discount for the three months since October 1. This adjusting entry will be:

Bond Interest Expense..	*30,750*	
Bond Interest Payable		*30,000*
Discount on Bonds Payable		*750*

To adjust for accrued interest on bonds and to amortize discount for period from Oct. 1 to Dec. 31. Accrued interest: $1,000,000 × .12 × \frac{3}{12} = $30,000. Amortization: $30,000 × \frac{3}{120} = $750.

A similar adjusting entry will be required every December 31 throughout the life of the bond issue.

In the December 31, 1996 balance sheet, the bond interest payable of $30,000 will appear as a current liability. The long-term liability for bonds payable will appear as follows:

Long-term liabilities:		
12% Bonds payable, due Oct. 1, 2006	*$1,000,000*	
Less: Discount on bonds payable	*29,250*	*$970,750*

When the bonds were issued on October 1, the net liability for bonds payable was $970,000. Notice that the carrying value of the bonds has **increased** over the three months by the amount of discount amortized. When the entire discount has been amortized, the carrying value of the bonds will be $1 million, which is equal to their maturity value.

On April 1, we must record interest expense and discount amortization only for the **three-month period since year-end.** Of the semiannual $60,000 cash payment to bondholders, one-half, or $30,000, represents payment of the liability for bond interest payable recorded on December 31. The entry on April 1 is:

Bond Interest Expense.....................................	*30,750*	
Bond Interest Payable	*30,000*	
Discount on Bonds Payable		*750*
Cash		*60,000*

To record bond interest expense and amortization of discount for three-month period since year-end and to record semiannual payment to bondholders.

Straight-Line Amortization: A Theoretical Shortcoming

Although the straight-line method of amortizing bond discount or premium recognizes the full cost of borrowing over the life of a bond issue, the method has one conceptual weakness: The same dollar amount of interest expense is recognized each year. Amortizing a discount, however, causes a gradual increase in the liability for bonds payable; amortizing a premium causes a gradual decrease in the liability. If the uniform annual interest expense is expressed as a *percentage* of either an increasing or a decreasing liability, it appears that the borrower's cost of capital is changing over the life of the bonds.

This problem can be avoided by using the ***effective interest method*** of amortizing bond discount or premium. The effective interest method recognizes annual interest expense equal to a ***constant percentage of the carrying value of the related liability.*** This percentage is the effective rate of interest incurred by the borrower. For this reason, the effective interest method of amortization is considered theoretically preferable to the straight-line method. Whenever the two methods would produce ***materially different*** annual results, the use of the effective interest method is preferable. In fact, the Financial Accounting Standards Board in the United States has taken such a position.

Over the life of the bonds, both amortization methods recognize the ***same total amount*** of interest expense. Even on an annual basis, the results produced by the two methods are quite similar (unless the bonds were issued at an enormous discount, as are zero coupon bonds).

Effective Interest Method of Amortization

When bonds are sold at a discount, the effective interest rate incurred by the issuing corporation is ***higher*** than the contract rate printed on the bonds. Conversely, when bonds are sold at a premium, the effective rate of interest is ***lower*** than the contract rate.

When the effective interest method is used, bond interest expense is determined by multiplying the ***carrying value of the bonds*** at the beginning of the period by the ***effective rate of interest*** for the bond issue. The amount of discount or premium to be amortized is the ***difference*** between the interest expense computed in this manner and the amount of interest paid (or payable) to bondholders for the period. The computation of effective interest expense and the amount of discount or premium amortization for the life of the bond issue is made in advance in a specially designed ***amortization table.***

Sale of Bonds at a Discount To illustrate the effective interest method, assume that on May 1 a corporation issues $1 million face value, 9%, 10-year bonds with interest dates of November 1 and May 1. The bonds sell for **$937,689,** a price resulting in an effective interest rate of 10%.[5] An amortization table for this bond issue is shown below. (Amounts of interest expense have been **rounded to the nearest dollar.**)

Amortization Table for Bonds Sold at a Discount
($1,000,000, 10-year bonds, 9% interest payable semiannually,
sold at $937,689 to yield 10% compounded semiannually)

Six-Month Interest Period	(A) Interest Paid Semiannually (4½% of Face Value)	(B) Effective Semiannual Interest Expense (5% of Bond Carrying Value)	(C) Discount Amortization (B − A)	(D) Bond Discount Balance	(E) Carrying Value of Bonds, End of Period ($1,000,000 − D)
Issue date	—	—	—	$62,311	$937,689
1	$45,000	$46,884	$1,884	60,427	939,573
2	45,000	46,979	1,979	58,448	941,552
3	45,000	47,078	2,078	56,370	943,630
4	45,000	47,182	2,182	54,188	945,812
5	45,000	47,291	2,291	51,897	948,103
6	45,000	47,405	2,405	49,492	950,508
7	45,000	47,525	2,525	46,967	953,033
8	45,000	47,652	2,652	44,315	955,685
9	45,000	47,784	2,784	41,531	958,469
10	45,000	47,923	2,923	38,608	961,392
11	45,000	48,070	3,070	35,538	964,462
12	45,000	48,223	3,223	32,315	967,685
13	45,000	48,384	3,384	28,931	971,069
14	45,000	48,553	3,553	25,378	974,622
15	45,000	48,731	3,731	21,647	978,353
16	45,000	48,918	3,918	17,729	982,271
17	45,000	49,114	4,114	13,615	986,385
18	45,000	49,319	4,319	9,296	990,704
19	45,000	49,535	4,535	4,761	995,239
20	45,000	49,761*	4,761	-0-	1,000,000

* In the last period, interest expense is equal to interest paid to bondholders plus the remaining balance on the bond discount. This compensates for the accumulated effects of rounding amounts.

This amortization table can be used to illustrate the concepts underlying the effective interest method of determining interest expense and discount amortization. Note that the "interest periods" in the table are the **semiannual** (six-month) interest periods. Thus, the interest payments (column A), interest expense (column B), and discount amortization (column C) are for six-month periods. Similarly, the balance of the Discount on

---

[5] Computation of the exact effective interest rate involves mathematical techniques beyond the scope of this discussion. A close approximation of the effective interest rate can be obtained by dividing the **average** annual interest expense by the **average** carrying value of the bonds.

Bonds Payable account (column D) and the carrying value of the liability (column E) are shown as of each semiannual interest payment date.

The original issuance price of the bonds ($937,689) is entered at the top of column E. This represents the carrying value of the liability throughout the first six-month interest period. The semiannual interest payment, shown in column A, is $4\frac{1}{2}\%$ (one-half of the original contract rate) of the $1 million face value of the bond issue. The semiannual cash interest payment does not change over the life of the bonds. The interest expense shown in column B, however, *changes every period.* This expense is always a *constant percentage* of the carrying value of the liability as of the end of the preceding period. The "constant percentage" is the effective interest rate of the bond issue. The bonds have an effective annual interest rate of 10%, indicating a semiannual rate of 5%. Thus, the effective interest expense for the first six-month period is $46,884 (5% of $937,689). The discount amortization for Period 1 is the difference between this effective interest expense and the contract interest paid to bondholders.

After the discount is reduced by $1,884 at the end of Period 1, the carrying value of the bonds in column E *increases* by $1,884 (from $937,689 to $939,573). In Period 2, the effective interest expense is determined by multiplying the effective semiannual interest rate of 5% by this new carrying value of $939,573 (5% × $939,573 = $46,979).

Semiannual interest expense may be recorded every period directly from the data in the amortization table. For example, the entry to record bond interest expense at the end of the first six-month period is:

Amortization of discount increases interest expense

Bond Interest Expense..	*46,884*	
Discount on Bonds Payable		*1,884*
Cash		*45,000*
To record semiannual interest payment and amortize discount for six months.		

Similarly, interest expense at the end of the *fifteenth* six-month period would be recorded by the following journal entry:

Bond Interest Expense..	*48,731*	
Discount on Bonds Payable		*3,731*
Cash		*45,000*
To record semiannual interest payment and amortize discount for six months.		

When bond discount is amortized, the carrying value of the liability for bonds payable *increases* every period toward the maturity value. Since the effective interest expense in each period is a constant percentage of this increasing carrying value, the interest expense also increases from one period to the next. This is the basic difference between the effective interest method and straight-line amortization.

Sale of Bonds at a Premium Let us now change our illustration by assuming that the $1 million issue of 9%, 10-year bonds is sold on May 1 at a price of ***$1,067,952***, resulting in an effective interest rate of 8% annually (4% per six-month interest period). An amortization table for this bond issue follows:

Amortization Table for Bonds Sold at a Premium
($1,000,000, 10-year bonds, 9% interest payable semiannually,
sold at $1,067,952 to yield 8% compounded semiannually)

Six-Month Interest Period	(A) Interest Paid Semiannually (4½% of Face Value)	(B) Effective Semiannual Interest Expense (4% of Bond Carrying Value)	(C) Premium Amorti-zation (A − B)	(D) Bond Premium Balance	(E) Carrying Value of Bonds, End of Period ($1,000,000 + D)
Issue date	—	—	—	$67,952	$1,067,952
1	$45,000	$42,718	$2,282	65,670	1,065,670
2	45,000	42,627	2,373	63,297	1,063,297
3	45,000	42,532	2,468	60,829	1,060,829
4	45,000	42,433	2,567	58,262	1,058,262
5	45,000	42,330	2,670	55,592	1,055,592
6	45,000	42,224	2,776	52,816	1,052,816
7	45,000	42,113	2,887	49,929	1,049,929
8	45,000	41,997	3,003	46,926	1,046,926
9	45,000	41,877	3,123	43,803	1,043,803
10	45,000	41,752	3,248	40,555	1,040,555
11	45,000	41,622	3,378	37,177	1,037,177
12	45,000	41,487	3,513	33,664	1,033,664
13	45,000	41,347	3,653	30,011	1,030,011
14	45,000	41,200	3,800	26,211	1,026,211
15	45,000	41,048	3,952	22,259	1,022,259
16	45,000	40,890	4,110	18,149	1,018,149
17	45,000	40,726	4,274	13,875	1,013,875
18	45,000	40,555	4,445	9,430	1,009,430
19	45,000	40,377	4,623	4,807	1,004,807
20	45,000	40,193*	4,807	-0-	1,000,000

*　In the last period, interest expense is equal to interest paid to bondholders minus the remaining balance of the bond premium. This compensates for the accumulated effects of rounding amounts.

In this amortization table, the interest expense for each six-month period is equal to **4%** of the carrying value of the liability at the beginning of that period. This amount of interest expense is **less** than the amount of cash being paid to bondholders, illustrating that the effective interest rate is less than the contract rate.

Based upon this amortization table, the entry to record the interest payment and amortization of the premium for the first six months of the bond issue is:

Amortization of premium decreases interest expense

Bond Interest Expense..	42,718	
Premium on Bonds Payable.....................................	2,282	
Cash		45,000

To record semiannual interest payment and amortization of premium.

As the carrying value of the liability declines, so does the amount recognized as bond interest expense.

Year-End Adjusting Entries Since the amounts recognized as interest expense change from one period to the next, we must refer to the appropriate interest period in the amortization table to obtain the dollar amounts for use in year-end adjusting entries. To illustrate, consider our example of the bonds sold at a premium on May 1. The entry shown on the previous page records interest and amortization of the premium through November 1. If the company keeps its accounts on a calendar-year basis, two months' interest has accrued as of December 31, and the following adjusting entry is made at year-end:

Year-end adjusting entry	*Bond Interest Expense*... 14,209	
	Premium on Bonds Payable................................... 791	
	Bond Interest Payable	15,000
	To record two months' accrued interest and amortize one-third of the premium for the interest period.	

This adjusting entry covers one-third (two months) of the second interest period. Consequently, the amounts shown as bond interest expense and amortization of premium are ***one-third*** of the amounts shown in the amortization table for the second interest period. Similar adjusting entries must be made at the end of every accounting period while the bonds are outstanding. The dollar amounts of these adjusting entries will vary, however, because the amounts of interest expense and premium amortization change in every interest period. The amounts applicable to any given adjusting entry will be the appropriate fraction of the amounts for the interest period then in progress.

Following the year-end adjusting entry illustrated above, the interest expense and premium amortization on May 1 of the second year, are recorded as follows:

Interest payment in the following year	*Bond Interest Expense*... 28,418	
	Bond Interest Payable 15,000	
	Premium on Bonds Payable................................... 1,582	
	Cash	45,000
	To record semiannual interest payment, a portion of which had been accrued, and amortize remainder of premium applicable to interest period.	

Bond Prices after Issuance

As stated earlier, many corporate bonds are traded daily on organized securities exchanges at quoted market prices. After bonds are issued, their market prices vary ***inversely*** with changes in market interest rates. As interest rates rise, investors will be willing to pay less money to own a bond that pays a given contract rate of interest. Conversely, as interest rates decline, the market prices of bonds rise.

CASE IN POINT   A large corporation sold to underwriters $500 million of 9⅜%, 25-year debenture bonds. The underwriters planned to sell the bonds to the public at a price of 99⅝. Just as the bonds were offered for sale, however, a change in general business conditions and government policy started an upward surge in interest rates. The underwriters encountered great difficulty selling the bonds. Within one week, the market price of the bonds had fallen to 94½. The underwriters dumped their unsold inventory at this price and sustained one of the largest underwriting losses in the history of the underwriting business.

During the months subsequent to the issuance, interest rates soared to record levels. Within five months, the price of the bonds had fallen to 76⅜. Thus, nearly one-fourth of the market value of these bonds evaporated in less than half a year. The financial strength of the corporation was never in question; this dramatic loss in market value was caused entirely by rising interest rates.

Changes in the current level of interest rates are not the only factor influencing the market prices of bonds. The length of time remaining until the bonds mature is another major force. As a bond nears its maturity date, its market price normally moves closer and closer to the maturity value. This trend is dependable because the bonds are redeemed at par value on the maturity date.

CASE IN POINT   Ontario Hydro has outstanding two issues of 10% bonds, one issue maturing in 5 years and the other in 12 years. When the going market rate of interest was much greater than 10%, both bonds were selling at a discount. The bonds maturing in 5 years, however, were selling at a market price of $91.10, whereas the bonds maturing in 12 years were selling at a price of only $86.20. Both bonds pay the same amount of interest, were issued by the same company, and have the same credit ratings. Thus, the difference in the market prices is caused mainly by the difference in the bonds' maturity dates.[6]

Volatility of Short-Term and Long-Term Bond Prices   When interest rates fluctuate, the market prices of long-term bonds are affected to a far greater extent than are the market prices of bonds due to mature in the near future. To illustrate, assume that market interest rates suddenly soar from 9% to 12%. A 9% bond scheduled to mature in but a few days will still have a market value of approximately $1,000—the amount to be collected in a few days from the issuing corporation. However, the market price of a 9% bond maturing in 10 years will drop significantly. Investors who must accept these "below market" interest payments for many years will buy the bonds only at a discounted price.

In summary, fluctuations in interest rates have a far greater effect upon the market prices of long-term bonds than upon the prices of short-term bonds.

Remember that after bonds have been issued, they belong to the bondholder, ***not to the issuing corporation.*** Therefore, changes in the market price of bonds subsequent to their issuance ***do not*** affect the amounts shown in the financial statements of the issuing corporation, and these changes are not recorded in the company's accounting records.

---

[6]   The expected future interest rate is also a factor. The yield rates for these two bonds are 12.60% and 12.32% respectively, suggesting an expected decline in future long-term interest rates.

Early Retirement of Bonds Payable

Bonds are sometimes retired before the maturity date. The principal reason for retiring bonds early is to relieve the issuing corporation of the obligation to make future interest payments. If interest rates decline to the point that a corporation can borrow at an interest rate below that being paid on a particular bond issue, the corporation may benefit from retiring those bonds and issuing new bonds at a lower interest rate.

Bond issues generally contain a call (redemption) provision, permitting the corporation to redeem the bonds by paying a specified price, usually a few points above par. Even without a call provision, the corporation may retire its bonds before maturity by purchasing them in the open market. If the bonds can be purchased by the issuing corporation at less than their carrying value, a *gain* is realized on the retirement of the debt. If the bonds are acquired by the issuing corporation at a price in excess of their carrying value, a *loss* must be recognized. If material in dollar amount, any gain or loss from the early retirement of debt should be presented separately in the income statement.

For example, assume that Briggs Corporation has outstanding a 13%, $10 million bond issue, callable on any interest date at a price of 104. Assume also that the bonds were issued at par and will not mature for nine years. Recently, however, market interest rates have declined to less than 13%, and the market price of Briggs' bonds has increased to 104.[7]

Regardless of the market price, Briggs can call these bonds at 104. If the company exercises this call provision for 10% of the bonds ($1 million face value), the entry will be:

Bonds called at a price above carrying value	Bonds Payable	1,000,000	
	Loss on Early Retirement of Bonds	40,000	
	Cash		1,040,000
	To record the call of $1,000,000 in 13% bonds payable at a call price of 104.		

Notice that Briggs *called* these bonds, rather than purchasing them at market prices, which may be higher than the call price. Therefore, Briggs is able to retire these bonds at their call price of 104.

Classification of Bonds Payable in a Balance Sheet

Bonds payable generally are classified as *long-term* liabilities, even when the bonds are within one year of maturity. This is because the obligation for maturing bonds usually is paid either (1) by issuing new bonds and using the proceeds to retire the maturing bond issue or (2) from a bond *sinking fund.*

If new bonds are issued, the maturing bond liability has been *refinanced.* As explained in Chapter 11, maturing obligations that will be

---

[7] Falling interest rates cause bond prices to rise. On the other hand, falling interest rates also provide the issuing company with an incentive to call the bonds and, perhaps, replace them with bonds bearing a lower rate of interest. For this reason, call prices often serve as an approximate "ceiling" on market prices.

refinanced on a long-term basis are classified as long-term liabilities rather than current liabilities. Now consider maturing bonds that will be repaid from a sinking fund accumulated over the years specifically for this purpose. A sinking fund is not regarded as a current asset, because its contents *cannot be used* for paying operating expenses or the claims of most short-term creditors. The bonds payable, therefore, do not become a current liability, as they will be paid from the sinking fund *rather than from current assets.*

Accrued interest payable on long-term bonds *is* regarded as a current liability, because accrued interest normally is paid in cash within six months or less.

Commercial Paper

The term *commercial paper* describes *very short-term* notes payable issued by financially strong corporations. These notes mature generally in 30 days to 270 days and are issued in denominations of $25,000 or more. Commercial paper is similar to bonds payable in that it splits a large loan into small units, enabling many different investors to act as the lender. Also, an organized marketplace exists in which the holders of commercial paper may sell their investment immediately at a quoted market price.

Because commercial paper matures so quickly, it is regarded as a safer and more liquid investment than are stocks or bonds. The market price of commercial paper does not fluctuate significantly as a result of changes in interest rates. Rather, the market price tends to progress day by day toward maturity value.

Many investors purchase commercial paper as a means of earning interest revenue on idle cash balances for very short periods of time—perhaps over a weekend. For this reason, investors usually regard commercial paper as a cash equivalent. The issuing corporation, of course, views these notes as a current liability.

Commercial paper is issued at a discount; that is, with the interest charges included in the face amount. (Accounting for short-term notes payable with interest charges included in the face amount was discussed in Chapter 11.)

OTHER "CORPORATE" LIABILITIES

Bonds payable and commercial paper are issued only by large corporations. These debt instruments are attractive to investors only if the continued existence and solvency of the business enterprise can be taken for granted.

We now will discuss the liabilities arising from lease agreements, pension plans, and the deferral of income taxes. These liabilities appear primarily in the financial statements of large corporations, but they may also affect smaller business organizations. Many small businesses, however, do not have financial reporting obligations to investors and creditors. Therefore, these businesses sometimes use income tax rules, rather than accounting principles, in recording the liabilities and expenses. Our discussion of these topics emphasizes generally accepted accounting principles—the accounting standards used in the financial statements of publicly owned companies.

Lease Payment Obligations

OBJECTIVE 7
Explain the
accounting
treatment of
operating
leases and
of capital
leases.

A company may purchase the assets needed in its business operations or, as an alternative, it may lease them. A *lease* is a contract in which the lessor gives the lessee the right to use an asset for a specified period of time in exchange for periodic rental payments. The *lessor* is the owner of the property; the *lessee* is a tenant or renter. Examples of assets frequently acquired by lease include automobiles, building space, computers, and equipment. Two types of leases—operating and capital—are presented below.

Operating Leases

When the lessor gives the lessee the right to use leased property for a limited period of time but retains the usual risks and rewards of owner-ship, the contract is known as an *operating lease.* An example of an oper-ating lease is a contract leasing office space in an office building. If the building increases in value, the *lessor* can receive the benefits of this in-crease by either selling the building or increasing the rental rate once the lease term has expired. On the other hand, if the building declines in value, it is the lessor who bears the loss.

In accounting for an operating lease, the lessor views the monthly lease payments received as rental revenue, and the lessee regards these pay-ments as rental expense. No asset or liability (other than a short-term liability for rent payable) relating to the lease appears in the lessee's bal-ance sheet. Thus, operating leases are sometimes termed off-balance-sheet financing.

Capital Leases

Some lease contracts are intended to provide financing to the lessee for the eventual purchase of the property or to provide the lessee with use of the property over most of its useful life. These lease contracts are called *capi-tal leases* (or sales-type or direct financing leases). In contrast to an oper-ating lease, a capital lease transfers most of the risks and rewards of own-ership from the lessor to the *lessee.* Assume, for example, that City Realty leases a new automobile for a period of three years. Also assume that at the end of the lease, title to the automobile transfers to City Realty at no addi-tional cost. Clearly, City Realty is not merely "renting" the use of the auto-mobile; rather, it is using the lease agreement as a means of *financing the purchase* of the car.

From an accounting viewpoint, capital leases are regarded as *essen-tially equivalent to a sale* of the property by the lessor to the lessee, even though title to the leased property has not been transferred. Thus, a capi-tal lease should be recorded by the *lessor as a sale* of property and by the *lessee as a purchase.* In such lease agreements, an appropriate interest charge usually is added to the regular sales price of the property in deter-mining the amount of the lease payments.

Some companies use capital lease agreements as a means of financing the sale of their products to customers. In accounting for merchandise "sold" through a capital lease, the lessor debits *Lease Payments Receiv-able* and credits *Sales* for an amount equal to the *present value* of the future lease payments.[8] In most cases, the present value of these future payments is equal to the regular sales price of the merchandise. In addition, the lessor transfers the cost of the leased merchandise from the Inventory account to the Cost of Goods Sold account. When lease payments are received, the lessor should recognize an appropriate portion of the payment as representing interest revenue and the remainder as a reduction in Lease Payments Receivable.

When equipment is acquired through a capital lease, the lessee should **debit an asset account,** Leased Equipment, and **credit a liability account,** Lease Payment Obligation, for the present value of the future lease payments. Lease payments made by the lessee are allocated between Interest Expense and a reduction in the liability, Lease Payment Obligation. The portion of the lease payment obligation that will be repaid within the next year is classified as a current liability, and the remainder is classified as long-term.

No rent expense is involved in a capital lease. The asset account, Leased Equipment, is depreciated over the life of the equipment rather than the life of the lease. (The journal entries used in accounting for a capital lease are illustrated in Appendix A at the end of this chapter.)

Distinguishing between Capital Leases and Operating Leases The *CICA Handbook* recommended the following distinction.[9]

1 A lease that transfers substantially all of the benefits and risks of ownership related to the leased property from the lessor to the lessee should be accounted for as a capital lease by the lessee and as a sales-type or direct financing lease by the lessor.

2 A lease where the benefits and risks of ownership related to the leased property are substantially retained by the lessor should be accounted for as an operating lease by the lessee and lessor.

Liabilities for Pensions and Other Postretirement Benefits

Pensions Many employers agree to pay their employees a pension; that is, monthly cash payments for life, beginning upon retirement. Pensions are not an expense of the years in which cash payments are made to retired workers. Employees earn the right to receive the pension *while they are working for their employer.* Therefore, the employer's cost of future pension payments *accrues* over the years that each employee is "on the payroll."

OBJECTIVE 8 Account for the costs of pensions and other postretirement benefits.

Of course, the amounts of the retirement benefits that will be paid to today's workers after they retire is not known with certainty. Among other things, these amounts depend upon how long retired employees live.

---

8   We have elected to record the present value of the future lease payments by a single debit entry to Lease Payments Receivable. An alternative is to debit Lease Payments Receivable for the total amount of the future payments and to credit Discount on Lease Payments Receivable, a contra-asset account, for the unearned finance charges included in the contractual amount. Either approach results in the lessor recording a net receivable equal to the present value of the future lease payments.

9   CICA, *CICA Handbook* (Toronto), section 3065.09 and .10.

Therefore, the employer's obligation for future pension payments arising during the current year *can only be estimated.*

Employers do not usually pay retirement pensions directly to retired employees. Most employers meet their pension obligations by making periodic deposits in a *pension fund* (or pension plan) throughout the years of each worker's employment.

A pension fund is *not an asset* of the employer. Rather, it is an *independent entity* managed by a trustee (usually a bank or an insurance company). As the employer makes deposits in the pension fund, the trustee invests the money in securities such as stocks and bonds. Over time, the pension fund earns investment income and normally accumulates to a balance far in excess of the employer's deposits. It is the *pension fund*—not the employer—that disburses monthly pension benefits to retired workers.

If the employer meets *all* of its estimated pension obligations by promptly depositing cash in a pension fund, the pension fund is said to be *fully funded.* The operation of a fully funded pension plan is summarized in the following illustration:

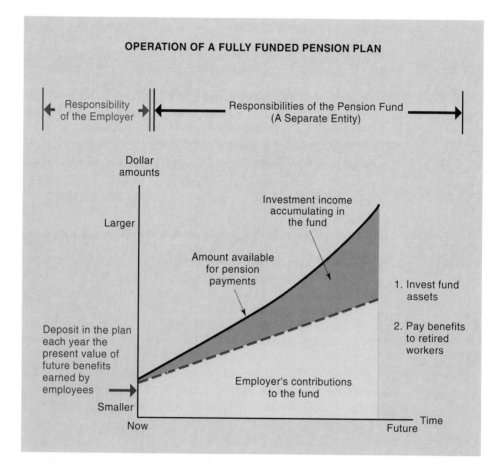

If a pension plan is fully funded, *no liability* for pension payments appears in the employer's balance sheet. The employer's obligation is discharged in the *current period* through the payments made to the pension fund. The employer records each payment to this fund by debiting Pension Expense and crediting Cash.

Most pension plans are fully funded; therefore, most corporations do *not* report any pension liability. However, an employer must credit a liability account, Unfunded Pension Liability, for any portion of its periodic pension expense that *is not* paid immediately to the pension fund.

Determining Pension Expense From a conceptual point of view, the pension expense of a given period is the ***present value*** of the future pension rights granted to employees as a result of their services during the period. The computation of annual pension expense is complex and involves many assumptions. The amount of this expense is not computed by accountants, but rather by a professional ***actuary.*** Among the factors considered by the actuary are:

■ Average age, retirement age, and life expectancy of employees.

■ Employee turnover rates.

■ Compensation levels and estimated rate of pay increases.

■ Expected rate of return to be earned on pension fund assets.

As a step in determining the pension expense for the year, the actuary estimates the employer's total pension liability as of year-end. Thus, the estimates are updated annually, and estimating errors in prior years are "corrected" in the current year.

Postretirement Benefits Other Than Pensions In addition to pension plans, many companies have promised their employees other types of postretirement benefits, such as dental or other health insurance. In most respects, these "nonpension" postretirement benefits are accounted for in the same manner as are pension benefits. Most companies, however, have not fully funded their obligations for nonpension postretirement benefits. Thus, recognition of the annual expense often involves a credit to an unfunded liability.

To illustrate, assume that at the end of 1996 Cable Corporation receives the following report from its actuaries:

CABLE CORPORATION
Summary of Postretirement Benefits Expenses
For the Year Ended December 31, 1996
Prepared by Gibson & Holt, Professional Actuaries

Pension Plan:

Estimated liability at Dec. 31, 1996	$4,500,000
Estimated liability at Dec. 31, 1995	4,100,000
Pension expense for 1996	$ 400,000
Payments during the year to National Trust (trustee for the pension plan) ...	400,000
Increase (decrease) in unfunded pension liability	$ -0-

Nonpension Postretirement Benefits:

Estimated liability at Dec. 31, 1996	$1,600,000
Estimated liability at Dec. 31, 1995	1,350,000
Nonpension postretirement benefits expense for 1996	$ 250,000
Payments during the year to National Trust (trustee for the nonpension postretirement benefits plan)...	140,000
Increase (decrease) in unfunded liability......................................	$ 110,000

As the pension plan is fully funded, an entry summarizing Cable Corporation's pension expense for 1996 is shown as follows:[10]

Pension Expense	*400,000*	
Cash		*400,000*

Pension expense for the year as determined by actuarial
firm of Gibson & Holt. Fully funded by payments to
National Trust.

The company's "nonpension" postretirement benefits expense was only partially paid in cash. The entry to summarize this expense for the year is:

Nonpension Postretirement Benefits Expense	*250,000*	
Cash		*140,000*
Unfunded Liability for Nonpension Postretirement		
Benefits		*110,000*

To record nonpension postretirement benefits expense per
report of Gibson & Holt, actuaries. Expense funded to the
extent of $140,000.

Any portion of the unfunded liability that the company intends to fund during the next year is classified as a current liability; the remainder is classified as a long-term liability.

There are many complex issues involved in computing and reporting unfunded liabilities for postretirement benefits. These issues will be discussed in more advanced accounting courses.

Deferred Income Taxes

OBJECTIVE 9
Explain the
nature of
deferred in-
come taxes.

Differences sometimes exist between the dates certain types of revenue or expense are recognized in financial statements and the dates these items are reported in income tax returns. For example, the amount of depreciation reported for financial purposes may be different for income tax purposes. Because of such ***timing differences*** between accounting principles and tax rules, income or expense may be reported in the income statement of one year but in the income tax return of a different year. Most timing differences result in ***postponing*** (deferring) the recognition of income or in early recognition of expenses for tax purposes.[11] The recognition of income in income tax returns is postponed by those tax rules that enable taxpayers either to (1) delay the recognition of revenue or (2) accelerate the recognition of expense.

In summary, income appearing in the income statement today may not be subject to income taxes until future years. However, the ***matching principle*** requires that the income shown in an income statement be offset by all related income taxes expense, regardless of when these taxes will be paid. Thus, the entry to record a corporation's income taxes expense often appears as follows:

---

[10] This entry summarizes the pension expense and payments to the trustee for the ***entire year.*** In practice, payments to the trustee often are made on a monthly or quarterly basis.

[11] In some situations, income may be subject to income taxes ***prior*** to recognition of the income for financial reporting purposes. In these instances, the taxpayer ***prepays*** its income taxes expense. Prepaid income taxes is an asset, similar to prepaid rent. In this chapter, we limit our discussion to the more common situation in which the payment of income taxes is ***deferred*** to later periods.

Payment of some taxes expense often can be deferred	*Income Taxes Expense* *1,000,000*	
	Income Taxes Payable............................	*800,000*
	Deferred Income Taxes	*200,000*
	To record corporate income taxes applicable to the income of the current year.	

Income Taxes Payable is a current liability representing the portion of the income taxes expense that must be paid when the company files its income tax return for the current year. That portion of the income taxes expense that is deferred to future tax returns is credited to a liability account entitled Deferred Income Taxes. Notice that deferred income taxes are tax obligations that have been **postponed** to future periods; the company has **not eliminated** its obligation to pay these taxes.

Growing businesses often are able to defer part of their income taxes expense every year. Of course, some of the income taxes deferred in prior years constantly are coming due. Nonetheless, the liability for deferred taxes usually continues to grow as the company grows.

Accounting for deferred taxes involves a number of complex issues that will be addressed in the intermediate accounting course.

Disclosures about Financial Instruments

Except for deferred income taxes, all the liabilities discussed in this chapter are among the contracts often regarded as financial instruments. The term **financial instruments** describes cash, equity investments in another business, and any contracts calling for the receipt or payment of cash. Notice that this term applies to certain assets, as well as to most liabilities.

Many financial instruments, such as bonds payable, investments in stocks and bonds, and long-term loans receivable or payable, have market values that can **differ substantially** from their carrying values in financial statements. In such cases, current practices require companies to **disclose** the **fair value** of these instruments, usually in notes accompanying the financial statements.

Fair value generally means **current market value.** As the disclosures of fair value generally appear in **notes** to the financial statements, these disclosures do **not** affect the carrying values of the financial instruments in the company's balance sheet.

There are two basic reasons for requiring disclosures of fair values. First, the fair value represents the current "economic" value of the financial instruments. Thus, it is the best indication of the **value today** of the resources owned or owed. Second, financial instruments often can be settled (sold or discharged) at their fair value. If these settlement prices differ from the book values of the financial instruments, the settlement transactions will result in the recognition of gains or losses. Disclosures of the fair values of these instruments may alert investors to the possibility—or probability—of such future gains or losses.

Measuring Fair Value Bonds payable usually have quoted market prices. Thus, the fair value of an issue of bonds payable is determined by multiplying the quoted price by the number of bonds outstanding. Investments in stocks and bonds also are financial instruments that usually have readily determinable market values. For financial instruments that **do not** have quoted market prices, fair value often is considered to be the **present value** of the future cash flows, computed under current market conditions. (Computation of the present value of future cash flows is explained and illustrated in Appendix A, at the end of this chapter.)

The fair market value of financial instruments must be disclosed only if this value (1) is reasonably determinable and (2) is **significantly different** from the carrying value in the financial statements. These conditions greatly limit the types of financial instruments for which this disclosure is required. Cash, accounts receivables, accounts payable, and commercial paper, for example, normally have carrying values that **closely approximate** their fair values.

Bonds payable, long-term notes payable or receivable, and investments in stocks and bonds, however, often **do** have fair values differing substantially from their carrying values. Thus, the requirement for disclosure of fair value applies primarily to these types of financial instruments.

Disclosure of Off-Balance-Sheet Risk   Some financial instruments do not create assets or liabilities that appear in financial statements but still create a risk of **future losses.** When a financial instrument does not appear in the balance sheet, the risk of loss created by the instrument is called an **off-balance-sheet risk.**

The possibility of **future losses** ordinarily is **not** disclosed in financial statements, because all of the situations that may cause future losses cannot be identified. However, if the risk of a future loss **is created by an existing contract** (financial instrument), current practices require disclosure of the potential for loss.

As an example, large and financially strong corporations sometimes guarantee bank loans or other specific liabilities of less financially sound corporations. In these situations, the guarantor promises to repay the loan if the original borrower is unable to do so. The basic purpose of a loan guarantee is to enable the weaker company to borrow money at more favourable terms than its own credit rating would justify.

Why would one company guarantee the debts of another? Often the borrower pays the guarantor a fee for this service. In other cases, the borrower may be an important customer or supplier of the guarantor.

A loan guarantee (also called an **accommodation endorsement**) creates a contingent loss for the guarantor.[12] Unless a loss is considered **likely** and **reasonably determinable,** however, no liability appears in the guarantor's financial statements. Therefore, the guarantor's risk of loss—that is, the possibility of having to assume responsibility for the guaranteed loan—is an **off-balance-sheet risk.**

Current practices require companies to disclose any material off-balance-sheet risk created by financial instruments. The required disclosure is to include a written explanation of the nature and terms of the financial instrument, and the maximum amount of loss that might be sustained.

---

[12]   Accounting for contingent losses is discussed in Chapter 11.

Some Old Ratios Take on New Importance

In Chapter 11, we discussed two ratios widely used by long-term creditors in evaluating the safety of their investments: the ***debt ratio*** and the ***interest coverage ratio.***

The debt ratio, which is total liabilities divided by total assets, indicates the percentage of total assets financed with borrowed money. Creditors prefer a ***low*** debt ratio, as this indicates that their claims amount to only a small percentage of the company's total assets. The interest coverage ratio, which equals operating income divided by interest expense, indicates how many times the company's earnings for the period "covered" its interest obligations. Creditors prefer a high interest coverage ratio.

The ability of large corporations to meet their interest obligations has taken on new importance in recent years. During the 1980s, a number of well-known corporations borrowed startling amounts of money by issuing "junk bonds" bearing interest rates of 12, 14, and 16 percent—and sometimes even higher. As a result, the very existence of some of these corporations now is threatened by the size of the companies' annual interest obligations. Such a long-established company as Federated Department Stores in the United States (owned by Campeau Corporation, a Canadian company) already has declared bankruptcy, and others are sure to follow.

Bankruptcy affects much more than the claims of long-term creditors. Shareholders have only a residual claim to assets; therefore, capital stocks are the first securities to lose value. Top management often is replaced, and many employees usually lose their jobs. Perhaps most devastating in human terms, bankrupt companies may be unable to meet unfunded postretirement obligations.

In conclusion, debt ratios and interest coverage ratios have become measurements of importance to ***everyone*** concerned with the long-run survival and health of a business organization.

■ ■ ■ **** Supplemental Topic***
Convertible Bonds Payable

OBJECTIVE 10
Explain the accounting treatment of convertible bonds payable.

Convertible bonds represent a popular form of financing, particularly during periods when common stock prices are rising. The conversion feature gives bondholders an opportunity to profit from a rise in the market price of the issuing company's common stock while still maintaining their status as creditors rather than shareholders. Because of this potential gain, convertible bonds generally carry lower interest rates than nonconvertible bonds.

The number of shares of common stock into which each bond may be converted is termed the ***conversion ratio.*** The market value of this number of shares represents the ***stock value*** of the bond. When the bond is originally issued, a conversion ratio is selected that sets the stock value well below the face value of the bond. In future periods, however, both the price of the stock and the stock value of the bond may increase without limit.

For example, assume that the current market rate of interest on long-term bonds with a face value of $1,000 each is 9%, and that the common stock of Ling Corporation has a current market price of *$27* per share. Instead of issuing 9% bonds payable, the company might issue *7% convertible bonds,* with a conversion ratio of 20 to 1 or a *conversion price* of $50 ($1,000 face value ÷ by 20 shares). At the issuance date, the stock value of each convertible bond would be only $540 (20 shares × $27). If the value of the common stock rises above *$50* per share, however, the stock value will rise above the $1,000 face value of the bond.

When the price of the common stock rises above the conversion price, the stock value of the bond becomes far more important than the current level of interest rates in establishing the market price of a convertible bond. (See, for example, the Case in Point below.)

Ling Corporation benefits from issuing these convertible bonds because it is able to pay less than the going market rate of interest. The bondholders also may benefit from the conversion feature, *but only if the price of the common stock rises above the conversion price* ($50 per share) during the life of the bonds.

Let us assume that Ling Corporation issues $5 million of these convertible bonds at par. Some years later, when the price of the common stock has risen to $90 per share, holders of 100 bonds decide to convert their bonds into common stock. Ling Corporation will record this conversion as follows:

Conversion of bonds into common stock

Convertible Bonds Payable	*100,000*	
Common Stock		*100,000*
To record the conversion of 100 bonds payable into 2,000 shares of common stock.		

Notice that the current market price of the stock ($90 per share) *does not* affect this entry. The carrying value of the bonds is simply assigned to the common stock issued in exchange. Thus, the effect of the entry is to transfer the carrying value of the bonds from the liability section to the shareholders' equity section of the balance sheet. (If the bonds had been issued at a price above or below the face amount, any unamortized premium or discount relating to the converted bonds would be written off at the time of conversion in order to assign the carrying value of the bonds to the common stock.)

CONVERSION OF BONDS FROM THE INVESTOR'S VIEWPOINT

Investors do not always convert their investment in convertible bonds into capital stock as soon as the market value of the capital stock they would receive rises above the $1,000 maturity value of their bonds. As the bonds easily can be converted into capital stock, their market value *rises right along* with that of the capital stock.

CASE IN POINT Norcen had an outstanding issue of more than $149 million of 6% bonds payable (maturing December 15, 2006) in which each bond was convertible into 64.52 shares of the company's capital stock. The company's capital stock was selling at $24 per share, indicating a market value for 64.52 shares of $1,548. The market value of the convertible bonds was quoted at 154 (that is, $1540 for a $1,000 bond), even though the bonds would mature at a price of only 100 (that is, at $1,000 for a $1,000 bond) in the near future. Also, the going market interest rate of about 13% was more than twice the 6% for the bonds, indicating that the stock value of the bonds was more important than the market interest rate in establishing the market price of a convertible bond.

When are the owners of convertible bonds likely to exchange their bonds for shares of capital stock? The exchange point is reached when the dividends that would be received from the capital stock *exceed the interest payments* currently being received from the investment in bonds. When the capital stock dividends increase to this level, the bondholders can *increase their cash receipts* by converting their bonds into shares of capital stock. Regardless of the relationship between interest and dividends, convertible bonds should be converted prior to their maturity date if the market price of the common stock exceeds the conversion price.

CHAPTER REVIEW

KEY TERMS INTRODUCED OR EMPHASIZED IN CHAPTER 16

Amortization of discount or premium on bonds payable   The process of systematically writing off a portion of bond discount to increase interest expense or writing off a portion of bond premium to decrease interest expense each period the bonds are outstanding.

Capital lease   A lease contract that, in essence, finances the eventual purchase by the lessee of leased property. The lessor accounts for a capital lease as a sale of property; the lessee records an asset and a liability equal to the present value of the future lease payments. Also called a *sales-type* or *direct financing lease.*

Commercial paper   Very short-term notes payable issued by financially strong corporations. Highly liquid from the investors' point of view.

Contract interest rate   The contractual rate of interest printed on bonds. The contract interest rate, applied to the face value of the bonds, determines the amount of the annual cash interest payments to bondholders. Also called the *nominal interest rate.*

Convertible bond   A bond that may be exchanged (at the bondholders' option) for a specified number of shares of the company's capital stock.

Deferred income taxes   Income taxes upon income that already has been reported for financial reporting purposes but that will not be reported in income tax returns until future periods.

Discount on bonds payable   Amount by which the face amount of the bond exceeds the price received by the corporation of the date of issuance. Indicates that the contractual rate of interest is lower than the market rate of interest.

Effective interest method of amortization   A method of amortizing bond discount or premium that causes bond interest expense to be a constant percentage of the carrying value of the liability.

---

*   *Supplemental Topic, "Convertible Bonds Payable"*

Effective interest rate The actual rate of interest expense to the borrowing corporation, taking into account the contractual cash interest payments and the discount or premium to be amortized.

Fair value A measure of current economic value. Usually means current market value, if determinable.

Financial instrument Cash, equity investments in another business, and contracts involving the receipt or payment of cash.

Junk bonds Bonds payable that, when issued, were abnormally risky but also offered an abnormally high contract rate of interest.

Lessee The tenant, user, or renter of leased property.

Lessor The owner of property leased to a lessee.

Off-balance-sheet financing An arrangement in which the use of resources is financed without the obligation for future payments appearing as a liability in the balance sheet. An operating lease is a common example of off-balance-sheet financing.

Off-balance-sheet risk The risk of future losses resulting from an existing financial instrument that does not currently appear on the balance sheet. An example is the risk of loss from a loan guarantee.

Operating lease A lease contract that is in essence a rental agreement. The lessee has the use of the leased property, but the lessor retains the usual risks and rewards of ownership. The periodic lease payments are accounted for as rent expense by the lessee and as rental revenue by the lessor.

Pension fund A fund managed by an independent trustee into which an employer company makes periodic payments. The fund is used for the purpose of paying retirement benefits to company employees.

Premium on bonds payable Amount by which the issuance price of a bond exceeds the face value. Indicates that the contractual rate of interest is higher than the market rate.

Present value of a future amount The amount of money that an informed investor would pay today for the right to receive the future amount, based upon a specific rate of return required by the investor.

Zero coupon bonds Bonds payable that do not provide for periodic interest payments. Instead, the bonds are issued at a large discount, and all interest charges are included in the face amount.

ASSIGNMENT MATERIAL

DISCUSSION QUESTIONS

1 Distinguish between the two terms in each of the following pairs:
   a Bonds payable; commercial paper
   b Mortgage bond; debenture
   c Callable bond; convertible bond
   d Junk bond; zero coupon bond

2 A financial newspaper recently quoted a market price of *102* for an issue of 8% bonds of a large corporation. What would be the market price for $25,000 face value of these bonds (ignoring accrued interest)? Is the market rate of interest for bonds of this quality higher or lower than 8%? Explain.

3 Briefly explain the income tax advantage of raising capital by issuing bonds rather than by capital stock.

4 Tampa Boat Limited pays income taxes at a rate of 30% on taxable income. Compute the company's annual **after-tax** cost of borrowing on a 10%, $5 million bond issue. Express this after-tax cost as a percentage of the borrowed $5 million.

5 Why is the **present value** of a future amount always less than the future amount?

6 Does issuing bonds at a discount increase or decrease the issuing company's cost of borrowing? Explain.

7 Explain why the effective rate of interest differs from the contract rate when bonds are issued (a) at a discount and (b) at a premium.

8 Why do bond prices **vary inversely** with interest rates?

9 When the effective interest method is used to amortize bond discount or premium, the amount of bond interest expense will differ in each period from that of the preceding period. Explain how the amount of bond interest expense changes from one period to another when the bonds are issued (a) at a discount and (b) at a premium.

10 Explain why the effective interest method of amortizing bond discount or premium is considered to be theoretically preferable to the straight-line method.

11 Some bonds now being bought and sold by investors on organized securities exchanges were issued when interest rates were much higher than they are today. Would you expect these bonds to be trading at prices above or below their face values? Explain.

12 The 6% bonds of Central Gas & Electric Limited are selling at a market price of 72, whereas the 6% bonds of Power Corporation are selling at a price of 97. Does this mean that Power has a better credit rating than Central Gas & Electric? Explain. (Assume current long-term interest rates are in the 11% to 13% range.)

13 Discuss the advantages and disadvantages of a **call (redemption) provision** in a bond contract from the viewpoint of (a) the bondholder and (b) the issuing corporation.

14 Explain how the lessee accounts for an operating lease and a capital lease. Why is an operating lease sometimes called **off-balance-sheet financing?**

15 Ortega Industries has a fully funded pension plan. Each year, pension expense runs in excess of $10 million. At the present time, employees are entitled to receive pension benefits with a present value of $125 million. Explain what liability, if any, Ortega Industries should include in its balance sheet as a result of this pension plan.

16 What is meant by the term **deferred income taxes?** Explain.

17 Define **financial instruments.** What are the basic reasons for disclosing the fair value of these instruments when this value differs significantly from the carrying values shown in the balance sheet?

18 Why does the requirement for disclosure of fair value often apply to financial instruments such as bonds payable, long-term notes payable and receivable, and investments in stocks and bonds, but usually **not** to cash, accounts payable or receivable, or commercial paper?

19 What is meant by a financial instrument creating *off-balance-sheet risk?* Provide an example.

20 As a result of issuing 20-year bonds payable, Low-Cal Foods now has an interest coverage ratio of *.75 to 1.* Should this ratio be of greater concern to short-term creditors or to shareholders? Explain.

21 A $200 million bond issue of Waterloo Corporation (a solvent company) recently matured. The entire maturity value was paid from a bond sinking fund. What effect did this transaction have upon the company's current ratio? Upon its debt ratio? Explain.

*22 What is a *convertible bond?* Discuss the advantages and disadvantages of convertible bonds from the standpoint of (a) the investor and (b) the issuing corporation.

*23 What situation or condition is most likely to cause the holders of convertible bonds to convert their bonds into shares of common stock? (Do not assume that the bonds have been called or that they are about to mature.)

MULTIPLE CHOICE QUESTIONS

1 Which of the following statements are correct? (More than one statement may be correct.)

a A bond issue is a technique for subdividing a very large loan into a great many small, transferable units.

b Bond interest payments are contractual obligations, whereas the board of directors determines whether or not dividends will be paid.

c As interest rates rise, the market prices of bonds fall; as interest rates fall, bond prices tend to rise.

d Bond interest payments are deductible in determining income subject to income taxes, whereas dividends paid to shareholders are not deductible.

2 A few years ago, Glasco issued 30-year, 9% bonds payable, callable at 105. At the issuance date, the market interest rate for such bonds was about $8\frac{1}{2}\%$; today, it is about 11%. Indicate statement(s) with which you agree. (More than one answer may be correct.)

a The bonds probably were issued at a discount.

b Glasco's disclosure of current fair value probably shows these bonds trading at a discount.

c The market price of these bonds probably has increased since the issuance date.

d Glasco is unlikely to call these bonds in the near future even if it has the resources to do so.

3 Lawton International leases its manufacturing equipment from Atlas under an arrangement that qualifies as a capital lease. Lawton's financial statements should include which of the following? (More than one answer may be correct.)

a Depreciation expense on the leased equipment.

b Rent expense each period for the amount of the lease payment made.

c A liability for the present value of all future lease payments.

d A liability for the total amount of all future lease payments.

---

* *Supplemental Topic, "Convertible Bonds Payable"*

4 Silverado maintains a fully funded pension plan. During 1996, $1 million was paid to retired workers, and workers currently employed by the company earned the right to receive pension payments expected to total $3 million *over their lifetimes.* Silverado's pension *expense* for 1996 amounts to:

   a $1

   b $3 million

   c $4 million

   d   Some other amount

5 Deferred income taxes result from:

   a   The fact that bond interest is deductible in the computation of taxable income.

   b   Depositing income taxes due in future years in a special fund managed by an independent trustee.

   c   Timing differences between when income or expense is recognized in financial statements and in income tax returns.

   d   The inability of a bankrupt company to pay its income tax liability on schedule.

6 Waste Disposal Corporation issued 30-year bonds at a price very close to par value. The company uses the effective interest method of amortizing bond discount and premium. Indicate any of the following statements with which you *agree.* (More than one statement may be correct.).

   a   If these bonds were issued at a discount, bond interest expense will *increase* from year to year.

   b   If these bonds were issued at a premium, bond interest expense will *decrease* from year to year.

   c   Total interest expense over the life of the bond issue will be the *same* as would result from use of the straight-line method of amortization.

   d   The annual differences between interest expense computed by the effective interest method and the straight-line method will not be material in dollar amount.

EXERCISES

EXERCISE 16-1
Accounting
Terminology

Listed below are nine technical accounting terms introduced or emphasized in this chapter.

Unfunded pension liability	*Deferred income taxes*	*Effective interest method (of amortization)*
Off-balance-sheet risk	*Present value of future amounts*	*Straight-line method (of amortization)*
Operating lease	*Bond premium*	*Commercial paper*

Each of the following statements may (or may not) describe one of these technical terms. For each statement, indicate the term described, or answer "None" if the statement does not correctly describe any of the terms.

   a   The measurement concept applied to the liabilities for capital lease obligations and to unfunded pension liabilities.

   b   Income taxes applicable to earnings that have already been included in the income statement but that appear in the income tax returns of a future year.

c   Cash, equity investments in another business organization, or contracts calling for receipts or payments of cash.

d   Amortizing bond discount or premium in a manner that results in the same amount of interest expense every period.

e   Future interest charges included in the maturity value of bonds payable.

f   A long-term liability appearing in the balance sheet of any company that offers a pension to retired workers.

g   A lease agreement that results in the lessee recording ownership of an asset and a long-term liability to the lessor.

h   Potential future losses that could result from existing financial instruments that are not listed either as assets or as liabilities.

EXERCISE 16-2
Effects of Bond Transactions upon the Accounting Equation

Listed below are seven events relating to debt instruments issued by Wizard Computer, Inc.:

a   Issued 30-year bonds payable at a discount.

b   Issued 90-day commercial paper at a discount.

c   Made a semiannual interest payment and amortized discount on the bond issue described in part **a,** above.

d   Made a semiannual interest payment and amortized premium on a 20-year bond issue that has been outstanding for nine years.

e   Due to a decline in interest rates, the market value of the bond issues described in both parts **a** and **d** have increased in market value.

f   Called bonds payable described in part **d,** above, at a price above carrying value but below current market value. (Assume all interest expense already has been properly recorded.)

g   Redeemed at face value the commercial paper described in part **b,** above.

INSTRUCTIONS

Indicate the effects of each of these transactions upon the financial statement categories shown below. Organize your answer in tabular form, using the illustrated column headings. Use the following code letters to indicate the effects of each transaction upon the accounting element listed in the column heading:

I = Increase   *D* = Decrease   *NE* = No Effect

	Income Statement			Balance Sheet			
Trans-action	Revenue −	Expenses and Losses =	Net Income	Assets =	Current Liab. +	Long-Term Liab. +	Owners' Equity
a							

EXERCISE 16-3
Effects upon the Accounting Equation— Transactions Other Than Bonds

The following seven items are among the transactions of Commuter Train Corporation during the current year:

a   Leased equipment, signing a five-year capital lease payable in monthly instalments.

b   Leased land to be used as a storage yard, signing a one-year lease payable in monthly instalments.

c   Paid a monthly instalment on a capital lease (assume all remaining payments on this particular lease are due within one year).

d   Made a monthly payment on an operating lease (assume all remaining payments on this particular lease are due within one year).

e Recorded pension expense on a fully funded pension plan and remitted in cash the amount owed to the trustee.

f Recorded expense relating to postretirement benefits other than pensions earned by employees during the current period. This liability is **partially** funded; no payments are made now, but 50% of the obligation arising this period will be funded within the next 12 months.

g Made an adjusting entry recording income taxes expense for the period, including a considerable amount of deferred taxes.

INSTRUCTIONS   Indicate the effects of each of these transactions upon the financial statement categories shown below. Organize your answer in tabular form, using the illustrated column headings. Use the following code letters to indicate the effects of each transaction upon the accounting element listed in the column heading:

I = Increase   *D* = Decrease   *NE* = No Effect

Trans-action	Income Statement			Balance Sheet			
	Revenue −	Expenses =	Net Income	Assets =	Current Liab. +	Long-Term Liab. +	Owners' Equity
a							

EXERCISE 16-4
After-Tax Cost of Borrowing

NY Central, Inc., issued $20 million of 12% bonds payable at face value. The company pays income taxes at an average rate of 35% of its taxable income.

Compute the company's annual **after-tax** cost of borrowing on this bond issue, stated as (a) a total dollar amount and (b) a percentage of the amount borrowed.

EXERCISE 16-5
Bond Interest (Bonds Issued at Par)

On March 31, Bancor Corporation received authorization to issue $30 million of 12%, 20-year debenture bonds. Interest payment dates were March 31 and September 30. The bonds were all issued at par on April 30, one month after the interest date printed on the bonds.

INSTRUCTIONS   a Prepare the journal entry at April 30, to record the sale of the bonds.

b Prepare the journal entry at September 30, to record the semiannual bond interest payment.

c Prepare the adjusting entry at December 31, to record bond interest accrued since September 30.

EXERCISE 16-6
Basic Entries for a Bond Issue: Issuance, Interest Payment, and Retirement

La Paloma Corporation issued $10 million of 15-year, 10½% bonds on July 1, 1995, at 98¼. Interest is due on June 30 and December 31 of each year, and the bonds mature on June 30, 2010. The fiscal year ends on December 31; bond discount is amortized by the straight-line method. Prepare the following journal entries:

a July 1, 1995, to record the issuance of the bonds

b December 31, 1995, to pay interest and amortize the bond discount (make two entries)

c June 30, 2010, to pay interest, amortize the bond discount, and retire the bonds at maturity (make three entries)

EXERCISE 16-7
Amortizing Bond Discount and Premium: Straight-line Method

North Corporation issued $80 million of 12%, 10-year bonds on January 1. Interest is payable semiannually on June 30 and December 31. The bonds were sold to an underwriting group at 105.

South Limited issued $80 million of 11%, 10-year bonds on January 1. Interest is payable semiannually on June 30 and December 31. The bonds were sold to an underwriting group at 95.

Prepare journal entries to record all transactions during the year for (a) the North bond issue; and (b) the South bond issue; assume that both companies amortize bond discount or premium by the straight-line method at each interest payment date. (c) Comment on the effect of the bond premium and discount on the interest expense for the two companies.

EXERCISE 16-8
Bond Prices and Accrued Interest

On August 1, 1996, Cellular Industries issued $10 million face value, 9%, 20-year bonds payable to an underwriter for total cash proceeds of $10,064,000. The bonds were dated April 1, 1996, and pay interest semiannually at October 1 and April 1.

a State the issue price of these bonds as a ***percentage*** of the face amount. (Round to the nearest $\frac{1}{10}$ of 1%.)

b Compute the amount of cash paid to bondholders at each semiannual interest date.

c Compute the company's semiannual bond interest expense (for a full six-month period), assuming that any discount or premium is amortized by the straight-line method.

EXERCISE 16-9
Effective Interest Method— Bond Discount

Three Flags Corporation issued on the authorization date $1 million of 10-year, 9% bonds payable and received proceeds of $937,689, resulting in an effective interest rate of 10%. The discount is amortized by the effective interest method; the amortization table for this bond issue is illustrated in this chapter. Interest is payable semiannually.

INSTRUCTIONS

a Show how the liability for the bonds would appear on a balance sheet prepared immediately after issuance of the bonds.

b Show how the liability for the bonds would appear on a balance sheet prepared after ***14*** semiannual interest periods (three years prior to maturity).

c Show the necessary calculations to determine interest expense by the effective interest method for the ***second*** six-month period; the discount amortized at the end of that second period; and the cash payment of interest. Round all amounts to the nearest dollar.

EXERCISE 16-10
Effective Interest Method— Premium

On April 1, Financial Publications issued $1 million of 10-year, 9% bonds payable and received proceeds of $1,067,952 resulting in an effective interest rate of 8%. Interest is payable on September 30 and March 31. The effective interest method is used to amortize bond premium; an amortization table for this bond issue is illustrated in this chapter.

INSTRUCTIONS

Prepare the necessary journal entries (rounding all amounts to the nearest dollar) on:

a April 1, to record the issuance of the bonds

b September 30, to record the payment of interest and amortization of premium at the first semiannual interest payment date

c December 31, to accrue bond interest expense through year-end

d March 31, to record payment of interest and amortization of bond premium at the second semiannual interest payment date.

EXERCISE 16-11
Partial Retirement of a Bond Issue

The following liability appears on the balance sheet of Pearl Limited on December 31, 1995:

Long-term liabilities:
Bonds payable, 11%, due Dec. 31, 2009 .... $10,000,000
Premium on bonds payable 210,000 $10,210,000

On January 1, 1996, 25% of the bonds are retired at 98. Interest had been paid on December 31, 1995.

a Record the retirement of $2,500,000 of bonds on January 1, 1996.

b Record the interest payment for the six months ending December 31, 1996, and the amortization of the premium on December 31, 1996 (using the straight-line method).

EXERCISE 16-12
Accounting for Leases

On July 1, City Hospital leased equipment from MedTech Instruments for a period of five years. The lease calls for monthly payments of $2,000, payable in advance on the first day of each month, beginning July 1.

INSTRUCTIONS

Prepare the journal entry needed to record this lease in the accounting records of City Hospital on July 1 under each of the following independent assumptions:

a The lease represents a simple rental arrangement.

b At the end of five years, title to this equipment will be transferred to City Hospital at no additional cost. The present value of the 60 monthly lease payments is $90,809, of which $2,000 is paid in cash on July 1.

EXERCISE 16-13
Pension Plans

During the current year, Deltron Corporation paid $3 million into a fully funded pension plan for the company's employees. At year-end, the plan has total assets of $42 million, and the present value of all future pension payments earned to date is estimated at $40 million. During the current year, the plan paid $5 million in pension benefits to retired Deltron employees.

INSTRUCTIONS

a What is Deltron's pension expense for the year?

b Identify any assets or liabilities relating to this pension plan that will appear in Deltron's balance sheet, and indicate the appropriate dollar amount.

c If Deltron becomes insolvent in future years, what prospects, if any, do today's employees have of receiving the pension benefits that they have earned to date?

EXERCISE 16-14
Accounting for Retirement Benefits

At the end of the current year, Krepshaw Power Tools, Inc., received the following information from its actuary:

Pension expense	*$1,790,000*
Nonpension postretirement benefits	*316,000*

The pension plan is fully funded. Krepshaw has funded only $23,000 of the non-pension postretirement benefits this year.

Prepare a separate journal entry to summarize for the entire year (a) the pension expense and (b) the nonpension postretirement benefits expense.

EXERCISE 16-15
Deferred Income Taxes

The following journal entry summarizes for the current year the income taxes expense of Kowloon Coachworks:

Income Taxes Expense	*14,000,000*	
Cash		*9,000,000*
Income Taxes Payable		*2,900,000*
Deferred Income Taxes Payable		*2,100,000*
To record income taxes expense for the current year.		

Of the deferred income taxes, only $240,000 is classified as a current liability.

INSTRUCTIONS

a Define ***deferred income taxes payable.***

b What is the amount of income taxes that the company has paid or expects to pay in conjunction with its income tax return for the current year?

c Illustrate the allocation of the liabilities shown in the above journal entry between the classifications of *current liabilities* and *long-term liabilities.*

*EXERCISE 16-16
Convertible
Bonds

A recent annual report of a large corporation shows that 406 of the company's $3\frac{7}{8}\%$, $1,000 face amount, convertible bonds are still outstanding. These bonds mature in less than 3 years and have a conversion ratio of 32 to 1. The company's common stock has a current market price of $60 per share, and currently pays dividends of $1.68 per share.

INSTRUCTIONS

a Prepare the journal entry that would be made by the corporation to record the conversion of these outstanding convertible bonds into shares of common stock. (Assume the bonds originally were issued at par.)

b Under the circumstances described above, would it be advantageous for the bondholders to exchange the bonds for common stock? Explain.

PROBLEMS

Note: In this chapter, we provide an unusually wide variety of problem assignments. In order to make the full range of these assignments available to all users of the text, we present them in one consecutive series, rather than in the usual A and B groups. This entire series is supported in both the Group A and Group B accounting work sheets.

PROBLEM 16-1
Bond Interest
(Bonds Issued
at Par)

Bar Harbor Gas & Electric obtained authorization to issue $90 million face value of 10%, 20-year bonds, dated May 1, 1995. Interest payment dates were November 1 and May 1. Issuance of the bonds did not take place until August 1, 1995. On this date all the bonds were sold at a price of 100 plus accrued interest.

INSTRUCTIONS

Prepare the necessary entries in general journal form on:

a August 1, 1995, to record the issuance of the bonds

b November 1, 1995, to record the first semiannual interest payment on the bond issue

c December 31, 1995, to accrue bond interest expense through year-end

d May 1, 1996, to record the second semiannual interest payment

PROBLEM 16-2
Amortization of
Bond Dis-
count:
Straight-line
Method

On May 1, 1996, Festival Cruise Ships, Inc., sold a $60 million face value, 11%, 10-year bond issue to an underwriter at a price of 98. Interest is payable semiannually on May 1 and November 1. Company policy is to amortize bond discount by the straight-line method at each interest payment date and at year-end. The company's fiscal year ends at December 31.

INSTRUCTIONS

a Prepare journal entries to record the issuance of these bonds, the payment of interest at November 1, 1996, and the bond interest expense through year-end.

b Show the proper balance sheet presentation of all liabilities relating to this bond issue at December 31, 1996. Include captions indicating whether the liabilities are classified as current or long-term.

c Why do you think that Festival was able to receive a price of only 98 for these bonds, rather than being able to issue them at par? What will issuing these bonds at a discount mean about the relationship between Festival's annual

---

* *Supplemental Topic, "Convertible Bonds Payable"*

bond interest expense and the amount of cash paid annually to bondholders? Explain.

PROBLEM 16-3
Amortizing Bond Discount and Premium: Straight-line Method

On September 1, 1995, North American Farm Equipment issued $60 million in 10% debenture bonds. Interest is payable semiannually on March 1 and September 1, and the bonds mature in 20 years. Company policy is to amortize bond discount or premium by the straight-line method at each interest payment date and at year-end. The company's fiscal year ends at December 31.

INSTRUCTIONS

a Make the necessary adjusting entries at December 31, 1995, and the journal entry to record the payment of bond interest on March 1, 1996, under each of the following assumptions:

1 The bonds were issued at 98.

2 The bonds were issued at 101.

b Compute the carrying value of bond liability at December 31, 1996, under assumptions 1 and 2 above.

PROBLEM 16-4
Comprehensive Problem: Straight-line Amortization

Country Recording Studios obtained the necessary approvals to issue $30 million of 12%, 10-year bonds, dated March 1, 1995. Interest payment dates were September 1 and March 1. Issuance of the bonds did not occur until June 1, 1995. On this date, the entire bond issue was sold to an underwriter at a price that included three months' accrued interest. Country Recording Studios follows the policy of amortizing bond discount or premium by the straight-line method at each interest date as well as for year-end adjusting entries at December 31.

INSTRUCTIONS

a Prepare all journal entries necessary to record the issuance of the bonds and bond interest expense during 1995, assuming that the total proceeds from issuance of the bonds on June 1 amounted to **$30,315,000** including accrued interest.

b Assume that the proceeds received from the underwriter on June 1 had amounted to **$31,180,800** including accrued interest. Prepare journal entries for 1995 parallel to those in part **a** above.

c Show the proper balance sheet presentation of the liability for bonds payable (including accrued interest) in the balance sheet prepared at December 31, **2000,** assuming that the total proceeds from issuance of the bonds (including accrued interest) had been:

1 $30,315,000, as described in part **a**

2 $31,180,800, as described in part **b**

PROBLEM 16-5
An Alternate to Problem 16-4

Liberty Broadcasting Corporation obtained authorization to issue $80 million of 12%, 10-year bonds, dated May 1, 1995. Interest payment dates were May 1 and November 1. Issuance of the bonds did not take place until July 1, 1995. On this date, the entire bond issue was sold to an underwriter at a price that included the two months' accrued interest. Liberty Broadcasting follows the policy of amortizing bond discount or premium by the straight-line method at each interest date as well as for year-end adjusting entries at December 31.

INSTRUCTIONS

a Prepare all journal entries necessary to record the issuance of the bonds and bond interest expense during 1995, assuming that the sales price of the bonds on July 1 was $83,960,000 ***including accrued interest.***

b Assume that the total proceeds from issuance of the bonds on July 1 had been $79,830,000 including accrued interest. Prepare journal entries for 1995 parallel to those in part **a** above.

c Show the proper balance sheet presentation of the liability for bonds payable in the balance sheet prepared at December 31, **2001,** assuming that the total proceeds from issuance of the bonds (including accrued interest) had been:

1 $83,960,000, as described in part **a**

2 $79,830,000, as described in part **b**

PROBLEM 16-6
Accrual and Payment of Interest, Amortization of Bond Premium, and Bond Redemption

The items shown below appear in the balance sheet of Majestic Corporation at December 31, 1995:

Current liabilities:
Bond interest payable (for three months from Sept. 30
  to Dec. 31) .... $ 200,000
Long-term debt:
  Bonds payable, 10%, due Sept. 30, 2000 .... $8,000,000
  Add: Premium on bonds payable 136,800   8,136,800

The bonds are redeemable on any interest date. On September 30, 1996, Majestic redeemed $2 million of the bonds at 101.

INSTRUCTIONS

a Prepare journal entries to record the semiannual interest payment on March 31, 1996. Premium is amortized by the straight-line method at each interest payment date and was amortized to December 31, 1995.

b Prepare journal entries to record the amortization of bond premium and payment of bond interest at September 30, 1996, and also to record the redemption of $2,000,000 of the bonds at this date.

c Prepare a journal entry to record the accrual of interest at December 31, 1996. Include the amortization of bond premium to the year-end.

PROBLEM 16-7
Accrual and Payment of Interest, Amortization of Bond Discount, and Bond Redemption

The following items appear in the balance sheet of International Limited at December 31, 1995:

Current liabilities:
Bond interest payable (for three months from
  Sept. 30 to Dec. 31) .... $ 300,000
Long-term debt:
  Bonds payable, 12%, due Mar. 31, 2006 .... $10,000,000
  Less: Discount on bonds payable 196,800   9,803,200

The bonds are redeemable on any interest date. On September 30, 1996, International redeemed $2,000,000 of the bonds at 102.

INSTRUCTIONS

a Prepare journal entries to record the semiannual payment on March 31, 1996. Discount is amortized by the straight-line method at each interest payment date and was amortized to December 31, 1995.

b Prepare journal entries to record the amortization of bond discount and payment of bond interest at September 30, 1996, and also to record the redemption of $2,000,000 of the bonds at this date.

c Prepare a journal entry to record the accrual of interest at December 31, 1996. Include the amortization of bond discount to the year-end.

PROBLEM 16-8
Effective Interest Method: Bonds Issued at Discount

Arcades R Fun maintains its accounts on a calendar-year basis. On June 30, 1996, the company issued $6 million face value of 7.6% bonds at a price of $97\frac{1}{4}$, resulting in an effective rate of interest of 8%. Semiannual interest payment dates are June 30 and December 31. Bond discount is amortized by the effective interest method. The bonds mature on June 30, 2006.

INSTRUCTIONS **a** Prepare the required journal entries on:

    1 June 30, 1996, to record the sale of the bonds.

    2 December 31, 1996, to pay interest and amortize the discount using the effective interest method.

    3 June 30, *2006,* to pay interest, amortize the discount, and retire the bonds. Assume that at the beginning of this last interest period, the carrying value of the bonds is *$5,988,462.* (Use a separate journal entry to show the retirement of the bonds.)

b Show how the accounts Bonds Payable and Discount on Bonds Payable should appear on the balance sheet at December 31, *1996.*

PROBLEM 16-9
Effective Interest Method of Amortizing Bond Discount

On December 31, 1994, city of Glenview issued $10 million face value, 10%, 10-year bonds to an underwriter at a price of 94. This price results in an effective annual interest rate of 11%. Interest is payable semiannually on June 30 and December 31. City of Glenview amortizes bond discount by the effective interest method.

INSTRUCTIONS **a** Prepare an amortization table for the first two years (four interest periods) of this bond issue. Round all amounts to the nearest dollar and use the following column headings for your table:

Six Month Interest Period	(A) Interest Paid Semi-annually ($10,000,000 × 5%)	(B) Effective Semi-annual Interest Expense (Carrying Value × 5½%)	(C) Discount Amorti-zation (B − A)	(D) Bond Discount Balance	(E) Carrying Value of Bonds, End of Period ($10,000,000 − D)
Issue date	—	—	—	$600,000	$9,400,000

b Using the information from your amortization table, prepare all journal entries necessary to record issuance of the bonds in *1994,* and bond interest for *1995.* (Use a compound entry for interest payment and amortization of bond discount at each semiannual interest payment date.)

c Show the proper balance sheet presentation of Bonds Payable and Discount on Bonds Payable at December 31, *1996.*

PROBLEM 16-10
Effective Interest Method: Bonds Issued at Premium

On December 31, 1995, Rocky Mountain Railroad sold a $10 million, 10¼%, 20-year bond issue to an underwriter at a price of 102. This price results in an effective annual interest rate of 10%. The bonds were dated December 31, and the interest payment dates were June 30 and December 31. Rocky Mountain Railroad follows a policy of amortizing the bond premium by the effective interest method at each semiannual payment date.

INSTRUCTIONS **a** Prepare an amortization table for the first two years (four interest periods) of the life of this bond issue. Round all amounts to the nearest dollar and use the following column headings:

Six-Month Interest Period	(A) Interest Paid Semi-annually ($10,000,000 × 5⅛%)	(B) Effective Semi-annual Interest-Expense (Carrying Value × 5%)	(C) Premium Amortization (A − B)	(D) Bond Premium Balance	(E) Carrying Value of Bonds, End of Period ($10,000,000 + D)

b Using the information in your amortization table, prepare all journal entries necessary to record the issuance of the bonds in *1995,* and the bond interest expense during *1996.*

c Show the proper balance sheet presentation of the liability for bonds payable at December 31, *1997.*

PROBLEM 16-11
Effective Interest Method: Discount and Premium

On September 1, 1995, Camelot Hotel & Casino issued $9 million face (par) value, $8\frac{1}{2}\%$, 10-year bonds payable with interest dates of March 1 and September 1. The company maintains its accounts on a calendar-year basis and follows the policy of amortizing bond discount and bond premium by the effective interest method at the semiannual interest payment dates as well as at the year-end adjusting of the accounts.

INSTRUCTIONS

a Prepare the necessary journal entries to record the following transactions, assuming that the bonds were sold for *$8,700,000,* a price resulting in an effective annual interest rate of *9%.*

1 Sale of the bonds on September 1, 1995

2 Adjustment of the accounts at December 31, 1995, for accrued interest and amortization of a discount

3 Payment of bond interest and amortization of discount on March 1, 1996

b Assume that the sales price of the bonds on September 1, 1995, had been *$9,300,000,* resulting in an effective annual interest rate of *8%.* Prepare journal entries parallel to those called for in **a** above at the dates of September 1, 1995; December 31, 1995; and March 1, 1996.

c State the amounts of bond interest expense for 1995 and the amount of the liability for the bonds payable at December 31, 1995, under the independent assumptions set forth in both **a** and **b** above. Show your computations.

PROBLEM 16-12
Factors Affecting Bond Prices

Shown below are three independent cases, each involving two bond issues of a large corporation. In each case, both bond issues have identical credit ratings.

a **Ontario Hydro** has two bond issues maturing in the year 2010; one has a contract interest rate of 10.5%, and the other, a contract rate of 13.375%.

b **Bell Canada** has outstanding two issues of $10\frac{1}{2}\%$ bonds—one issue maturing in 1998 and the other in 2009.

*c **John Labatt Limited** has issued the following convertible bonds: (1) 6% bonds maturing in 2006, with a conversion price of $17.875 per share of common stock, and (2) 5% bonds maturing in 2007, with a conversion price of $27 per share of common stock. In February, 1994, the market price of Labatt's common stock was $22\frac{1}{2}$ per share.

INSTRUCTIONS

For each case, explain which of the two bonds you would expect to have been selling at the higher market price in February, *1994.* Also indicate whether each bond should have been selling at a premium or a discount at that time. Explain the reasoning behind your answers. Assume that in February, 1994, market interest rates for bonds of this quality were as follows:

Maturity	Market Interest Rate
Years 1994–1996	13%
Years 1997–1999	12%
Year 2000 and beyond	11%

---

* *Supplemental Topic, "Convertible Bonds Payable"*

PROBLEM 16-13
Capital Leases:
A Comprehen-
sive Problem

Beach Equipment frequently uses long-term contracts as a means of financing the sale of its products. On November 1, 1996, Beach Equipment leased to Star Industries a machine carried in the perpetual inventory records at a cost of $18,120. The terms of the lease called for 48 monthly payments of $650 each, beginning November 30, 1996. The present value of these payments, after considering a built-in interest charge of 1% per month, is equal to $24,680, the regular sales price of the machine. At the end of the 48-month lease, title to the machine will transfer to Star Industries.

INSTRUCTIONS

a Prepare journal entries for 1996 in the accounts of Beach Equipment on:

   1 November 1 to record the sale financed by the lease and the related cost of goods sold.

   2 November 30, to record receipt of the first $650 monthly payment.

   3 December 31, to record receipt of the second monthly payment.

b Prepare journal entries for 1996 in the accounts of Star Industries on:

   1 November 1, to record acquisition of the leased machine.

   2 November 30, to record the first monthly lease payment.

   3 December 31, to record the second monthly lease payment.

   4 December 31, to recognize depreciation on the leased machine through year-end. Compute the depreciation expense by the straight-line method, using a 10-year service life and an estimated salvage value of $6,680.

c Compute the net carrying value of the leased machine in the balance sheet of Star Industries at December 31, 1996.

d Compute the amount of Star Industries' lease payment obligation at December 31, 1996.

PROBLEM 16-14
Reporting Lia-
bilities in a
Balance Sheet

Listed below are selected items from the accounting records of Gulf Coast Telephone Limited (GulfTel) for the year ended December 31, *1996* (dollar amounts in thousands):

Accounts payable	$ 65,600
Accrued expenses payable (other than interest)	11,347
$6\frac{3}{4}$% Bonds payable, due Feb. 1, 1997	100,000
$8\frac{1}{2}$% Bonds payable, due June 1, 1997..	250,000
Unamortized bond discount ($8\frac{1}{2}$% bonds of 1997)	260
11% Bonds payable, due June 1, 2006..	300,000
Unamortized bond premium (11% bonds of '06)..............................	1,700
Accrued interest payable	7,333
Bond interest expense...	61,000
Other interest expense	17,000
Commercial paper (net of unamortized discount)	110,000
Lease payment obligations—capital leases	23,600
Pensions obligation	410,000
Unfunded obligation for postretirement benefits other than pensions	72,000
Deferred income taxes...	130,000
Income taxes expense	66,900
Income taxes payable	17,300
Accommodation endorsements (loan guarantees).............................	28,600
Operating income	280,800
Net income...	134,700
Total assets	2,093,500

OTHER INFOR-MATION (dollar amounts in thousands)

1 The 6¾% bonds due in February 1997 will be refinanced in January 1997 through the issuance of $150,000 in 9%, 20-year general debentures.

2 The 8½% bonds due June 1, 1997, will be repaid entirely from a bond sinking fund.

3 GulfTel is committed to total lease payments of $14,400 in 1997. Of this amount, $7,479 is applicable to operating leases, and $6,921 to capital leases. Payments on capital leases will be applied as follows: $2,300 to interest expense and $4,621 to reduction in the capitalized lease payment obligation.

4 GulfTel's pension plan is fully funded with an independent trustee.

5 The obligation for postretirement benefits other than pensions consists of a commitment to maintain dental and other health insurance for retired workers. During 1997, GulfTel will fund $18,000 of this obligation.

6 The $17,300 in income taxes payable relates to income taxes levied in 1996 and must be paid on or before March 15, 1997. No portion of the deferred tax liability is regarded as a current liability.

7 The accommodation endorsements are guarantees of bank loans and other indebtedness of various suppliers of specialized telecommunications equipment. In the opinion of management, the risk of material losses arising from these loan guarantees is not likely.

INSTRUCTIONS

a Using this information, prepare the current liabilities and long-term liabilities sections of a classified balance sheet as of December 31, 1996. (Within each classification, items may be listed in any order.)

b Explain briefly how the information in each of the seven numbered paragraphs affected your presentation of the company's liabilities.

c Compute as of December 31, 1996, the company's (1) debt ratio and (2) interest coverage ratio.

d Based solely upon information stated in this problem, indicate whether this company appears to be an outstanding, medium, or poor long-term credit risk. State specific reasons for your conclusion.

ANALYTICAL AND DECISION PROBLEMS AND CASES

A&D 16-1
Don't Call Us . . . We'll Call You

On December 31 of the current year, Synex Corporation has outstanding $200 million of 14½% bonds payable that mature in 20 years. These bonds were issued at par and are callable at a price of 106. Because of a recent decline in market interest rates, the company today can issue, at par, $200 million of 20-year bonds with an interest rate of only 11% and use the proceeds to call the 14½% bonds; the issuing cost is $3,000,000.

INSTRUCTIONS

a Would you recommend that Synex replace the 14½% bond issue, or leave it outstanding? Justify your recommendation.

b Assume that you are an investor willing to earn the current market rate of return of 11%. If you were to purchase the Synex 14½% bonds at a price of 113 and hold these bonds until their maturity date, you would earn a return slightly greater than 11%. Does this investment sound attractive? Explain.

A&D 16-2
Accounting for Leases

At the beginning of the current year, Cable TV entered into the two long-term lease agreements described below:

Building Lease. Leased from Lamden Properties the use of an office building for a period of 5 years. The monthly lease payments are based upon the square metres of the building and increase by 5% each year. The estimated useful life of the building is 40 years.

Satellite Lease. Leased from SpaceNet, Inc., the use of a communications satellite for a period of 5 years. The monthly payments are intended to pay SpaceNet the current sales price of the satellite, plus a reasonable charge for interest. At the end of the lease, ownership of the satellite will transfer to Cable TV at no additional cost. The estimated useful life of the satellite is 15 years.

INSTRUCTIONS   Answer each of the following questions as they relate to the building lease. After answering all four questions, answer them again as they relate to the satellite lease.

a   Is this agreement an operating lease or a capital lease? Why?

b   Will this lease result in any assets or liabilities being included in Cable TV's future balance sheets? If so, identify these assets and liabilities.

c   Indicate the nature of any expenses that will appear in Cable TV's future income statements as a result of the lease, and indicate the number of years for which the expense will be incurred.

d   Briefly explain how the ***lessor*** should account for this lease agreement, including the receipt of future lease payments. Indicate whether the lessor should recognize depreciation on the leased asset.

*A&D 16-3
Convertible
Bonds

Dreyer's Grand Ice Cream, Inc., has outstanding $50 million face value of $6\frac{1}{2}\%$ convertible bonds payable, callable at $106\frac{1}{2}$, maturing in 2011. Each $1,000 bond is convertible into 31.25 shares of the company's common stock. Today's newspaper indicates a market price for the company's common stock, which pays a dividend of 20 cents per share, of $36. On this date, the market rate of interest for bonds of similar quality and maturity date but ***without*** a conversion feature is approximately 10%.

INSTRUCTIONS   a   Compute the conversion price and the stock value for one of these bonds.

b   Prepare journal entries in the company's accounting records to record the following alternative possibilities:

  1   Dreyer's calls the bonds (assume the bonds were originally issued at par).

  2   Bondholders convert the entire bond issue into common stock.

c   Given the circumstances described above, would you expect:

  1   The bonds to be selling at a discount or a premium?

  2   Dreyer's to call the bonds in the immediate future?

  3   Bondholders to convert the bonds into common stock in the immediate future?

Explain the reasons for your answers to each question in part **c.**

COMPREHENSIVE PROBLEM 4

SHADOW MOUNTAIN HOTEL

A CORPORATE "PRACTICE SET"

Note to Students and Instructors: This problem ***requires*** use of the partially completed working papers that accompany this textbook.

---

*   *Supplemental Topic, "Convertible Bonds Payable"*

Shadow Mountain Hotel is a profitable resort hotel and convention centre that has been in operation for several years. Max Griffith, a motion picture producer, organized a new corporation called Shadow Mountain Corporation to purchase and operate the Shadow Mountain Hotel. The new corporation raised capital by issuing both capital stock and bonds payable, and on July 1, 1996, purchased the Shadow Mountain Hotel from the previous owners.

You have been hired as the corporation's controller. The hotel's accounting staff records and posts all the routine transactions, but you have instructed them **not** to record any transaction that they do not understand. Rather, they are to prepare a written description of these items for your review, and you will handle the recording of these transactions. You also perform the end-of-period procedures, including the preparation of a work sheet, adjusting and closing entries, and financial statements. The corporation adjusts and closes its accounting records at the end of each *calendar quarter* (three-month period).

It is now September 30, 1996, the end of the first calendar quarter after Shadow Mountain Corporation acquired the Shadow Mountain Hotel. Management has asked you to provide an income statement and statement of retained earnings for this three-month period, and also a balance sheet as of September 30. Almost all of the routine transactions have **already been recorded** in the accounting records and posted to ledger accounts by your staff. Per your instructions, they have prepared the following written description of each transaction or event **not yet recorded,** as well as information necessary for end-of-period adjustments.

Transactions or Events Not Recorded by Staff

Date 1996	Transaction or Event
June 2	Max Griffith organized Shadow Mountain Corporation, with an unlimited number of authorized no-par common stock, and $100 par value, 6% convertible preferred stock (each convertible into six shares of common stock).
June 3	Griffith and other investors subscribed to 480,000 shares of the corporation's common stock at a price of $16 per share. Griffith states that he expects to have another 70,000 shares subscribed by the end of the month.
June 4	Issued to Dianna Trump all 25,000 shares of the convertible preferred stock at par, receiving $2,500,000 cash.
June 6	Underwriters Milken & Burnham agreed to purchase $10 million of 15%, 20-year bonds payable to be issued by the corporation on July 1, 1996. The bonds will pay interest every December 31 and June 30. The exact issue price will be determined at the date of issuance, based upon an index of interest rates and bond prices.
June 25	Collected in cash all $7,680,000 receivable from subscribers to the common stock. Issued stock certificates for 480,000 shares.
June 29	Issued an additional 2,000 shares of common stock to Griffith for his services in organizing the corporation. The board of directors agrees that these services were worth the $32,000 market value of these shares.

July 1 Issued the $10 million of 15%, 20-year bonds payable, dated today, to underwriters Milken & Burnham. The issue price was 98, and the corporation received $9,800,000 in cash from the underwriters.

July 1 Purchased Shadow Mountain Hotel by assuming the liabilities of the hotel and paying an additional $19 million cash to National Resorts, Inc. Exhibit 1 indicates the current values of the specific assets purchased, and also the amounts of the liabilities assumed. The excess of our $19 million purchase price over the current value of the net ***identifiable*** assets is regarded as a purchase of unrecorded goodwill.

Exhibit 1
Shadow Mountain Hotel
Valuation of Assets Purchased and Liabilities Assumed
July 1, 1996

Assets acquired:		
Accounts receivable	$ 50,800	
Allowance for doubtful accounts	(1,000)	(credit)
Inventory	36,200	
Supplies	44,000	
Land	10,570,000	
Buildings	14,000,000	
Furnishings & equipment	1,200,000	
Total identifiable assets	$25,900,000	
Liabilities assumed:		
Accounts payable	$ 99,000	
Interest payable	41,000	
Unearned deposits	615,000	
Income taxes payable	305,000	
Mortgage note payable (10%)	9,840,000	
Total liabilities	$10,900,000	
Current value of net identifiable assets purchased	$15,000,000	
Purchase price	$19,000,000	

July 4 Isadora Duncan, a shareholder who owned 12,000 shares of common stock in Shadow Mountain Corporation, was killed in an automobile accident. Duncan was a personal friend of Max Griffith.

July 10 Shadow Mountain Corporation purchased 12,000 shares of its common stock from the estate of Isadora Duncan at a price of $18 per share. These shares will be held temporarily as treasury stock and will be reissued in the near future.

July 11 Milken & Burnham, the underwriters of the bond issue, reported that they had resold all the bonds to investors at an average price of 101.

July 12 As part of the normal refurbishing of hotel rooms, older furniture was sold to Freight Liquidators for $119,900 cash. In the acquisition transaction on July 1, these furnishings had been assigned a cost of $200,000. (As these assets were sold less than one-half month after acquisition, there is no related accumulated depreciation, and no depreciation need be computed through the date of sale.)

July 14 Purchased new furnishings for $500,000 cash to replace those sold on July 12.

Aug. 10 Dianna Trump converted 10,000 shares of her $100 par value convertible preferred stock into 60,000 shares of no-par value common stock.

In light of her increased voting rights, Trump was given a seat on the corporation's board of directors.

Aug. 18 The City of Shadow Mountain gave to Shadow Mountain Corporation several hectares of land including the riverbed along the western boundary of the hotel parking lot. The land was given to the corporation at no cost, but with the understanding that the corporation would build a flood control channel in this riverbed to prevent land erosion. The corporation intends to build this flood control channel underground, and then to expand the parking lot on top of the riverbed and the donated land.

The donated land currently is estimated to be worth $320,000 in its present condition.

Sept. 2 Received a $48,000 advance deposit from the Canadian Academic Accounting Association to reserve a block of 300 rooms for its national convention next June.

Sept. 10 The board of directors declared the regular quarterly dividend of $1.50 per share on the shares of 6% convertible preferred stock still outstanding. The dividend is payable on October 10 to shareholders of record on September 20.

Sept. 10 The board of directors declared a 2% stock dividend on currently outstanding shares of common stock. The current market price of the common stock is $20 per share. The dividend will be distributed on September 30 to shareholders of record on September 20.

Sept. 20 Date of record for the stock dividend declared on September 10. The market value of the stock today is $21 per share.

Sept. 24 Reissued 10,400 shares of the common stock held in the treasury at a price of $21, receiving $218,400 in cash.

Sept. 26 The provincial government paid Shadow Mountain Corporation cash of $310,000 in compensation for land that was expropriated by the province to permit widening of a highway. The cost of this land to the corporation, based upon the July 1 purchase transaction, was $200,000. In this case, the transaction also is *material in dollar amount.*

Sept. 27 Max Griffith sold 100,000 shares of his common stock in Shadow Mountain Corporation to Dianna Trump at a price of $20 per share. On this date, Griffith resigned as the corporation's chief executive officer, and the board named Trump as his replacement.

You remain the company's controller.

Sept. 30 Distributed the 10,600 share stock dividend declared on September 10. The market price of the common stock today is $22 per share.

Sept. 30 Although paycheques have been prepared and distributed, no entries have yet been made in the accounting records to record the biweekly payroll occurring on this date. Your accounting staff has provided you with the following information:

The wages and salaries earned by employees in the two weeks ended September 30 amounted to $108,000. Amounts withheld from employees' cheques consisted of $14,320 in income taxes, unemployment insurance of $4,300, and Canada Pension Plan of $3,500. Shadow Mountain contributes an equal amount for unemployment insurance and 1.4 times for Canada Pension Plan.

Company policy is to make two entries to record biweekly payrolls: one recording the payroll and amounts withheld and the other recording the payroll taxes upon the employer.

Sept. 30 Paid in cash all the liabilities at month-end for unemployment insurance and Canada Pension Plan, as well as for income taxes withheld from employees. This payment included the liabilities arising from the September 30 payroll. (Make one compound journal entry to record payment of these liabilities.)

Information for End-of-Period Adjustments

a Hotel guests normally are billed for their room rental when they check out. As of September 30, guests currently registered at the hotel owe $44,100 in room rental charges that have not yet been recorded or billed.

b The hotel's accounts receivable consist primarily of amounts owed by current guests who have not yet checked out. Based upon experience, the company's policy is to provide an allowance for uncollectible accounts equal to 2% of these receivables. The amount of the allowance determined in this manner is rounded to the nearest $100.

c The Unearned Deposits account represents advance deposits made by conventions and other groups to reserve large blocks of rooms for future dates. As of September 30, $402,300 of the amounts credited to this account have been earned, and $642,000 remains unearned.

d Supplies on hand at September 30 amount to $40,000.

e The insurance policies were purchased on July 1 for $300,000 and cover a period of 12 months.

f Depreciation on the hotel building and other structures is computed by the *straight-line* method, assuming a 25-year life and no salvage value.

g Depreciation on furniture and equipment is computed by the *double-declining-balance* method, assuming a 5-year life. (Depreciation for fractional periods is rounded to the nearest full month. In this case, you are to take 3 full months' depreciation on all assets included in the Furniture & Equipment account at September 30.)

h Goodwill is amortized by the straight-line method over a 40-year amortization period.

i Organization costs are amortized by the straight-line method over a five-year period.

j Property taxes payable accrue at the rate of $30,000 per month, beginning on July 1. These taxes are payable within a year.

k Interest accrues on the mortgage note payable at the annual rate of 10%, and accrued interest is payable on the 15th of each month. Thus, at September 30, one-half month's interest expense has accrued. (The principal amount of this note is not due until April 30, 1997.)

l In recognizing interest expense on the 15% bonds payable, bond discount is amortized by the straight-line method.

m A public accountant has determined that the company's income taxes applicable to the quarter ended September 30 amount to $256,000, including $212,000 in taxes applicable to normal operations, and $44,000 in taxes resulting from the gain from the condemnation of land by the state government. The $44,000 in taxes relating to this gain should be debited to *account no. 600,* Gains on Disposals of Plant Assets, rather than to the Income Taxes Expense account.
   All income tax obligations will be paid within 90 days.

INSTRUCTIONS a Prepare general journal entries to record any of the transactions and events listed above that should be recorded in the accounting records of Shadow Mountain Corporation.

Next, post your journal entries to the general ledger accounts in the partially completed accounting work sheets (a supplement to the text). You will find the company's chart of accounts in the work sheets.

Remember, your accounting staff *already* has recorded and posted the routine transactions occurring during the quarter ended September 30. Entries summarizing the transactions recorded by your staff *already appear* in the general ledger accounts and are identified by the caption "Summary of entries posted by staff." After *you* post an entry to the ledger, enter the new balance of the ledger account.

b Prepare a 10-column work sheet for the *three months* ended September 30, 1996 using the information for end-of-period adjustments provided. (We have included in this work sheet a *correct and complete unadjusted trial balance* as of September 30, 1996. By comparing your September 30 account balances to the amounts shown, you may determine whether or not you have correctly completed the earlier portions of this problem.)

c Prepare the following financial statements:

1 An income statement for the three months ended September 30, 1996 using single-step format.

Your income statement is to include the *earnings per share figures* normally found in the income statement of a publicly owned corporation. (Round per-share amounts to the nearest cent. Fully diluted amounts are not required.)

2 A statement of retained earnings for the three months ended September 30, 1996.

3 A classified balance sheet as of September 30, 1996. Include a separate classification in your balance sheet for Intangible Assets, immediately following the Plant and Equipment section. For retained earnings, show only the ending balance as of September 30.

d Journalize and post the adjusting and closing entries.

e Prepare an after-closing trial balance as of September 30, 1996.

Applications of Present Value

Several chapters have included brief references to the concept of present value in discussions of the valuation of certain assets and liabilities. The purpose of this appendix is to discuss this concept more fully and also to demonstrate the use of present value tables as an aid to making present value computations. In addition, the appendix summarizes in one location the various applications of the present value concept that have been discussed throughout the book.

Learning Objectives

After studying this appendix you should be able to:

1 *Explain the concept of present value.*
2 *Identify the three factors that affect the present value of a future amount.*
3 *Compute the present value of a future amount and of an annuity using present value tables.*
4 *Discuss accounting applications of the present value concept.*

The Concept of Present Value

OBJECTIVE 1
Explain the concept of present value.

The concept of present value has many applications in accounting, but it is most easily explained in the context of evaluating investment opportunities. In this context, the present value of an expected future cash receipt is the amount that a knowledgeable investor would pay **today** for the right to receive that future amount. The present value is always **less** than the future amount, because the investor will expect to earn a return on the investment. The amount by which the future cash receipt exceeds its present value represents the investor's profit; in short, this difference may be regarded as **interest revenue** included in the future amount.

OBJECTIVE 2
Identify the three factors that affect the present value of a future amount.

The present value of a particular investment opportunity depends upon three factors: (1) the expected dollar amount to be received in the future, (2) the length of time until the future amount will be received, and (3) the rate of return (called the **discount rate**) required by the investor. The process of determining the present value of a future cash receipt or payment is called **discounting** the future amount.

To illustrate the present value concept, assume that a specific investment is expected to result in a $1,000 cash receipt at the end of one year. An investor requiring a 10% annual rate of return would be willing to pay $909 today (computed as $1,000 ÷ 1.10) for the right to receive this future amount. This computation may be verified as follows (amounts rounded to the nearest dollar):

Amount to be invested (present value)	$ 909
Required return on investment ($909 × 10%)...................................	91
Amount to be received in one year (future value)	$1,000

If the $1,000 is to be received **two years** in the future, the investor would pay only $826 for the investment today [($1,000 ÷ 1.10) ÷ 1.10]. This computation may be verified as follows (amounts rounded to the nearest dollar):

Amount to be invested (present value)	$ 826
Required return on investment in first year ($826 × 10%)........................	83
Amount invested after one year..	$ 909
Required return on investment in second year ($909 × 10%).....................	91
Amount to be received in two years (future value)	$1,000

The amount that our investor would pay today, $826, is the **present value** of $1,000 to be received two years later, discounted at an annual rate of 10%. The $174 difference between the $826 present value and the $1,000 future amount may be regarded as the return (interest revenue) to be earned by the investor over the two-year period.

Present Value Tables

Although we can compute the present value of future amounts by a series of divisions as illustrated above, a more convenient method is available. We can use a **table of present values** to find the present value of $1 at a specified discount rate and then multiply that value by the future amount. For example, in *Table 1* below, the present value of $1 to be received in two years, discounted at an annual rate of 10%, is ***$0.826.*** If we multiply .826 by the expected future cash receipt of $1,000, we get an answer of $826, the same amount produced by the series of divisions in our previous illustration.

TABLE 1
Present Values of $1 Due in *n* Periods*

Number of Periods (*n*)	Discount Rate								
	1%	1½%	5%	6%	8%	10%	12%	15%	20%
1	.990	.985	.952	.943	.926	.909	.893	.870	.833
2	.980	.971	.907	.890	.857	.826	.797	.756	.694
3	.971	.956	.864	.840	.794	.751	.712	.658	.579
4	.961	.942	.823	.792	.735	.683	.636	.572	.482
5	.951	.928	.784	.747	.681	.621	.567	.497	.402
6	.942	.915	.746	.705	.630	.564	.507	.432	.335
7	.933	.901	.711	.665	.583	.513	.452	.376	.279
8	.923	.888	.677	.627	.540	.467	.404	.327	.233
9	.914	.875	.645	.592	.510	.424	.361	.284	.194
10	.905	.862	.614	.558	.463	.386	.322	.247	.162
20	.820	.742	.377	.312	.215	.149	.104	.061	.026
24	.788	.700	.310	.247	.158	.102	.066	.035	.013
36	.699	.585	.173	.123	.063	.032	.017	.007	.001

˙ The present value of $1 is computed by the formula $p = 1/(1 + i)^n$, where p is the present value of $1, i is the discount rate, and n is the number of periods until the future cash flow will occur. Amounts in this table have been rounded to three decimal places and are shown for a limited number of periods and discount rates. Many calculators are programmed to use this formula and can compute present values when the future amount is entered along with values for i and n.

Selecting an Appropriate Discount Rate

The ***discount rate*** may be viewed as the investor's required rate of return. All investments involve some degree of risk that actual future cash flows may turn out to be less than expected. Investors usually will expect a rate of return that justifies taking this risk. Under today's market conditions, investors require annual returns of between 7% and 9% on low-risk investments, such as government bonds and term deposits. For relatively high-risk investments, such as the introduction of a new product line, investors may expect to earn an annual return of perhaps 15% or more.

In addition to the amount of risk involved, the "appropriate" discount rate for determining the present value of a specific investment depends upon the investor's cost of capital and the returns available from other investment opportunities. When a higher discount rate is used, the resulting present value will be lower and the investor, therefore, will be interested in the investment only at a lower price.

Discounting Annual Cash Flows

OBJECTIVE 3
Compute the
present
value of a
future
amount and
of an annu-
ity using
present
value tables.

Let us now assume that an investment is expected to produce an **annual net cash flow** of $10,000 in **each of the next three years.**[1] If Camino Company expects a 12% return on this type of investment, it may compute the present value of these cash flows as follows:

Year	Expected Net Cash Flow	×	Present Value of $1 Discounted at 12%	=	Present Value of Net Cash Flows
1	$10,000		.893		$ 8,930
2	10,000		.797		7,970
3	10,000		.712		7,120
Total present value of the investment					$24,020

This analysis indicates that the present value of the expected net cash flows from the investment, discounted at an annual rate of 12%, amounts to $24,020. This is the maximum amount that Camino Company could afford to pay for this investment and still expect to earn the 12% required rate of return.

In the preceding schedule, we multiplied each of the expected annual cash flows by the present value of $1 in the appropriate future period, discounted at 12% per year. The present values of the annual cash flows were then added to determine the total present value of the investment. Separately discounting each annual cash flow to its present value is neces- sary only when the cash flows vary in amount from one year to the next. Since the annual cash flows in our example are **uniform in amount,** there are two easier ways to compute the total present value.

One way is to add the three decimal figures representing the present value of $1 in the successive years (.893 + .797 + .712) and then to multi- ply this total (2.402) by the $10,000 annual cash flow. This approach pro- duces the same result ($10,000 × 2.402 = $24,020) we obtained by deter- mining the present value of each year's cash flow separately and adding the results.

An even easier approach to determining the present value of uniform annual cash flows is to refer to an **annuity table,** which shows the present value of **$1 to be received periodically** for a given number of periods. An annuity table appears on the following page and is labelled as **Table 2.**[2]

Note that the present value of $1 to be received periodically (annually) for three years, discounted at 12% per year, is **$2.402.** Thus, $10,000 re- ceived annually for three years, discounted at 12%, is **$24,020** ($10,000 × 2.402).

---

[1]   An "annual net cash flow" normally is the net result of a series of cash receipts and cash payments occurring throughout the year. For convenience, we follow the common practice of as- suming that the entire net cash flow for each year occurs at **year-end.** This assumption causes relatively little distortion and greatly simplifies computations.

[2]   This table assumes that the periodic cash flows occur at the **end** of each period.

TABLE 2
Present Values of $1 to Be Received Periodically for *n* Periods

Number of Periods (*n*)	Discount Rate								
	1%	1½%	5%	6%	8%	10%	12%	15%	20%
1	0.990	0.985	0.952	0.943	0.926	0.909	0.893	0.870	0.833
2	1.970	1.956	1.859	1.833	1.783	1.736	1.690	1.626	1.528
3	2.941	2.912	2.723	2.673	2.577	2.487	2.402	2.283	2.106
4	3.902	3.854	3.546	3.465	3.312	3.170	3.037	2.855	2.589
5	4.853	4.783	4.329	4.212	3.993	3.791	3.605	3.352	2.991
6	5.795	5.697	5.076	4.917	4.623	4.355	4.111	3.784	3.326
7	6.728	6.598	5.786	5.582	5.206	4.868	4.564	4.160	3.605
8	7.652	7.486	6.463	6.210	5.747	5.335	4.968	4.487	3.837
9	8.566	8.361	7.108	6.802	6.247	5.759	5.328	4.772	4.031
10	9.471	9.222	7.722	7.360	6.710	6.145	5.650	5.019	4.192
20	18.046	17.169	12.462	11.470	9.818	8.514	7.469	6.259	4.870
24	21.243	20.030	13.799	12.550	10.529	8.985	7.784	6.434	4.937
36	30.108	27.661	16.547	14.621	11.717	9.677	8.192	6.623	4.993

Discount Periods of Less Than One Year

The interval between regular periodic cash flows is termed the ***discount period.*** In our preceding examples we have assumed cash flows and, therefore, discount periods of one year. Often a note or a contract may call for cash payments on a more frequent basis, such as monthly, quarterly, or semiannually. The illustrated present value tables can be used with discount periods of any length, ***but the discount rate must relate to the time interval of the discount period.*** Thus, if we use the annuity table to find the present value of a series of equal monthly cash payments, the discount rate must be expressed as a monthly interest rate.

To illustrate, assume that StyleMart purchases merchandise from Western Fashions, issuing in exchange a $96,000 note payable to be paid in 24 monthly instalments of $4,000 each. Both companies should record this transaction at the present value of the note. If a reasonable ***annual*** interest rate for this type of note is 12%, we should discount the monthly cash payments at the ***monthly*** rate of *1%.* The annuity table shows the present value of $1 to be received (or paid) for 24 monthly periods, discounted at 1% per month, is 21.243. Thus, the present value of the instalment note issued by StyleMart is ***$84,972*** ($4,000 × 21.243).

ACCOUNTING APPLICATIONS OF THE PRESENT VALUE CONCEPT

Accounting applications of the concept of present value have been discussed at appropriate points throughout this textbook. We will now demon-

OBJECTIVE 4
Discuss ac-
counting
applications
of the pres-
ent value
concept.

strate these applications with examples that make use of our present value tables.

Valuation of Long-Term Notes Receivable and Payable (Chapters 8 and 11)

When a long-term note receivable or payable does not bear a realistic stated rate of interest, a portion of the face amount of the note should be regarded as representing an interest charge. The amount of this interest charge can be determined by discounting the note to its present value using as a discount rate a realistic rate of interest.

To illustrate, consider our preceding example in which StyleMart purchases merchandise from Western Fashions by issuing an instalment note payable with a face amount of $96,000 and no stated rate of interest. The present value of this note, discounted at the realistic market interest rate of 1% per month, was $84,972. The difference between the $96,000 face amount of the note and its present value of $84,972 is $11,028, which represents the interest charge included in the face amount.

StyleMart should use the **present value** of the note in determining the cost of the merchandise and the amount of the related net liability, as shown by the following entry:

The net liability is recorded at its present value

Inventory..	84,972	
Discount on Notes Payable	11,028	
Notes Payable		96,000

Purchased merchandise by issuing a 24-month instalment note payable with a 1% monthly interest charge included in the face amount.

The $11,028 discount represents the interest charges included in the face amount of the note. To determine how much of this discount will be recognized as interest expense each month, StyleMart should prepare an **amortization table** similar to the one illustrated in Chapter 11. This table will be based upon 24 monthly payments of $4,000, a monthly interest rate of 1%, and an original unpaid balance (principal amount) of $84,972. Therefore, the interest expense for the first month (rounded to the nearest dollar) will be $850 ($84,972 × 1%), and the remaining $3,150 ($4,000 payment, less $850 interest expense) will reduce the unpaid principal amount. Interest expense will decline in each successive month, as a result of the decline in the unpaid principal amount.

The entries to record the first $4,000 payment on the face amount of this note and the related monthly interest expense are illustrated below:

Notes Payable..	4,000	
Cash		4,000

To record $4,000 payment on a note payable.

Interest Expense	850	
Discount on Notes Payable		850

To record interest expense and amortize discount on an instalment note payable with interest included in the face amount (interest expense equal to unpaid principal amount, $84,972, times 1% monthly interest rate).

Capital Budgeting (Chapter 10)[3]

Capital budgeting is the process of planning and evaluating proposals for capital expenditures, such as the acquisition of plant assets or the introduction of a new product line. Perhaps the most widely used approach in the evaluation of proposed capital expenditures is ***discounting*** the expected future cash flows to their ***present value.***

Assume that Globe Mfg. Ltd. is considering a proposal to purchase new equipment in order to produce a new product. The equipment costs $400,000, has an estimated 10-year service life, and has an estimated salvage value of $50,000. Globe estimates that production and sale of the new product will increase the company's annual net cash flow by $100,000 per year for the next 10 years. If Globe requires a 15% annual rate of return on investments of this nature, the present value of these cash flows may be computed as shown below:

Present value of expected annual net cash inflows of $100,000 for 10 years,	
discounted at 15% per year: $100,000 × 5.019 (from Table 2, page 795)	**$501,900**
Present value of estimated salvage value to be received at the end of the tenth	
year: $50,000 × .247 (from Table 1, page 793)	12,350
Present value of estimated future cash inflows	**$514,250**
Less: *Amount to be invested (already a present value)*	400,000
Net present value of proposal	**$114,250**

This analysis indicates that the present value of the expected net cash flows from this investment, discounted at an annual rate of 15%, amounts to $514,250. This is the maximum amount that Globe could afford to invest in this project and still expect to earn the required 15% annual rate of return. As the cost of this investment is only $400,000, Globe can expect to earn more than its required 15% return.

The ***net present value*** of a proposal is the ***difference*** between the total present value of the future net cash flows and the cost of the investment. When the net present value is equal to zero, the investment provides a rate of return exactly equal to the rate used in discounting the cash flows. A ***positive*** net present value means that the investment provides a rate of return ***greater*** than the discount rate; a ***negative*** net present value means that the investment yields a return of ***less*** than the discount rate.

Since the discount rate usually is the minimum rate of return required by the investor, proposals with a positive net present value are considered acceptable, and those with a negative net present value are viewed as unacceptable.

Capital budgeting techniques are discussed further in courses in management accounting, cost accounting, and finance.

Estimating the Value of Goodwill (Chapter 10)

The asset goodwill may be defined as the present value of expected future earnings in excess of the normal return on net identifiable assets. One

---

[3]   Capital budgeting also is discussed in Chapter 26.

method of estimating goodwill is to estimate the annual amounts by which earnings are expected to exceed a normal return and then to discount these amounts to their present value.

To illustrate, assume that LiteHouse, a chain of restaurants, is negotiating to purchase Little Nell's, a highly profitable restaurant in Toronto. In addition to paying for the fair market value of Little Nell's net identifiable assets, LiteHouse is willing to pay an appropriate amount for goodwill. The management of LiteHouse estimates that Little Nell's will earn at least $80,000 in excess of "normal earnings" for this size restaurant in each of the next five years. If LiteHouse requires a 20% annual return on purchased goodwill, it can pay as much as $239,280 for this expected 5-year $80,000 annuity. [$80,000 × 2.991 (from Table 2) = $239,280.]

Market Prices of Bonds (Chapter 16)

The market price of bonds may be regarded as the ***present value*** to bondholders of the future principal and interest payments. To illustrate, assume that a corporation issues $1,000,000 face value of 10-year, 9% bonds when the going market rate of interest is 10%. Since bond interest generally is paid semiannually, we must use 20 ***semiannual*** periods as the life of the bond issue and a 5% ***semiannual*** market rate of interest in our present value calculations. The expected issuance price of this bond issue may be computed as follows:

Present value of future principal payments:
  $1,000,000 due after 20 semiannual periods, discounted at 5% per period:
  $1,000,000 × .377 (from Table 1, page 793) **$377,000**
Present value of future interest payments:
  $45,000 per period ($1,000,000 × 9% × ½) for 20 semiannual periods,
  discounted at 5%: $45,000 × 12.462 (from Table 2, page 795)   560,790
Expected issuance price of bond issue **$937,790**

Capital Lease (Chapter 16)

A capital lease is regarded as a sale of the leased asset by the lessor to the lessee. At the date of this sale, the lessor recognizes sales revenue equal to the ***present value*** of the future lease payments receivable, discounted at a realistic rate of interest. The lessee also uses the present value of the future payments to determine the cost of the leased asset and the valuation of the related liability.

To illustrate, assume that on December 1, Pace Tractor uses a ***capital lease*** to finance the sale of a tractor to Kelly Grading Co. The tractor was carried in Pace Tractor's perpetual inventory records at a cost of $15,000. Terms of the lease call for Kelly Grading Co. to make ***24*** monthly payments of ***$1,000*** each, beginning on December 31. These lease payments include an interest charge of ***1%*** per month. At the end of the 24-month lease, title to the tractor will pass to Kelly Grading Co. at no additional cost.

Accounting by the Lessor (Pace Tractor) ***Table 2*** shows that the present value of $1 to be received monthly for 24 months, discounted at 1% per month, is **21.243.** Therefore, the present value of the 24 future lease payments is $1,000 × 21.243, or **$21,243.** Pace Tractor should record this capital lease as a sale of the tractor at a price equal to the present value of the lease payments, as follows:

Lease Payment Receivable (net).............................	*21,243*	
Sales		*21,243*
Financed sale of a tractor to Kelly Grading Co. using a capital lease requiring 24 monthly payments of $1,000. Payments include a 1% monthly interest charge.		

Cost of Goods Sold	*15,000*	
Inventory		*15,000*
To record cost of tractor sold under capital lease.		

Notice that the sales price of the tractor is only $21,243, even though the gross amount to be collected from Kelly Grading Co. amounts to $24,000 ($1,000 × 24 payments). The difference between these two amounts, $2,757, will be recognized by Pace Tractor as interest revenue over the life of the lease.[4]

To illustrate the recognition of interest revenue, the entry on December 31 to record collection of the first monthly lease payment (rounded to the nearest dollar) is:

Cash..	*1,000*	
Interest Revenue		*212*
Lease Payments Receivable (net)		*788*
Received first lease payment from Kelly Grading Co.:		
Lease payment received	*$1,000*	
Interest revenue ($21,243 × 1%)	*(212)*	
Reduction in lease payments receivable	*$ 788*	

After this first monthly payment is collected, the present value of the lease payments receivable is reduced to $20,455 ($21,243 original balance, less $788). Therefore, the interest revenue earned during the **second** month of the lease (rounded to the nearest dollar) will be **$205** ($20,455 × 1%).[5]

Accounting by the Lessee (Kelly Grading Co.) Kelly Grading Co. also should use the present value of the lease payments to determine the cost of the tractor and the amount of the related liability, as shown below:

Leased Equipment..	*21,243*	
Lease Payment Obligation		*21,243*
To record acquisition of a tractor through a capital lease from Pace Tractor. Terms call for 24 monthly payments of $1,000, which include a 1% monthly interest charge.		

---

[4]   We have elected to record the present value of the future lease payments by a single debit entry to Lease Payments Receivable. An alternative is to debit Lease Payments Receivable for the total amount of the future payments and to credit Discount on Lease Payments Receivable, a contra-asset account, for the unearned finance charges included in the contractual amount. Either approach results in the lessor recording a net receivable equal to the present value of the future lease payments.

[5]   Both Pace Tractor and Kelly Grading Co. would prepare **amortization tables** showing the allocation of each lease payment between interest and the amount due.

The entry on December 31 to record the first monthly lease payment (rounded to the nearest dollar) is:

Interest Expense	*212*	
Lease Payment Obligation	*788*	
Cash		*1,000*
To record first monthly lease payment to Pace Tractor:		
Amount of payment	*$1,000*	
Interest expense ($21,243 × 1%)	*(212)*	
Reduction in lease payment obligation	*$ 788*	

ASSIGNMENT MATERIAL

PROBLEMS

PROBLEM 1
Using Present Value Tables

Use Tables 1 and 2 to determine the present value of the following cash flows.

a $10,000 to be paid annually for seven years, discounted at an annual rate of 10%. Payments are to occur at the end of each year.

b $7,500 to be received today, assuming that money can be invested to earn 15% annually.

c $350 to be paid monthly for 24 months, with an additional "balloon payment" of $15,000 due at the end of the twenty-fourth month, discounted at a monthly interest rate of $1\frac{1}{2}$%. The first payment is to be one month from today.

d $30,000 to be received annually for the first three years, followed by $20,000 to be received annually for the next two years (total of five years in which collections are received), discounted at an annual rate of 12%. Assume collections occur at year-end.

PROBLEM 2
Present Value and Bond Prices

On June 30 of the current year, Rural Gas & Electric Ltd. issued $10,000,000 face value, 11%, 10-year bonds payable, with interest dates of December 31 and June 30. The bonds were issued at a discount, resulting in an effective *semiannual* interest rate of 6%. The company maintains its accounts on a calendar-year basis and amortizes the bond discount by the effective interest method.

INSTRUCTIONS

a   Compute the issuance price for the bond issue that results in an effective semi-annual interest rate of 6%.

b   Prepare a journal entry to record the issuance of the bonds at the sales price you computed in part **a.**

PROBLEM 3
Valuation of a Note Payable

On December 1, Showcase Interiors purchased a shipment of furniture from Colonial House by paying $10,500 cash and issuing an instalment note payable in the face amount of $28,800. The note is to be paid in 24 monthly instalments of $1,200 each. Although the note makes no mention of an interest charge, the rate of interest usually charged to Showcase Interiors in such transactions is $1\frac{1}{2}$% per month.

INSTRUCTIONS

a   Compute the present value of the note payable, using a discount rate of $1\frac{1}{2}$% per month.

b   Prepare the journal entries in the accounts of Showcase Interiors on:

   1   December 1, to record the purchase of the furniture (debit Inventory).

   2   December 31, to record the first $1,200 monthly payment on the note and to recognize interest expense for one month by the effective interest method. (Round interest expense to the nearest dollar.)

c Show how the liability for this note would appear in the balance sheet at December 31. (Assume that the note is classified as a current liability.)

PROBLEM 4
Discounting Lease Agreements to Present Value

Metropolitan Transit District (MTD) plans to acquire a large computer system by entering into a long-term lease agreement with the computer manufacturer. The manufacturer will provide the computer system under either of the following lease agreements:

Five-year lease. MTD is to pay $2,500,000 at the beginning of the lease (delivery date) and $1,000,000 annually at the end of each of the next 5 years. At the end of the fifth year, MTD may take title to the system for an additional payment of $3,000,000.

Ten-year lease. MTD is to pay $2,000,000 at the beginning of the lease and $900,000 annually at the end of each of the next 10 years. At the end of the tenth year, MTD may take title for an additional payment of $1,300,000.

Under either proposal, MTD will buy the computer at the end of the lease. MTD is a governmental agency that does not seek to earn a profit and is not evaluating alternative investment opportunities. However, MTD does attempt to minimize its costs and it must borrow the money to finance either lease agreement at an annual interest rate of 10%.

INSTRUCTIONS

a Determine which lease proposal results in the lower cost for the computer system when the future cash outlays are discounted at an annual interest rate of 10%.

b Prepare a journal entry to record the acquisition of the computer system under the lowest cost lease agreement as determined in part **a.** (This journal entry will include the initial cash payment to the computer manufacturer required at the beginning of the lease.)

PROBLEM 5
Capital Leases: A Comprehensive Problem

Custom Truck Builders frequently uses long-term lease contracts to finance the sale of its trucks. On November 1, 1995, Custom Truck Builders leased to Central Van Lines a truck carried in the perpetual inventory records at $33,520. The terms of the lease call for Central Van Lines to make 36 monthly payments of $1,400 each, beginning on November 30, 1995. The present value of these payments, after considering a built-in interest charge of 1% per month, is equal to the regular $42,150 sales price of the truck. At the end of the 36-month lease, title to the truck will transfer to Central Van Lines.

INSTRUCTIONS

a Prepare journal entries for 1995 in the accounts of Custom Truck Builders on:

  1 November 1 to record the sale financed by the lease and the related cost of goods sold. (Debit Lease Payments Receivable for the $42,150 present value of the future lease payments.)

  2 November 30, to record receipt of the first $1,400 monthly payment. (Prepare a compound journal entry that allocates the cash receipt between interest revenue and reduction of Lease Payments Receivable. Round all interest computations to the nearest dollar.)

  3 December 31, to record receipt of the second monthly payment.

b Prepare journal entries for 1995 in the accounts of Central Van Lines on:

  1 November 1, to record acquisition of the leased truck.

  2 November 30, to record the first monthly lease payment. (Determine the portion of the payment representing interest expense in a manner parallel to that described in part **a.**)

3 December 31, to record the second monthly lease payment.

4 December 31, to recognize depreciation on the leased truck through year-end. Compute depreciation expense by the straight-line method, using a 10-year service life and an estimated salvage value of $6,150.

c Compute the net carrying value of the leased truck in the balance sheet of Central Van Lines at December 31, 1995.

d Compute the amount of Central Van Lines' lease payment obligation at December 31, 1995.

PROBLEM 6
Valuation of a Note Receivable with an Unrealistic Interest Rate

On December 31, Richland Farms sold a tract of land, which had cost $930,000, to Skyline Developers in exchange for $150,000 cash and a five-year, 4%, note receivable for $900,000. Interest on the note is payable annually, and the principal amount is due in five years. The accountant for Richland Farms did not notice the unrealistically low interest rate on the note and made the following entry on December 31 to record this sale:

Cash	*150,000*	
Notes Receivable	*900,000*	
Land		*930,000*
Gain on Sale of Land		*120,000*

Sold land to Skyline Developers in exchange for cash and a five-year note with interest due annually.

INSTRUCTIONS

a Compute the present value of the note receivable from Skyline Developers at the date of sale, assuming that a realistic rate of interest for this transaction is 12%.

b Prepare the journal entry on December 31 to record the sale of the land correctly. Show supporting computations for (1) the gain or loss on the sale and (2) the discount on the note receivable.

c Explain what effects the error made by Richland Farms' accountant will have upon (1) the net income in the year of the sale and (2) the combined net income of the next five years. Ignore income taxes.

17 Investments in Corporate Securities

In this chapter, we discuss investments in corporate securities (stocks and bonds) from the viewpoint of the investor. We first focus upon short-term investments in marketable securities—that is, highly liquid investments made primarily for the purpose of earning dividend or interest revenue. Next, we discuss long-term investments in common stock made for the purpose of exercising significant influence or control over the issuing corporation. We illustrate the equity method of accounting for these investments and explain how a parent company and its subsidiaries function as one economic entity. The chapter concludes with a discussion of consolidated financial statements.

Learning Objectives

After studying this chapter you should be able to:

1 Account for short-term investments in stocks and bonds.
2 Account for an investment in common stock by the equity method.
3 Explain how a parent company "controls" its subsidiaries.
4 Describe the distinctive feature of consolidated financial statements.
5 Explain why intercompany transactions must be eliminated as a step in preparing consolidated financial statements.
6 Prepare a consolidated balance sheet.

*T*he term ***corporate securities*** refers to the stocks and bonds issued by corporations. The securities issued by large, publicly owned corporations such as BCE, Inc., Canadian Pacific, and Alcan Aluminum are owned by literally millions of different investors. On the other hand, all of the common stock issued by a small, closely held corporation may be owned by one individual or by a small group of investors, such as the members of a family. From the investor's point of view, most investments in corporate securities fall into one of two broad categories: (1) investments in ***marketable securities*** and (2) investments for purposes of ***significant influence or control.***

INVESTMENTS IN MARKETABLE SECURITIES

Marketable securities consist primarily of government bonds and the bonds and stocks of large corporations. These securities are traded on organized securities exchanges, such as the Toronto Stock Exchange. Thus, they are easily purchased or sold at quoted market prices. Investments in marketable securities earn a return for the investor, yet are almost as liquid as cash itself. For this reason, marketable securities usually are listed in the balance sheet second among current assets, immediately after cash.

To qualify as a current asset, an investment in marketable securities must be readily marketable. ***Readily marketable*** means immediately salable at a quoted market price. In addition, management must be ***willing*** to use the invested funds to pay current liabilities or to use in current operations. Investments that are not readily marketable, or that management intends to hold on a long-term basis, are ***not*** current assets. Such investments should be shown in the balance sheet just below the current asset section under the caption Long-Term Investments.

Quoted Market Prices   The current market prices of most marketable securities are quoted daily by securities exchanges, by brokerage houses, and in the financial pages of major newspapers. The market prices of stocks are quoted in terms of dollars per share. As illustrated in Chapter 16, bond prices are stated as a percentage of the bond's maturity value, which usually is $1,000. Thus, a bond with a quoted price of **87** has a market value of **$870** ($1,000 × 87%).

Accounting for Marketable Securities

OBJECTIVE 1
Account for
short-term
investments
in stocks
and bonds.

Accounting differs somewhat between investments in marketable equity securities (stocks) and in marketable debt securities (bonds). The principal distinction in accounting for investments in stocks and in bonds is that ***interest on bonds accrues*** from day to day. An investor in bonds must account for this accrued interest when the bonds are purchased, at the end of each accounting period, and when the bonds are sold. Dividends on stock, however, ***do not accrue.*** For this reason, separate controlling accounts are used in the general ledger for each type of investment. For each controlling account, a subsidiary ledger is maintained, which shows for each security owned the acquisition date, total cost, number of shares (or bonds) owned, and the cost per share (or bond). This subsidiary ledger provides the information necessary to determine the amount of gain or loss when an investment in a particular stock or bond is sold.

Marketable Debt Securities (Bonds)

The amount of interest paid annually to bondholders is equal to a stated percentage of the bond's maturity value. Thus, the owner of a 10% bond receives $100 interest ($1,000 × 10%) every year. Since bond interest usually is paid semiannually, the bondholder receives two semiannual interest payments of $50 each.

When bonds are purchased between interest dates, the purchaser pays the quoted market price for the bond **plus** the interest accrued since the last interest payment date. By this arrangement the new owner becomes entitled to receive in full the next semiannual interest payment. An account called Bond Interest Receivable should be debited for the amount of accrued interest purchased.

To illustrate the accounting entries for an investment in bonds, assume that on August 1 an investor purchases ten 9%, $1,000 bonds of Rider Corporation that pay interest on June 1 and December 1. The investor buys the bonds on August 1 at a price of 99 (or $9,900), plus a brokerage commission of $50 and two months' accrued interest of $150 ($10,000 × 9% × $\frac{2}{12}$ = $150). The brokerage commission is viewed as part of the cost of the bonds. However, the accrued interest receivable at the time of purchase must be accounted for separately. Therefore, the journal entry made by the investor on August 1 is:

Separate account for accrued bond interest purchased	*Marketable Debt Securities*............................... *9,950*	
	Bond Interest Receivable *150*	
	Cash	*10,100*
	Purchased ten 9% bonds of Rider Corporation for $9,900 plus a brokerage commission of $50 and two months' accrued interest.	

On December 1, the semiannual interest payment date, the investor will receive an interest cheque for $450, which will be recorded as follows:

Note portion of interest cheque earned	*Cash*.. *450*	
	Bond Interest Receivable	*150*
	Bond Interest Revenue	*300*
	Received semiannual interest on Rider Corporation bonds.	

The $300 credit to Bond Interest Revenue represents the amount actually earned during the four months the bonds were owned by the investor (9% × $10,000 × $\frac{4}{12}$ = $300).

If the investor's accounting records are maintained on a calendar-year basis, the following adjusting entry is required at December 31 to record bond interest earned since December 1:

Bond Interest Receivable *75*		
Bond Interest Revenue		*75*
To accrue one month's interest earned (Dec. 1–Dec. 31) on Rider Corporation bonds ($10,000 × 9% × $\frac{1}{12}$ = $75).		

Amortization of Bond Discount or Premium from the Investor's Viewpoint

We have discussed the need for the corporation issuing bonds payable to amortize any bond discount or premium to measure correctly the bond interest expense. But what about the *purchaser* of the bonds? Should an investor in bonds amortize any difference between the cost of the investment and its future maturity value in order to measure investment income correctly? The answer to this question depends upon whether the investor considers the bonds to be a current asset (short-term investment) or a long-term investment.

When an investment in bonds is classified as a current asset, the investor usually *does not* amortize discount or premium. The justification for this practice is the accounting principle of *materiality.* Given that the investment may be held for but a short period of time, amortization of bond discount or premium probably will not have a material effect upon reported net income. When an investment in bonds will be held for the long term, however, the investor should amortize discount or premium. Amortization of a discount will increase the amount of interest revenue recognized by the investor; amortization of a premium will reduce the amount of interest revenue recognized.

Marketable Equity Securities (Stocks)

Since dividends on stock do not accrue, the *entire cost* of purchasing stock (including brokerage commissions) is debited to the Marketable Equity Securities account. Dividend revenue usually is recognized when the dividend cheque arrives; the entry consists of a debit to Cash and a credit to Dividend Revenue. No adjusting entries are needed to recognize dividend revenue at the end of an accounting period.

Additional shares of stock received in stock splits or stock dividends *are not income* to the shareholder, and only a *memorandum entry* is used to record the increase in the number of shares owned. The *cost basis per share* is decreased, however, because of the larger number of shares comprising the investment after receiving additional "free" shares from a stock split or a stock dividend.

As an example, assume that an investor purchases 100 shares of Delta Limited common stock at a total cost of $7,200, including commission. The investor's original cost basis is $72 per share ($7,200 ÷ 100 shares). Later the investor receives an additional 20 shares as the result of a 20% stock dividend. The investor's cost basis per share is thereby reduced to *$60* per share, computed by dividing the total cost of $7,200 by the *120* shares owned after the stock dividend. The memorandum entry to be made in the investor's general journal would be:

July 10   Memorandum: Received 20 additional shares of Delta Limited common stock as a result of 20% stock dividend. Now own 120 shares with a cost basis of $7,200, or $60 per share.

Gains and Losses from Sales of Investments

The sale of an investment in *stocks* is recorded by debiting Cash for the amount received and crediting the Marketable Equity Securities account for the cost of the securities sold. Any difference between the proceeds of the sale and the cost of the investment is recorded by a debit to Loss on Sale of Marketable Securities or by a credit to Gain on Sale of Marketable Securities.

At the day of sale of an investment in **bonds,** any interest that has accrued since the last interest payment date (or year-end) should be recognized as interest revenue. For example, assume that 10 bonds of the Elk Corporation carried in the accounts of an investor at $9,600 are sold at a price of **94,** plus accrued interest of **$90,** and less a brokerage commission of **$50.** The gain or loss may be computed as follows:

Proceeds from sale ($9,400 + $90 − $50)	$9,440
Less: Proceeds representing interest revenue	90
Sales price of investment in bonds..	$9,350
Cost of investment in bonds..	9,600
Loss on sale	$ 250

This sale should be recorded by the following journal entry:

<table>
<tr><td>**Investment in bonds sold at a loss**</td><td>Cash...
Loss on Sale of Marketable Securities.............................
    Marketable Debt Securities ....
    Bond Interest Revenue ....
Sold 10 bonds of Elk Corporation at 94 and accrued interest
of $90, less broker's commission of $50.</td><td>9,440
250</td><td>

9,600
90</td></tr>
</table>

Balance Sheet Valuation of Marketable Securities

The market values of securities such as bonds and stocks fluctuate from day to day. An investor who sells an investment in marketable securities at a price above or below cost will recognize a gain or loss on the sale. But what if the investor continues to hold securities after a significant change in their market value? In this case, should any gain or loss be recognized in the financial statements? The answer depends on whether the securities are short-term or long-term investments and whether the change in market value is temporary in nature.

Short-term marketable securities should be shown as a current asset in the balance sheet at the **lower** of their aggregate cost and market value. The effect of the **lower-of-cost-and-market** (LCM) rule is to recognize losses from drops in market value without recognizing gains from rising prices.

Marketable securities classified as long-term investments are accounted for in the balance sheet by either the cost method or the equity method. The **cost method** is used for long-term **portfolio investments** where the investor is not able to exercise significant influence over the investee. The account title for this type of investment is commonly called Marketable Securities—Long-Term. The **equity method** is used for those long-term investments where **the investor is able to exercise significant influence over the investee.** The common account title for this type of investment is Investment in X Corporation. When there is a decline in the market value of these long-term investments that is other than a temporary decline, these investments should be shown in the balance sheet at their lower market value. Consequently, a lower market value is also used for long-term investments if the decline in market value is not temporary in nature.

The lower-of-cost-and-market rule produces ***conservative results*** in both the balance sheet and the income statement. In the balance sheet, the investment in marketable securities is shown at the lowest justifiable amount—that is, the lower of its cost and market value. In the income statement, declines in market value below cost immediately are recognized as losses. Increases in market value above cost or the carrying value (if lower), however, are not recognized until the securities are sold.

Accountants traditionally have applied different criteria in recognizing gains and losses. One of the basic principles in accounting is that gains shall not be recognized until they are ***realized,*** and the usual test of realization is the sale of the asset in question. Losses, on the other hand, are recognized as soon as ***objective evidence*** indicates that a loss has been incurred.

Applying the Lower-of-Cost-and-Market Rule: An Illustration

In applying the lower-of-cost-and-market rule, the total cost of the marketable securities is compared with their current market value, and the ***lower*** of these two amounts is used as the balance sheet valuation. If the market value is below cost, an entry is made to reduce the carrying value of the marketable securities to current market value and to recognize a ***loss*** for the amount of the market decline. The write-down of an investment in marketable securities to a market value below cost is an end-of-period adjusting entry and should be based upon market prices at the balance sheet date.

To illustrate the lower-of-cost-and-market adjustment, assume the following facts for the investment of Eagle Corporation at December 31, 1996:

	Cost	Market Value
Common stock of Adams Corporation........................	$100,000	$106,000
Common stock of Barnes Limited	60,000	52,000
Preferred stock of Parker Industries.........................	200,000	182,000
Other marketable securities.................................	25,000	25,000
Totals..	$385,000	$365,000

Since the total market value of the securities in our example is less than their cost to Eagle Corporation, the balance sheet valuation would be the lower amount of $365,000. This downward adjustment of $20,000 means that a loss of $20,000 will be included in the determination of the year's net income. Also the $365,000 market value becomes the ***carrying value*** for these securities and is used as the "new cost" for future applications of the lower-of-cost-and-market rule. The balance sheet presentation would be:

Current assets:
  Marketable securities (at the lower of cost and market,
    cost—$385,000) $365,000

The significance of the carrying value deserves an explanation. Since the carrying value is considered to be the "new cost" for the marketable securities, if there is a further decline in market value, this carrying value will be adjusted to the lower market value.[1] However, if there is a recovery in market value, the recovery is not recognized because the market value is higher than the carrying value even though it is still lower than the original cost. For example, if the marketable securities of Eagle Corporation were held until December 31, 1997, and the market value were $380,000 (still $5,000 below the original cost of $385,000), these securities would be stated in the balance sheet at the carrying value of $365,000 because it is lower than the current market value of $380,000. Consequently, the recovery in market value of $15,000 was not recognized. This practice of not recognizing the recovery in the decline of market value below cost lacks logical support.

In the United States, the FASB recommended that for marketable equity securities such as common stock the recovery in the decline of market value below cost should be recognized. The decline and recovery in market value are considered as **unrealized loss** and **unrealized gain,** so as to distinguish them from a loss or a gain by an actual sale of securities. Based on the Eagle Corporation example, the $20,000 decline in market value would be recorded as follows:

1996

Dec. 31	*Unrealized Loss on Marketable Securities*	*20,000*	
	Valuation Allowance for Marketable Securities ...		*20,000*
	To reduce the cost of the investment in marketable equity securities to the lower of cost and market.		

The Valuation Allowance for Marketable Securities is a **contra-asset** account or **valuation** account. In the balance sheet, this valuation account is offset against the asset Marketable Securities in the same manner as the Allowance for Doubtful Accounts is offset against Accounts Receivable. The following partial balance sheet illustrates the use of the Valuation Allowance for Marketable Securities:

Current assets:

Marketable securities	*$385,000*	
Less: Valuation allowance for marketable securities	*20,000*	*365,000*

At the end of every period, the balance of the valuation account is adjusted so that marketable equity securities will be shown in the balance sheet at the lower of cost and current market value. If the valuation allowance must be increased because of further declines in market value, the adjusting entry will recognize an additional unrealized loss. On the other hand, if market prices have gone up since the last balance sheet date, the adjusting entry will reduce or eliminate the valuation allowance and recognize an **unrealized gain.**

To illustrate the adjustment of the valuation account, let us assume that by the end of 1997 the market value of Eagle Corporation's investment has **increased** to an amount greater than cost. Since market value is no longer below cost, the valuation allowance, which has a credit balance of $20,000, is no longer needed. Thus, the following entry would be made to eliminate the balance of the valuation allowance:

---

[1] CICA, *CICA Handbook* (Toronto), paragraph 3010.06.

Unrealized gain
cannot exceed
the former bal-
ance of the
valuation ac-
count

1997
Dec. 31 Valuation Allowance for Marketable Securities *20,000*
                Unrealized Gain on Marketable Securities *20,000*
            To increase the carrying value of marketable
            equity securities to original cost following recovery
            of market value.

Note that the amount of unrealized gain recognized is limited to the amount in the valuation account. ***Increases in market value above cost are not recognized in the accounting records.*** In brief, when marketable equity securities have been written down to the lower of cost and market, they can be written back up only ***to original cost*** if the market prices recover.

Because the valuation allowance is based upon a comparison of ***total*** cost and market value, the allowance cannot be directly associated with individual investments. The valuation allowance reduces the carrying value of the total investment but does not affect the individual carrying values of the investments. Lower-of-cost-and-market adjustments, therefore, have ***no effect*** upon the gain or loss recognized when an investment is sold. When specific securities are sold, the gain or loss realized from the sale is determined by comparing the ***cost*** of the securities (without regard to lower-of-cost-and-market adjustments) to their selling price.[2]

Presentation of Marketable Securities in Financial Statements

Gains and losses from the decline in market value of marketable securities or on the sale of marketable securities, as well as interest and dividend revenue, are types of nonoperating income. These items should be specifically identified in the income statement and shown after the determination of operating income.

Those marketable securities classified as current assets should be presented in the balance sheet at the lower of cost and market; those classified as long-term investments should be presented in the balance sheet at cost, unless the decline in market value is permanent, in which case the lower of cost and market should be used.

We mentioned earlier that separate controlling accounts are usually used in the general ledger for marketable equity securities and marketable debt securities. In the balance sheet, however, these two types of investments are combined and shown under a single caption, such as ***Marketable Securities.***

Presentation of Investments That Are Not Readily Marketable   Securities
issued by small businesses may not be traded on securities exchanges and, therefore, may not have quoted market prices. These securities are not

---

[2]   The reader may notice that a decline in the market value of securities owned could be reported in the income statement on two separate occasions: first, as an unrealized loss in the period in which the price decline occurs; and second, as a realized loss in the period in which the securities are sold. However, after securities with market values below cost have been sold, the valuation allowance may be reduced or eliminated. The entry to reduce the valuation allowance involves the recognition of an unrealized gain, which offsets the unrealized losses reported in earlier periods.

"readily marketable"; an investor owning such securities should classify the investment as long-term, rather than as a current asset. Also, such investments should be identified as "Other Long-Term Investments," rather than as marketable securities. As these securities do not have quoted market prices, the lower-of-cost-and-market rule is not applied. These investments normally are shown in the investor's balance sheet at *cost.*[3]

INVESTMENTS FOR PURPOSES OF SIGNIFICANT INFLUENCE OR CONTROL

An investor may acquire enough of a company's common stock to *significantly influence or control* that company's strategic operating, investing, and financing policies through the voting rights of the shares owned. Such large holdings of common stock create an important business relationship between the investor and the issuing company (called the *investee*). Since investments of this type cannot be sold without disrupting this relationship, they are not included in the portfolio of marketable securities. Such investments are shown in the investor's balance sheet under the caption Long-Term Investments and are accounted for quite differently from an investment in marketable securities.

If an investor is able to exercise *significant influence* over the investee's management, dividends paid by the investee may no longer be a good measure of the investor's income from the investment. This is because the investor may influence the investee's dividend policy. In such cases, dividends paid by the investee are likely to reflect the *investor's* cash needs and income tax considerations, rather than the profitability of the investment.

For example, assume that Sigma Corporation owns 49% of the common stock of Davis Limited. For three years Davis is very profitable but pays no dividends, because Sigma has no need for additional cash. In the fourth year, Davis pays a large cash dividend to Sigma despite operating at a loss for that year. Clearly, it would be misleading for Sigma to report no investment income while the company it owns is operating profitably, and then to show large investment income in a year when Davis incurred a net loss.

The investor does not have to own 49% of the common stock of the investee to exercise a significant degree of influence. An investor with much less than 49% of the voting stock may have significant influence, since the remaining shares are not likely to vote as an organized block. In the absence of other evidence (such as another large shareholder), ownership of *20% or more* (but below 50%) of the investee's common stock is viewed as giving the investor significant influence over the investee's policies and operations. In such cases, the investor should account for the investment by using the *equity method.*[4]

---

[3] As with any asset valued at cost, the asset should be written down to an estimated recoverable amount if it becomes apparent that the original cost cannot be recovered.

[4] CICA, *CICA Handbook* (Toronto), section 3050.06.

The Equity Method

OBJECTIVE 2
*Account for
an invest-
ment in com-
mon stock by
the equity
method.*

When the equity method is used, an investment in common stock is first recorded at cost but later is adjusted each year for changes in the shareholders' equity in the investee. As the investee earns net income, the shareholders' equity in the company increases. An investor using the equity method recognizes its ***proportionate share of the investee's net income*** as an increase in the carrying value of its investment. A proportionate share of a net loss reported by the investee is recognized as a decrease in the investment.

When the investee pays dividends, the shareholders' equity in the company is reduced. The investor, therefore, treats dividends received from the investee as a conversion of part of the investment into cash, thus reducing the carrying value of the investment. In effect, the equity method causes the carrying value of the investment (the amount reported in the balance sheet) to rise and fall with changes in the book value of the shares. As mentioned earlier, if the market value is lower than cost (or carrying value) and the decline is not temporary, the lower market value should be used.[5]

Illustration of the Equity Method   Assume that Cove Corporation purchases 10,000 shares (25%) of the common stock of Bay Limited for $200,000, which corresponds to 25% of the underlying book value of Bay. During the following year, Bay earns net income of $120,000 and pays dividends of $80,000. Cove Corporation would account for its investment as follows:

Investment in Bay Limited	*200,000*	
Cash		*200,000*
To record acquisition of 25% of the common stock of Bay Limited.		

Investment in Bay Limited	*30,000*	
Investment Income		*30,000*
To increase the investment for 25% share of net income earned by Bay Limited (25% × $120,000).		

Cash..	*20,000*	
Investment in Bay Limited		*20,000*
To reduce investment for dividends received from Bay Limited (25% × $80,000).		

The net result of these entries by Cove Corporation is to increase the carrying value of the Investment in Bay Limited account by $10,000, to $210,000. This corresponds to 25% of the increase reported in Bay Limited's retained earnings during the period [25% × ($120,000 − $80,000) = $10,000]. Cove Corporation ***reports in its balance sheet*** the investment in Bay Limited at $210,000 under the caption Long-Term Investments.

In this illustration of the equity method, we have made several simplifying assumptions: (1) Cove Corporation purchased the stock of Bay Limited at a price equal to the underlying book value; (2) Bay Limited had issued common stock only and the number of shares outstanding did not

---

[5]   Ibid., section 3050.25.

change during the year; and (3) there were no intercompany transactions between Cove Corporation and Bay Limited. If we were to change any of these assumptions, the computations in applying the equity method would become more complicated. Application of the equity method in more complex situations is discussed in advanced accounting courses.

Parent and Subsidiary Companies

OBJECTIVE 3
Explain how
a parent
company
"controls"
its subsidi-
aries.

A corporation that owns **all or a majority** of another corporation's outstanding voting stock is called a **parent** company, and the corporation that is wholly owned or majority-held is called a **subsidiary**.[6] Through the voting rights of the owned shares, the parent company can elect the board of directors of the subsidiary company and thereby control the subsidiary's resources and policies. In effect, the **affiliated companies** (the parent and its subsidiaries) function as a **single economic unit** controlled by the directors of the parent company. This relationship is illustrated in the following diagram.

PARENT COMPANY AND TWO SUBSIDIARIES

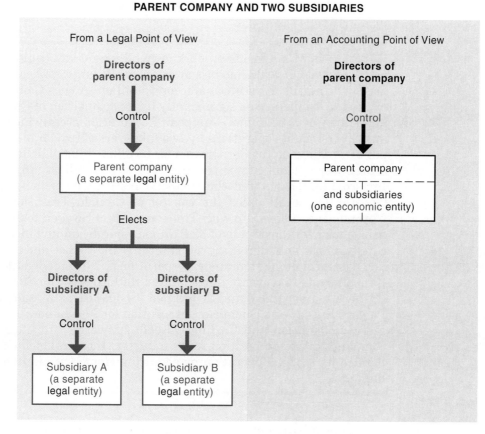

For simplicity, our illustration shows a parent company with only two subsidiaries. It is not unusual, however, for a parent company to own and control a dozen or more subsidiaries.

---

[6] Ownership of a majority of a company's voting stock means holding at least 50% plus one share.

There are a number of economic, legal, and income tax advantages that encourage large business organizations to operate through subsidiaries rather than through a single legal entity. Although we think of BCE, Inc., Canadian Pacific, or George Weston Ltd. as single companies, each of these organizations is really a parent company with many subsidiaries. Since the parent company in each case controls the resources and policies of its subsidiaries, it is logical for us to consider an organization such as BCE (which owns 100% of Bell Canada) as one *economic* entity.

Growth through the Acquisition of Subsidiaries

A parent company may acquire another corporation as a subsidiary by purchasing more than 50% of the other corporation's voting stock. The purchase of one corporation by another may be termed a *merger,* a *business combination,* an *acquisition,* or a *takeover.* The acquisition of new subsidiaries is a fast and effective way for a company to grow, to diversify into new product lines, and to acquire new technology. In recent years, the price tag for these acquisitions and mergers has run into billions of dollars.

CASE IN POINT   Just a few well-known billion-dollar acquisitions or mergers: Imperial Oil reaffirmed its position as the largest oil company in Canada by acquiring Texaco Canada for $5 billion. Amoco Canada Petroleum expanded its operations significantly by its acquisition of Dome Petroleum for slightly over $5 billion. Campeau Corporation greatly increased its size and diversified its operations by two takeovers of two large American companies—Allied Stores Corporation for $5 billion ($3.6 billion U.S.) and Federated Department Stores Incorporated at $8.2 billion ($6.6 billion U.S.). Imasco Limited entered the financial institution business by acquiring Genstar Corporation for the control of Canada Trust for $2.6 billion. Noranda Inc. teamed up with Trelleborg AB of Sweden to acquire Falconbridge for a total price tag of $2.2 billion, thereby adding nickel as another core business and increasing substantially the copper and zinc production and reserves. Stone Container Corporation (U.S) extended its operation to Canada by its takeover of Consolidated Bathurst Inc. for $2.6 billion. Nova Corporation expanded and diversified its operations by the acquisition of Polysar Energy and Chemical Corporation for $1.4 billion. The $1.6 billion merger of Molson and Carling O'Keefe Breweries propelled the merged company to the top position in its industry. Interprovincial Pipe Line expanded its scope of operation by acquiring Home Oil Limited for $1.1 billion.

The acquisition of one corporation by another is, perhaps, the largest and most interesting of all business transactions. Such transactions may involve billions of dollars, bidding wars among prospective buyers, and dramatic increases in the value of a sought-after company's capital stock. Sometimes a company borrows vast amounts of money and acquires a corporation much larger than itself, thus doubling or tripling the size of the parent company overnight.

Financial Statements for a Consolidated Economic Entity

OBJECTIVE 4
Describe the
distinctive
feature of
consolidated
financial
statements.

Because the parent company and its subsidiaries are separate legal entities, separate financial statements are prepared for each company. In the **separate** financial statements of the parent company, the subsidiaries appear only as assets classified as long-term investments. Since the affiliated companies function as a single economic unit, the parent company also prepares **consolidated financial statements** that show the financial position and operating results of the **entire group of companies.**[7] It is these consolidated financial statements that are of greatest interest to the investing public and that are included in the parent company's annual report to its shareholders.

In consolidated financial statements, the parent company and its subsidiaries are viewed as **one economic** or **business entity.** The distinctive feature of these statements is that the assets, liabilities, revenue, and expenses of **two or more separate legal entities** are combined in a single set of financial statements. For example, the amount shown as cash in a consolidated balance sheet is the total of the cash owned by all of the affiliated companies. Liabilities of the parent and subsidiary companies also are combined. Similarly, in a consolidated income statement, the revenue and expenses of the affiliated companies are combined to show the operating results of the consolidated economic entity.

Shareholders and creditors of the parent company have a vital interest in the financial results of all operations under the parent company's control, including those conducted by subsidiaries. Therefore, it is the consolidated financial statements that are included in the parent company's annual and quarterly reports to shareholders.

There are many interesting accounting issues involved in the preparation of consolidated financial statements. A brief introduction to some of these issues is provided in the following section of this chapter. However, **no special problems are posed in reading a set of consolidated financial statements.** The number of separate legal entities within the consolidated organization is an unimportant detail. For most purposes, consolidated financial statements may be interpreted as if the parent company and its subsidiaries **were just one organization.**

CONSOLIDATED FINANCIAL STATEMENTS: CONCEPTS AND MECHANICS

Methods of Consolidation

The purchase of an entire corporation usually is a very big investment. To accumulate the money necessary to buy another corporation, the parent company often needs to issue capital stock or bonds payable. If the parent

---

[7]   In the past, some subsidiaries were omitted from the consolidated financial statements for such reasons as the subsidiaries being engaged in business activities substantially different from those of the parent company. New rules, however, require every subsidiary controlled by the parent company to be included in the consolidated statements unless this control will be temporary. In this case, the investment in the subsidiary is shown in the balance sheet at cost and is classified as a long-term investment; dividends received are recorded as revenue.

company pays cash or issues debt securities to purchase the other corporation's capital stock, the business combination is accounted for by the ***purchase method.***

A second method of accounting for a business combination is called a ***pooling of interests.*** The pooling method may be appropriate if the stock of a subsidiary is obtained in direct exchange for shares of the parent company's capital stock and neither company can be identified as the acquirer.[8] A key aspect of such a transaction is that the former shareholders of the subsidiary ***become shareholders in the parent corporation.*** The vast majority of business combinations are viewed as purchases, rather than poolings. In this textbook, we shall illustrate only the purchase method of accounting for business combinations. The special case of a pooling of interests will be covered in more advanced accounting courses.

Consolidated financial statements are prepared by combining the amounts that appear in the separate financial statements of the parent and subsidiary companies. In the combining process, however, certain adjustments are made to ***eliminate the effects of intercompany transactions*** and thus to reflect the assets, liabilities, and shareholders' equity as those of a single economic entity.

Intercompany Transactions   The term ***intercompany transactions*** refers to transactions between affiliated companies. These transactions may include, for example, the sale of merchandise, the leasing of property, and the making of loans. When the affiliated companies are viewed separately, these transactions may create assets and liabilities for the individual companies. However, when the affiliated companies are viewed as a single business entity, these assets and liabilities are merely the result of internal transfers within the business organization and should ***not appear*** in the consolidated financial statements.

For example, if a subsidiary borrows money from the parent company, a note payable will appear as a liability in the balance sheet of the subsidiary company and a note receivable will appear as an asset in the separate balance sheet of the parent. When the two companies are viewed as a single consolidated entity, however, this "loan" is nothing more than a transfer of cash from one part of the business to another. Transferring assets between two parts of a single business entity does not create either a receivable or a payable for that entity. Therefore, the parent company's note receivable and the subsidiary's note payable should not appear in the consolidated financial statements.

Preparing Consolidated Financial Statements   Separate accounting records are maintained for each company in an affiliated group, but no accounting records are maintained for the consolidated entity. The amounts shown in consolidated financial statements ***do not come from a ledger;*** they are determined on a ***working paper*** by combining the amounts of like items on the financial statements of the affiliated companies. For example, the inventories of all the affiliated companies are combined into one amount for inventories. Entries to eliminate the effects of intercompany

OBJECTIVE 5
Explain why intercompany transactions must be eliminated as a step in preparing consolidated financial statements.

8   CICA, *CICA Handbook* (Toronto), section 1580.08.

transactions are made *only* on this working paper. These elimination entries are *not recorded in the accounting records* of either the parent company or its subsidiaries.

Consolidation at the Date of Acquisition

OBJECTIVE 6
Prepare a
consolidated
balance
sheet.

To illustrate the basic principles of consolidation, we will now prepare a consolidated balance sheet. Assume that on January 1 Post Corporation purchases for cash 100% of the capital stock of Sun Limited at its book value of $3,000,000. (The shares are purchased from Sun's former shareholders.) Also on this date, Post Corporation lends $200,000 cash to Sun, receiving a note as evidence of the loan. Immediately after these two transactions, the separate balance sheet accounts of Post Corporation and Sun Limited are as shown in the first two columns of the following working paper:

POST CORPORATION AND SUBSIDIARY
Working Paper—Consolidated Balance Sheet
January 1, 19___ (Date of Acquisition)

	Post Corpo-ration	Sun Limited	Intercompany Eliminations		Consol-idated Balance Sheet
			Debit	Credit	
Cash & cash equivalents	500,000	350,000			850,000
Notes receivable	200,000			(b) 200,000	—
Accounts receivable (net).....	300,000	400,000			700,000
Inventories	1,100,000	950,000			2,050,000
Investment in Sun Limited	3,000,000			(a) 3,000,000	—
Plant & equipment (net).......	2,800,000	1,800,000			4,600,000
Totals....................	7,900,000	3,500,000			8,200,000
Notes payable...............		200,000	(b) 200,000		—
Accounts payable	425,000	300,000			725,000
Capital stock—					
Post Corporation	4,000,000				4,000,000
Sun Limited		2,000,000	(a) 2,000,000		—
Retained earnings—					
Post Corporation	3,475,000				3,475,000
Sun Limited		1,000,000	(a) 1,000,000		—
Totals....................	7,900,000	3,500,000	3,200,000	3,200,000	8,200,000

Explanation of elimination:
(a) To eliminate the Investment in Sun Limited against Sun Limited's shareholders' equity.
(b) To eliminate intercompany note receivable against related note payable.

Intercompany Eliminations

Before the balance sheet amounts of Post Corporation and Sun Limited are combined, entries are made in the working paper to eliminate the effects of intercompany transactions. Intercompany eliminations may be classified into three basic types:

1 Elimination of intercompany stock ownership
2 Elimination of intercompany debt
3 Elimination of intercompany revenue and expenses

The first two types of eliminations are illustrated in our example of Post Corporation and Sun Limited. The elimination of intercompany revenue and expenses will be discussed later in this chapter.

To understand the need for elimination entries, we must adopt the viewpoint of the consolidated entity, in which Post Corporation and Sun Limited are regarded as two business operations within a single company.

Entry (a): Elimination of Intercompany Stock Ownership The purpose of entry (*a*) in the working paper on page 817 is to eliminate from the consolidated balance sheet both the asset account and the shareholders' equity accounts representing the parent company's ownership of the subsidiary.

Post Corporation's ownership interest in Sun Limited appears in the ***separate*** balance sheets of both corporations. In the parent's balance sheet, this ownership interest is shown as the asset Investment in Sun Limited. In the separate balance sheet of the subsidiary, the parent company's ownership interest is represented by the shareholders' equity accounts Capital Stock and Retained Earnings. In the ***consolidated*** balance sheet, however, this "ownership interest" is neither an asset nor a part of shareholders' equity.

From the viewpoint of the single consolidated entity, ***there are no shareholders in Sun Limited.*** "Shareholders" are outside investors who have an ownership interest in the business. All of Sun's capital stock is "internally owned" by another part of the consolidated entity. A company's "ownership" of its own stock does not create either an asset or shareholders' equity. Therefore the asset account Investment in Sun Limited and Sun Limited's related shareholders' equity accounts must be eliminated from the consolidated balance sheet.

Entry (b): Elimination of Intercompany Debt When Post Corporation loaned $200,000 to Sun Limited, the parent company recorded a note receivable and the subsidiary recorded a note payable. This "receivable" and "payable" exist only when Post Corporation and Sun Limited are viewed as two separate entities. When both corporations are viewed as a single company, this "loan" is merely a transfer of cash from one part of the business to another. Such internal transfers of assets do not create either a receivable or a payable for the consolidated entity. Therefore, entry (*b*) is made to eliminate Post Corporation's note receivable and Sun Limited's note payable from the consolidated balance sheet.

After the necessary eliminations have been entered in the working paper, the remaining balance sheet amounts of Post Corporation and Sun Limited are combined to determine the assets, liabilities, and shareholders' equity of the consolidated entity. The following consolidated balance sheet is then prepared from the last column of the working paper.

POST CORPORATION AND SUBSIDIARY
Consolidated Balance Sheet
January 1, 19__

Assets

Current assets:

Cash & cash equivalents		$ 850,000
Accounts receivable (net)		700,000
Inventories		2,050,000
Total current assets		$3,600,000
Plant & equipment (net)		4,600,000
Total assets		$8,200,000

Liabilities & Shareholders' Equity

Current liabilities:

Accounts payable		725,000
Shareholders' equity:		
Capital stock	$4,000,000	
Retained earnings	3,475,000	
Total shareholders' equity		7,475,000
Total liabilities & shareholders' equity		$8,200,000

Notice the shareholders' equity is that of the parent company

Acquisition of Subsidiary's Stock at a Price above Book Value

When a parent company purchases a controlling interest in a subsidiary, it usually pays a price for the shares *in excess of* their book value.[9] We cannot ignore a difference between the cost of the parent company's investment and the underlying book value of these shares. In consolidation, the parent's investment is offset against the shareholders' equity accounts of the subsidiary, and if the two amounts are not equal, we must determine what the difference between them represents.

To illustrate, let's use the preceding example with one significant change. Assume that on January 1 Post Corporation purchases all of the outstanding shares of Sun Limited for $3,400,000 instead of $3,000,000. On this date, Sun Limited's balance sheet shows total shareholders' equity of $3,000,000, consisting of capital stock of $2,000,000 and retained earnings of $1,000,000. In preparing the elimination entry on the working papers for a consolidated balance sheet, we must determine what to do with the $400,000 difference between the price paid, $3,400,000, and the shareholders' equity (book value) of Sun Limited, $3,000,000.

Why would Post Corporation pay a price in excess of book value for Sun Limited's stock? Post's management must believe that either (1) the fair market value of certain specific assets of Sun (such as land or buildings) is in excess of book value or (2) Sun's future earnings prospects are so favourable as to justify paying $400,000 for Sun's unrecorded *goodwill.*

If we assume that the $400,000 represents unrecorded goodwill, entry

---

[9] The parent company also might acquire the shares of the subsidiary at a price below book value. This situation will be discussed in an advanced accounting course.

(*a*) in the working papers to eliminate Post Corporation's investment account against the shareholders' equity accounts of Sun Limited would be:

Note: This	*Capital Stock—Sun Limited*	*2,000,000*
entry is made	*Retained Earnings—Sun Limited*	*1,000,000*
only in the	*Goodwill*	*400,000*
working pa-	*Investment in Sun Limited (Post Corporation's*	
pers, not in the	*asset account)*	*3,400,000*
accounting	*To eliminate the cost of Post Corporation's 100% interest*	
records of ei-	*in Sun Limited against Sun's shareholders' equity*	
ther company	*accounts and to recognize Sun Limited's unrecorded*	
	goodwill.	

Although we have shown this entry in general journal form, it actually would be made **only** in the Intercompany Eliminations columns of the working paper for a consolidated balance sheet, as illustrated below:

POST CORPORATION AND SUBSIDIARY
Working Paper—Consolidated Balance Sheet
January 1, 19__ (Date of Acquisition)

	Post Corpo- ration	Sun Limited	Intercompany Eliminations		Consol- idated Balance Sheet
			Debit	*Credit*	
Cash & cash equivalents	*100,000*	*350,000*			*450,000*
Notes receivable	*200,000*			*(b) 200,000*	—
Accounts receivable (net)	*300,000*	*400,000*			*700,000*
Inventories	*1,100,000*	*950,000*			*2,050,000*
Investment in Sun Limited	*3,400,000*			*(a) 3,400,000*	
Plant & equipment (net)	*2,800,000*	*1,800,000*			*4,600,000*
Goodwill			*(a) 400,000*		*400,000*
Totals	*7,900,000*	*3,500,000*			*8,200,000*
Notes payable		*200,000*	*(b) 200,000*		—
Accounts payable	*425,000*	*300,000*			*725,000*
Capital stock—					
Post Corporation	*4,000,000*				*4,000,000*
Sun Limited		*2,000,000*	*(a) 2,000,000*		
Retained earnings—					
Post Corporation	*3,475,000*				*3,475,000*
Sun Limited		*1,000,000*	*(a) 1,000,000*		
Totals	*7,900,000*	*3,500,000*	*3,600,000*	*3,600,000*	*8,200,000*

Explanation of elimination:
(a)   To eliminate the Investment in Sun Limited against Sun Limited's shareholders' equity, and to recognize goodwill.
(b)   To eliminate intercompany note receivable against related note payable.

The following consolidated balance sheet is then prepared from the last column of the working paper. It is important to note that the $400,000 of goodwill will appear as an asset only in the **consolidated** balance sheet, *not* in the accounting records of Sun Limited or Post Corporation.[10] This asset will be amortized to expense over its useful life.

POST CORPORATION AND SUBSIDIARY
Consolidated Balance Sheet
January 1, 19__

Assets

Current assets:

Cash & cash equivalents		$ 450,000
Accounts receivable (net)		700,000
Inventories		2,050,000
Total current assets		$3,200,000
Plant & equipment (net)		4,600,000
Goodwill		400,000
Total assets		$8,200,000

Liabilities & Shareholders' Equity

Current liabilities:

Accounts payable		725,000
Shareholders' equity:		
Capital stock	$4,000,000	
Retained earnings	3,475,000	
Total shareholders' equity		7,475,000
Total liabilities & shareholders' equity		$8,200,000

Notice that goodwill appears only in the consolidated balance sheet

Less Than 100% Ownership in Subsidiary

If a parent company owns a majority interest in a subsidiary but less than 100% of the outstanding shares, a new kind of ownership equity known as the ***non-controlling (minority) interest*** will appear in the consolidated balance sheet. This non-controlling interest represents the ownership interest in the subsidiary held by shareholders other than the parent company.

When there are non-controlling (minority) shareholders, only the portion of the subsidiary's shareholders' equity owned by the parent company is eliminated. The remainder of the shareholders' equity of the subsidiary is included in the consolidated balance sheet under the caption Non-controlling Interest.

To illustrate, assume that on January 1 Park Limited purchases 75% of the outstanding capital stock of Sims Corporation for $150,000 cash, an amount equal to 75% of the book value (shareholders' equity) of Sims. The working paper to prepare a consolidated balance sheet on the date that control of Sims Corporation is acquired appears as follows:

---

[10] If specific assets of Sun Limited had been undervalued, the $400,000 would be allocated to increase the valuation of those assets in the consolidated working papers. The revaluation of specific assets is beyond the scope of our introductory discussion.

PARK LIMITED AND SUBSIDIARY
Working Paper—Consolidated Balance Sheet
January 1, 19__ (Date of Acquisition)

	Park Limited	Sims Corporation	Intercompany Eliminations		Consolidated Balance Sheet
			Debit	Credit	
Cash.........................	200,000	50,000			250,000
Other assets	500,000	210,000			710,000
Investment in Sims Corporation	150,000			(a) 150,000	
Totals.....................	850,000	260,000			960,000
Liabilities	250,000	60,000			310,000
Capital stock—					
Park Limited	500,000				500,000
Sims Corporation..........		120,000	(a) 90,000 (b) 30,000		
Retained earnings—					
Park Limited	100,000				100,000
Sims Corporation..........		80,000	(a) 60,000 (b) 20,000		
Non-controlling interest (25% of $200,000)...................				(b) 50,000	50,000
Totals.....................	850,000	260,000	200,000	200,000	960,000

Explanation of elimination:
(a)   To eliminate Park Limited's investment in 75% of Sims Corporation's shareholders' equity.
(b)   To classify the remaining 25% of Sims Corporation's shareholders' equity as a non-controlling interest.

Entry (a) in this working paper offsets Park's asset, Investment in Sims Corporation, against 75% of Sims Corporation's capital stock and retained earnings. The purpose of this entry is to eliminate intercompany stock ownership from the assets and shareholders' equity shown in the consolidated balance sheet. Entry (b) reclassifies the remaining 25% of Sims Corporation's capital stock and retained earnings into a special account entitled Non-controlling Interest. The CICA recommends that the non-controlling interest appear separately from the shareholders' equity section of the consolidated balance sheet usually between total liabilities and shareholders' equity.[11]

Non-Controlling Interest   Why is the non-controlling interest shown separately in the consolidated balance sheet instead of being included in the amounts shown for capital stock and retained earnings? The reason for this separate presentation is to distinguish between the ownership equity of the controlling shareholders and the equity of the non-controlling shareholders.

The shareholders in the parent company own the controlling interest in the consolidated entity. Because these shareholders elect the directors of the parent company, they control the entire group of affiliated companies.

---

[11]   CICA, *CICA Handbook* (Toronto), section 1600.69.

The non-controlling interest, however, has **no control** over any of the affiliated companies. Because they own shares only in a subsidiary, they cannot vote for the directors of the parent company. Also, they can never outvote the parent shareholder (the parent company) in electing the directors or establishing the policies of the subsidiary.

The non-controlling shareholders receive 25% of the dividends declared by Sims but do not participate in dividends declared by the parent company. The controlling shareholders, on the other hand, receive all the dividends declared by Park but do not receive directly dividends declared by the subsidiary.

Consolidated Income Statement

At date of acquisition of a controlling interest, the consolidated balance sheet is the only appropriate financial statement, as no revenue or expenses have yet occurred. Once operations begin, however, a complete set of four corporate financial statements is required: consolidated income statement, consolidated statement of retained earnings, consolidated balance sheet, and consolidated statement of changes in financial position. We shall discuss briefly some of the basic concepts involved in the preparation of a consolidated income statement.

A **consolidated income statement** is prepared simply by combining the revenue and expense accounts of the parent and subsidiary. Revenue or expenses that are the result of **intercompany transactions** are eliminated because they do not change the net assets from a consolidated viewpoint—they merely reflect transfers of assets from one affiliated company to another. Assume a subsidiary pays $12,000 to its parent company for rent of warehouse facilities during the year. The subsidiary's $12,000 rent expense as well as the parent's $12,000 rental income should be disregarded (eliminated) in reporting the results of operations for the consolidated entity. This rental transaction neither increased nor decreased the net assets **of the consolidated entity.**

Elimination of Intercompany Revenue and Expenses Some of the more common examples of intercompany items that should be eliminated in preparing a consolidated income statement are:

- Sales to affiliated companies
- Cost of goods sold resulting from sales to affiliated companies
- Interest expense on loans from affiliated companies
- Interest revenue on loans made to affiliated companies
- Rent or other revenue received for services rendered to affiliated companies
- Rent or other expenses paid for services received from affiliated companies

Because of the complexity of the intercompany eliminations, the preparation of a consolidated income statement, a consolidated statement of retained earnings, and a consolidated statement of changes in financial position are topics appropriately deferred to an advanced accounting course.

Accounting for Investments in Corporate Securities: A Summary

In this chapter, we have discussed the accounting principles applied to investments in corporate securities under various circumstances. The accounting treatment accorded to investments in **bonds** depends upon whether the investment is viewed as a current asset or a long-term investment. The accounting treatment of an investment in **stock** depends primarily upon the **degree of influence** or **control** that the investor is able to exercise over the issuing corporation. These relationships are summarized as follows:

Situation	Accounting Practice
Investments in bonds: Classified as current asset	*Combined with current asset portfolio of stocks and shown as marketable securities. Interest revenue accrues each period. Difference between cost and maturity value (discount or premium) generally not amortized.*
Classified as a long-term investment	*Combined with long-term portfolio of stocks and shown as marketable securities, under the classification Long-Term Investments. Interest revenue accrues each period. Difference between cost and maturity value is amortized.*
Investment in stocks: Noninfluential interest (ownership of less than 20% of the voting stock)	*(Readily marketable) Shown as a marketable security (may be classified as a current asset or a long-term investment). For those classified as current assets, each portfolio is valued at lower-of-cost-and-market. For those classified as long-term investments, each portfolio is valued at cost; when the decline in the lower market value is not temporary in nature, the lower market value is used. Dividends recorded as revenue when received.* *(Not readily marketable) Shown as a long-term investment and carried at cost. Dividends recorded as revenue when received.*
Influential but noncontrolling interest (ownership from 20% to 49% of the voting stock)	*Shown as a long-term investment, accounted for by the equity method. A lower market value is used if the decline in market value is not temporary in nature.*
Controlling interest (ownership of more than 50% of voting stock)	*The assets, liabilities, revenue, and expenses of controlled subsidiary are combined with those of the parent corporation in consolidated financial statements.*

CHAPTER REVIEW

KEY TERMS INTRODUCED OR EMPHASIZED IN CHAPTER 17

Business combination   The combining of two or more companies into a single economic or business entity. Also called a *merger,* an *acquisition,* or a *takeover.*

Consolidated financial statements   A set of statements presenting the combined financial position and operating results of a consolidated entity consisting of a parent company and one or more subsidiaries.

Equity method   The method of accounting used when the investment by one corporation in another is large enough to significantly influence the policies of the *investee.* The investor recognizes as investment income its proportionate share of the investee's net income, rather than considering dividends received as income.

Intercompany transactions   Transactions between two affiliated companies. The effects of intercompany transactions, such as intercompany loans, are eliminated as a step in preparing consolidated financial statements.

Lower-of-cost-and-market (LCM)   The conservative practice of valuing marketable securities in the balance sheet at the lower of total cost and current market value.

Marketable securities   Investments in stocks (equity securities) and bonds (debt securities). These are highly liquid investments that may be sold at any time. Classified as a current asset second only to cash in liquidity.

Non-controlling (minority) interest   Shares of a subsidiary owned by investors other than the parent.

Parent company   A corporation that owns a controlling interest in another company.

Purchase method   The method used in preparing consolidated financial statements when the parent company has purchased the shares of its subsidiary by paying cash or issuing debt securities. The purchase method is not used for those special transactions that qualify as a *pooling of interests.*

Subsidiary   A corporation in which a controlling stock interest is held by another corporation (the parent).

ASSIGNMENT MATERIAL

DISCUSSION QUESTIONS

1 Why are investments in marketable securities usually regarded as current assets?

2 Why must an investor who owns numerous marketable securities maintain a marketable securities subsidiary ledger?

3 If an investor buys a bond between interest dates, he or she pays as a part of the purchase price the accrued interest since the last interest date. On the other hand, if the investor buys a share of common or preferred stock, no "accrued dividend" is added to the quoted price. Explain why this difference exists.

4 Should stock dividends received be considered revenue to an investor? Explain.

5 In the current asset section of its balance sheet at December 31, 1995, Delta Industries shows marketable securities at a market value of $3,000,000, which

is $190,000 below cost. If the market value of these securities rises by $250,000 during 1996, how should Delta Industries account for such an increase in its 1996 income statement under the recommendations of the CICA and the FASB?

6 Ancaster Corporation has a large investment in stocks and bonds. The market value of this investment is significantly below cost at December 31, 1995, but is slightly above cost at April 30, 1996. Explain how Ancaster should value this investment in the balance sheet if it is (a) a short-term investment (b) a long-term portfolio investment.

7 When should investors use the equity method to account for an investment in common stock?

8 Dividends on stock owned are usually recognized as income when they are received. Does an investor using the **equity method** to account for an investment in common stock follow this policy? Explain fully.

9 When the equity method is used to account for an investment in common stock that is traded on organized exchanges, is the investment adjusted to the lower-of-cost-and-market at the end of each accounting period? Explain your answer.

10 Alexander Corporation owns 80% of the outstanding stock of Benton Limited. Explain the basis for the assumption that these two companies constitute a single economic entity operating under unified control.

11 What are consolidated financial statements? Explain briefly how these statements are prepared.

12 List the three basic types of intercompany eliminations that should be made as a step in the preparation of consolidated financial statements.

13 Explain why the price paid to acquire a controlling interest in a subsidiary company may be different from the book value of the equity acquired.

14 The following items appear on a consolidated balance sheet: "Non-controlling interest in subsidiary . . . $620,000." Explain the nature of this item, and where you would expect to find it on the consolidated balance sheet.

15 Briefly explain when a business combination is viewed as a **purchase** and when it might be viewed as a **pooling of interests.**

16 As a general rule, when are consolidated financial statements appropriate?

17 What groups of investors are likely to be primarily interested in consolidated financial statements? Why?

MULTIPLE CHOICE QUESTIONS

1 During 1995, Bonner Company bought and sold a short-term investment in $200,000 face value, 9% bonds that pay interest each April 1 and October 1. Bonner purchased the bonds at 98 plus accrued interest on February 1, 1995, and held the bonds until December 1, 1995, when the entire investment was sold for $200,000, including accrued interest. Each of the following is true, **except:**

a Bonner recognizes bond interest revenue of $15,000 for 1995.

   b Bonner paid a total of $202,000 to acquire the investment on February 1, 1995.

   c Bonner recognizes a gain of $1,000 on the sale of these marketable securities on December 1, 1995.

   d Bonner received semiannual interest cheques in the amounts of $3,000 on April 1 and $9,000 on October 1.

2 Early in 1993, Rodgers Corp. purchased for $1,000,000 several marketable equity securities as a short-term investment. The market value of this investment was $900,000 at the end of 1993, $990,000 at the end of 1994, and $1,180,000 at the end of 1995. Based on these facts:

   a Rodgers will recognize in its income statement a loss of $100,000 in 1993, and a gain of $90,000 in both 1994 and 1995.

   b At the end of 1994, Rodgers will recognize a gain of $90,000.

   c In 1995, Rodgers will report the investment in the balance sheet at $1,000,000.

   d Rogers will recognize in its 1993 income statement a loss of $100,000.

3 Which of the following is *true* with regard to investments in corporate securities?

   a When an investor acquires more than 20% of the common stock of a company, the investment is no longer classified as a marketable security even if it is traded on the stock exchanges.

   b An investor who owns more than 20% of the outstanding bonds of a company should account for this investment by using the equity method.

   c Whenever an investor owns less than 50% of the common stock of a corporation, the investment is valued at the lower-of-cost-and-market value.

   d Regardless of percentage ownership, an investor in the common stock of another corporation records dividends as revenue when they are received.

4 On January 1, 1996, Stockdale Limited purchased 30% (30,000 shares) of the common stock of Equus, Inc., for $600,000. At December 31, 1996, Equus reported net income of $200,000 and paid cash dividends of $80,000. At December 31, 1996, Equus' stock is trading at $19 per share. With regard to this investment, Stockdale's financial statements for 1996 should report:

   a Dividend revenue of $24,000.

   b Investment in Equus, Inc., of $636,000.

   c Investment income of $36,000.

   d A loss on marketable securities of $30,000.

5 When consolidated financial statements are issued by a parent and a subsidiary:

   a The consolidated balance sheet includes the shareholders' equity accounts of both the parent and the subsidiary.

   b Intercompany transactions are reported in separate sections of the income statement and the balance sheet.

   c There is no need for the parent and the subsidiary to maintain separate accounting records or prepare separate financial statements.

   d Non-controlling interest appears in the consolidated balance sheet whenever the parent does not own 100% of the outstanding shares of the subsidiary.

EXERCISES

EXERCISE 17-1
Accounting Terminology

Listed below are nine technical accounting terms emphasized in this chapter:

Consolidated financial statements	Lower-of-cost-and-market	Elimination of intercompany transactions
Parent company	Non-controlling interest	Equity method
Goodwill	Subsidiary	Marketable securities

Each of the following statements may (or may not) describe one of these technical terms. For each statement, indicate the accounting term described, or answer "None" if the statement does not correctly describe any of the terms.

a A separate legal entity owned and controlled by another corporation.

b An accounting procedure that is a necessary step in preparing consolidated financial statements, but that does not involve making entries in the ledger accounts.

c A single set of financial statements showing the assets, liabilities, revenue, and expenses of all companies in a given industry.

d An investment in voting stock of a large corporation that is too small to give the investor significant influence within the issuing company and that is almost as liquid an asset as cash.

e Procedures used to account for an investment in which a corporate investor has significant influence over the policies of another corporation.

f An unrecorded asset that often explains why a parent company pays far more than book value to acquire the capital stock of a subsidiary.

g The equity in a subsidiary held by shareholders other than the parent company.

h Method used in the balance sheet valuation of an investment in marketable securities.

EXERCISE 17-2
Investment in Bonds

Yamato Limited purchased as a short-term investment $300,000 face value of the 7% bonds of Lorenzo, Inc., on May 31 of the current year, at a total cost of $305,750, including interest accrued since January 1. Interest is paid by Lorenzo, Inc., on June 30 and December 31. On October 31, five months after the purchase, Yamato sold the bonds and interest accrued since July 1 for a total price of $304,900.

INSTRUCTIONS

Prepare in general journal form all entries required in the accounting records of Yamato relating to the investment in Lorenzo, Inc., bonds. (Commissions are to be ignored.)

EXERCISE 17-3
Investment in Stocks

During the current year, the following events occurred with respect to the Deutz Corporation's investments in stocks:

Jan. 17 Purchased as a short-term investment 5,000 shares of Cooper Industries common stock at a price of $83.50 per share, plus a brokerage commission of $2,500.

Mar. 10 Received a cash dividend of $1.25 per share on the investment in Cooper Industries stock.

July 9 Received an additional 250 shares of Cooper Industries common stock as a result of a 5% stock dividend.

Sept. 11 Sold 2,500 shares of Cooper Industries common stock at a price of $85 per share, less a brokerage commission of $1,450.

INSTRUCTIONS

a Prepare the journal entries in the accounting records of the Deutz Corporation to record the above transactions. Include a memorandum entry on July 9 to show the change in the cost basis per share.

b Assume the stock of Cooper Industries is widely traded and has a quoted market price of $87 per share at the end of the current year. What is the amount reported in Deutz company's year-end **balance sheet** for this investment?

EXERCISE 17-4
Valuation at Lower-of-Cost-and-Market

The cost and market value of Escobar Corporation's marketable securities (in common stock) at the end of 1995 and 1996 are shown below. The marketable securities are viewed as a current asset.

	Cost	Market Value
1995	$395,000	$334,000
1996 (carrying value $334,000)	395,000	415,000

INSTRUCTIONS

Show how the investment would appear **in the balance sheet** at the end of 1995 and at the end of 1996, based on the recommendations of the CICA and FASB. If appropriate, use a valuation account in your presentation.

EXERCISE 17-5
The Equity Method

On January 1, 1995, Southern Transport purchases 40% of the common stock of Delta Shipping, Inc., for $900,000, which corresponds to the underlying book value. Delta Shipping, Inc., has issued common stock only. At December 31, 1995, Delta Shipping reported net income for the year of $400,000 and paid cash dividends of $180,000. Southern Transport uses the equity method to account for this investment.

INSTRUCTIONS

a Prepare all journal entries in the accounting records of Southern Transport relating to the investment during 1995.

b During 1996, Delta Shipping, Inc., reports a net loss of $300,000 and pays no dividends. Compute the carrying value of Southern Transport's investment in Delta Shipping, Inc., at the end of 1995 (refer to your answer to part **a**) and at the end of 1996.

c Based upon quoted market prices, the fair market value of Southern Transport's investment in Delta Shipping, Inc. was $995,000 at the end of 1995 but has temporarily fallen to $850,000 at the end of 1996. Do these market values affect amounts reported **in the balance sheet** for this investment? Are these market values reflected **in any way** in the financial statements?

EXERCISE 17-6
Eliminating Intercompany Stock Ownership; Recording Goodwill

Merit Brands, Inc., has purchased all the outstanding shares of Eduardo Foods for $670,000. At the date of acquisition, Eduardo Foods' balance sheet showed total shareholders' equity of $600,000, consisting of $250,000 capital stock and $350,000 retained earnings. The excess of this purchase price over the book value of Eduardo Foods' shares is regarded as payment for Eduardo Foods' unrecorded goodwill.

In general journal entry form, prepare the eliminating entry necessary on the working paper to consolidate the balance sheets of these two companies.

EXERCISE 17-7
Computing Consolidated Amounts

Selected account balances from the separate balance sheets of Primis Corporation and its wholly owned subsidiary, Syntech, Inc., immediately after acquisition, are as follows:

	Primis Corporation	Syntech, Inc.	Consolidated
Accounts receivable	$ 300,000	$ 140,000	$
Rent receivable—Primis Corporation		7,000	
Investment in Syntech, Inc.	1,475,000		
Accounts payable	390,000	120,000	
Accrued expenses payable	29,000		
Bonds payable	1,400,000	900,000	
Capital stock	4,000,000	1,000,000	
Retained earnings	2,934,000	475,000	

Primis Corporation owes Syntech, Inc., $7,000 in accrued rent payable and Syntech, Inc., owes Primis Corporation $24,000 on account for services rendered prior to acquisition.

INSTRUCTIONS Indicate the amount that should appear in the consolidated balance sheet for each of these selected accounts. If the account would not appear in the consolidated balance sheet, enter –0– as the consolidated account balance. Show supporting computations.

EXERCISE 17-8
Preparing a Consolidated Balance Sheet; Non-controlling Interest

On June 30 Peabody, Inc., **purchased** 80% of the stock of Stern Ltd. for $1,200,000 in cash. The separate condensed balance sheets immediately after the purchase are as follows:

	Peabody, Inc.	Stern Ltd.
Cash...	$ 350,000	$ 225,000
Investments in Stern Ltd.	1,200,000	
Other assets	5,450,000	1,775,000
	$7,000,000	$2,000,000
Liabilities	$1,500,000	$ 500,000
Capital stock	3,000,000	1,000,000
Retained earnings	2,500,000	500,000
	$7,000,000	$2,000,000

INSTRUCTIONS Prepare a consolidated balance sheet immediately after Peabody, Inc., acquired control of Stern Ltd.

PROBLEMS

Group A

PROBLEM 17A-1
Investments in Marketable Debt Securities

On April 1, 1995, Imperial Motors purchased $450,000 face value of the 8% bonds of Crest Theatres, Inc., at a price of 98 plus accrued interest. The bonds pay interest semiannually on March 1 and September 1. Imperial regards these bonds as a short-term investment.

INSTRUCTIONS a In general journal form, prepare the entries required in 1995 to record:
   1 Purchase of the bonds on April 1.
   2 Receipt of the semiannual interest payment on September 1.

3 Adjustment of the accounts at December 31 for bond interest earned since September 1. (Imperial Motors adjusts and closes its accounts annually, using the calendar year.)

b Assume that on January 31, 1996, Imperial Motors sells the entire investment in Crest Theatres bonds for $444,700 plus accrued interest. Prepare the entries to:

1 Accrue bond interest earned from December 31, 1995 through the date of sale.

2 Record the sale of the bonds on January 31, 1996.

PROBLEM 17A-2
Investments in Marketable Equity Securities

During the current year, the following transactions occurred relating to Talley Manufacturing Limited's investments in marketable equity securities:

Jan. 31   Purchased as a short-term investment 4,000 shares of Raleigh Corporation common stock at $64.75 per share, plus broker's commission of $1,400.

Mar. 31   Received a cash dividend of $1.25 per share from Raleigh Corporation. Raleigh declared the dividend on February 15, payable on March 31 to shareholders of record on March 15.

June 30   Raleigh Corporation distributed a 5% stock dividend.

July 31   Raleigh Corporation shares were split 2 for 1; Talley Manufacturing received additional shares pursuant to this stock split.

Sept. 30   Raleigh Corporation paid a cash dividend of 70 cents per share. Dividend was declared on August 25 payable on September 30 to shareholders of record on September 15.

Dec. 21   Talley Manufacturing sold 3,000 shares of Raleigh Corporation stock at $29 per share. Commission charges on the sale amounted to $600.

As of December 31, Raleigh Corporation common stock had a market value of $28.50 per share. Talley Manufacturing classifies its Raleigh Corporation stock as a current asset and owns no other marketable equity securities.

INSTRUCTIONS

Prepare journal entries to account for this investment in Talley Manufacturing's accounting records. Include memorandum entries when appropriate. For journal entries involving computations, the explanation portion of the entry should include the computation. Also show how the investment should appear in the balance sheet at December 31.

PROBLEM 17A-3
Accounting for Marketable Securities: A Comprehensive Problem

The marketable securities owned by Freitag Development at the beginning of the current year are listed below. Management considers all investments in marketable securities to be current assets.

$300,000 maturity value of Micro Computer 12% bonds due Apr. 30, 1999. Interest payable on Apr. 30 and Oct. 31 of each year. Cost basis $990 per bond *$297,000*

4,000 shares of Ryan Corporation common stock. Cost basis $52.50 per share *210,000*

Transactions relating to marketable securities during the current year were as follows:

Jan. 21   Received semiannual cash dividend of 90 cents per share on the 4,000 shares of Ryan Corporation common stock.

Feb. 8 Purchased 1,500 shares of Gramm Ltd. common stock at $39\frac{3}{4}$ per share. Brokerage commissions amounted to $375.

Mar. 15 Received an additional 1,500 shares of Gramm Ltd. common stock as a result of a 2-for-1 split.

Apr. 30 Received semiannual interest on Micro Computer 12% bonds. Accrued interest of $6,000 had been recorded on December 31 of last year in the Bond Interest Receivable account.

May 31 Sold $200,000 face value of Micro Computer 12% bonds at a price of 103, plus one month's accrued interest, less a brokerage commission of $575.

July 21 Received cash dividend on 4,000 shares of Ryan Corporation common stock. Amount of dividend has increased to $1.05 per share.

Oct. 18 Received an additional 200 shares of Ryan Corporation common stock as a result of a 5% stock dividend.

Oct. 19 Sold 1,200 shares of Ryan Corporation common stock at $47 per share, less a brokerage commission of $250.

Oct. 31 Received semiannual interest payment on remaining $100,000 face value of Micro Computer 12% bonds.

At December 31 of the current year, the quoted market prices of the marketable securities owned by Freitag Development were as follows: Ryan Corporation, $46 per share; Gramm Ltd. $21.50 per share; Micro Computer 12% bonds, $1,025 per bond.

INSTRUCTIONS

a Prepare journal entries to record the transactions listed above. Include an adjusting entry to record the accrued interest on the remaining Micro Computer bonds through December 31.

b Prepare a schedule showing the cost and market value of the marketable securities owned by Freitag Development at December 31.

c Show how the marketable securities should appear in the balance sheet at December 31.

PROBLEM 17A-4
Equity Method—Financial Statement Effects

On January 1, 1995, Minelli Foods purchased 30% (300,000 shares) of the widely traded common stock of Kansas Grain Products, Inc., for $5,100,000. (This price was equal to 30% of Kansas Products' book value at that date.) The following data is available regarding Kansas Grain Products, Inc., for 1995 and 1996:

	1995	1996
Net income (loss)	$2,500,000	$(900,000)
Dividends declared & paid	$1,300,000	$ 650,000
Quoted market price per share at December 31	$ 19	$ 14

INSTRUCTIONS

a Briefly describe how Minelli Foods should account for this investment. Identify the principal factors that determine the accounting treatment.

b Compute each of the following amounts relating only to Minelli's investment in Kansas Grain Products, Inc.

1 Cash dividends received by Minelli in 1995 and in 1996.

2 Amounts (if any) reported in Minelli's ***income statement*** in 1995 and in 1996 for each of the following: Dividend Revenue; Investment Income (or Loss).

3 Carrying value of this investment reported in Minelli's ***balance sheet*** at December 31, 1995, and at December 31, 1996.

c Compute the **market value** of Minelli Foods' investment in Kansas Grain Products, Inc., at the end of 1995 and 1996. How are these market values reflected in Minelli Foods' financial statements, if at all? Assume that the market value of Kansas' stock went up to $17.50 per share in early 1997.

PROBLEM 17A-5
Basic Elements of a Consolidated Balance Sheet

On December 31, 1995, the Home Club, Inc., purchased for cash 70% of the capital stock of Winston Paint Ltd. The separate year-end balance sheets of the two companies include the following items:

	Home Club, Inc.	Winston Paint Ltd.
Accounts receivable—Home Club, Inc.	–0–	315,000
Investments in Winston Paint Ltd.	1,050,000	–0–
Total assets	6,500,000	2,180,000
Accounts payable—Winston Paint Ltd.	315,000	–0–
Total liabilities...	3,900,000	980,000
Total shareholders' equity	2,600,000	1,200,000

The excess of the $1,050,000 purchase price over the book value of the acquired shares in Winston Paint Ltd. is regarded as a purchase of Winston Paint's unrecorded goodwill.

INSTRUCTIONS

Compute the amounts to appear in the year-end consolidated balance sheet for each of the following (show supporting computations):

a Goodwill

b Non-controlling interest

c Total assets

d Total liabilities

e Total shareholders' equity.

PROBLEM 17A-6
Preparing a Consolidated Balance Sheet

On January 1, 1996, Maxwell Entertainment purchased all the outstanding common stock of Video Scene, Inc., for $800,000. Immediately **before** the acquisition, the condensed separate balance sheets of the two companies were as shown below. (As these balance sheets were prepared just **before** the purchase, the current assets of Maxwell Entertainment still include the $800,000 in cash that was paid to acquire Video Scene, Inc.)

Assets	Maxwell Entertainment	Video Scene, Inc.
Current assets	$1,630,000	$240,000
Other assets	1,970,000	660,000
Total assets	$3,600,000	$900,000

Liabilities & Shareholders' Equity		
Current liabilities	$ 580,000	$120,000
Long-term debt...	900,000	208,000
Capital stock	1,000,000	200,000
Retained earnings	1,120,000	372,000
Total liabilities & shareholders' equity	$3,600,000	$900,000

The excess, if any, of the purchase price over the book value of Video Scene's acquired shares is regarded as payment for Video Scene's unrecorded goodwill.

INSTRUCTIONS Prepare a consolidated balance sheet for Maxwell Entertainment and its newly acquired subsidiary (Video Scene, Inc.) on January 1, 1996, the date of acquisition.

PROBLEM 17A-7
Working Paper for a Consolidated Balance Sheet

On March 31, 1996, Connor Yacht Design purchased for $375,000 cash 90% of the capital stock of Wing Sails, Inc. The separate balance sheets of the two corporations immediately *after* this purchase are as follows:

Assets	Connor Yacht Design	Wing Sails, Inc.
Cash...	$ 69,000	$ 40,000
Accounts receivable	150,000	60,000
Inventories	120,000	80,000
Investment in Wing Sails, Inc....................................	375,000	
Plant and equipment	500,000	360,000
Accumulated depreciation	(100,000)	(80,000)
Total assets	$1,114,000	$460,000

Liabilities & Shareholders' Equity		
Accounts payable	$ 80,000	$ 80,000
Accrued liabilities	50,000	20,000
Common stock	600,000	200,000
Retained earnings	384,000	160,000
Total liabilities & shareholders' equity	$1,114,000	$460,000

ADDITIONAL INFORMATION

1 Connor Yacht's asset account, Investment in Wing Sails, Inc., represents ownership of 90% of Wing Sails' shareholders' equity, which has a book value of $324,000 [90% × ($200,000 + $160,000) = $324,000]. The remainder of the Investment account balance represents the purchase of Wing Sails, Inc.'s unrecorded goodwill.

2 Wing Sails owes Connor Yacht Design $14,000 in accrued rent payable. This amount is included in the accrued liabilities of the subsidiary and the accounts receivable of the parent company.

3 Connor Yacht Design owes Wing Sales $32,000 for services rendered. This amount is included in the parent company's accounts payable and the subsidiary's accounts receivable.

INSTRUCTIONS Prepare a working paper for a consolidated balance sheet at March 31, 1996—the date of this business acquisition. Include at the bottom of the working paper explanations of the elimination entries.

Group B

PROBLEM 17B-1
Investments in Marketable Debt Securities

On June 1, 1995, Allied Chemical purchased $600,000 face value of the 9% bonds of Tiger Trucking at a price of 102 plus accrued interest. The bonds pay interest semiannually on April 1 and October 1. Allied Chemical regards these bonds as a short-term investment.

INSTRUCTIONS a In general journal form, prepare the entries required in 1995 to record:

1 Purchase of the bonds on June 1.

2 Receipt of the semiannual interest payment on October 1.

3 Adjustment of the accounts at December 31 for bond interest earned since October 1. (Allied Chemical adjusts and closes its accounts annually, using the calendar year.)

b Assume that on February 28, 1996, Allied Chemical sells the entire investment in Tiger Trucking bonds for total proceeds of $628,900, which includes accrued interest. Prepare the entries to:

  1 Accrue bond interest earned from December 31, 1995, through the date of sale.

  2 Record the sale of the bonds on February 28, 1996.

PROBLEM 17B-2
Investments in Marketable Securities

During the current year, Overnight Air Freight (OAF) engaged in the following transactions relating to marketable securities in stock:

Feb. 28 Purchased 5,000 shares of National Products common stock for $88.50 per share plus a broker's commission of $1,500.

Mar. 15 National Products paid a cash dividend of 75 cents per share that had been declared on February 20, payable on March 15 to shareholders of record on March 6.

May 31 National Products distributed a 20% stock dividend.

Nov. 15 National Products distributed additional shares as the result of a 2-for-1 stock split.

Dec. 5 OAF sold 3,500 shares of its National Products stock at $39 per share, less a broker's commission of $450.

Dec. 10 National Products paid a cash dividend of 30 cents per share. Dividend was declared November 20, payable December 10 to shareholders of record on November 30.

As of December 31, National Products common stock had a market value of $35 per share. OAF classifies its National Products stock as a current asset and owns no other marketable securities.

INSTRUCTIONS

Prepare journal entries to account for this investment in OAF's accounting records. Include memorandum entries when appropriate. For journal entries involving computations, the explanation portion of the entry should include the computation. Also show how the investment should appear in the balance sheet at December 31.

PROBLEM 17B-3
Accounting for Marketable Securities: A Comprehensive Problem

The marketable securities owned by Bar Harbour Corporation at January 1 consisted of the three securities listed below. All marketable securities are classified as current assets.

$200,000 maturity value Copper Products Ltd. 9% bonds due Apr. 30, 2002.
  Interest is payable on Apr. 30 and Oct. 31 of each year. Cost basis $990 per
  bond *$198,000*
3,000 shares of Aztec Corporation common stock. Cost basis $38.50 per share . *115,500*
1,500 shares of Donner-Pass, Inc., $7.00 cumulative preferred stock. Cost basis
  $55 per share *82,500*

Jan. 10 Acquired 1,000 shares of Rhodes Ltd. common stock at $65.50 per share. Brokerage commissions paid amounted to $500.

Jan. 21 Received quarterly dividend on $1.75 per share on 1,500 shares of Donner-Pass, Inc., preferred stock.

Mar. 5 Sold all 1,500 shares of Donner-Pass, Inc., preferred stock at $58 per share less a brokerage commission of $375.

Apr. 1 Received additional 2,000 shares of Rhodes Ltd. common stock as a result of a 3-for-1 split.

Apr. 30 Received semiannual interest on Copper Products Ltd. 9% bonds. Accrued interest of $3,000 had been recorded on December 31 of last year in the Bond Interest Receivable account.

June 30 Sold $100,000 face value of Copper Products Ltd. 9% bonds at 93, plus two months' accrued interest, less a commission of $125.

July 10 Received additional 300 shares of Aztec Corporation common stock as a result of 10% stock dividend.

Sept. 24 Sold 1,300 shares of Aztec Corporation common stock at $40 per share, less a brokerage commission of $250.

Oct. 31 Received semiannual interest payment on remaining $100,000 face value of Copper Products Ltd. 9% bonds.

At December 31, 19__, the quoted market prices of the marketable securities owned by Bar Harbour Corporation were as follows: Aztec Corporation common stock, $37; and Rhodes common stock, $18. Copper Products 9% bonds, $960 per bond.

INSTRUCTIONS
a Prepare journal entries to record the transactions listed above. Include an adjusting entry to record accrued interest on the remaining Copper Products bonds through December 31.

b Prepare a schedule showing the cost and market value of the marketable securities owned by Bar Harbour Corporation at December 31.

c Show how the marketable securities should be presented in the balance sheet at December 31.

PROBLEM 17B-4
Equity Method— Financial Statement Effects

On January 1, 1996, Bishop Industries purchased 60,000 shares of the widely traded common stock of Franklin-Parker Corporation for $1,500,000. On this date, Franklin-Parker had 150,000 shares of a single class of stock outstanding and total shareholders' equity of $3,750,000. The following data is available regarding Franklin-Parker Corporation for 1996 and 1997:

	1996	*1997*
Net income (loss)	*$(300,000)*	*$1,500,000*
Dividends declared & paid	*$ 75,000*	*$ 600,000*
Quoted market price per share at December 31	*$ 22*	*$ 30*

INSTRUCTIONS
a Briefly describe how Bishop Industries should account for this investment. Identify the principal factors that determine the accounting treatment.

b Compute each of the following amounts relating only to Bishop's investment in Franklin-Parker Corporation.

1 Cash dividends received by Bishop in 1996 and in 1997.

2 Amounts (if any) reported in Bishop's *income statement* in 1996 and in 1997 for each of the following: Dividend Revenue; Investment Income (or Loss).

3 Carrying value of this investment reported on Bishop's *balance sheet* at December 31, 1996, and at December 31, 1997.

c Compute the *market value* of Bishop Industries' investment in Franklin-Parker at December 31, 1996, and December 31, 1997. How are these market values reflected in Bishop's financial statements, if at all?

PROBLEM 17B-5
Basic Elements of a Consolidated Balance Sheet

On December 31, 1996, Northwest Building Materials purchased for cash 80% of the capital stock of Corning Electrical Supply. The separate year-end balance sheets of the two companies include the following items:

	Northwest Building Materials	Corning Electrical Supply
Accounts receivable—Corning Electrical Supply	130,000	–0–
Investment in Corning Electrical Supply	1,600,000	–0–
Total assets	9,800,000	2,200,000
Accounts payable—Northwest Building Materials	–0–	130,000
Total liabilities...	3,600,000	700,000
Total shareholders' equity	6,200,000	1,500,000

The excess of the $1,600,000 purchase price over the book value of the acquired shares in Corning is regarded as a purchase of Corning's unrecorded goodwill.

INSTRUCTIONS Compute the amounts to appear in the year-end consolidated balance sheet for each of the following (show supporting computations):

a   Goodwill

b   Non-controlling interest

c   Total assets

d   Total liabilities

e   Total shareholders' equity.

PROBLEM 17B-6
Preparing a Consolidated Balance Sheet

On June 30, 19__, Pokfulam Sportswear paid $1,800,000 cash to acquire all the outstanding capital stock of Jeans by Jorge. Immediately *before* this acquisition, the condensed separate balance sheets of the two companies were as shown below. (As these balance sheets were prepared immediately *before* the acquisition, the current assets of Pokfulam Sportswear still include the $1,800,000 in cash that will be paid to acquire Jeans by Jorge.)

Assets	Pokfulam Sportswear	Jeans by Jorge
Current assets	$3,760,000	$ 640,000
Plant and equipment	3,040,000	1,800,000
Total assets	$6,800,000	$2,440,000

Liabilities & Shareholders' Equity		
Current liabilities	$1,080,000	$ 560,000
Long-term debt...	2,400,000	400,000
Capital stock...	1,200,000	300,000
Retained earnings	2,120,000	380,000
Total liabilities & shareholders' equity	$6,800,000	$2,440,000

The excess, if any, of the purchase price over the book value of Jeans by Jorge shares acquired is regarded as payment for unrecorded goodwill.

INSTRUCTIONS Prepare a consolidated balance sheet for Pokfulam Sportswear and its newly acquired subsidiary (Jeans by Jorge) on June 30, 19__, the date of acquisition.

PROBLEM 17B-7
Working Paper for a Consolidated Balance Sheet

On September 30, 1996, Morse Communications purchased 80% of the stock of Graham Cable for cash. The separate balance sheets of the two companies immediately after this purchase are as follows:

Assets	Morse Communications	Graham Cable
Cash...	$ 52,000	$ 45,000
Note receivable from Graham Cable......................	50,000	
Accounts receivable.....................................	108,000	60,000
Inventories..	120,000	174,000
Investment in Graham Cable.............................	570,000	
Plant and equipment	420,000	540,000
Accumulated depreciation...............................	(168,000)	(100,000)
Total assets...	$1,152,000	$719,000

Liabilities & Shareholders' Equity		
Notes payable...	$ 120,000	$ 50,000
Accounts payable	144,000	45,000
Accrued liabilities	36,000	24,000
Common stock...	500,000	350,000
Retained earnings	352,000	250,000
Total liabilities & shareholders' equity..................	$1,152,000	$719,000

ADDITIONAL INFORMATION

1 Morse Communications' asset account Investment in Graham Cable represents ownership of 80% of Graham Cable's shareholders' equity, which has a book value of $480,000 [80% × ($350,000 + $250,000) = $480,000]. The remainder of the investment account balance represents the purchase of Graham Cable's unrecorded goodwill.

2 Graham Cable's $50,000 note payable is owed to Morse Communications. (All interest has been paid through September 30.)

3 The accounts payable of Morse Communications include $15,000 owed to Graham Cable. This amount also is included in the accounts receivable of Graham Cable.

INSTRUCTIONS Prepare a working paper for a consolidated balance sheet at September 30, 1996— immediately after the purchase of Graham Cable. Include at the bottom of the working paper explanations of the elimination entries.

ANALYTICAL AND DECISION PROBLEMS AND CASES

A&D 17-1
Apples and Oranges

Dane Electronics has the following investments in the securities of other corporations:

a 2,000 shares of the common stock of Apple Computer. Apple is a large publicly owned corporation and sells at a quoted market price in excess of Dane's cost. Dane's management stands ready to sell these shares at any time.

b $100,000 face amount of Central Telephone's $3\frac{5}{8}$% bonds maturing in 10 years. The bonds were acquired at a substantial discount. These bonds are readily marketable, and Dane's management stands ready to sell them to meet any current cash requirements.

c 5 million of the 15 million voting shares in Micro-Desk, Inc. Micro-Desk is a publicly owned corporation, and its quoted stock price recently has declined to a level below Dane's cost.

d $300,000 face value of Carver Stores $12\frac{1}{4}$% bonds maturing in 10 years. These bonds are readily marketable at a quoted price. However, Dane intends to hold these bonds until their maturity date. The bonds were acquired at a premium.

e   51% of the voting stock in Consumer Corp. Consumer is a profitable company, but it is not publicly owned. There is no quoted market price for Consumer's capital stock.

f   50,000 of the 1 million outstanding shares of SIMCO Products, a publicly owned corporation. The market price of SIMCO's shares has declined steadily since Dane purchased its shares. Dane's management, however, believes in the long-run prospects of SIMCO and intends to hold this investment for at least 10 years.

g   5,000 shares of voting stock of Orange Express. Orange Express operates profitably, but it is not publicly owned and has no quoted market value. This investment does not give Dane an influential interest in Orange Express. Dane's management stands ready to sell these shares at any time that an attractive offer is received.

INSTRUCTIONS   Explain how Dane Electronics should account for each of these investments. Your explanations should include discussion of the three topics listed below.

1   Whether the investment qualifies for consolidation and, if not, the appropriate balance sheet classification of the investment account.

2   The basis for balance sheet valuation (e.g., consolidation, equity method, cost, cost adjusted for amortization of bond discount or premium, or lower-of-cost-and-market).

3   The factors involved in the recognition of income (or loss) from the investment (e.g., Does the lower-of-cost-and-market rule enter into the determination of net income? Is bond discount or premium amortized? Are dividends recorded as income when received? Is the equity method in use?).

A&D 17-2
Success or
Failure and
Why?

There have been many well-known, well-publicized business acquisitions and mergers in recent years. The results of these acquisitions and mergers have been mixed—some successes, some failures, and a few disasters. In addition, the fate of the more recent acquisitions and mergers is still pending.

INSTRUCTIONS   Select one of the acquisitions or mergers cited in the "CASE IN POINT" in this chapter and determine why it has been a success or a failure.

6 Special Purpose Reports and Financial Statement Analysis

In the next three chapters we discuss several specialized uses of accounting information, including the determination of taxable income, the measurement of cash flows, and the analysis of financial statements by investors.

Part 6 also includes Comprehensive Problem 5, which provides an opportunity to analyze and evaluate the financial statements of a well-known corporation.

CHAPTER

18 Income Taxes and Business Decisions

For many college and university students, this chapter may be their only academic exposure to the truly remarkable system known as income taxes. The early part of the chapter presents a brief history, rationale, and basic structure of the federal tax structure, including the tax reform measures introduced in 1988. This introduction also stresses the pervasive influence of income taxes upon economic activity. The next section portrays the basic process of determining taxable income and the tax liability for individual taxpayers. The income tax computations for a corporation are also explained and illustrated. The final section of the chapter gives students an understanding of the important role that tax planning can play in the affairs of individuals and also in the decision-making of a business entity.

Learning Objectives

After studying this chapter you should be able to:

1 *Describe the history of the federal income tax, the highlights of the tax reform measures introduced in 1988, and the basic structure of the tax system.*

2 *Explain the formula for determining the taxable income and tax liability of an individual taxpayer.*

3 *Explain the income tax treatment of dividends received by individuals.*

4 *Determine the tax liability of an individual.*

5 *Determine the taxable income and income tax of a corporation.*

6 *Determine the amount of capital cost allowance.*

7 *Describe the circumstances that create a liability for deferred income taxes.*

8 *Explain how tax planning is used in choosing the form of business organization, timing and nature of transactions, and the capital structure.*

The Federal Income Tax: History and Objectives

OBJECTIVE 1
Describe the
history of
the federal
income tax,
the high-
lights of the
tax reform
measures
introduced
in 1988, and
the basic
structure of
the tax sys-
tem.

The federal income tax legislation, the **Income Tax Act,** has undergone many changes since its inception as the **Income War Tax Act** in 1917. The more significant changes occurred in the years 1948, 1952, and 1972. In 1988, major tax reform measures were introduced, as highlighted in the following section and discussed in this chapter. Similarly, the objectives of income tax legislation also have been changed and expanded over the years. The administration and enforcement of the Income Tax Act rest with the Department of National Revenue for Taxation, commonly known as Revenue Canada, Taxation.

Originally, the objective of the federal income tax was simply to obtain revenue to help meet Canada's growing war expenditures. It was intended as a temporary measure and the tax rates were quite low. Today, the objectives are many and the tax rates are significantly higher.

The objectives of federal income tax today include a number of broad ones in addition to raising revenue. Among these broad objectives are to combat inflation, to influence the rate of economic growth, to encourage full employment, to provide incentive for small businesses, and to redistribute national income on a more equal basis.

Tax Reform Measures of 1988

In 1988, the federal government enacted new income tax legislation that brought sweeping changes in income tax rules and rates. Although annual changes in the income tax law have become normal practice, the changes in this new legislation represented some of the most drastic in the history of the federal income tax. Annual changes, however, will continue. The five most striking characteristics of this major tax legislation are the broadening of the tax base, the lowering of tax rates, the reduction of the number of tax brackets, the replacement of various exemptions and deductions with tax credits, and a shifting of the tax burden from individuals to corporations and to sales tax.

Provincial Income Tax

All ten provinces as well as the Northwest Territories and Yukon levy income tax. The federal government collects the income tax of individuals and corporations except for the Provinces of Ontario, Alberta, and Quebec; Ontario and Alberta collect their corporate income tax and Quebec collects its income tax on both individuals and corporations. The rate of income tax varies among the jurisdictions. The tax rate for individuals is expressed as a percentage of the individual's basic federal tax. The tax rate for corporations, on the other hand, applies to the corporation's taxable income. The computations of provincial income tax will be illustrated later.

Tax Planning versus Tax Evasion

Tax Planning   Taxpayers who manage their affairs in ways that **legally** minimize their income tax obligations are engaging in a practice called **tax planning.** Tax planning is both legal and ethical.

The goals of tax planning usually are either to minimize the total amount of taxes owed or to postpone into future years the dates at which the taxes become due. Tax planning may take many forms; for example: Should business automobiles be leased or purchased? Should needed capital be financed by issuing bonds or preferred stock? Should a business be incorporated? Some of these choices may significantly affect the amount and timing of the taxpayer's income tax obligations.

If tax planning is to be efficient, it should be undertaken **before** the taxpayer engages in the related transactions. Once a transaction is complete, it usually is **too late** to change its tax consequences. Every taxpayer, whether an individual or a corporation, can benefit from thoughtful tax planning. Tax planning is one of the major services that public accounting firms offer their clients.

Tax Evasion In contrast to tax planning, **tax evasion** refers to **illegal** efforts by taxpayers to avoid their tax obligations. Examples include failure to file an income tax return or fraudulently understating the amount of taxable income reported in the return. By definition, tax evasion is a crime, punishable by fines, imprisonment, or both.

CASE IN POINT Al Capone, one of the most infamous gangsters in American history, was believed to have committed many crimes, including bootlegging, extortion, and murder. Capone was the subject of an intense criminal investigation conducted by the American federal law enforcement agents—including the legendary Elliot Ness and "The Untouchables."

The only crime for which the American government was able to convict Capone was income tax evasion. The result, however, was the same as if he had been convicted of murder and given a life sentence. He died in prison while serving his term.

The Critical Importance of Income Taxes

Taxes levied by federal and provincial governments are a significant part of the cost of operating a typical household, as well as a business enterprise. Every manager who makes business decisions, and every individual who makes personal investments, urgently needs some knowledge of income taxes. A general knowledge of income taxes will help any business manager or owner to benefit more fully from the advice of the professional tax accountant.

Some understanding of income taxes will also aid the individual citizen in voting intelligently, because a great many of the issues decided in every election have tax implications. Such issues as pollution, inflation, foreign policy, and employment are quite closely linked with income taxes. For example, the offering of special tax incentives to encourage businesses to launch massive programs to reduce pollution is one approach to protection of the environment.

In terms of revenue generated, income taxes constitute one of the most important sources of revenue in Canada. Income taxes also exert a pervasive influence on all types of business decisions and affect millions of individuals. For example, tax returns filed annually in recent years were about 19 million for individuals and 900,000 for corporations. The annual income tax revenue from individuals and corporations in recent years was about

$96 billion. For this reason we shall limit our discussion to the basic federal and provincial income tax rules applicable to individuals and corporations.

Income tax returns are based on accounting information. In many respects this information is consistent with the accounting concepts we have discussed in earlier chapters. However, the measurement of *taxable income* includes some unique principles and computations that differ from those used for published financial statements. An understanding of the unique aspects of taxable income can assist an individual or a business in minimizing the amount of income taxes owed.

Classes of Taxpayers and Liability of Tax

In the eyes of the income tax law, the classes of taxpayers are: individuals, corporations, and trusts. Since trusts are taxed as individuals, there are in essence two classes of taxpayers.

Proprietorships and partnerships are not taxed as business units; their income is taxed directly to the individual proprietor or partners, *whether or not actually withdrawn from the business.* A proprietor reports his or her business income on an individual tax return; the members of a partnership include on their individual tax returns their respective shares of the partnership net income. An individual taxpayer's income tax return must include not only any business income from a proprietorship or partnership, but also any salary or income from other sources and any deductions affecting the tax liability.

A corporation is a separate taxable entity; it must file an income tax return and pay a tax on its annual taxable income. In addition, individual shareholders must report dividends received as part of their personal taxable income. This is sometimes called "double taxation" of corporate income—once to the corporation and again when it is distributed as dividends to shareholders. However, this double taxation is minimized by the "dividend tax credit" claimed by the shareholders.

The income tax law stipulates that income tax is payable on the taxable income for each taxation year of every person resident in Canada. Moreover, income tax is payable on the taxable income earned in Canada by a nonresident person. The word "person" may include an individual or a corporation.

Enforcement of Income Tax Laws

Our system of income taxes relies upon taxpayers measuring their own taxable income, computing the taxes that they owe, and filing an income tax return in which these amounts are reported to governmental income tax authorities. For this reason, our system of collecting income taxes often is described as a system of *self-assessment.*

However, income tax authorities have several means of enforcing this "self-assessment" system. To begin with, much of the taxable income earned by taxpayers is reported to the tax authorities by a third party. For example, employers must send *T4* forms to the government indicating the total salary or wages paid to each employee during the year. Corporations and banks are required to send *T5* forms reporting to the government the dividends and interest earned by each investor and creditor. Through the use of its computers, Revenue Canada traces many of these reported amounts directly into the recipient's income tax return.

Next, each year income tax authorities *audit* selected tax returns filed by taxpayers. Only a small percentage of the returns filed each year are audited; however, Revenue Canada has considerable experience in identifying those returns in which taxable income may be understated. Many of the returns selected for audit are those that appear "suspicious" in some way, or in which taxpayers have claimed deductions to which they might not be entitled. Thus, by claiming certain deductions (such as expenses relating to a "home office" or a large business loss), a taxpayer may increase the chances that his or her return will be audited.

An interesting quirk in the tax law is that when a tax return is audited, *the burden of proof rests with the taxpayer.* Thus, taxpayers who do not maintain adequate records may lose deductions to which they otherwise would be entitled.

Finally, tax authorities may impose financial penalties upon taxpayers who have understated their taxable incomes. First, the taxpayer must pay interest on any additional taxes owed. In addition, substantial fines and penalties may be levied if the taxpayer has been careless or fraudulent. As previously stated, fraudulent tax evasion is a criminal offense and may be punishable by imprisonment, as well as by financial penalties.

INCOME TAXES: INDIVIDUALS

Cash Basis of Accounting for Individual Tax Returns

Most of the individual tax returns are prepared on the cash basis of measuring income. The cash basis is advantageous for the individual taxpayer for several reasons. It is simple and requires a minimum of record keeping. Moreover, the income of most individuals comes in the form of salaries, interest, and dividends. At the end of each year, employers are required to inform each employee (and Revenue Canada, Taxation) of the salary earned and the income tax withheld during the year. The report (a T4 form) must be prepared on the cash basis without any accrual of unpaid wages. Generally, companies paying interest and dividends also use the cash basis in reporting the amounts paid during the year. Thus, most individuals are provided with reports prepared on a cash basis for use in preparing their individual tax returns. However, businesses and professional practices, with rare exceptions such as a farming business, are not allowed to use the cash basis for tax purposes.

Tax Rates for Individuals

All taxes may be characterized as progressive, proportional, or regressive with respect to any given base. A *progressive* tax becomes a larger portion of the base as that base increases. A *proportional* tax remains a constant percentage of the base no matter how that base changes. For example, an 8% sales tax remains a constant percentage of sales regardless of changes in the dollar amount of sales. A *regressive* tax becomes a smaller percentage of the base as the base increases. Regressive taxes, however, are extremely rare.

Federal income tax is *progressive* with respect to income, since a higher tax *rate* applies as the amount of taxable income increases. Since provincial income tax is expressed as a percentage of "basic federal tax," it is also progressive with respect to income. The 1993 federal and provincial tax rates for individuals are as follows:

Federal Tax Rates for Individuals—1993

Taxable Income	Marginal Tax Rate
$0–29,590	17%
$29,591–59,180	26%
over $59,180	29%

Provincial Tax Rates for Individuals*—1993

Alberta	45.5%
British Columbia	52.5%
Manitoba	52%
New Brunswick	62%
Newfoundland	69%
Nova Scotia	59.5%
Ontario	58%
Prince Edward Island	59.5%
Saskatchewan	50%

* There was a surtax or flat tax or both for all provinces except Newfoundland.

(The province of Quebec collects its own individual income tax. The 1993 rate ranges from 16% to 24%, and the rate applies to taxable income as computed under the Quebec Taxation Act.)

As mentioned earlier, two of the most striking characteristics of the 1988 tax reform legislation are the reduction of the number of tax brackets and the lowering of tax rates. In contrast to the 10 tax brackets and marginal tax rates ranging from 6% to 34% prior to the tax reform, the current tax legislation provides for only 3 tax brackets and 3 marginal tax rates ranging from 17% to 29%.

To minimize the impact of severe inflation, the tax legislation provides for the indexing of the three tax brackets and tax credits relating to "personal amount" by any annual increase in the Consumers Price Index in excess of 3%.

Income Tax Formula for Individuals

*OBJECTIVE 2
Explain the
formula for
determining
the taxable
income and
tax liability
of an indi-
vidual tax-
payer.*

The federal government supplies a standard income tax form (T1 General) on which individual taxpayers are guided to a proper computation of their taxable income and the amount of the tax. It is helpful to visualize the computation in terms of an income tax formula. Moreover, it is easier to understand the structure and logic of income tax and to analyze tax rules and their effect by referring to a tax formula. The general income tax formula, based on the standard income tax form for individuals, is outlined on the next page. The items in the formula are explained in more detail in the following paragraphs.

Total Income

The total income of an individual taxpayer is his or her world income from all sources except those explicitly excluded by the income tax law. If an amount received by an individual is income and not a return of capital and it is not explicitly excluded by the tax law, then it should be included as income. To identify whether an amount is excluded as income for tax purposes, it is necessary to refer to the income tax law, regulations, and court decisions.

The major categories of income for tax purposes are on page 850.

General Income Tax Formula for Individuals

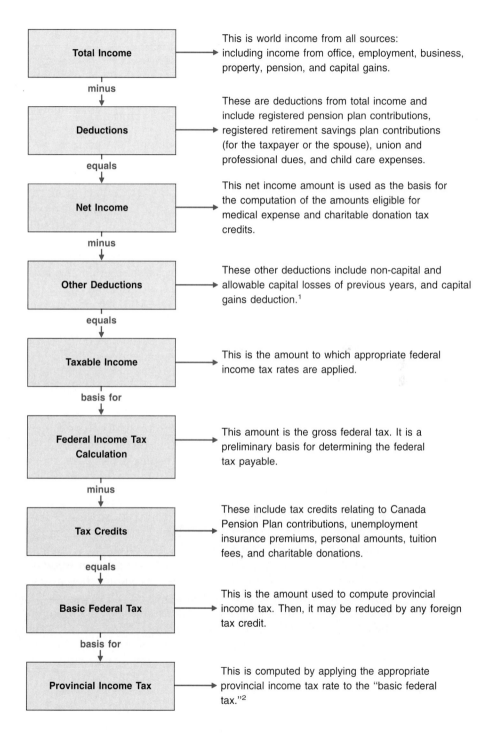

Total Income — This is world income from all sources: including income from office, employment, business, property, pension, and capital gains.

minus

Deductions — These are deductions from total income and include registered pension plan contributions, registered retirement savings plan contributions (for the taxpayer or the spouse), union and professional dues, and child care expenses.

equals

Net Income — This net income amount is used as the basis for the computation of the amounts eligible for medical expense and charitable donation tax credits.

minus

Other Deductions — These other deductions include non-capital and allowable capital losses of previous years, and capital gains deduction.[1]

equals

Taxable Income — This is the amount to which appropriate federal income tax rates are applied.

basis for

Federal Income Tax Calculation — This amount is the gross federal tax. It is a preliminary basis for determining the federal tax payable.

minus

Tax Credits — These include tax credits relating to Canada Pension Plan contributions, unemployment insurance premiums, personal amounts, tuition fees, and charitable donations.

equals

Basic Federal Tax — This is the amount used to compute provincial income tax. Then, it may be reduced by any foreign tax credit.

basis for

Provincial Income Tax — This is computed by applying the appropriate provincial income tax rate to the "basic federal tax."[2]

---

[1] Only those capital gains accrued as of February 22, 1994 are eligible for the $100,000 lifetime capital gains exemption. This capital gains exemption is no longer available after February 22, 1994.

[2] As mentioned earlier, the province of Quebec applies its tax rate to taxable income under the Quebec Taxation Act.

1 **Income from an office or employment**   This category includes salaries, wages, directors' fees, and other remuneration and taxable fringe benefits[3] such as bonuses, tips, honoraria, and certain allowances for personal or living expenses.

2 **Income from a business or property**   This category includes net income from a proprietorship, partnership, or a professional business, as well as rental, royalty, interest, and dividend income. Also, income from a business of an illegal nature is to be included in income for tax purposes.

3 **Capital gains**   This category includes gains from selling capital assets such as stocks, bonds, and depreciable properties used in the business at prices higher than their costs or adjusted costs. For 1993, ***three-quarters*** of capital gains (known as "taxable capital gains") were to be included as income for tax purposes. These gains may be offset by the same proportion of capital losses (known as "allowable capital losses") for a given year. Any remaining allowable capital losses may be carried back against taxable capital gains of the three preceding years and may be carried forward indefinitely against taxable capital gains in future years. However, there is a cumulative lifetime capital gains exemption of $100,000. In other words, up to $100,000 of the capital gain is not subject to tax.[4]

4 **Other sources of income**   This category includes all income items not covered by the preceding three categories. The more common items are: benefits from Old Age Security Pension, Canada or Quebec Pension Plan, other pensions or superannuation, and unemployment insurance benefits.

As mentioned earlier, certain items are explicitly excluded as income for tax purposes; the more common items include lottery winnings, war disability pensions, inheritance, and income from personal injury awards.[5]

Deductions

There are a number of deductions from total income. The more common ones include: registered pension plan contributions, registered retirement savings plan contributions, annual union and professional dues, child care expenses, moving expenses, alimony or separation allowance paid, carrying charges such as interest expense on money borrowed to earn investment income, safety deposit box charges for storing investment documents, and social benefits repayment for unemployment insurance and old age security when the amount of net income before the repayment, called "net income before adjustments," is over a certain limit. The amount of repayment is first deducted from "net income before adjustments" and then added back to the federal and provincial taxes to arrive at the total amount of taxes payable to the government.

---

[3]   Effective July 1, 1994, the premium on group term life insurance paid by the employer is considered to be a taxable fringe benefit. Previously, only the premium on coverage exceeding $25,000 was taxable.

[4]   As indicated in footnote 1, the lifetime capital gains exemption is no longer available after February 22, 1994.

[5]   Workers' compensation payments are first included in total income and then deducted, as "other deductions," from net income.

Net Income

The net income of an individual taxpayer is his or her total income minus the deductions. This amount is important because it is the basis for computing the amounts eligible for medical expense and charitable donation tax credits.

Other Deductions

There are very few items in this category. The deductions for 1993 include: workers' compensation payments, social assistance payments, non-capital and net capital losses of previous years, and capital gain deductions (i.e., taxable capital gain). For many taxpayers, their net income would be the same as taxable income unless they had business and allowable capital losses in prior years to be carried forward to the current year, or they have capital gains eligible for exemption from tax this year (the cumulative lifetime capital gains exemption of $100,000 was mentioned earlier).[6]

Taxable Income

This is the amount subject to federal income tax. It is computed by deducting from total income the allowable deductions to arrive at net income and then deducting from net income the allowable other deductions. The concept of taxable income is most important because it is the amount to which the appropriate tax rate is applied to determine the amount of "gross" federal income tax.

Federal Income Tax Calculation

This is the amount of "gross" federal income tax. It is not the amount of tax payable because there are a number of tax credits to be deducted from it to determine the basic federal tax and the federal tax payable.

Tax Credits

As mentioned earlier, one of the most striking characteristics of the tax reform legislation was the replacement of various deductions and exemptions with tax credits. Deductions such as Canada Pension Plan contributions, unemployment insurance premiums, tuition fees, education deductions, medical expenses in excess of 3% of net income, and charitable donations were substituted by tax credits. Similarly, all the personal exemptions—basic, married, infirm dependant aged 18 and over, and age—were replaced by tax credits. While some of the tax credits may be transferred to a spouse or a parent, any unused tax credits are not refundable. Since the tax credits are set at the lowest rate of 17%, this is an example of the broadening of the tax base as taxpayers with taxable income above the 17% bracket will be paying more income tax. The more common tax credits and the amounts for 1993 are:

---

[6]   As indicated in footnote 1, the lifetime capital gains exemption is no longer available after February 22, 1994.

1 **Personal tax credits**[7]

    (a) basic, for the taxpayer ($6,456 × 17%) $1,098

    (b) married, for the taxpayer's spouse ($5,380 × 17%)*   915

    (c) infirm dependants aged 18 and over ($1,583 × 17%)*   269

    (d) age, 65 and over ($3,482[8] × 17%)   592

* A spouse and an infirm dependant aged 18 and over can earn a net income of $538 and $2,690 respectively without reduction in the amount of tax credits. The tax credit will be reduced by 17% of net income in excess of these limits.

2 **Deduction tax credits** based on 17% of the amount of the allowable deductions.

    (a) Canada Pension Plan contributions

    (b) Unemployment insurance premiums

    (c) Tuition fees

    (d) Education amount of $80 for each month in full-time attendance at a designated educational institution and enrolled in a qualifying educational program.

    (e) Medical expenses in excess of $1,614 or 3% of net income (this excess is commonly called "allowable medical expenses"), ***whichever is less***

    (f) Charitable donations (the 17% is for the first $250 in donations and 29% for the amount in excess of $250, up to a maximum of 20% of net income)[9]

It should be mentioned that the tax reform legislation eliminated two common deductions—the employment expense deduction and the interest and dividend income deduction. Such an elimination is an example of the broadening of the tax base, one of the most striking characteristics of this tax reform legislation that was mentioned earlier.

Basic Federal Tax

The amount of basic federal tax is "gross" federal income tax (federal income tax calculation) minus tax credits. It is the basis for computing the provincial income tax. This amount plus the federal surtax of 3% on basic federal tax and 5% of basic federal tax over $12,500 and minus any foreign tax credit becomes the amount of federal tax payable.

Provincial Income Tax

The amount of provincial income tax is determined by applying the appropriate provincial tax rate to the amount of basic federal tax. Since the tax

---

[7]   On January 1, 1993, the tax credit for dependants under age 18 (as well as the family allowance payments) was replaced by the "child tax benefits." However, these benefits do not affect the computation of taxable income or income taxes.

[8]   This amount is reduced by the amount of net income exceeding $25,921 times 7.5% in 1994 and 15% in 1995. For example, if net income is $49,134 in both 1994 and 1995, the reduction for 1994 is $1,741 [($49,134 − $25,921) × 7.5%] and the reduction for 1995 is $3,482 [($49,134 − $25,921) × 15%]. In other words, for 1995 and subsequent years, if a senior's net income is $49,134 or more, he or she is not entitled to the age tax credit.

[9]   Commencing in 1994, the threshold amount is decreased from $250 to $200; that is, the 17% is applied to the first $200 of donations and the 29% to donations exceeding $200.

rate varies among provinces, an average rate of 58% (surtax or flat tax included) will be used as a provincial tax rate for illustration purposes and for the assignment materials.

Federal Dividend Tax Credit for Individuals

OBJECTIVE 3
Explain the
income tax
treatment of
dividends
received by
individuals.

To minimize the impact of double taxation on corporate income upon its subsequent distribution as dividends to individual shareholders, income tax law allows a special deduction from tax called "federal dividend tax credit." However, an individual taxpayer must first include in his or her income the dividends from taxable Canadian corporations at 125% for 1993 (known as the "gross-up" or "taxable" amount of dividends). This "gross-up" amount is taxed at the normal rate of the taxpayer. The federal income tax is then reduced by the dividend tax credit at 13⅓% of the "gross-up" amount of dividends. Since income tax is progressive, the dividend tax credit provides more tax benefit to taxpayers with lower income. To illustrate, let us assume that the federal tax rates for three individuals are 17%, 26%, and 29% and each has $8,000 of dividends from taxable Canadian corporations.

		17%	26%	29%
Tax Rate		*17%*	*26%*	*29%*
Dividends	*(a)*	*$ 8,000*	*$ 8,000*	*$ 8,000*
Add: "gross-up" of 25%		*2,000*	*2,000*	*2,000*
Taxable (gross-up) amount of dividends				
(125% of dividends received)......................		*$10,000*	*$10,000*	*$10,000*
Federal income tax on taxable amount				
of dividends......................................		*$ 1,700*	*$ 2,600*	*$ 2,900*
Less: dividend tax credit of 13⅓% on taxable				
(gross-up) amount of dividends (13⅓% × $10,000) .		*1,333*	*1,333*	*1,333*
Federal tax on dividends............................	*(b)*	*$ 367*	*$ 1,267*	*$ 1,567*
Effective rate of federal tax on dividends				
(b) ÷ (a)...		*4.6%*	*15.8%*	*19.6%*

It is clear from the preceding illustration that the difference in the effective tax rate on the dividend income between the lowest and the highest tax brackets is very substantial—a 15% difference. The 15% difference is greater than the 12% (29% − 17%) difference between the tax rates for these two tax brackets. This is, of course, in keeping with the progressive nature or the "ability to pay" philosophy of our current income tax system.

Instalment Payment of Estimate Tax for Individuals

For self-employed persons such as public accountants, doctors, dentists, and owners of unincorporated businesses, there is, of course, no salary and no tax withholding. Other examples of income on which no withholding occurs are rental income, dividends, and interest income. In these cases, instalment tax is required if tax is not withheld from at least three-quarters of a taxpayer's net income and if the taxpayer's tax in the year or in the preceding year is $1,000 or more.[10] The amount of instalment payments, due on or before March 15, June 15, September 15, and December 15, is based either on a reasonable estimate or on the tax applicable to the taxable income of the preceding year, whichever is lower. Any additional tax is due on or before April 30 of the following year.

Tax Returns, Tax Refunds, and Payment of the Tax

All individuals with tax owing must file an income tax return on or before April 30 for the preceding calendar year; otherwise, late filing penalties and interest will be charged. The payment of income taxes is on a "pay as you go" basis. The procedure by which employers withhold income taxes from the salaries of employees has been discussed previously in Chapter 11. The amounts withheld from an employee's salary for income taxes can be considered as payment on account. If the amount of income taxes as computed by preparing a tax return is less than the amount withheld during the year, the taxpayer is entitled to a refund. On the other hand, if the tax computed is more than the amount withheld, the balance should be paid with the filing of the tax return. Individuals who are entitled to a refund will have to file a tax return (within three years from the end of the year for which a refund is due) to obtain a refund.

Computation of Individual Income Tax Illustrated

OBJECTIVE 4
Determine the tax liability of an individual

The computation of the 1993 federal and provincial income tax for Sam Lee is illustrated on the next page. The illustration highlights some of the main features of the income tax law and is based on the following assumed data:

1 Mr. Sam Lee is married and has a sixteen-year-old son who has $860 net income from various part-time jobs. Also, Mrs. Lee has a net income of $500.

2 Mr. Lee's income, withholdings, and disbursements include:

Income:
Salary from employment (before tax withholding)	$60,000
Dividends from taxable Canadian corporations	8,000
Interest from Canada Savings Bonds	1,800
Gain on sale of shares of Canadian Ltd.	1,200

Withholdings:
Income taxes	16,000
Canada Pension Plan contributions	753
Unemployment insurance premiums	1,162
Contribution to a registered pension plan*	4,869
Union membership dues	530

Disbursements:
Medical expenses	900
Charitable donations	1,600
Professional membership dues	690

* Assumed amount for the year. The determination of the maximum amount can be very complex, depending on the types of pension plan and such elements as pensionable earnings, years of services, etc.

---

[10] Effective September 15, 1994, instalment tax is required if the difference between tax payable (federal and provincial) and tax withheld at source is greater than $2,000 in both the current year and either of the two preceding years.

3 Provincial tax rate is 58%.

SAM LEE
Illustrative Federal and Provincial Income Tax Computation
For the Year 1993

Total income:

Salary..		$60,000
Dividends ($8,000 plus 25% gross-up).....................................		10,000
Interest		1,800
Taxable capital gain (¾ of the $1,200 gain)		900
		$72,700

Deductions

Registered pension plan contributions	$4,869	
Union and professional dues...................................	1,220	6,089
Net income..		$66,611

Other deductions

Capital gains deduction (¾ of the $1,200 gain)*		900
Taxable income		$65,711

Federal income tax calculation:

$29,590 at 17%		$ 5,030
$29,590 at 26%		7,693
$ 6,531 at 29%		1,894
$65,711		$14,617

Tax credits:

Canada Pension Plan contributions credit	$ 128	
Unemployment insurance premiums credit	198	
Basic personal credit	1,098	
Spousal (married) credit	915	
Charitable donations credits		
($250 at 17% and $1,350 at 29%)**............................	434	
Dividend credit (13⅓% of the gross-up amount of $10,000).......	1,333	4,106
Basic federal tax		$10,511
3% federal surtax...		315
Federal tax payable..		$10,826

Add:

Provincial tax—58% of "basic federal tax"		6,096
Total tax payable		$16,922
Less: income taxes withheld		16,000
Amount to be paid		$ 922

* Assuming the $100,000 lifetime capital gains exemption has not been reached. Also note, this exemption is no longer available after February 22, 1994.
** As mentioned in footnote 9, the threshold amount of $250 is decreased to $200 for 1994 and subsequent years.
Note: Since the amount of medical expenses of $900 is less than 3% of net income, there is no tax credit for medical expenses.

INCOME TAXES: CORPORATIONS

Taxation and Tax Rates

A corporation is a separate taxable entity. Every corporation, unless specifically exempt from taxation, must file an income tax return (Form T2) within six months from the end of its taxation year, whether or not it has taxable income or owes any tax. Also, corporations are required to pay their income taxes on a monthly instalment basis. Our discussion is focussed on the ordinary business public corporations, with only brief references to certain other types of corporations for which special tax treatment applies.

As with individuals, the federal income tax rate applies to the corporation's taxable income. The tax rates for 1993 are as shown below:

Type of Business	Tax Rate
General business	28%
Manufacturing business	22%[11]
Small business	12%[12]

Also, there is a 3% surtax on federal corporate income tax that increases all the above rates by 0.8%.

In addition to federal tax, all provinces levy income tax on corporations. The provincial tax rate for 1993 for general business public corporations ranges from 9% to 17%. Also, provincial rates are lower for certain businesses, such as manufacturing and processing and small businesses.

Computation of Taxable Income of Corporations

While the taxable income of corporations is computed in much the same way as for individuals there are a number of differences. The major ones include:

1 **Tax credits of a personal nature** Corporations are not allowed tax credits of a personal nature, such as basic personal, married, dependant (for infirm dependant aged 18 and over) tax credits and medical expenses tax credits, which are allowed for individuals.

2 **Dividends received** The dividends received by a corporation from other taxable Canadian corporations are **not** included in the corporation's taxable income. Since these dividends are not taxable, the dividend tax credit for individuals does not apply to corporations. However, certain private corporations pay a special refundable tax on certain dividends received, which will be refunded when the corporation subsequently pays a taxable dividend to its shareholders.

---

[11] The 1994 tax rate for a manufacturing business is 21%.

[12] This low tax rate is no longer available to those corporations with taxable capital employed in Canada of $15 million or more for taxation years ending after June 30, 1994. Also, for corporations with taxable capital between $10 and $15 million, the amount subject to this low rate is reduced on a straight-line basis.

Capital gains and losses   Corporations, like individuals, may deduct the **allowable** capital losses **only** to the extent of **taxable** capital gains. Also, corporations may carry back and forward the remaining allowable capital losses against taxable capital gains in the same manner as for individuals, as discussed earlier. However, the lifetime cumulative capital gains exemption of $100,000 for individuals is **not** available for corporations.[13]

Computation of Taxable Income and Federal Income Tax for Corporation Illustrated

OBJECTIVE 5
Determine the taxable income and income tax of a corporation.

To highlight some of the main features of income tax law as it applies to corporations, the computation of federal tax for Stone Corporation, a general business operation, for the 1993 taxation year follows. Remember this illustration is not an income statement and does not show items in the sequence of an income statement.

STONE CORPORATION
Illustrative Federal Tax Computation
(In thousands of dollars)

Revenue:

Sales		$780,000
Dividends received from taxable Canadian corporations......................		10,000
Total revenue		$790,000

Expenses:

Cost of goods sold...	$510,000	
Other expenses (includes capital loss of $2,000)	96,000	606,000
Income for accounting purposes		$184,000

Add back:

Notice the difference between accounting income ($184,000) and taxable income ($176,000)

Capital loss deducted as part of operating expenses.........................		2,000
Subtotal...		$186,000
Deduct (item not subject to tax)		
Dividends received from taxable Canadian corporations......................		10,000
Taxable income		$176,000

Federal tax computation:

28% on $176,000	$49,280	
3% surtax (3% × $49,280)	1,478	$ 50,758
Deduct: Monthly instalment payments		50,600
Balance of federal tax payable		$ 158

Accounting Income versus Taxable Income

In the determination of **accounting income,** the objective is to measure business operating results as accurately as possible in accordance with generally accepted accounting principles. **Taxable income,** on the other hand, is a legal concept governed by statute and subject to frequent change

---

[13]   As indicated in footnote 1, the lifetime capital gains exemption is no longer available after February 22, 1994.

by Parliament. In setting the rules for determining taxable income, Parliament is interested not only in meeting the revenue needs of government but also in achieving certain public policy objectives. Since accounting income and taxable income are determined with different purposes in mind, it is not surprising that they often differ by material amounts.

The following are some of the major areas of difference between accounting income and taxable income:

1 Certain income and expense items included in computing accounting income are either excluded or partly excluded from computing taxable income. For example, dividends received by a taxable Canadian corporation from other taxable Canadian corporations are included in accounting income but are excluded from taxable income; goodwill and organization costs incurred after 1971 may be amortized for accounting purposes, but only three-quarters of them can be amortized for tax purposes.

2 Capital gains and losses are fully included in computing accounting income, but only a portion (¾) of these gains and losses is included in computing taxable income.

3 Methods used for computing accounting income may differ from those used for computing taxable income. For example, lifo method of inventory may be used for accounting purposes, but is not allowed for tax purposes; straight-line or sum-of-the-years'-digits method of depreciation may be used for computing accounting income, but a declining balance method based on tax regulations is used to compute depreciation, called "capital cost allowance," for tax purposes.

Capital Cost Allowance

OBJECTIVE 6 Determine the amount of capital cost allowance.

There are special tax regulations for recognizing a portion of a depreciable asset as an expense each year. This expense is called **capital cost allowance** rather than depreciation. The recognition of capital cost allowance for tax purposes differs significantly from depreciation for accounting purposes. The main features of capital cost allowance are:

1 Depreciable assets of a similar nature are grouped into a particular class or pool.

2 Costs of additions are added to, and proceeds of disposals (up to the original cost of the asset) and capital cost allowances are deducted from, the balance of the class or pool.

3 When a class or pool has a credit balance at the end of a taxation year, the credit balance, known as "recaptured capital cost allowance," is to be included in income for tax purposes.

4 A stipulated rate is applied to the balance of each class or pool to obtain the amount of capital cost allowance for the year. However, in the year where there is net addition of assets (i.e., total addition exceeds total disposal), only one-half of such net addition is eligible for capital cost allowance for that year.

Some of the more common classes of depreciable assets and their stipulated rates are:

Class		Maximum Rate
1	Brick, stone, cement buildings, and most buildings (other than those in Classes 6, 31, or 32).................	4%*
8	Machinery, equipment, and furniture**.......................	20%
10	Automobiles, trucks, and tractors	30%

* For buildings acquired in 1988 and subsequent years. Buildings acquired prior to 1988 are in class 3, with a 5% rate.
** If the machinery and equipment are for manufacturing, they are included in class 43.

Taxpayers may claim an amount of capital cost allowance in each taxation year up to the maximum amount allowed for each class. The following example illustrates the application of the main features of capital cost allowance.

X Ltd. has a number of trucks (Class 10) used in its business operations. The beginning balance is $100,000. During the year, two trucks costing $48,000 were purchased and one old truck, with an original cost of $12,000, was sold for $8,000.

The capital cost allowance for the year is computed as follows:

Beginning balance...	$100,000
Add: purchase of two trucks..	48,000
	$148,000
Deduct: proceeds of disposal of one truck	8,000
Ending balance...	$140,000
Capital cost allowance: 30% on beginning balance of $100,000	$ 30,000
30% on ½ of net asset addition of $40,000	
[($48,000 − $8,000) × ½ × 30%)]......................	6,000
	$ 36,000

X Ltd. may claim a capital cost allowance for class 10 of up to a maximum of $36,000 for the year.

Deferred Income Taxes

OBJECTIVE 7 Describe the circumstances that create a liability for deferred income taxes.

We have seen that differences between generally accepted accounting principles and income tax rules can be material. Some businesses might consider it more convenient to maintain their accounting records in conformity with the tax rules, but the result would be to distort financial statements. It is clearly preferable to maintain accounting records by the principles that produce relevant information about business operations. The data in the records can then be adjusted by use of work sheets to arrive at taxable income.

When a corporation follows one method in its accounting records and financial statements but uses a different method for its income tax return, a financial reporting problem arises. The difference in method will usually have the effect of postponing the recognition of income on the tax return. The items causing this difference fall into two broad categories: permanent differences and timing (temporary) differences.

Permanent differences are revenue or expenses that enter into the computation of one type of income, but never are considered in determining the other. Most permanent differences are the result of special tax law provisions unrelated to accounting principles. For example, dividends received by a corporation from other taxable Canadian corporations are included in the determination of accounting income but are excluded from the computation of taxable income. Also, certain expenses such as political contributions are deducted from accounting income but are not deducted from the computation of taxable income.

Timing differences arise when the ***same dollar amount*** of revenue or expense is recognized for tax purposes and for accounting purposes, but the ***timing*** of the recognition under tax rules differs from that under accounting principles. For example, a company may use an accelerated method of depreciation in its income tax return but use the straight-line method in its income statement. Over the life of the depreciable asset, however, the total amount of depreciation claimed in the tax returns will be the same as that reported in the company's income statements.

Most businesses have a policy of using in their income tax returns those accounting methods that will ***accelerate as much as possible the recognition of expenses, and delay as long as possible the recognition of revenue.*** As a result of using these methods, many businesses are able to defer the recognition of significant portions of their pretax accounting income into the tax returns of future years. Hence, they are able to defer payment of the related income taxes.

Accounting for Deferred Taxes: An Illustration

When differences between pretax accounting income and taxable income are caused by timing differences, a business bases its income tax expense for the period upon its pretax accounting income. This practice achieves a proper ***matching*** of income taxes expense with the related earnings. However, some of this income taxes expense will not be paid until later years, when the income is included in future tax returns. Through timing differences, payment of part of a company's income taxes expense may be deferred on a long-term basis.

To illustrate, let us consider a very simple case involving only one timing difference. Assume that Pryor Corporation has before-tax accounting income of $600,000 in both 1995 and 1996. However, the company takes as a tax deduction in 1995 an expense of $200,000, which is not deducted as expense in the income statement until 1996. The company's accounting income, taxable income, and the actual income taxes due (assuming an average federal and provincial tax rate of 46%) are shown below.

	1996	1995
Accounting income (before income taxes)	$600,000	$600,000
Taxable income	800,000	400,000
Actual income taxes due each year at 46% rate:		
1995: $600,000 − $200,000 = $400,000 taxable income × 46%		$184,000
1996: $600,000 + $200,000 = $800,000 taxable income × 46%	$368,000	

Let us assume the Pryor Corporation reports as an expense in its income statement each year the amount of income taxes due for that year. The effect on reported net income as shown in the company's financial statements would be as follows:

	1996	**1995**
Accounting income (before income taxes)	$600,000	$600,000
Income taxes expense (amount actually due)	368,000	184,000
Net income...	$232,000	$416,000
Income taxes expense as a percentage of pretax accounting income..	61%	31%

(margin note: Company reports actual taxes)

The readers of Pryor Corporation's income statement might well wonder why the same $600,000 accounting income before income taxes in the two years produced such widely varying amounts of tax expense and net income.

To deal with this distortion between pretax income and after-tax income, an accounting policy known as ***interperiod income tax allocation*** is required for financial reporting purposes.[14] Briefly, the objective of income tax allocation is to ***accrue income taxes expense*** in ***relation to accounting income,*** even if the items comprising accounting income will be taxable or deductible in a different period.

In the Pryor Corporation example, this means we would report in the 1995 income statement a tax expense based on $600,000 of accounting income even though a portion of this income ($200,000) will not be subject to income tax until the second year. The effect of this accounting procedure is demonstrated by the following journal entries to record the income tax expense in each of the two years:

(margin note: Entries to record income tax allocations)

1995	Income Taxes Expense..	276,000	
	Income Taxes Payable		184,000
	Deferred Income Taxes		92,000
	To record current and deferred income taxes at 46%		
	of accounting income of $600,000.		

Deferred income taxes are a liability. As explained in Chapter 16, classification of deferred income taxes as current or long-term depends upon the nature of the items causing the tax deferral.[15]

In 1996, the timing difference will "reverse," and Pryor will report taxable income of $200,000 in excess of its pretax accounting income. Thus, the income taxes deferred in 1995 are coming due. The entry to record income taxes expense in 1996 is:

---

[14]   For a more complete discussion of tax allocation procedures, see *CICA Handbook,* section 3470, on "Corporate income taxes."

[15]   Timing differences also may require a company to pay some income taxes ***before*** the related income appears in accounting income. This situation creates an asset, which might be called Prepaid Income Taxes. In this chapter, we illustrate only the more common situation in which the payment of taxes is deferred, thereby creating a liability.

1996	Income Taxes Expense	276,000	
	Deferred Income Taxes	92,000	
	Income Taxes Payable		368,000

To record income taxes at 46% of accounting income of $600,000 and to record actual income taxes due.

Notice that as in 1995, income tax expense is based upon the pretax accounting income shown in the company's income statement.

Using these interperiod tax allocation procedures, Pryor Corporation's financial statements would report net income during the two-year period as follows:

	1996	1995
Accounting income (before income taxes)	$600,000	$600,000
Income taxes expense (tax allocation basis)	276,000	276,000
Net income	$324,000	$324,000
Income taxes expense as a percentage of pretax accounting income	46%	46%

Deferred Taxes: An Evaluation In 1996, Pryor Corporation faces the unpleasant prospect of paying an amount of income taxes that is **greater** than its income taxes expense for the current year. Although this situation can arise, it does not usually happen as long as a company continues to grow.

A growing company usually defers more taxes each year than the previous deferrals that are coming due. Thus, a growing company may pay less in taxes each year than the amount of its current tax expense, and its liability for deferred income taxes continues to grow. The liability for deferred taxes is, in essence, an **interest-free loan**—capital made available to the business by selecting advantageous accounting methods for use in the company's income tax returns. Hence, deferring income taxes generally is viewed as a desirable business strategy.

CASE IN POINT The balance sheets of many companies showed large amounts of deferred income taxes. As of a recent year, the deferred income taxes for Petro-Canada were $460 million; Canadian Pacific, $420 million; Dofasco, $394 million; and Bow Valley Industries, $133 million.

TAX PLANNING OPPORTUNITIES

Income tax laws have become so complex that careful tax planning has become a way of life for most business firms. Almost all companies today engage professional tax specialists to review the tax aspects of major business decisions and to develop plans for legally minimizing income taxes. We will now consider some areas in which tax planning may offer substantial benefits.

Form of Business Organization

Tax factors should be carefully considered at the time a business is organized. As a sole proprietor or partner, a business owner will pay taxes at individual rates on the business income earned in any year **whether or not it is withdrawn from the business.** On the other hand, corporations deduct salaries paid to owners for services but cannot deduct dividends paid to shareholders. Both **salaries and dividends** are taxable income to the persons receiving them. However, the tax on dividends is reduced by a dividend tax credit.

These and other factors must be weighed in deciding in any given situation whether the corporate or noncorporate form of business organization is preferable. There is no simple answer, even considering only these basic differences. To illustrate, suppose that Able, a married man, starts a small business that he expects will produce, before any compensation to himself and before income taxes, an average annual income of $80,000. Able plans to recognize a salary of $20,000 and to withdraw all income from the business. The combined corporate and individual taxes (based on 1993 tax rates) under the corporate and sole proprietorship form of business organization are summarized below (surtax is excluded to simplify the computations).

Which form of business organization produces a lower tax?

	Corporation	Sole Proprietorship
Business income	$80,000	$80,000
Salary to Able	20,000	
	$60,000	$80,000
Corporate taxes (on the $60,000 taxable income of a small business)		
Federal 12% $7,200		
Provincial 10%* 6,000	13,200	
Amount to Able (the $46,800 as dividends)	$46,800	$80,000
Combined corporate and individual tax:		
Corporate tax on $60,000 taxable income	$13,200	
Individual tax (assume a total deduction of $8,500, tax credits of $2,123, and dividend tax credit of $7,800)		
On Able's $20,000 salary and $46,800 dividends	9,382	
On Able's $80,000 share of business income		$22,393
Total income taxes on business income	$22,582	$22,393

* The more common rate for 1993.

Under these assumptions, the formation of a corporation is not favourable from an income tax viewpoint. However, the tax difference between the corporation and sole proprietorship of $189 is very small. Another factor to be considered is that, with the corporation, Able can postpone the amount of tax payable by retaining the income in the corporation rather than paying it out as dividends. Of course, factors other than income tax (such as limited liability) must be considered in deciding whether to incorporate the business.

Planning Business Transactions to Minimize or Postpone Income Taxes

Business transactions may often be arranged in such a way as to produce favourable tax treatment. For example, timing of disposal of investments (usually at or near the year-end date) in securities can postpone income taxes because capital losses from securities can be offset against capital gains. However, the sale of an investment in securities to generate a capital loss must not be accompanied by the purchase of the same securities within 30 days or the capital loss would be disallowed as it would be considered as a "wash transaction."

Sometimes sellers try to arrange a transaction one way to their tax benefit and buyers try to shape it another way to produce tax savings for them. Income tax effects thus become a part of price negotiation. For example, in buying business property, the purchasers will try to allocate as much of the cost of the property to the building and as little to the land as possible, since building costs can be depreciated for tax purposes. Similarly, in buying a business, the buyers will want as much as possible of the total purchase price to be attributed to inventories or to depreciable assets rather than goodwill. The cost of goods sold and depreciation are deductible against income, whereas only three-quarters of goodwill can be amortized for tax purposes. Thus, the main point is: *any failure to consider tax effects on major business transactions can be costly.*

Tax Planning in the Choice of Financial Structure

In deciding upon the best means of raising capital to start or expand a business, consideration should be given to income taxes. Different forms of business financing produce different amounts of tax expense. Interest on debt, for example, is *fully deductible,* but dividends on preferred or common stock are not. This factor operates as a strong incentive to finance expansion by borrowing.

Let us suppose that a company subject to a 45% marginal tax rate needs $100,000 to invest in productive assets on which it can earn a 16% annual return. If the company obtains the needed money by issuing $100,000 in 9% preferred stock, it will earn *after taxes* only $8,800, which is not even enough to cover the $9,000 preferred dividend. (This after-tax amount is computed as $16,000 income less taxes at 45% of $16,000.)

Now let us assume, on the other hand, that the company borrowed $100,000 at 12% interest. (Interest rate is usually higher than dividend rate because interest is tax deductible and dividend provides a dividend tax credit.) The additional gross income would be $16,000 but interest expense of $12,000 would be deducted, leaving taxable income of $4,000. The tax on the $4,000 at 45% would be $1,800, leaving after-tax income of $2,200. Analysis along these lines is also needed in choosing between debt financing and financing by issuing common stock.

CHAPTER REVIEW

KEY TERMS INTRODUCED OR EMPHASIZED IN CHAPTER 18

Basic federal tax   The gross amount of federal tax minus tax credits. The basic federal tax is the basis for computing provincial tax.

Capital cost allowance   The amount of expense for depreciable assets for tax purposes.

Capital gain or loss   The difference between the cost or adjusted-cost base of a capital asset and the amount received from its sale.

Dividend tax credit   This credit is intended to minimize the impact of "double taxation" on corporate income. It is computed by applying $13\frac{1}{3}\%$ to the taxable (gross-up) amount of dividends and is deducted from federal income tax.

Gross federal tax   Taxable income times federal tax rate equals gross federal tax.

Interperiod tax allocation   Allocation of income tax expense among accounting periods because of timing differences between accounting income and taxable income. Causes income tax expense reported in financial statements to be in logical relation to accounting income.

Marginal tax rate   The tax rate to which a taxpayer is subject on the additional dollar of income received.

Tax credit   An amount to be subtracted from gross federal income tax to arrive at basic federal tax, including credits for Canada Pension Plan contributions, unemployment insurance premiums, basic personal, married, dependant (infirm and aged 18 and over), tuition fees, and charitable donations.

Tax planning   A systematic process of legally minimizing income taxes by considering in advance the tax consequences of alternative business or investment actions.

Taxable income   The computed amount to which the appropriate tax rate is to be applied to arrive at the gross amount of federal tax.

Total income   An individual's world income from all sources, including income from office, employment, business, property and pension, and capital gain.

ASSIGNMENT MATERIAL

DISCUSSION QUESTIONS

1 What are some broad objectives of the federal income tax legislation other than providing revenue for the government?

2 List the five most striking characteristics of the 1988 tax reform legislation.

3 List three examples of tax credits other than dividend tax credit.

4 Explain the differences between *tax planning* and *tax evasion,* and give an example of each.

5 What are the major classes of taxpayers under the federal income tax law?

6 It has been claimed that corporate income is subject to "double taxation." Explain the meaning of this expression, and indicate whether there is provision in the tax law to minimize it.

7 Why is the income tax system described as one of ***self-assessment?*** What means do tax authorities have of enforcing this system?

8 Taxes are characterized as either ***progressive, proportional,*** or ***regressive*** with respect to any given base. Describe an income tax rate structure that would fit each of these characterizations.

9 State whether you agree with the following statement and explain your reasoning: A person in a very high tax bracket who makes a cash contribution to a charitable organization will reduce his or her federal income tax liability by more than the amount of the donation.

10 State the federal income tax formula for individuals, beginning with total income and ending with basic federal tax.

11 From an individual taxpayer's viewpoint, it is better to have a $10,000 capital gain than $10,000 of ordinary income. Explain.

12 Cite two examples to illustrate the broadening of the tax base originated from the tax reform legislation.

13 Even when a corporation uses the accrual method of accounting, taxable income may differ from accounting income. Give four ***examples*** of differences between the tax treatment and accounting treatment of items that are included in the determination of income.

14 Under what circumstances is the accounting procedure known as ***interperiod income tax allocation*** appropriate? Explain the objective of this procedure.

15 The depreciation expense computed by Zane Corporation as the capital cost allowance (permitted by the income tax law) appeared in the tax return as $150,000. In the accounting records and financial statements, Zane's depreciation was computed on the straight-line basis and amounted to $100,000. Under interperiod tax allocation procedures, would Zane's balance sheet show deferred income taxes as a debit or credit? Explain.

16 List some tax factors to be considered in deciding whether to organize a new business as a corporation or as a partnership.

17 Explain the principal factors that should be considered by a taxpayer in determining ***when*** it would be most advantageous to sell an investment that will result in the recognition of a capital loss.

18 Explain how the corporate income tax makes debt financing in general more attractive than financing through the issuance of preferred stock.

19 Some of the decisions that business owners must make in the organization and operation of a business will affect the amount of income taxes to be paid. List some of these decisions that affect the amount of income taxes legally payable.

MULTIPLE CHOICE QUESTIONS

1 Which of the following is applicable to the income tax system?

   a The only objective of income tax laws is to raise as much revenue as possible to finance government spending.

   b A taxpayer is required to pay instalment tax if tax withheld at source is greater than $2,000.

   c One of the most striking characteristics of the 1988 tax reform legislation is the lowering of tax rates and the broadening of the tax base.

d   The three classes of taxpayers are: individuals, partnerships, and corporations.

2   In preparing the income tax return for an individual taxpayer:

a   Income taxes withheld from an individual's salary are deducted from total income.

b   Income from sources outside Canada must be included in the determination of total income.

c   Income from illegal sources is excluded from the computation of total income.

d   Receipt of a large refund each year indicates better tax planning than receipt of a small refund.

3   Which of the following are eligible for tax credits? (More than one answer may be correct.)

a   Registered pension plan contributions and unemployment insurance premiums.

b   Tuition fees, charitable donations, and education amount.

c   Basic personal amount for the taxpayer, Canada Pension Plan contributions, and unemployment insurance premium.

d   Medical expenses, union dues, and allowable capital losses.

4   When a business is organized as a corporation:

a   Income taxes expense recorded in the accounting records is based upon accounting income and may differ from the income taxes liability shown in the corporate income tax return.

b   The treatment of capital gains and losses is the same as for individuals, including the cumulative capital gain exemption of $100,000.

c   Taxable income is the same as net income before income taxes in the income statement.

d   Dividends received from other taxable Canadian corporations must be included in the corporation's taxable income.

5   Which of the following are valid statements regarding tax planning and the choice of business organization? (More than one answer may be correct.)

a   When a business is organized as a corporation, no income tax is paid on earnings that remain invested in the business.

b   In computing a corporation's taxable income, the corporation may deduct salaries paid to owners, but may not deduct dividends.

c   When a business is organized as a sole proprietorship, the owner must pay taxes at individual rates on the entire amount of business income, regardless of amounts withdrawn by the owner.

d   An individual who organizes a business as a corporation must pay individual income taxes on any salary and dividends received from the corporation after deducting the appropriate amount of dividend tax credit.

EXERCISES

EXERCISE 18-1
Accounting and Tax Terminology

Listed below are nine technical accounting and tax terms introduced in this chapter:

Capital gain	*Taxable income*	*Interperiod tax allocation*
Tax credit	*Gross federal tax*	*Cash basis of accounting*
Basic federal tax	*Tax planning*	*Capital cost allowance*

Each of the following statements may (or may not) describe one of these technical terms. For each statement, indicate the term described, or answer "None" if the statement does not correctly describe any of the terms.

a Net income minus other deductions, which serves as a basis to compute gross federal tax.

b Taxable income multiplied by an appropriate federal tax rate.

c Gross federal tax minus tax credits.

d Income tax recognized each period as a constant percentage of net sales.

e Causes income tax expense reported in financial statements to be in logical relationship to accounting income.

f Profit from disposal of such assets as stock and bonds acquired as long-term investments.

g Revenue recorded when received in cash and expenses recorded in period payment is made.

h An amount to be subtracted from gross federal tax.

i Depreciation calculated according to tax law and regulations.

EXERCISE 18-2
Inclusion or
Exclusion?

Some of the following items should be included in income; others on the list should be excluded. For each item listed, write the identifying letter and the word *included* or *excluded* to show whether the item belongs in income on the income tax return of an individual.

a Kickbacks received by automobile salespeople from insurance brokers to whom they referred customers.

b Dividends from investment in a taxable Canadian corporation.

c Compensation received for damages suffered in automobile accident.

d Gain on sale of shares of Canadian Ltd. common stock.

e Gift from an uncle.

f Money received from lottery winnings.

g Tips received by waiter.

h Interest received on investment bonds.

EXERCISE 18-3
Deductible or
Nondeduct-
ible?

Susan Rooney has a total income of $68,000 and a net income of $54,000. For each item listed, write the identifying letter and the word *deductible* or *nondeductible*.

a Interest paid on instalment contract on automobile	$ 180
b Gift to an unemployed relative	300
c Professional dues	660
d Contribution to Red Cross...	575
e Cost of commuting between home and work	800
f Canada Pension Plan contributions	753
g Unemployment insurance premiums	1,162
h Registered pension plan contributions	4,800
i Medical expenses (not covered by insurance)	500
j Cash stolen while on business trip	80
k Interest paid on a bank loan for investment purposes	450
l Safety deposit box fee (to keep investment certificates).......................	35

**EXERCISE 18-4
Determine
Total, Net, and
Taxable In-
come, and
Federal Tax for
an Individual**

Angela Lambert has the following information for her first tax return, one year after graduation from a top university.

Salary	*$88,000*
Interest from a bank account	*388*
Canada Pension Plan contributions	*753*
Unemployment insurance premiums	*1,162*
Professional dues	*800*
Registered pension plan contributions	*3,500*
Basic personal tax credits	*1,098*
Dental expenses	*2,980*
Charitable donations	*2,600*

Compute (a) total income, (b) net income, (c) taxable income, (d) gross federal tax, and (e) basic federal tax for Angela Lambert. The federal tax rates are assumed to be: 17% the first $29,590, 26% on the second $29,590, and 29% on the remaining taxable income.

**EXERCISE 18-5
Determine Tax-
able Income
for an Individ-
ual**

Pier Fiorino has the following sources of income for 1993:

Interest from Canada Savings Bonds	*$ 1,000*
Dividends from taxable Canadian corporations	*12,000*
Gains on sales of shares in Canadian National Ltd.	*3,000*

Compute the ***net*** amount that should be included as taxable income, assuming no capital gain was reported in prior years.

**EXERCISE 18-6
Determine Tax-
able Income
and Federal
Tax Liability
for a Corpora-
tion**

Sunset Limited reports the following income during Year 1:

Operating income (after deducting depreciation of $100,000)	*$600,000*
Capital gains	*180,000*
Dividends received from taxable Canadian corporations	*60,000*
Capital cost allowances	*116,000*

Compute the taxable income and ***federal*** income tax liability for Sunset Limited for Year 1. Assume a 28% federal tax rate and ignore any surtax.

**EXERCISE 18-7
Interperiod Tax
Allocation**

Sea King Corporation deducted on its tax return for Year 1 an expense of $50,000 that was not recognized as an expense for accounting purposes until Year 2. The corporation's accounting income before income taxes in each of the two years was $485,000. The company uses tax allocation procedures.

a Prepare the journal entries required at the end of Year 1 and Year 2 to record income tax expense, assuming a combined federal and provincial tax rate of 46%.

b Prepare a two-column schedule showing the net income to appear on the financial statements for Year 1 and Year 2, assuming tax allocation procedures are used. Also prepare a similar schedule on the assumption that tax allocation procedures are not used.

PROBLEMS

Group A

PROBLEM 18A-1
Inclusion in or Exclusion from Income?

State whether each item listed below should be included in or excluded from an individual's income for federal income tax purposes. Add explanatory comments if needed.

1 Lottery winnings.

2 Cash dividends received on stock of Canadian Ltd.

3 Proceeds of life insurance policy received on death of a taxpayer.

4 Tips received by a door attendant at a luxury hotel.

5 Income from a business of an illegal nature.

6 Unemployment insurance benefits.

7 Drawing received from a proprietorship in excess of its income.

8 Income from personal injury awards.

9 Interest received on a savings account in Scotia Bank.

10 Gain on sale of Loris Ltd. shares of common stock.

11 Painted a building owned by the creditor in return for the cancellation of a note payable of $1,000.

12 Las Vegas vacation paid by employer as reward for outstanding service.

PROBLEM 18A-2
Deductible or Not Deductible?

State whether each item listed below is deductible or not deductible by an individual for federal income tax purposes, and if deductible, whether it is from total income or net income, or as a tax credit.

1 Fees for preparation of personal income tax return.

2 Lawyer's fee for appealing an assessment by Revenue Canada, Taxation.

3 Registered pension plan contributions.

4 Professional membership fee.

5 Interest on a loan that was used to invest in a taxable Canadian corporation.

6 Interest paid on mortgage covering personal residence.

7 Capital loss on the sale of securities.

8 Life insurance premium paid by a taxpayer.

9 Lottery losses.

10 Expenses incurred in moving from Calgary to Vancouver to accept a new position with a different company, not reimbursed by employer.

11 Alimony paid.

12 Education amount.

PROBLEM 18A-3
Determine Income Tax for an Individual

The following information is related to Gloria Hoysum, a resident of a province with a tax rate of 58%.

Income:

Salary from employment	$70,000
Director's fee (on the board of directors of Toysun Ltd.)	8,000
Dividends from taxable Canadian corporations	6,000
Interest from savings account with Bank of Nova Scotia	600
Gain on sale of shares of Halifax Ltd.	1,800

Withholdings:

Income taxes	22,000
Canada Pension Plan contributions	753
Unemployment insurance premiums	1,162
Contribution to a registered pension plan	4,980

Disbursements:

Charitable donations	3,200
Professional membership fees	1,200

Others:

Loss on sale of shares of Sydney Mines Ltd.	600
Lottery losses	890
Tax credits relating to the taxpayer	1,098

INSTRUCTIONS Compute Hoysum's federal and provincial income tax for the year by using the following federal tax rates: 17% on the first $29,590, 26% on the second $29,590, and 29% on the remaining amount. Assume that Hoysum had not reported any capital gains or losses in prior years and that there is a 3% federal surtax on basic federal tax and a 5% surtax on basic federal tax in excess of $12,500. The provincial rate is 58%.

PROBLEM 18A-4
Determine Capital Cost Allowance, Federal Tax, and Deferred Tax

The following information is related to Macri Corporation for the current year:

Operating income (before depreciation, dividends, capital gains, and capital losses)	$980,000
Depreciation (automobiles and trucks, straight-line basis)	150,000
Dividends received from taxable Canadian corporations	80,000
Capital gains from sale of securities	30,000
Capital losses from sale of securities	50,000
Automobiles and trucks (class 10, maximum rate 30%):	
Beginning balance	700,000
Additions during the last month of the year	350,000
Proceeds from disposal of trucks (original cost $460,000) during the year	250,000

INSTRUCTIONS
a Compute the amount of capital cost allowance for the current year.

b Compute the federal income tax for the current year, based on a 28% tax rate.

c Compute the amount of federal income tax deferred by claiming the maximum capital cost allowance rather than the amount of depreciation for accounting purposes.

PROBLEM 18A-5
Determine Accounting and Taxable Income, Income Tax and Deferred Tax, and Tax Advantage of Financing Method

The accounting records of Garden Corporation included the following information for the current year:

Net sales	$8,600,000
Cost of goods sold	6,000,000
Dividends received from a taxable Canadian corporation	53,000
Operating expenses (including depreciation of $250,000)	1,700,000
Capital gains from sales of securities	28,000
Capital losses from sales of securities	12,000
Capital cost allowance	360,000

Garden is considering expanding its facilities as a result of increased sales, financed either by issuing $500,000, 12% bonds or 9% cumulative preferred stock.

INSTRUCTIONS

a Compute the accounting income for the current year.

b Compute the taxable income for the current year.

c Compute the federal and provincial income taxes for the current year. Assume that the federal rate is 28% and provincial rate is 14%.

d Prepare the journal entry to record the current and deferred income taxes for the year.

e Explain which method of financing the $500,000 expansion is more beneficial to the company from an income tax viewpoint.

Group B

PROBLEM 18B-1
Inclusion in or Exclusion from Income?

State whether each item listed below should be included in or excluded from an individual's income for federal income tax purposes. Add explanatory comments if they are necessary.

1 Share of income from partnership in excess of drawings.

2 An honorarium of $100 for a speech to charitable organizations.

3 Interest received on Canada Savings Bonds.

4 Salary received from a corporation by a shareholder who owns directly or indirectly all the shares of the corporation's outstanding stock.

5 Amount received as damages in a libel lawsuit.

6 Trip to Hawaii given by employer as reward for outstanding service.

7 Taxpayer owed $1,500 on a note payable. During the current year the taxpayer painted a building owned by the creditor, and in turn the creditor cancelled the note.

8 Gain on sale of taxable Canadian Ltd. capital stock.

9 Value of a colour TV set won as a prize in a quiz contest.

10 Inheritance received on death of a rich uncle.

11 Cash dividends received from Canadian Oil Ltd.

12 Unemployment insurance benefits.

PROBLEM 18B-2
Deductible or Not Deductible?

State whether each of the following items is deductible or not deductible by an individual for federal income tax purposes, and if deductible, whether it is from total income or net income, or as a tax credit.

1 Tuition fees.

2 Fee paid to chartered accountant for services in contesting assessment of additional income taxes by Revenue Canada, Taxation.

3 Expenses incurred in moving across country to accept a position with different employer. Not reimbursed.

4 Charitable donations.

5 Loss on sale of investment in securities.

6 Cost of commuting between home and place of employment.

7 Registered retirement savings plan contributions for spouse.

8 Unemployment insurance premiums.

9 Registered pension plan contributions.

10 Interest paid on mortgage on personal residence.

11 Union dues.

12 Interest expense for a loan to finance investment in securities.

PROBLEM 18B-3
Determine Income Tax for an Individual

Christine Levy, a resident of a province with a 58% tax rate, asks you to prepare her tax return for the current year. She provides you with the following information:

Income:

Salary from employment...	$68,000
Dividends from taxable Canadian corporations	3,000
Interest from Canada Savings Bonds.......................................	1,200
Gains on sale of shares of B.C. Ltd.'s common stock.........................	2,000
Rental income (net)..	8,000

Withholdings:

Income taxes..	20,000
Canada Pension Plan contributions	753
Unemployment insurance premiums..	1,162
Registered pension plan contributions	4,680

Disbursements:

Dental expenses..	2,200
Charitable donations	2,500
Professional membership fees	800

Others:

Loss on sale of shares in Victoria Mines Ltd................................	5,000
Lottery winnings	9,600
Basic personal tax credit	1,098

INSTRUCTIONS

Compute Levy's federal and provincial income taxes for the year by using the following federal tax rates: 17% on the first $29,590, 26% on the second $29,590 and 29% on the balance. There is also a 3% federal surtax on basic federal tax and a 5% surtax on basic federal tax in excess of $12,500.

PROBLEM 18B-4
Determine Capital Cost Allowance, Federal Tax, and Deferred Tax

Colitti Limited has the following operation results for the current year:

Operating income (after depreciation of $138,000 and before capital gains and losses and dividends)	$800,000
Net capital gains from sale of securities (capital gains of $30,000 less capital losses of $18,000)	12,000
Dividends received from taxable Canadian corporations.......................	45,000

The company's only depreciation assets are machinery, equipment, and furniture. The ending balance from last year's tax return was $600,000. During the current year, the company added equipment and furniture at a cost of $450,000 and sold a machine (original cost $66,000) for $50,000. The capital cost allowance rate for tax purposes is 20%.

INSTRUCTIONS

a Compute the amount of capital cost allowance for the current year.

b Compute the federal income tax for the current year, based on 28% tax rate.

c Compute the amount of federal income tax deferred by claiming the maximum capital cost allowance rather than the amount of depreciation for accounting purposes.

PROBLEM 18B-5
Determine Accounting and Taxable Income, Income Tax and Deferred Tax, and Tax Advantage of Financing Method

The following information appears in the records of Macor Corporation for the current year:

Net sales..	$988,000
Cost of goods sold	707,000
Operating expenses (including depreciation of $90,000)	151,000
Dividends received from taxable Canadian corporations........................	38,000
Net capital losses from sale of securities (capital losses of	
$37,000 less capital gains of $19,000)	18,000
Capital cost allowance..	190,000

The company is considering whether it should issue bonds or cumulative preferred stock to finance its expanded operations. The amount needed would be $600,000. The interest rate would be 11% and the dividend rate would be at 8%.

INSTRUCTIONS

a Compute the accounting income for the current year.

b Compute the taxable income for the current year.

c Compute the federal and provincial income taxes for the current year, based on the respective rates of 28% and 14%.

d Prepare the journal entry to record the current and deferred income taxes for the year.

e Explain which method of financing the $600,000 expansion is more beneficial to the company from an income tax viewpoint.

ANALYTICAL AND DECISION PROBLEMS AND CASES

A&D 18-1
What's Wrong with My Tax Return?

After one look at his tax return, Tim Pearl is stunned by the income tax he has to pay. "After I inherited $500,000 from Uncle Tom and won a $30,000 lottery this year, I thought I was O.K. for life. Now, this year's tax is more than double last year's and I have to pay thousands of dollars on April 30. I just don't have this much cash every April 30 to pay the taxes," Tim complains to his wife. The tax return that Tim is complaining about shows the following information:

Total income:	
Salary...	$ 46,000
Dividends received	22,000
Interest	25,500
Capital gains	6,000
Lottery winnings	30,000
	$129,500
Deduct: union dues	500
Net income and taxable income	$129,000

Federal income tax calculation:

$ 29,590 at 17%	$ 5,030
29,590 at 26%	7,693
69,820 at 29%	20,248
$129,000	$ 32,971

Tax credits

Registered pension plan contributions (17% × $3,820)...............	$ 649	
Canada Pension Plan contributions (17% × $753)	128	
Unemployment insurance premium (17% × $1,162)..................	198	
Basic personal amount (17% × $6,456)	1,098	
Married amount (17% × $5,380)	915	
Medical (17% × $2,188)	372	3,360
Basic federal tax		$ 29,611
Provincial tax: 57% of basic federal tax..		16,878
Total tax payable		$ 46,489
Deduct: amount withheld (on salary)		10,966
Tax payable		$ 35,523

INSTRUCTIONS   Explain how each of the errors in Tim's return should be corrected. (Do *not* prepare a corrected return.) Assume that Tim has not claimed any capital gains before and is subject to a 57% provincial tax and federal tax of: 17% on the first $29,590, 26% on the second $29,590, and 29% on the remaining taxable income. (Ignore surtax.) Also, comment on Tim's concern regarding the cash need on April 30 in future years.

A&D 18-2
Investors Choose between Debt and Equity

Bill and Hannah Bailey own a successful small company, Bailey Corporation. The outstanding capital stock consists of 1,000 shares, of which 400 shares are owned by Bill and 600 by Hannah. In order to finance a new branch operation, the corporation needs an additional $100,000 in cash. Bill and Hannah have this amount on deposit with a bank and intend to put these personal funds into the corporation in order to establish the new branch. They will either arrange for the corporation to issue to them an additional 1,000 shares of stock, or they will make a loan to the corporation at an interest rate of 12%.

Income before taxes of the corporation has been consistently averaging $150,000 a year, and annual dividends of $64,000 have been paid regularly on the $100,000 of capital stock. It is expected that the new branch will cause income before taxes to increase by $30,000. If new common stock is issued to finance the expansion, the total annual dividend of $64,000 will be continued unchanged. If a loan of $100,000 is arranged, the dividend will be reduced by $12,000, the amount of annual interest on the loan.

INSTRUCTIONS   a   From the income tax standpoint of Bill and Hannah Bailey (with a federal marginal tax rate of 29%), would there be any savings as between the stock issuance and the loan? Explain.

b   From the standpoint of getting their money out of the corporation (assuming that the new branch is profitable), should Bill and Hannah choose capital stock or a loan for the infusion of new funds to the corporation?

c Prepare a two-column schedule, with one column headed If New Stock Is Used and the other headed If Loan Is Used. For each of these proposed methods of financing, show (1) the present corporate income *before taxes;* (2) the corporate income *before taxes* after the expansion; (3) the corporate income taxes (12% federal tax rate) after the expansion; and (4) the corporate net income after the expansion.

A&D 18-3

Tax Advantage: Sole Proprietorship versus Corporation

Stephen Glenn is in the process of organizing a business that is expected to produce, before any compensation to him and before income taxes, an income of $98,000 per year. In deciding whether to operate as a sole proprietorship or as a corporation, he is willing to make the choice on the basis of the relative income tax advantage under either form of organization.

If the business is organized as a sole proprietorship, Glenn plans to withdraw the entire income of $98,000 each year.

If the business is organized as a corporation, Glenn will own all the shares and will pay himself a salary of $32,000. He will distribute the remaining after-tax income as dividends.

It may be assumed that the accounting income and the taxable income for the corporation would be the same and that the corporation would be qualified as a small business for income tax purposes.

Glenn is a resident of a province where the tax rate for individuals is 58% and has a total deduction of $8,000, and a total tax credit (not including any dividend tax credit) of $1,800.

INSTRUCTIONS Determine the relative income tax advantage to Stephen Glenn of operating the business as a sole proprietorship or as a corporation, and make a recommendation as to the form of organization he should adopt. Would it be beneficial to Glenn, from an income tax viewpoint, to keep the remaining after-tax income in the corporation rather than distribute it as dividend? Assume a combined federal and provincial tax rate of 20% for a corporation qualified as a small business and that the federal income tax rates for individuals are: 17% for the first $29,590, 26% for the second $29,590, and 29% on the balance. (Ignore surtax.)

19 Statement of Changes in Financial Position

In this chapter we introduce a new major financial statement—a statement of changes in financial position. First, we differentiate this statement from the balance sheet and the income statement. Second, we explain the nature and objective of, as well as the disclosure and presentation requirements for, a statement of changes in financial position. Third, we explain how cash flows are determined and the underlying rationale. Fourth, we show step-by-step how a statement of changes in financial position can be developed, using both a simple and a comprehensive case. Finally, we demonstrate how a statement of changes in a financial position may be analyzed and interpreted. Also, the T account method for the preparation of the statement of changes in financial position is presented in Appendix B.

Learning Objectives

After studying this chapter you should be able to:

1 *Differentiate a statement of changes in financial position from an income statement and a balance sheet.*

2 *Explain the nature and objective of the statement of changes in financial position.*

3 *Explain the disclosure and presentation requirements for a statement of changes in financial position.*

4 *Explain how cash flows are determined and why.*

5 *Develop a statement of changes in financial position—a simple and a comprehensive illustration.*

6 *Analyze and interpret a statement of changes in financial position.*

OBJECTIVE 1
Differentiate a statement of changes in financial position from an income statement and a balance sheet.

In Chapter 1, we introduced two key financial objectives of every business organization: ***operating profitably*** and ***staying solvent.*** Operating profitably means increasing the amount of the owners' equity through the activities of the business; in short, providing the owners with a satisfactory return on their investment. Staying solvent means being able to pay the debts and obligations of the business as they come due.

An income statement is designed to measure the success or failure of the business in achieving its objective of profitable operations. To some extent, a balance sheet shows whether or not the business is solvent. It shows, for example, the nature and amounts of current assets and current liabilities. From this information, users of the financial statements may compute such measures of solvency as the current ratio and the amount of working capital.

However, assessing the ability of a business to remain solvent involves more than just evaluating the liquid resources on hand at the balance sheet date. In this chapter we introduce a major financial statement, the ***statement of changes in financial position,*** which provides ***additional*** information on the solvency and liquidity of a business. Liquidity means the ability to generate and maintain an adequate amount of the most liquid financial resources—cash and cash equivalents. Thus, this statement complements the balance sheet and the income statement.

STATEMENT OF CHANGES IN FINANCIAL POSITION

Nature and Objective

OBJECTIVE 2
Explain the nature and objective of the statement of changes in financial position.

A statement of changes in financial position summarizes the operating, financing, and investing activities of a business for a period on a ***cash basis*** (i.e., cash and cash equivalents).[1] Thus, it explains how and why the cash position of a business has changed during a period. The objective of this statement is to provide information to financial statement users to assess the liquidity and solvency of a business, that is, its ability to generate cash from internal and external sources to finance its operations and investments.[2] With this information on how cash has flowed into the business and how cash has been used, we can begin to answer such important questions as: Do the normal operations of the business generate sufficient cash to enable the company to continue paying dividends? Did the company have to borrow to finance the acquisition of new plant assets, or was it able to generate the cash from current operations? Is the business becoming more or less solvent? And perhaps the most puzzling question: How can a ***profitable*** business be running low on cash? Even though a business operates profitably, its cash may decline and the business may even become insolvent.

The statement of changes in financial position gives us answers to these questions, because it shows in detail the amount of cash inflows (or sources) and outflows (or uses) relating to the operating, financing, and investing activities throughout the year. In fact, this statement is also called a "cash flow statement," a "statement of changes in cash resources,"

---

[1] CICA, *CICA Handbook* (Toronto), section 1540.01, 1540.02, and 1540.03.

[2] The terms "operations" and "operating activities" are used interchangeably.

and a "statement of changes in cash position." However, the most commonly used title for this statement is the ***statement of changes in financial position.***[3]

Prior to 1985, the statement of changes in financial position was prepared on a working capital (current assets less current liabilities) basis, that is, it focussed on the sources and uses of working capital. In September, 1985, the Accounting Standards Board, through Section 1540 of the *CICA Handbook,* recommended that the statement of changes in financial position should be prepared on a basis of cash rather than of working capital. The reason for this change is to accommodate the financial statement users' increasing interest and preference for information on cash flows.

Cash Defined

Section 1540 of the *CICA Handbook* recommends that the statement of changes in financial position "should report the changes in ***cash and cash equivalents*** resulting from the activities of the enterprise during the period." (Emphasis added.) Thus, this statement shows the changes not only for cash but also for cash equivalents. Cash and cash equivalents are described in Section 1540 as follows: "Cash and cash equivalents would normally include cash, net of short-term borrowings, and temporary investments and may, in some cases, include ***certain other elements of working capital when they are equivalent to cash.***" (Emphasis added.) It should be noted that it is the short-term ***borrowings*** (such as bank loans), not short-term debts (such as accounts payable), that are included in the calculation of cash and cash equivalents.

Unfortunately, Section 1540 neither identifies these "other elements" nor explains the conditions under which these elements are considered as equivalent to cash. It has been suggested that these elements would include such working capital items as "receivables, inventories, and payables when they are equivalent to cash."[4]

Disclosure and Presentation

OBJECTIVE 3 Explain the disclosure and presentation requirements for a statement of changes in financial position.

While the exact format of the statement of changes in financial position may vary from company to company, Section 1540 stipulates the items that should be disclosed and the manner in which these items should be presented. To ensure that the statement of changes in financial position is as informative as possible, Section 1540 recommends that it disclose the components of cash and cash equivalents and that it contain separate disclosures of at least the following items:

1 Cash from operations: the amount of cash from operations should be reconciled to the income statement, or the components of cash from operations should be disclosed.[5]

---

[3]   According to the CICA's *Financial Reporting in Canada,* 20th ed. (Toronto), 1993, p. 212, of the 300 companies surveyed, 205 used this title.

[4]   Sam Marinucci, "Changes to Statement of Changes," *CA Magazine,* October, 1985, p. 68.

[5]   *Financial Reporting in Canada,* p. 213. Of the 300 companies surveyed, 294 reconcile the amount of cash from operations to net income in the income statement. This approach is used here in Chapter 19.

2 Cash flows resulting from discontinued operations.

3 Cash flows resulting from extraordinary items.

4 Outlays for acquisition and proceeds on disposal of assets, by major category, not included in **1, 2** or **3** above.

5 The issue, assumption, redemption, and repayment of debt not included in **1, 2** or **3** above.

6 The issue, redemption, and acquisition of share capital (capital stock).

7 The payment of dividends, identifying separately dividends paid by subsidiaries to non-controlling interests.

Furthermore, it recommends that the above items be classified into three categories: **operating, financing,** and **investing.** Cash flows from **operating activities** relate to cash from operations and would include net income (or income from continuing operations if there are discontinued operations and extraordinary items) and changes in noncash current accounts. Cash flows from **financing activities** refer to those items affecting the size and composition of a company's long-term debt and equity capital structure and would include items **5** and **6** above. Also, cash dividends (item **7** above) are usually treated as a financing activity even though Section 1540 of the *CICA Handbook* allows a choice of presenting them as a financing activity, as an operating activity, or as an activity apart from both financing and operating.[6] It is more logical to treat cash dividends as a financing activity because they are an important factor in attracting equity capital. The amount of cash dividends affects the market price of a company's stock and the ability of the company to raise equity capital. Cash flows from **investing activities** pertain to those items affecting the non-current assets such as long-term investments, plant, and equipment implied in item **4** above.

Certain financing and investing activities such as the acquisition of plant assets or long-term investments by issuing long-term debt or capital stock, the conversion of long-term debt to equity or of preferred stock to common stock, and stock dividends where the shareholder has an option of receiving cash or shares (optional stock dividend), even though they do not involve cash, are to be disclosed, since the effect of these activities is "similar to a cash inflow followed immediately by a cash outflow, or vice versa."[7] These activities are often referred to as **exchange transactions.**

While most transactions affecting **only long-term (noncurrent) accounts** are exchange transactions, there are four exceptions: (1) stock dividends where shareholders can only receive shares of capital stock (non-optional stock dividends); (2) stock splits; (3) transfers to and from reserve accounts; and (4) appraisal adjustments.[8] These exceptions do not involve an exchange and **are not** regarded as financing and investing activities. For this reason, they are not shown in a statement of changes in financial position.

---

[6] *Financial Reporting in Canada,* p. 214. Of the 212 companies surveyed, 134 presented dividends as a financing activity and 55 classified dividends as a separate category.

[7] CICA, *CICA Handbook,* Section 1540.20.

[8] Ibid., Section 1540.21.

The rationale for the recommended disclosure and presentation is to provide information to financial statement users to assess a company's ability to generate cash from internal and external sources to finance its operating and investing activities, as well as to show the changes in the structure of a company's long-term assets, long-term debts, and equity capital. Consequently, these users are better able to evaluate the company's liquidity and solvency position, and its cash policies on operating, financing, and investing activities.

The cash flow from operations is of critical importance because, in the long run, a business must generate a positive net cash flow from operations if the business is to survive. A business with a negative net cash flow from operations will not be able to raise cash from other sources indefinitely. In fact, the ability of a business to raise cash through financing activities is highly dependent upon its ability to generate cash from operations. Creditors and shareholders are reluctant to invest in a company that does not generate enough cash from operations to assure prompt payment of maturing liabilities, interest, and dividends.

DETERMINATION OF CASH FLOWS

OBJECTIVE 4 Explain how cash flows are determined and why.

Transactions involving a debit to cash represent an inflow (source) of cash. The sales of merchandise for cash, the collection of accounts receivable and the issuance of long-term debt or equity instruments for cash are the common examples of sources of cash inflows. On the other hand, transactions involving a credit to cash represent an outflow (use) of cash. The purchase of merchandise for cash, the payment of accounts payable or expenses, and the payment for redemption or retirement of long-term debt or preferred stock are common examples of cash outflows (uses of cash).

However, since the statement of changes in financial position is on a cash and cash equivalent basis, transactions affecting only the cash and cash equivalent accounts ***equally*** do not produce an inflow or outflow of cash. The reason is that there is no change in the amount of cash and cash equivalents. For example, the purchase of temporary investments such as marketable securities with cash (debiting marketable securities and crediting cash for an equal amount) changes the components but does not change the total amount of cash and cash equivalents. Similarly, short-term borrowings such as bank loans (debiting cash and crediting bank loans for an equal amount) change the components but do not change the total amount of cash and cash equivalents. Of course, if a transaction affects more than the cash and cash equivalent accounts, there will be either an inflow or outflow of cash. For example, selling temporary investments at a gain will increase the amount of cash and cash equivalents (that is, increased by the amount of the gain) and the increase is included in the net income. Also, obtaining a short-term bank loan at a discount (that is, with prepaid interest deducted from the loan) or selling temporary investments at a loss will decrease the amount of cash and cash equivalents and the decrease is included in net income.

Since the accounting records and the other financial statements are on an accrual basis, how do we determine the cash inflows and outflows for the statement of changes in financial position? We will answer this question by presenting explanations under the three categories of the statement of changes in financial position—operating, financing, and investing activities.

Operating Activities

The determination of cash flow for operating activities requires the reconciliation or conversion from net income (the accrual basis of accounting) to net cash flow (cash basis of accounting).[9] Thus, **changes** in the **noncash current asset** and **current liability** accounts such as accounts receivable, inventory, unexpired insurance, accounts payable, and accrued liabilities, which have a **different effect on net income than on cash flows,** must be taken into account in the reconciliation. However, certain current liability accounts, such as dividends payable, and the current portion of the long-term debts are **not** related to the income statement and therefore have no effect on cash flow for operation. Now, let's explain how the changes in the noncash current assets and current liability accounts are handled in the reconciliation from net income to net cash flow resulting from operating activities.

Changes in Accounts Receivable   Accounts receivable increases as credit sales are made, and decreases as cash is collected from customers. A net increase in accounts receivable over an accounting period indicates that revenue from credit sales exceeds collections from customers. In other words, the increase represents the portion of credit sales (which have been recognized as revenue and reflected in net income) that have not been collected. Thus, net income measured on the accrual basis is greater than net cash flow. Consequently, a net increase in accounts receivable is deducted from net income in the reconciliation from net income to net cash flow.

On the other hand, a net decrease in accounts receivable indicates that revenue from credit sales is less than collections from customers. Thus, net income on the accrual basis is smaller than net cash flow. Consequently, a net decrease in accounts receivable is added to net income in the reconciliation from net income to net cash flow.

Changes in Inventory   The balance in the Inventory account increases as merchandise is purchased, and decreases as goods are sold. A net increase during the accounting period in the Inventory account indicates that purchases during the period exceed the cost of goods sold. Thus, to reconcile net income with net cash flow, we deduct from net income the amount of these additional purchases (the net increase in the balance of the Inventory account).

A net decrease over the period in the balance of the Inventory account indicates that the cost of goods sold exceeds purchases made during the

---

[9]   The cash basis of accounting was explained in Chapter 3. Under the cash basis, revenue is not recorded until cash is collected from the customer; purchases of merchandise and expenses incurred are recorded in the period in which payment is made. Under the accrual basis, on the other hand, revenue is recognized at the date of sale and expenses are recorded when the related goods or services are used.

period. Thus, to reconcile net income with net cash flow, we add to net income the net decrease in inventory.

It should be noted that the adjustment of the increase or decrease of inventory to net income is really to convert the amount of cost of goods sold to the amount of credit purchases. The amount of credit purchases will be converted to cash payments for purchases (as required by the cash basis of accounting) by incorporating the change in accounts payable, as discussed later.

Changes in Prepaid Expenses Prepaid expenses are current assets. Increases in these assets result from cash payments, and decreases result from recognizing the expired portion as expenses. Thus, a net increase of prepaid expenses over the period indicates that cash payments made for these items exceed the amount recognized as expenses. Consequently, we deduct from net income the net increase in prepaid expenses in determining net cash flows for operating activities.

A net decrease in prepaid expenses indicates that cash outlays during the period are less than the amounts deducted as expenses in the determination of net income. Consequently, a net decrease in prepaid expenses is added back to net income in determining net cash flows for operating activities.

Changes in Accounts Payable Accounts payable are increased by purchases on account and are reduced by cash payments to suppliers. A net increase in accounts payable indicates that the credit purchases are greater than the cash payments made to suppliers. Thus, in converting net income to net cash flow, we add back to net income the amount of purchases financed by a net increase in accounts payable. (In the earlier discussion on changes in inventory, we *deduct* a net increase in inventory to net income to convert the amount of cost of goods sold to credit purchases. An increase in accounts payable means that the portion of the credit purchases has not been paid. Therefore, such an increase must be added back to net income to arrive at the amount of cash payments for purchases.)[10]

A net decrease in accounts payable indicates that cash payments to suppliers exceed the purchases during the period. Thus, a net decrease in accounts payable is deducted from net income to arrive at the cash flows for operating activities.

Changes in Accrued Expenses (Accrued Liabilities) The liability for accrued expenses rises with the recognition of expenses that will be paid in the future, and decreases as cash payments are made. A net increase in accrued expenses indicates that expenses in the period exceed the related cash payments. Thus, net income is less than net cash flow, and the increase in accrued expenses should be added to net income in determining the net cash flow for operating activities.

A net decrease in accrued expenses indicates that cash payments exceed the related amounts of expense. This decrease, therefore, is deducted from net income in determining the net cash flow from operating activities.

---

[10] This situation is illustrated in the Claire Company example in a later section.

Income Statement Items Not Affecting Cash Items such as depreciation, amortization of intangible assets, and amortization of discount on bonds payable reduce net income, but do not reduce cash flow. Thus, the amount of depreciation and amortization must be added back to net income to convert it to net cash flow.

Let us use depreciation as an example to illustrate this point. Assume that on December 31, 1995, City Delivery Service buys two trucks for cash at a cost of $30,000. As of January 1, 1996, the company does business on a cash basis, collecting revenue of $40,000 and paying expenses of $22,000, thus showing an $18,000 increase in cash. The company then records depreciation expense of $6,000 on its trucks, resulting in a $12,000 net income for 1996. What is the amount of cash provided by operations in 1996? The recording of depreciation expense reduces net income, ***but it does not reduce cash flow;*** cash flow for operating activities remains at $18,000. The $12,000 net income figure therefore ***understates*** the amount of cash flow for operating activities by the amount of depreciation expense recorded during the period. Thus, to convert the $12,000 net income of City Delivery Service to the amount of cash flow for operating activities of $18,000, we must ***add back*** the depreciation expense of $6,000.

On the other hand, certain items in the income statement increase net income without increasing cash flow; such items must be deducted from net income in the conversion of net income to net cash flow for operating activities. An example is the amortization of premium on bonds payable, which causes interest expense to be less than the cash payments of interest to bondholders.

"Nonoperating" Gains and Losses These gains and losses usually result from the disposal of long-term assets or the retirement of long-term debts. While these gains and losses do not affect operating activities, they do enter into the determination of net income. Therefore, in converting net income to net cash flow for operating activities, we ***add back any nonoperating losses*** and ***deduct any nonoperating gains*** included in net income.

Discontinued Operations and Extraordinary Items The income or loss from discontinued operations as well as gains or losses for discontinued operations and extraordinary items are included in the determination of net income (as presented in Chapter 15). To determine the net cash flow for "normal" operating activities, we must exclude such income or loss as well as gains or losses. Consequently, we add back to net income the losses and deduct from net income the income or gains in the conversion of net income to net cash flow. (The resulting figure represents income from continuing operations.) The income or loss from discontinued operations is converted to net cash flow and presented as a separate item called "cash from discontinued operations" under the operating activities. The gains or losses are combined with the related proceeds for discontinued operations and extraordinary items, and presented separately under the investing activities.

A Summary for Cash Flows of Operating Activities The foregoing discussion on the determination of cash flows of operating activities can be summarized by the following formula:

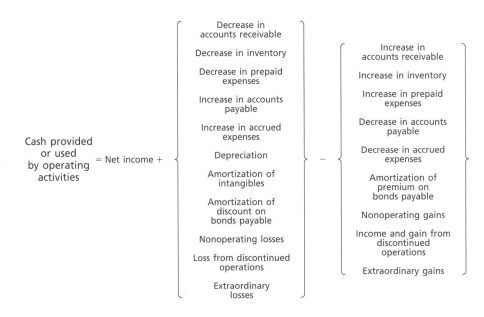

A few observations may be noted from the formula. First, decreases in noncash current asset accounts are added to net income because they cause a lower net income to be reported than net cash flow. Second, increases in noncash current asset accounts are deducted from net income because they cause a higher net income to be reported than net cash flow. Third, increases in current liability accounts (other than short-term borrowings, such as bank loans, which are included in the computation of cash and cash equivalents) are added because they cause a lower net income to be reported than net cash flow. Fourth, decreases in current liability accounts are deducted because they cause a higher net income to be reported than net cash flow. As mentioned earlier, the changes in the dividends payable or the current instalment of long-term debt have no effect on cash flow for operations as these two liabilities are not related to the income statement.

Financing Activities

Cash flows for financing activities are determined by analyzing the debit and credit changes recorded during the period in the long-term liability and shareholders' equity accounts. Credit changes in such accounts as bonds payable and preferred or common stock indicate cash receipts (inflow of cash), while debit changes of these accounts indicate cash payments (outflow of cash), unless these changes are the result of exchange transactions (which are discussed later).

The amount of cash dividends can be determined by analyzing the debit changes recorded during the period in the Retained Earnings account and the changes in the Dividends Payable account.

As mentioned earlier, exchange transactions such as issuing long-term debt or capital stock for plant assets, conversion of long-term debt or preferred stock into common stock, and optional stock dividends where shareholders have a choice of receiving cash or shares of common stock are considered financial activities even though no cash is involved. Thus, the debits and credits recorded during the period in the plant asset, long-term debt, preferred stock, common stock, and retained earnings account must be analyzed to determine exchange transactions.

Investing Activities

Cash flows for investing activities can be determined by analyzing the changes in such noncurrent accounts as long-term investments, intangible assets, plant, and equipment. Debit entries in these accounts represent purchases of the assets or cash outlay (unless an exchange transaction is involved as discussed in the paragraph below). Credit entries in these accounts, however, represent only the **cost** or **book value** of the assets sold. Therefore, to determine the cash proceeds from these sales transactions, we must adjust the amount of the credit entries for any gains or losses recognized on the sales (unless an exchange transaction is involved as discussed in the paragraph below). Also, the gains will be deducted from, and the losses added to, net income in the determination of cash flow for operating activities.

Similar to the discussion in the section on financing activities, exchange transactions—such as the acquisition of long-term investments or plant assets by issuing long-term debt or capital stock and the exchange of long-term investments or plant assets for other noncurrent assets—are considered investing activities even though no cash is involved. Thus, the debits and credits recorded during the period in these noncurrent asset accounts must be analyzed to determine exchange transactions.

DEVELOP A STATEMENT OF CHANGES IN FINANCIAL POSITION

Cash Flow: A Simple Illustration

OBJECTIVE 5 Develop a statement of changes in financial position—a simple and a comprehensive illustration.

Assume that John Claire started a business, Claire Company, as a sole proprietorship on April 30 by investing $40,000 cash; the company rented a building on May 1 and completed the following transactions during the month of May:

(1) Claire invested an additional $27,000 cash in the business.

(2) Purchased merchandise costing $40,000 on credit and sold three-fourths of this, also on credit, for $58,000.

(3) Collected $45,000 on receivables; paid $31,000 on accounts payable.

(4) Incurred $20,500 of operating expenses, of which $18,500 was paid, $2,000 was accrued.

(5) Purchased land for the construction of a store by issuing a six-year mortgage note for $17,000.

(6) Paid $30,000 for equipment purchased on May 31.

(7) Paid $1,000 for a one-year insurance policy that begins on June 1.

(8) Withdrew $2,000 cash from the business for personal use.

The company's income statement and balance sheet at May 31 follow:

CLAIRE COMPANY
Income Statement
For the Month Ended May 31

Sales	$58,000
Cost of goods sold (three-fourths of purchases)	30,000
Gross profit	$28,000
Operating expenses	20,500
Net income	$7,500

CLAIRE COMPANY
Comparative Balance Sheet

Assets	May 31	Apr. 30
Cash	$ 29,500	$40,000
Accounts receivable	13,000	
Inventory	10,000	
Unexpired insurance	1,000	
Land	17,000	
Equipment	30,000	
Total assets	$100,500	$40,000

Liabilities & Owner's Equity		
Accounts payable	$ 9,000	
Accrued liabilities (Accrued expenses)	2,000	
Mortgage payable (due in six years)	17,000	
John Claire, capital	72,500	$40,000
Total liabilities & owner's equity	$100,500	$40,000

The cash account amounted to $40,000 on April 30 but was only $29,500 on May 31, a decrease of $10,500. In analyzing the transactions completed during the month of May, we see that cash was increased and decreased as follows:

Transactions increasing cash:		
Additional investment by owner		$27,000
Collection of accounts receivable		45,000
Total increases in cash		$72,000
Transactions decreasing cash:		
Payment of accounts payable	$31,000	
Payment of operating expenses	18,500	
Payment for purchase of equipment	30,000	
Payment for unexpired insurance	1,000	
Withdrawal of cash by owner	2,000	
Total decrease in cash		82,500
Decrease in cash during May		$10,500

A complete list of transactions for a fiscal period may not be readily available, and even if it were, analysis of such a list would be a laborious process. In practice, a statement of changes in financial position is prepared by analyzing the changes that occurred *in the noncash accounts* (that is, all accounts other than the accounts for cash, temporary investment, and short-term borrowing such as bank loans) during the fiscal period. An analysis of the comparative balance sheet for Claire Company indicates the following changes in the noncash accounts:

(1) Increase in accounts receivable, $13,000.

(2) Increase in inventory, $10,000.

(3) Increase in unexpired insurance, $1,000.

(4) Increase in land, $17,000.

(5) Increase in equipment, $30,000.

(6) Increase in accounts payable, $9,000.

(7) Increase in accrued liabilities, $2,000.

(8) Increase in mortgage payable, $17,000.

(9) Increase in Claire's capital, $32,500, resulting from additional cash investment of $27,000, net income of $7,500, and a withdrawal of cash of $2,000.

Based on this analysis and the discussion on the determination of cash flows in the preceding section, we can prepare the following statement of changes in financial position for the month of May to account for the $10,500 decrease in cash.

A simple statement of changes in financial position

CLAIRE COMPANY
Statement of Changes in Financial Position
For Month of May

Operating activities:		
Net income..		$ 7,500
Deduct: Increase in accounts receivable.........................	$(13,000)	
Increase in inventory.....................................	(10,000)	
Increase in unexpired insurance	(1,000)	(24,000)
Add: Increase in accounts payable.............................	$9,000	
Increase in accrued liabilities..............................	2,000	11,000
Cash used by operating activities		$ (5,500)
Financing activities:		
Additional investment by owner.................................	$27,000	
Withdrawal by owner	(2,000)	
Issuance of mortgage note for land	17,000	
Cash provided by financing activities		42,000
Investing activities:		
Purchase of land in exchange for a mortgage note	$(17,000)	
Purchase of equipment	(30,000)	
Cash used in investing activities..........................		(47,000)
Decrease in cash...		$(10,500)

The difference between net income and net cash flow should be carefully noted in this example. Although Claire Company's net income for May was $7,500, it experienced a *cash deficiency* of $5,500 from operating activities and its cash account *decreased* by $10,500. This is not unusual for a company just beginning its business. However, a company will experience financial difficulty if there is a continuing cash deficiency from its operations and a continuing decline in its most liquid asset—cash.

The Claire Company illustrates clearly the application of many of the concepts on the determination of cash flows presented in the preceding section.

Operating Activities

To determine the net cash flows for operating activities, we have to reconcile the net income to net cash flow. This reconciliation is a conversion of net income on an accrual basis to a cash basis. Thus, changes in such noncash current accounts as accounts receivable, inventory, unexpired insurance, accounts payable, and accrued liabilities must be accounted for as follows:

Increase in Accounts Receivable The $13,000 increase in accounts receivable is deducted from net income because it represents the portion of credit sales that has not been collected but that has been reflected in net income.

Increase in Inventory The $10,000 increase in inventory is deducted from net income to convert the amount of cost of goods sold to the amount of credit purchases. (Deducting the increase in inventory from net income has the same effect as adding the increase to the cost of goods sold.) This amount of credit purchases will be converted to cash payments for purchases with the adjustment of the change in accounts payable, as explained later.

Increase in Unexpired Insurance The $1,000 increase in unexpired insurance is deducted from net income because this prepayment has not been recognized as an expense in the determination of net income.

Increase in Accounts Payable The $9,000 increase in accounts payable is added to net income to convert the amount of credit purchases (which was determined by deducting the $10,000 increase in inventory from net income as presented earlier) to cash payments for purchases. The following will further clarify this point.

Cost of goods sold	$30,000
Add: Increase in inventory*	10,000
Credit purchases	$40,000
Deduct: Increase in accounts payable for purchases*	9,000
Cash payments for purchases	$31,000

* In converting the accrual basis to the cash basis of accounting, adding the increase in inventory to cost of goods sold has the same effect as deducting the increase from net income, and deducting the increase in accounts payable from credit purchases has the same effect as adding the increase to net income.

It should also be observed from the above example that if the increase in inventory is equal to the increase in accounts payable, then cost of goods sold is equal to cash payments for purchases. Consequently, the equal but opposite adjustments have no net effect on net income.

Increase in Accrued Liabilities   The $2,000 increase in accrued liabilities is added back to net income because the expenses recognized ($20,500) are more than the cash payments for expenses ($18,500) by $2,000.

Financing Activities

The additional investment and the withdrawal by the owner represent financial activities. The investment increases cash and the withdrawal decreases cash. The issuance of a mortgage note for land is an exchange transaction. Thus, this transaction should be shown as both a financing activity and an investing activity. The issuance of a mortgage note is treated in the same manner as if it is for cash.

Investing Activities

The purchase of equipment is an investing activity involving a cash outflow. The purchase of land in exchange for a mortgage note, an exchange transaction (as pointed out in the preceding section), constitutes an investing activity, as if it is purchased with cash from the issuance of the mortgage note.

Cash Flow: A Comprehensive Illustration

To illustrate more fully the concepts discussed in the section on determination of cash flows, we shall prepare a statement of changes in financial position for the Allison Corporation from the comparative balance sheet and the condensed income statement that appear on page 891. A summary of the transactions completed by Allison Corporation that resulted in a change in **noncash accounts** during 1996 follows:

1 **Changes in noncash current accounts:**
   a Increase in accounts receivable, $20,000
   b Increase in inventory, $80,000
   c Increase in prepaid expenses, $13,000
   d Increase in accounts payable, $55,000
   e Decrease in accrued expenses, $19,500
2 **Changes in noncurrent assets:**
   a A plant asset costing $50,000 was sold for $53,000 cash. This asset was acquired in 1995 and was not used in operation. Thus, no depreciation was recorded.
   b A segment of business with a book value of $215,000 was sold for $180,000 cash (ignore the income tax effect and assume no operating income or loss, as these matters are more appropriate for a higher level accounting course).
   c A parcel of land was acquired for $150,000 by issuing a long-term note payable for the entire purchase price.

d Equipment was purchased for $140,000; the invoice was paid within 10 days.

e Depreciation of $67,500 was recorded.

Analysis of these financial statements will explain the sources and uses of cash

ALLISON CORPORATION
Comparative Balance Sheet
At December 31

Assets	1996	1995
Current assets:		
Cash...	$ 12,000	$ 35,000
Marketable securities	23,000	–0–
Accounts receivable (net).....................................	105,000	85,000
Inventory...	150,000	70,000
Prepaid expenses	25,000	12,000
Total current assets	$315,000	$202,000
Land...	300,000	150,000
Plant and equipment	470,000	380,000
Less: accumulated depreciation................................	(192,500)	(125,000)
Other: assets of a business segment............................	–0–	215,000
Total assets	$892,500	$822,000

Liabilities & Shareholders' Equity

	1996	1995
Current liabilities:		
Bank loan...	$ 20,000	$ –0–
Accounts payable (for purchases).............................	145,000	90,000
Accrued expenses...	22,500	42,000
Total current liabilities	$187,500	$132,000
Notes payable, long-term	170,000	20,000
Bonds payable, due June 30, 2008	60,000	300,000
Capital stock, no-par	310,000	160,000
Retained earnings	165,000	210,000
Total liabilities & shareholders' equity.......................	$892,500	$822,000

ALLISON CORPORATION
Condensed Income Statement
For Year Ended December 31, 1996

Sales (net)	$900,000
Cost of goods sold..	500,000
Gross profit..	$400,000
Operating expenses and income taxes	
(less $3,000 gain on sale of plant asset).....................................	340,000
Income from continuing operations	$ 60,000
Loss on sale of a business segment	35,000
Net income...	$ 25,000

3 Changes in noncurrent liabilities:

a As stated in transaction **2c,** a $150,000 long-term note payable was issued in exchange for land.

b Bonds payable of $240,000 were retired at a price equal to face value.

4 Changes in shareholders' equity accounts:

    a A stock dividend (non-optional) was declared in January, requiring a transfer of $30,000 from the Retained Earnings account to the Capital Stock account.

    b In February, 8,000 shares of no-par value stock were issued for $120,000 cash.

    c Cash dividends of $40,000 were declared and paid, causing a reduction in retained earnings.

    d The net income for the year, $25,000 (including the $3,000 nonoperating gain on sale of a plant asset and the $35,000 loss on sale of a business segment), was transferred to the Retained Earnings account.

From the comparative balance sheets, the income statement, and the summary of transactions affecting noncash accounts, we can prepare a statement of changes in financial position by completing the following three steps:

1 Compute the change in cash (i.e., cash and cash equivalents) during the period.

2 Prepare a working paper for analysis of changes in noncash accounts.

3 Prepare the statement of changes in financial position.

Computation of Increase in Cash during the Period The first step in preparing a statement of changes in financial position is to determine the net increase or decrease in cash during the period covered by the statement.

Cash of the Allison Corporation decreased by $20,000 during 1996, determined as follows:

<table>
<tr><td rowspan="2">**Uses of cash exceed sources by $20,000**</td><td colspan="3" align="center">**ALLISON CORPORATION**
Computation of Decrease in Cash during 1996</td></tr>
<tr><td></td><td align="center">*Dec. 31
1996*</td><td align="center">*Dec. 31
1995*</td></tr>
<tr><td></td><td>*Cash and cash equivalents*
  (cash and marketable securities) ....</td><td align="right">*$35,000*</td><td align="right">*$35,000*</td></tr>
<tr><td></td><td>*Less: Short-term borrowing (bank loan)* ....</td><td align="right">*20,000*</td><td align="right">*–0–*</td></tr>
<tr><td></td><td>*Cash and cash equivalents* ....</td><td align="right">*$15,000*</td><td align="right">*$35,000*</td></tr>
<tr><td></td><td>*Decrease in cash during 1996 ($15,000 – $35,000)* ....</td><td align="right">*$20,000*</td><td></td></tr>
</table>

The purpose of the statement of changes in financial position is to explain the *reasons* for the change in cash. This is accomplished by listing the specific sources (inflows) and uses (outflows) of cash during the period. Since cash for the Allison Corporation decreases by $20,000, the uses of cash during 1996 exceeded the sources by this amount. But before a statement of changes in financial position can be prepared, we must analyze the changes that took place during the year in the noncash accounts.

Preparation of Working Paper for Analysis of Changes in Noncash Accounts
A working paper showing the analysis of changes in noncash accounts for
Allison Corporation is illustrated below and on page 894. The amount of
cash and the balances in noncash accounts at the beginning of the period
are listed in the first column of the working paper; balances at the end of
the year are listed in the last (right-hand) column. The two middle columns
are used to **explain the changes** in each **noncash** account during the
year and to indicate whether each change represents a source or a use of
cash. Transactions for the year (in summary form) are recorded in these
middle columns, and an offsetting entry is made in the lower section of the
working paper indicating the effect of each transaction upon cash.

ALLISON CORPORATION
Working Paper for Statement of Changes in Financial Position
For Year Ended December 31, 1996

Debits	Account Balances, End of 1995	Analysis of Transactions for 1996		Account Balances, End of 1996
		Debit	Credit	
Cash and marketable securities,				
net of bank loan..........................	35,000		(x) 20,000	15,000
Accounts receivable (net).................	85,000	(7) 20,000		105,000
Inventory...................................	70,000	(8) 80,000		150,000
Prepaid expenses	12,000	(9) 13,000		25,000
Land.......................................	150,000	(12) 150,000		300,000
Plant and equipment	380,000	(13) 140,000	(4) 50,000	470,000
Assets of a business segment	215,000		(5) 215,000	–0–
Total....................................	947,000			1,065,000
Credits				
Accumulated depreciation	125,000		(6) 67,500	192,500
Accounts payable	90,000		(10) 55,000	145,000
Accrued expenses.........................	42,000	(11) 19,500		22,500
Notes payable, long-term	20,000		(12) 150,000	170,000
Bonds payable, due June 30, 2008	300,000	(14) 240,000		60,000
Capital stock, no-par	160,000		(3) 30,000 ⎫ (15) 120,000 ⎭	310,000
Retained earnings	210,000	(2) 40,000 (3) 30,000	(1) 25,000 ⎫ ⎭	165,000
Total......................................	947,000	732,500	732,500	1,065,000

	Sources	Uses	
Operating activities:			
Net income...	(1) 25,000		Income from
Deduct: Gain on sale of plant..........................		(4) 3,000	continuing
Increase in accounts receivable................		(7) 20,000	operations,
Increase in inventory...........................		(8) 80,000	$60,000; cash
Increase in prepaid expenses..................		(9) 13,000	provided by
Decrease in accrued expenses.................		(11) 19,500	operating
Add: Loss on sale of a business segment..............	(5) 35,000		activities,
Depreciation......................................	(6) 67,500		$47,000
Increase in accounts payable....................	(10) 55,000		
Financing activities:			
Cash dividends......................................		(2) 40,000	Cash used in
Issuance of long-term note payable for land............	(12) 150,000		financing
Retirement of bonds payable..........................		(14) 240,000	activities,
Issuance of capital stock	(15) 120,000		$10,000
Investing activities:			
Sale of plant, including a gain of $3,000...............	(4) 53,000		
Sale of a business segment..........................	(5) 180,000		Cash used in
Purchase of land in exchange for long-term			investing
note payable		(12) 150,000	activities,
Purchase of equipment		(13) 140,000	$57,000
Total sources and uses of cash	685,500	705,500	
Decrease in cash during the year	(x) 20,000		
	705,500	705,500	

Explanation of transactions for 1996:
(1) Net income, $25,000 (including a gain of $3,000 on sale of plant asset and $35,000 loss on sale of a business segment), is transferred to Retained Earnings and is classified as a tentative source of cash [to be adjusted by entries (4) through (11) below].
(2) Cash dividends paid, $40,000, reduce retained earnings and cash, and this is a use of cash.
(3) A stock dividend has no effect on cash.
(4) Sale of plant asset for $53,000. Explains a $50,000 credit change in the Plant and equipment account. The $3,000 nonoperating gain on the sale is reclassified within the sources of cash from the "operating activities" section to the "investing activities" section.
(5) Sale of a business segment for $180,000. Explains the $215,000 credit in the assets of business segment account. The $35,000 loss is added back to net income to show income from continuing operations.
(6) Depreciation, $67,500, is added to net income in arriving at cash provided by operating activities.
(7) Increase in accounts receivable of $20,000 is deducted from net income in arriving at cash provided by operating activities.
(8) Increase in inventory of $80,000 is deducted from net income in arriving at cash provided by operating activities.
(9) Increase in prepaid expenses of $13,000 is deducted from net income in arriving at cash provided by operating activities.
(10) Increase in accounts payable of $55,000 is added to net income in arriving at cash provided by operating activities.
(11) Decrease in accrued expenses of $19,500 is deducted from net income in arriving at cash provided by operating activities.
(12) A $150,000 long-term note payable was issued (a source of cash) to acquire land (a use of cash).
(13) Cash of $140,000 was used to purchase equipment, an investing activity.
(14) Cash of $240,000 was used to retire bonds payable, a financing activity.
(15) Issued capital stock, increasing cash by $120,000, a financing activity.
(x) Balancing figure—decreases in cash during the year.

Explanation of Entries in the Middle Columns By studying the changes in the noncash accounts during 1996, we are able to find the specific reasons for the $20,000 decrease in cash. The noncash accounts may be analyzed in any sequence; however, we recommend the following approach.

1 Explain all transactions affecting the Retained Earnings account.

2 Explain the adjustment and reclassification of nonoperating gain and loss on sale of a business segment.

3 Explain the expense items that have no effect on cash.

4 Explain the changes in the ***noncash current*** accounts.

5 Explain any remaining changes in ***noncurrent*** accounts.

6 Make an entry explaining the net change in cash. This entry should bring both the upper and lower sets of middle columns into balance.

Using this approach, the entries in our illustrated working paper are explained as follows:

Entry

Step 1: Explain the changes in retained earnings

(1) Allison Corporation's net income explains a $25,000 credit change in the Retained Earnings account. In the bottom portion of the working papers, an offsetting entry is made identifying net income as a source of cash, which is shown in the "operating activities" section.

(2) Cash dividends of $40,000 declared and paid during 1996 caused a debit change in the Retained Earnings account and were a use of cash, which is shown in the "financing activities" section.

(3) The stock dividend (non-optional) caused a $30,000 debit change in the Retained Earnings account and a $30,000 credit change in the Capital Stock account. Notice that both the debit and credit portions of this entry appear in the ***top portion*** of the working papers. As previously stated, non-optional stock dividends (and stock splits) are an exception to the general rule that changes in noncurrent accounts represent either sources or uses of cash. Non-optional stock dividends have ***no effect*** upon cash.

With these first three entries, we have explained how the Retained Earnings account increased during 1996 from $210,000 to its ending balance of $165,000.

Step 2: Explain the adjustment and reclassification of non-operating gain and loss on sale of a business segment.

(4) To compute the cash provided by operating activities, we must remove from net income the $3,000 nonoperating gain from the sale of a plant asset from the "operating activities" section and show the entire $53,000 proceeds from the sale as a source of cash in the "investing activities" section in the bottom portion of the working paper. In the top portion of the working paper, entry (4) shows that the sale of this plant asset caused a $50,000 credit change in the Plant and Equipment account.

(5) The $35,000 loss on sale of a business segment is added back to net income to show the amount of income from continuing operations of $60,000. The $180,000 proceeds are treated as a source of cash under the "investing activities" section in the bottom portion of the working paper. In the top portion of the working paper, entry (5) shows that the sale of the business segment reduced the assets of a business segment account to zero.

Step 3: Explain the expense items having no effect on cash.

(6) The $25,000 net income figure appearing in the bottom portion of the working paper is only a tentative measure of the cash provided by operating activities. Depreciation expense, for example, must be added back to this figure, because the recording of depreciation expense reduced net income but did not reduce cash. Entry (6) shows that depreciation expense explains the $67,500 credit change in the Accumulated Depreciation account and adds this amount to net income as a step in determining cash provided by operating activities.

Step 4: Explain the changes in the noncash current accounts.

(7) To complete the computation of cash provided by operating activities, we must convert the net income of $25,000 from an accrual to a cash basis by also taking into consideration the changes in these noncash current accounts that are related to the income statement. The rationale for involving the changes of these accounts in the conversion has been explained in the section on the determination of cash flows and in the Claire Company example. The changes in the noncash current accounts of Allison Corporation are considered in entries (7) through (11) in the working paper.

Entry (7) shows the increase in accounts receivable of $20,000 as a deduction from net income in the "operating activities" section in arriving at cash provided by operating activities, and as a debit change in accounts receivable in the top portion of the working paper.

(8) This entry shows the $80,000 increase in inventory as a deduction from net income in the "operating activities" section and as a debit change in inventory in the top portion of the working paper.

(9) This entry shows the $13,000 increase in prepaid expenses as a deduction from net income in the "operating activities" section and as a debit change in the prepaid expenses in the top portion of the working paper.

(10) This entry shows the $55,000 increase in accounts payable as an addition to net income in the "operating activities" section and as a credit change in accounts payable in the top portion of the working paper.

(11) This entry shows the $19,500 decrease in accrued expenses as a deduction from net income in the "operating activities" section and as a debit change in accrued expenses in the top portion of the working paper.

We have now determined that cash of $47,000 was provided by operating activities, and income from continuing operations was $60,000.

Step 5: Explain any remaining changes in non-current accounts.

(12) The issuance of a $150,000 long-term note payable in exchange for land is an exchange transaction, representing both a source and a use of cash. First, an entry is made in the top portion of the working paper explaining the $150,000 increase in the Notes Payable account and an offsetting entry is made in the "financing activities" section below showing a $150,000 source of cash. Next, a debit entry is made in the upper portion of the working paper explaining the $150,000 increase

in the Land account, and an offsetting entry is made in the following "investing activities" section showing this $150,000 use of cash.

(13) The purchase of equipment explains the $140,000 debit change in the Equipment account and is a use of cash for investing activities.

(14) During the year, Allison Corporation retired $240,000 of bonds payable at par. A reduction in long-term debt is a use of cash. This transaction is recorded in the working paper by a debit to the Bonds Payable account and an offsetting entry describing the use of cash for financing activities.

(15) The issuance of capital stock in February for $120,000 is recorded in the upper section of the working paper by credits to Capital Stock. The issuance of capital stock is a source of cash; therefore, the offsetting entry in the lower section of the working papers is entered in the "financing activities" section as a source of cash.

At this point we should check carefully to determine that our entries in the Debit and Credit columns correctly explain the difference between the beginning and ending balances of each noncash account. If the top section of the working paper explains the change in every noncash account, the bottom section should include all of the sources and uses of cash for the year.

Step 6: Record the net change in cash. (x) We now total the Sources column ($685,500) and the Uses column ($705,500) in the bottom section of the working paper. The $20,000 difference between these column totals represents the net change in cash during the year. Since cash decreased, this $20,000 is entered as a credit to cash on the top line of the working paper and as the balancing figure in the Sources column at the bottom of the working paper.

Totals can now be determined for the Debit and Credit columns in the top section of the working paper. If these totals agree, we know that our analysis is correct, at least so far as the mechanics are concerned.

Preparation of Statement of Changes in Financial Position The preceding working paper analysis explained all changes in noncash accounts that took place during 1996. In making this analysis, we listed the sources and uses of cash in the lower section of the working paper on pages 893–894. The decrease of $20,000 in cash has been confirmed and a statement of changes in financial position, including a schedule showing the change in cash, can now be prepared as follows:

Statement of changes in financial position shows sources and uses of cash relating to operating, financing, and investing activities

ALLISON CORPORATION
Statement of Changes in Financial Position
For Year Ended December 31, 1996

Operating activities:

Income from continuing operations*....................................		$ 60,000
Deduct: *Gain on sale of plant asset*	$ (3,000)	
Increase in accounts receivable.....................	(20,000)	
Increase in inventory	(80,000)	
Increase in prepaid expenses	(13,000)	
Decrease in accrued expenses.......................	(19,500)	(135,500)
Add: *Expenses not requiring the use of cash—depreciation*....	$ 67,500	
Increase in accounts payable	55,000	122,500
Cash provided by operating activities		$ 47,000

Financing activities:

Cash dividends...	$ (40,000)	
Issuance of long-term note payable for land	150,000	
Retirement of bonds payable...............................	(240,000)	
Issuance of capital stock	120,000	
Cash used by financing activities		(10,000)

Investing activities:

Sale of a plant asset including a gain of $3,000...............	$ 53,000	
Sale of a business segment at a $35,000 loss	180,000	
Purchase of land in exchange for long-term note payable	(150,000)	
Purchase of equipment	(140,000)	
Cash used in investing activities		(57,000)
Decrease in cash and cash equivalents		$ (20,000)

* If there are no discontinued operations or extraordinary items, this will be "net income."

This supporting schedule shows the change in cash

Schedule of Changes in Cash and Cash Equivalents

	December 31	
	1996	**1995**
Cash..	$ 12,000	$35,000
Marketable securities	23,000	–0–
	$ 35,000	$35,000
Deduct: *Bank loan (short-term)*....................................	20,000	–0–
Cash and cash equivalents	$ 15,000	$35,000
	(35,000)	
Decrease in cash and cash equivalents	$(20,000)	

The preceding statement of changes in financial position illustrates the disclosure and presentation requirements of Section 1540 of the *CICA Handbook* in a clear and understandable manner. The schedule of changes in cash and cash equivalents is included here to enhance understanding of the "cash and cash equivalents" definition for cash. In published financial statements, such a schedule is seldom presented because the change can be easily determined from the few items involved. Instead, the items included as "cash and cash equivalents" are simply described in a note below the statement or in the last heading in the statement.

In published financial statements, the changes in noncash current accounts are usually presented in the statement of changes in financial position as one lump sum amount entitled "Changes in noncash working capital components" or "Changes in noncash working capital." This amount is sometimes supported by a schedule or a footnote showing the changes in the individual noncash current or working capital accounts.

ANALYSIS AND INTERPRETATION OF A STATEMENT OF CHANGES IN FINANCIAL POSITION

OBJECTIVE 6
Analyze and interpret a statement of changes in financial position.

As discussed in the early part of this chapter, the statement of changes in financial position provides information on the liquidity and solvency position of a business, as well as the cash policies on its operating, financing, and investing activities. The amount of cash and cash equivalents together with the changes in noncash current account in the statement will provide insights into the liquidity position and the cash policy on operating activities. The changes in the noncurrent accounts shown in the financing and investing activities sections of the statement will provide information on the cash policies regarding the extent of financing and investing activities. Thus, a careful analysis and interpretation of this statement will enable management and other users to logically assess the soundness of the business's liquidity position and its cash policies on operating, financing, and investing activities.

The following analysis and interpretation of a statement of changes in financial position is based on the Allison Corporation example.

The Allison Corporation's liquidity position is deteriorating; its cash and cash equivalents at the end of 1996 are less than half that in 1995, as shown in the Schedule of Changes in Cash and Cash Equivalents on page 898. Moreover, the amount of cash and cash equivalents of $15,000 seems to be inadequate to meet the need for paying the $167,500 of account payable and accrued expenses, especially if the company continues its existing policy on collection from customers, which is explained later.

The company does not appear to have a well-coordinated and satisfactory cash policy on operating activities. The increase in accounts receivable means that credit sales are greater than the cash collected from customers. Since there is an increase in both inventory and accounts payable and the increase in inventory exceeds the increase in accounts payable, more goods are being purchased on credit than are being sold and payments are less than the credit purchases. The increase in prepaid expenses indicates that more expenses are being prepaid than are being incurred. Similarly, the decrease in accrued liabilities means that payments are being made faster than the expenses are being incurred. These analyses show that the company seems to be slow in collecting its accounts receivable and in paying its suppliers but too quick in paying its other expenses. Consequently, the company should evaluate its credit, collection, and payment policies for their soundness and coordination. The fact that the cash provided from operating activities is much less than the amount of depreciation indicates that the company will have to borrow more, or issue additional capital stock, in order to maintain its present operating capacity, unless this is a temporary situation. However, this had already occurred in 1996 as the company had to issue long-term notes payable and capital stock to finance its purchase of land and equipment (in addition to the proceeds from the sale of a business segment).

The company's cash policy on financing activities seems unsound. The retirement of $240,000 bonds payable, in spite of an unsatisfactory cash position, was ill-advised. The cash dividends of about two-thirds of income from continuing operations and 80% of the amount of cash from operations were unusually large and caused a further strain on the cash resources. Consequently, the company should amend its policy in each of these areas. It should also be noted that, by presenting the information on financing activities in one place, it is easier for users to analyze and interpret the extent and reasonableness of these activities.

The company's cash policy on investing activities reflects the desire to finance its investments through long-term debt and capital stock. The heavier emphasis on debt than equity financing appeared to be logical in view of the relationship between the amount of long-term debts and the amount of long-term assets on the one hand, and the amount of long-term debts and the amount of shareholders' equity on the other. However, since the total amount of debts is about 50% of the total assets, the company may find borrowing increasingly difficult and risky in the future, unless there is a substantial increase in shareholders' equity. The sale of a business segment at a loss may have reflected the need to get rid of an unprofitable segment and to generate more cash. Since the investing activities are presented in one place, it is easier for users to analyze and interpret the extent and reasonableness of these activities.

CHAPTER REVIEW

KEY TERMS INTRODUCED OR EMPHASIZED IN CHAPTER 19

Accrual basis A method of summarizing operating results in terms of revenue earned and expenses incurred, rather than cash receipts or cash payments.

Cash basis A method of summarizing operating results in terms of cash receipts and cash payments rather than revenue earned and expenses incurred.

Cash and cash equivalents Cash and cash equivalents encompass cash, net of short-term borrowings, and temporary investments. In some cases, cash and cash equivalents may include certain other elements of working capital when they are equivalent to cash.

Cash flows from financing activities Cash flows that affect the size and composition of a company's long-term debt and equity capital structure.

Cash flows from investing activities Cash flows that affect the noncurrent assets such as long-term investments, plant, and equipment.

Cash flows from operating activities Cash flows from operations, including net income or income from continuing operation and changes in noncash current accounts.

Exchange transaction In the context of a statement of changes in financial position, exchange transactions are financing or investing activities that do not directly affect cash. An example of such a transaction is the purchase of plant assets by issuing common stock. Such transactions should be shown in a statement of changes in financial position as both a source and a use of cash.

Noncash current accounts All current asset and current liability accounts other than cash or cash equivalents. Also referred to as noncash working capital accounts.

Noncurrent account Any balance sheet account *other than* a current asset or a current liability. Noncurrent accounts include long-term investments, plant assets, intangible assets, long-term liabilities, and shareholders' equity accounts.

Noncurrent assets All long-term assets such as long-term investments, plant, and equipment; they are part of the noncurrent accounts.

Non-optional stock dividends Stock dividends where shareholders can only receive shares of capital stock.

Optional stock dividends Stock dividends where shareholders have an option of receiving cash or shares of capital stock.

Statement of changes in financial position A financial statement showing the sources and uses of cash from operating, financing, and investing activities during the accounting period. In addition, this statement shows financing and investing activities, such as exchange transactions, that do not directly affect cash.

Working capital Current assets minus current liabilities. Working capital represents the net amount of liquid resources available to a business.

DEMONSTRATION PROBLEM FOR YOUR REVIEW

Comparative financial data for Liquid Gas Limited for the last two years are shown on page 902.

OTHER DATA

(1) During 1996, the board of directors of the company authorized a transfer of $15,000 from retained earnings to reflect a stock dividend on the common stock. (This is a non-optional stock dividend.)

(2) Cash dividends of $6,000 were declared and paid on the preferred stock, and cash dividends of $50,000 were declared and paid on the common stock.

(3) Three hundred shares of preferred stock were retired for $30,000 cash.

(4) The only entries recorded in the Retained Earnings account were for dividends and to close the Income Summary account, which had a credit balance of $66,000 after the loss on the sale of the land.

(5) There were no sales or retirements of building and equipment during the year; land was sold for $8,000, resulting in a loss of $2,000.

	December 31	
Debits	**1996**	**1995**
Cash..	$ 29,220	$ 15,800
Marketable securities	20,000	28,000
Accounts receivable (net of allowance for doubtful accounts)	41,400	24,000
Inventories, lower of cost and market	27,600	36,800
Prepaid expenses	4,180	4,400
Land...	9,000	19,000
Buildings	280,000	250,000
Equipment	478,600	450,000
Total..	$890,000	$828,000

Credits		
Accumulated depreciation: buildings	$ 95,000	$ 77,000
Accumulated depreciation: equipment............................	153,000	120,000
Bank loan..	12,000	23,000
Accounts payable	67,200	35,000
Accrued expenses..	20,000	10,000
Bonds payable	90,000	90,000
Premium on bonds payable	2,800	3,000
Preferred stock (no-par)	70,000	100,000
Common stock (no-par)...	305,000	290,000
Retained earnings	75,000	80,000
Total..	$890,000	$828,000

INSTRUCTIONS

a Compute the change in cash and cash equivalents during 1996.

b Prepare a working paper for a statement of changes in financial position for 1996.

c Prepare a statement of changes in financial position for 1996, without showing the schedule of change in cash.

SOLUTION TO DEMONSTRATION PROBLEM

a Computation of change in cash and cash equivalents:

	December 31	
	1996	**1995**
Cash..	$29,220	$15,800
Marketable securities	20,000	28,000
	$49,220	$43,800
Less: Bank loan..	12,000	23,000
Cash and cash equivalents	$37,220	$20,800
Increase in cash during 1996 ($37,220 − $20,800)	$16,420	

b

LIQUID GAS LIMITED
Working Paper for Statement of Changes in Financial Position
For Year Ended December 31, 1996

Debits	Account Balances, End of 1995	Analysis of Transactions for 1996		Account Balances, End of 1996
		Debit	Credit	
Cash and marketable securities, net of bank loan.........................	20,800	(x) 16,420		37,220
Accounts receivable (net).................	24,000	(6) 17,400		41,400
Inventories...............................	36,800		(7) 9,200	27,600
Prepaid expenses	4,400		(8) 220	4,180
Land......................................	19,000		(4) 10,000	9,000
Buildings	250,000	(11) 30,000		280,000
Equipment	450,000	(12) 28,600		478,600
Total...................................	805,000			878,000
Credits				
Accumulated depreciation: buildings	77,000		(5) 18,000	95,000
Accumulated depreciation: equipment......	120,000		(5) 33,000	153,000
Accounts payable	35,000		(9) 32,200	67,200
Accrued expenses........................	10,000		(10) 10,000	20,000
Bonds payable	90,000			90,000
Premium on bonds payable...............	3,000	(13) 200		2,800
Preferred stock, no-par	100,000	(14) 30,000		70,000
Common stock, no-par	290,000		(2) 15,000	305,000
Retained earnings	80,000	(2) 15,000 (3) 56,000	(1) 66,000	75,000
Total...................................	805,000	193,620	193,620	878,000

	Sources	Uses	
Operating activities:			
Net income..	(1) 66,000		Cash
Add: Loss on sale of land	(4) 2,000		provided by
Depreciation	(5) 51,000		operating
Decrease in inventories	(7) 9,200		activities,
Decrease in prepaid expenses	(8) 220		$153,020.
Increase in accounts payable....................	(9) 32,200		
Increase in accrued expenses	(10) 10,000		
Deduct: Increase in accounts receivable..............		(6) 17,400	
Amortization of premium on bonds payable		(13) 200	
Financing Activities:			
Cash dividends.......................................		(3) 56,000	Cash used in
Retirement of preferred stock		(14) 30,000	financing
			activities,
			$86,000.
Investing activities:			Cash used in
Sale of land, at a loss of $2,000........................	(4) 8,000		investing
Purchase of building		(11) 30,000	activities,
Purchase of equipment		(12) 28,600	$50,600.
Total sources and uses of cash	178,620	162,200	
Increase in cash during the year		(x) 16,420	
	178,620	178,620	

Explanation of transactions for 1996:

(1) Net income, $66,000, including a loss of $2,000 on sale of land, transferred to Retained Earnings account.

(2) Entry to record stock dividend; no effect on cash.

(3) Cash dividends declared, $56,000 (preferred stock, $6,000, and common, $50,000).

(4) To record sale of land for $8,000; the $2,000 nonoperating loss is reclassified from the "operating activities" section to "investing activities" section.

(5) Depreciation, $51,000, is added to net income because it is an expense that did not reduce cash.

(6) Increase in accounts receivable of $17,400 is deducted from net income in arriving at cash provided by operating activities.

(7) Decrease in inventory of $9,200 is added to net income in arriving at cash provided by operating activities.

(8) Decrease in prepaid expenses of $220 is added to net income in arriving at cash provided by operating activities.

(9) Increase in accounts payable of $32,200 is added to net income in arriving at cash provided by operating activities.

(10) Increase in accrued expenses of $10,000 is added to net income in arriving at cash provided by operating activities.

(11) To record cash used for purchase of building.

(12) To record cash used for purchase of equipment.

(13) Amortization of premium on bonds payable decreased expense and thus increased net income but had no effect on cash.

(14) To record cash used for retirement of preferred stock.

(x) Balancing figure—increase in cash during the year.

c

LIQUID GAS LIMITED
Statement of Changes in Financial Position
For Year Ended December 31, 1996

Operating activities:

Net income...		$ 66,000
Add: Loss on sale of land	$ 2,000	
Expenses not requiring the use of cash—depreciation......	51,000	
Decrease in inventory	9,200	
Decrease in prepaid expenses	220	
Increase in accounts payable	32,200	
Increase in accrued expenses	10,000	104,620
Deduct: Increase in accounts receivable........................	$(17,400)	
Expense reduction that increased income but with no		
effect on cash—amortization of premium on bonds		
payable	(200)	(17,600)
Cash provided by operating activities		$153,020

Financing activities:

Cash dividends...	$(56,000)	
Retirement of preferred stock	(30,000)	
Cash used in financing activities...		(86,000)

Investing activities:

Sale of land at a loss of $2,000	$ 8,000	
Purchase of building	(30,000)	
Purchase of equipment	(28,600)	
Cash used in investing activities		(50,600)
Increase in cash and cash equivalents		$ 16,420

■ ■ ▒ ** Appendix B*

T Account Method for the Preparation of Statement of Changes in Financial Position

The "T account method," as the name suggests, utilizes T accounts to summarize the same information as the working paper method illustrated in the chapter. First, all the accounts required for the preparation of the statement of changes in financial position are set up in the T account format rather than in the working paper format. Second, the changes between the beginning and ending balances for these accounts are noted in the T accounts. (With the working paper method, the beginning and ending balances of a period rather than their changes are noted.) Third, these changes are accounted for by reconstructing the entries posted to these accounts during the period. (With the working paper method, the beginning and ending balances of a period are reconciled by reconstructing the entries posted to these accounts.) The following examples, selected from the demonstration problem—Liquid Gas Limited—delineate these three basic differences.

Working Paper Method

Debits	Account Balances, End of 1995	Analysis of Transactions for 1996		Account Balances, End of 1996
		Debit	Credit	
Buildings	250,000	(11) 30,000		280,000
Credits				
Preferred stock, no-par...................	100,000	(14) 30,000		70,000
		Sources	*Uses*	
Financing activities:				
Retirement of preferred stocks			(14) 30,000	
Investing activities:				
Purchase of building			(11) 30,000	

T Account Method

Buildings

Change	30,000		
(11) Purchase of building	30,000		

Preferred Stock, No-Par

Change	30,000		
(14) Retirement of Preferred Stock......................	30,000		

Financing Activities

		(14) Retirement of Preferred Stock	30,000

Investing Activities

		(11) Purchase of building	30,000

A careful study of these examples shows that both the working paper and the T accounts contain the same information needed for the preparation of the statement of changes in financial position. The T account method may be more efficient, particularly for solving relatively simple problems, but the essential difference is really the format in which the information is presented. In the above example, the two items in the credit column in the use of cash section of the working paper—purchase of building, $30,000, and retirement of preferred stock, $30,000—are the same as the two items in the credit column of the financing and investing activities accounts. Similar parallels can be made for all the other accounts in the Liquid Gas Limited demonstration problem.

The T account method generally involves the following steps:

1 Open a T account for "Cash" (that is, cash and cash equivalents) and debit or credit the account with the increase or decrease (change) in cash. Double underline this amount.

2 Open a T account for each noncash account with the change between the beginning and ending balances and debit or credit the change to these accounts. Double underline the amount in each of these accounts.

3 Add the debits and credits of the T account for cash and for the noncash accounts. The equality of the debit and credit totals proves that the amounts have been correctly noted on these accounts (unless there are exact offsetting errors, which are usually unlikely).

4 Open a T account for "Operating Activities" for the reconstruction of the posting of entries related to cash from operations such as net income, nonoperating gains or losses, items included in the income statement but not providing cash or requiring the use of cash (e.g., amortization of premium on bonds payable or depreciation), and changes in noncash current accounts. This account shows the details of cash provided or used by operating activities.

5 Open a T account for "Financing Activities" for the reconstruction of the postings of entries related to cash flows on such activities as the issuance, redemption, and retirement of long-term debt and capital stock. This account shows the details of cash provided by or used in financing activities.

6 Open a T account for "Investing Activities" for the reconstruction of the postings of entries related to cash flows on such activities as the acquisition and disposal of long-term assets such as plant and equipment. This account shows the details of cash provided by or used in investing activities.

7 Analyze all available information, and reconstruct the postings to account for the changes in the T accounts set up thus far.

8 Check that the changes in each noncash T account have been accounted for.

9 Add the Operating Activities, Financing Activities, and Investing Activities T accounts and transfer the balances (these are the amounts of cash provided by or used in operating, financing and investing activities) to the Cash T account.

10 Check that the total amount of the balances transferred from step 9 is the same amount and on the same side of the T account as that already noted in the cash T account.

11 Review all the noncurrent T accounts to ensure that exchange transactions have been accounted for.

12 Prepare the statement of changes in financial position from

  i The Operating Activities T account, which provides all the details on cash provided by or used in operations.

  ii The Financing Activities T account, which provides all the details on cash provided by or used in financing activities.

iii The Investing Activities T account, which provides all the details on cash provided by or used in investing activities.

These twelve steps are used to illustrate the T account method using the information of the Liquid Gas Limited demonstration problem.

a The information contained in the T accounts after steps 1 to 6 is as follows [the total of debits ($127,620) equals the total of credits ($127,620)]:

Cash*		Accounts Receivable	
16,420		17,400	

Inventories		Prepaid Expenses	
	9,200		220

Land		Buildings	
	10,000	30,000	

Equipment		Acc. Depr.—Buildings	
28,600			18,000

Acc. Depr.—Equipment		Accounts Payable	
	33,000		32,200

Accrued Expenses		Premium on Bonds Payable	
	10,000	200	

Preferred Stock		Common Stock	
30,000			15,000

Retained Earnings		Operating Activities	
5,000			

Financing Activities		Investing Activities	

* Cash and cash equivalents

b After analyzing all available information and reconstructing the postings to account for the differences in the T accounts as required by step 7, the T accounts are as follows. (Comparing the numbered items in these T accounts with the numbered items in the middle columns of the working paper on pages 903–904 will show that the information is identical in both places.)

Cash			Accounts Receivable	
16,420			17,400	
		(6)	17,400	

Inventories			Prepaid Expenses	
	9,200			220
(7)	9,200	(8)		220

Land			Buildings	
	10,000		30,000	
(4)	10,000	(11)	30,000	

Equipment			Acc. Depr.—Buildings	
28,600				18,000
(12)	28,600	(5)		18,000

Acc. Depr.—Equipment			Accounts Payable	
	33,000			32,200
(5)	33,000	(9)		32,200

Accrued Expenses			Premium on Bonds Payable	
	10,000			200
(10)	10,000	(13)		200

Preferred Stock			Common Stock	
30,000				15,000
(14)	30,000	(2)		15,000

Retained Earnings

	5,000		
(2)	15,000	(1)	66,000
(3)	56,000		
	71,000		
	5,000		

(Check that the difference in each noncash T account has been accounted for.)

Operating Activities

(1) Net income	66,000	(6) Increase in accounts		
(4) Loss on sale of land	2,000	receivable................		17,400
(5) Depreciation	51,000	(13) Amortization of premium		
(7) Decrease in inventories	9,200	on bonds payable		200
(8) Decrease in prepaid				
expenses	220			
(9) Increase in accounts payable...	32,200			
(10) Increase in accrued				
expenses	10,000			

Financing Activities

	(3) Cash dividends	56,000
	(14) Retirement of preferred	
	stock	30,000

Investing Activities

(4) Sale of land, at a loss of		(11) Purchase of building		30,000
$2,000	8,000	(12) Purchase of equipment		28,600

c Add the Operating Activities, Financing Activities, and Investing Activities T accounts and transfer the balances to the Cash T account. Check that the total amount of the balances transferred to and the amount already noted in the Cash T account are in agreement. These are required by steps 9 and 10. These four accounts, after the two steps have been performed, are as follows:

Operating Activities

(1) Net income	66,000	(6) Increase in accounts		
(4) Loss on sale of land	2,000	receivable..................		17,400
(5) Depreciation	51,000	(13) Amortization of premium		
(7) Decrease in inventories ..	9,200	on bonds payable		200
(8) Decrease in prepaid				
expenses	220			
(9) Increase in accounts				
payable.................	32,200			
(10) Increase in accrued				
expenses	10,000			
	170,620			17,600
		(x) Transfer to cash T acct.....		153,020
	170,620			170,620

Financing Activities

		(3) Cash dividends	56,000
		(14) Retirement of preferred	
		stock	30,000
(x) Transfer to cash			
T account	86,000		86,000

Investing Activities

(4) Sale of land, at a loss of		(11) Purchase of building	30,000
$2,000	8,000	(12) Purchase of equipment	28,600
	8,000		58,600
(x) Transfer to cash T			
account	50,600		
	58,600		58,600

Cash

	16,420		
(x) Transfer from operating		(x) Transfer from:	
activities	153,020	Financing activities.........	86,000
		Investing activities	50,600
	136,600		136,600
	16,420		

d Review all the noncurrent T accounts to ensure that exchange transactions have been accounted for.

e Use the information in the Operating Activities, Financing Activities, and Investing Activities T accounts to prepare the statement of changes in financial position. This statement is the same as that on page 905.

ASSIGNMENT MATERIAL

DISCUSSION QUESTIONS

1 Does a statement of changes in financial position or an income statement best measure the profitability of a financially sound business? Explain.

2 What is the nature and objective of the statement of changes in financial position?

3 What information can a reader gain from a statement of changes in financial position that is not apparent from reading a balance sheet?

4 How is "cash and cash equivalents" defined by Section 1540 of the *CICA Handbook*?

5 List the items required to be separately disclosed in a statement of changes in financial position by Section 1540 of the *CICA Handbook*.

6 How should the items in 5 be classified?

7 Briefly describe the meaning of: cash flows from operating activities; cash flows from financing activities; cash flows from investing activities.

8 Explain the rationale of Section 1540 of the *CICA Handbook* for the recommended disclosure and presentation for the statement of changes in financial position.

9 List six items that are added to or deducted from net income in computing cash provided or used by operating activities.

10 List four items that are included in computing cash provided by or used in financing activities.

11 List four items that are included in computing cash provided by or used in investing activities.

12 How should an increase and a decrease in accounts receivable be handled in converting net income to cash provided or used by operating activities? Why?

13 How should an increase and a decrease in inventory and in accounts payable be handled in converting net income to cash provided or used by operating activities? Why?

14 How should an increase and a decrease in prepaid expenses be handled in converting net income to cash provided or used by operating activities? Why?

15 How should an increase and a decrease in accrued expenses be handled in converting net income to cash provided or used by operating activities? Why?

16 In converting net income to cash provided or used by operating activities, are all

   (a) increases in noncash current asset accounts handled in the same manner? Explain.

   (b) decreases in noncash current asset accounts handled in the same manner? Explain.

17 In converting net income to cash provided or used by operating activities, are all

   (a) increases in current liability accounts other than bank loans handled in the same manner? Explain.

(b) decreases in current liability accounts other than bank loans handled in the same manner? Explain.

18 What is an "exchange transaction"? List two examples and explain how they are handled in a statement of changes in financial position.

19 List four exceptions to "exchange transactions" that are not disclosed in a statement of changes in financial position.

20 Sources of cash include long-term borrowing, sale of noncurrent assets, operations, and sale of capital stock. Which of these possible sources of cash do you consider to be most important to the long-run survival of a business?

21 Give examples of expenses, other than depreciation expense, that reduce net income but do not result in the use of cash during the period.

22 Give an example of an increase in net income that does not result in an increase in cash during the period.

23 Miller Corporation acquired a building for $300,000, paying $60,000 cash and issuing a long-term note payable for the balance. What is the effect of this transaction upon the cash of Miller Corporation? How should the transaction be shown in a statement of changes in financial position?

24 During the year, holders of $4 million of Sommersby Limited convertible bonds converted their bonds into shares of Sommersby common stock. The president of Sommersby Limited made the following statement: "By issuing common stock to retire these bonds, the company has saved $4 million in cash. Our statement of changes in financial position will not have to show the retirement of bonds among the uses of cash." Do you agree with this statement? Explain.

25 An outside member of the board of directors of a small corporation made the following comment after studying the comparative financial statements for the past two years: "I have trouble understanding why our cash has increased steadily during the past two years, yet our profits have been negligible; we have paid no dividends; and inventories, receivables, payables, cost of plant and equipment, long-term debt, and capital stock have remained essentially unchanged." Write a brief statement explaining how this situation might occur.

MULTIPLE CHOICE QUESTIONS

1 The statement of changes in financial position is designed to assist users in assessing each of the following, ***except:***
   a The ability of a company to remain solvent.
   b The company's profitability.
   c The major sources of cash receipts during the period.
   d The reasons why net cash flow from operating activities differ from net income.

2 Which of the following is ***not*** included in the statement of changes in financial position?
   a Disclosure of the amount of cash invested in temporary investments during the accounting period.
   b A reconciliation of net income to net cash flow from operating activities.
   c Disclosure of investing or financing activities that did not involve cash.
   d The amount of cash and cash equivalents owned by the business at the end of the accounting period.

3 The cash flows shown in the statement of changes in financial position are grouped into the following major categories:

   a Operating activities, investing activities, and financing activities.

   b Cash receipts, cash disbursements, and noncash activities.

   c Direct cash flows and indirect cash flows.

   d Operating activities, investing activities, and collecting activities.

4 The following information is obtained from Owen Limited.

Increase in accounts receivable	*$12,000*
Decrease in inventory..	*19,000*
Increase in accounts payable	*16,000*
Decrease in accrued expenses	*8,000*
Depreciation expense..	*67,000*
Gain on sale of plant assets	*3,000*

Based only upon the above items, net cash flow from operating activities is:

   a $85,000   b $15,000   c $79,000   d $125,000

5 During the current year, two transactions were recorded in the Land account of Cliffhanger Industries. One involved a debit of $320,000 to the Land account; the second was a $210,000 credit to the Land account. Cliffhanger Industries' income statement for the year reported a loss on sale of land in the amount of $25,000. All transactions involving the Land account were cash transactions. These transactions would be shown in the statement of cash flows as:

   a $320,000 cash provided by investing activities, and $210,000 cash disbursed for investing activities.

   b $210,000 cash provided by investing activities, and $320,000 cash disbursed for investing activities.

   c $235,000 cash provided by financing activities, and $320,000 cash disbursed for investing activities.

   d $185,000 cash provided by investing activities, and $320,000 cash disbursed for investing activities.

EXERCISES

EXERCISE 19-1
Accounting
Terminology

Listed below are nine technical accounting terms introduced in this chapter:

Operating activities	*Statement of changes in*	*Working capital*
Investing activities	*financial position*	*Accrual basis*
Financing activities	*Income statement*	*Cash basis*
	Cash equivalents	

Each of the following statements may (or may not) describe one of these technical terms. For each statement, indicate the accounting term described, or answer "None" if the statement does not correctly describe any of the terms.

   a A method of accounting that summarizes operating results in terms of cash receipts and cash payments.

   b The financial statement that shows the financial position of the business at a particular date.

   c An asset consisting of temporary investments in marketable securities.

d The financial statement that best describes the profitability of a business that receives most of its revenue in cash.

e Transactions involving the issuance and repayment of debt, investments by owners, and distributions to owners.

f The section of a statement of changes in financial position summarizing the cash effects of most transactions that enter into the determination of net income.

g The section of a statement of changes in financial position summarizing the acquisition and disposal of plant and equipment.

EXERCISE 19-2
Computing
Cash Equiva-
lents

Compute the amount of the increase or decrease in cash and cash equivalents during 1996 from the following information:

	December 31 1996	1995
Cash	*$ 26,000*	*$ 20,000*
Marketable securities	*32,000*	*28,000*
Accounts receivable (net)	*87,000*	*79,000*
Unexpired insurance	*6,000*	*1,500*
Bank loans	*30,000*	*38,000*
Accounts payable	*80,000*	*78,000*
Mortgage payable	*200,000*	*200,000*

EXERCISE 19-3
Effect of Trans-
actions on
Cash and Cash
Equivalents

Indicate the amount of the increase or decrease (if any) in cash and cash equivalents as a result of each of the following situations:

a In the first year of operations, cash sales were $240,000, credit sales were $600,000, and accounts receivable at the end of the year were $120,000.

b Issued $600,000 of bonds payable for an office building.

c Land costing $18,000 was sold for $26,000; the purchaser paid $12,000 and issued a mortgage note for $14,000.

d Issued capital stock to investors for $860,000 cash.

e Purchased temporary investments for $90,000 cash.

f Purchased equipment costing $300,000 for $100,000 cash and $200,000 mortgage payable.

g Declared cash dividends of $80,000.

h Obtained a short-term bank loan of $180,000.

EXERCISE 19-4
Items To Be
Reported in
the Statement
of Changes in
Financial Posi-
tion

Briefly explain how each of the following situations should be reported in the statement of changes in financial position for 1997.

a Cash of $80,000 was paid and capital stock with a market value of $450,000 was issued to acquire land worth $530,000.

b Depreciation of $200,000 was recorded for the year.

c In June, the 20,000 shares of no-par value capital stock of $500,000 were split 3 for 6, and in November, a 10% stock dividend in common stock was distributed to shareholders.

d Classified a portion of long-term debt as current liabilities, $190,000.

e Sold a plant asset for $2,160,000 cash, resulting in a gain of $160,000 that was reported in the income statement.

EXERCISE 19-5
Conversion of Accrual to Cash Basis

Indicate whether each of the following changes during the year should be added or deducted in converting net income to cash provided or used by operating activities:

a   Increase in accounts receivable.

b   Increase in accounts payable.

c   Decrease in inventory.

d   Decrease in prepaid expenses.

e   Decrease in accrued expenses.

EXERCISE 19-6
Classification of Items in the Statement of Changes in Financial Position

Indicate in which of the three categories of activities in the statement of changes in financial position each of the following items should be presented:

a   Redeemed preferred stock.

b   Purchased equipment for cash.

c   Sold land for cash.

d   Paid cash dividends of $800,000.

e   Depreciation expense.

f   Increase in inventory.

g   Decrease in accrued liabilities.

h   Purchased a building costing $60,000 by issuing capital stock.

i   Issued bonds payable for cash.

EXERCISE 19-7
Determine Cash from Operations

The London Corporation reported a net loss of $54,000 on its income statement. In arriving at this figure, the following items, among others, were included:

Gain on sale of a plant asset	$28,000
Depreciation expense	88,400
Amortization of patents	28,000
Amortization of premium on bonds payable	10,000

In addition, the changes in noncash current accounts were:

Increase in accounts receivable	$ 8,000
Decrease in inventory	12,000
Increase in prepaid expenses	2,200
Increase in accounts payable	13,000
Decrease in accrued expenses	2,000

From the information above, compute the amount of cash provided or used by operating activities.

EXERCISE 19-8
Converting Net Income to Cash from Operations

The following data are taken from the records of the Eaton Company:

	End of Year	Beginning of Year
Accounts receivable	$ 19,700	$ 7,700
Inventories	32,000	40,000
Prepaid expenses	2,800	2,000
Accounts payable (merchandise creditors)	28,000	25,000
Accrued expenses	1,000	1,200
Net credit sales	398,000	
Cost of goods sold	260,000	
Operating expenses (includes depreciation of $10,000)	100,000	

From the foregoing information prepare the operating activities section of the statement of changes in financial position.

EXERCISE 19-9
Converting Income Statement Items to a Cash Basis

From the information provided in Exercise 19-8, compute the following:

a Cash collected from customers during the year.

b Cash paid to merchandise creditors during the year.

c Cash paid for operating expenses during the year.

d Cash provided or used by operating activities during the year.

EXERCISE 19-10
Preparing a Statement of Changes in Financial Position

A summary of the comparative financial position for Landscape Consultants, Inc., for the current year appears as follows:

	End of Current Year	Beginning of Current Year
Cash (cash and cash equivalents).................................	$ 18,000	$ 14,000
Accounts receivable (net).......................................	98,000	88,000
Inventory..	64,000	73,000
Land..	90,000	50,000
Buildings	160,000	100,000
Less: Accumulated depreciation	(40,000)	(35,000)
Totals...	$390,000	$290,000
Accounts payable (for purchases)...............................	$ 42,000	$ 31,000
Accrued expenses...	8,000	9,000
Notes payable, due in five years	70,000	–0–
Capital stock, no-par value.....................................	220,000	210,000
Retained earnings	50,000	40,000
Totals...	$390,000	$290,000

The net income was $17,000. Depreciation expense for the current year was $5,000. A cash dividend of $7,000 was paid at the end of the current year.

Prepare a statement of changes in financial position for the current year without using a working paper.

PROBLEMS

Group A

PROBLEM 19A-1
Effect of Transactions on Cash and Cash Equivalents and on Net Income Conversion, and Identifying Exchange Transactions

For each of the following business transactions and adjustments, you are to indicate the effect, first, on cash and cash equivalents, and second, on net income in its conversion to cash provided or used by operating activities. In each case, the possible effects are an increase, decrease, or no change.

1 One-year fire insurance policy paid in advance at year-end date.

2 Inventory destroyed in an accident; one-half of its carrying value covered by insurance and paid by the insurance company.

3 Charging the portion of unexpired insurance expense that expired during the current year.

4 A plant asset sold for cash at a price below its carrying value.

5 Declaration of a cash dividend.

6 Payment of a previously declared cash dividend.

7 Purchase of patent, which gives 200 shares of the company's common stock in exchange.

8 Marketable securities (temporary investments) sold for cash at a price above cost.

9 Amortization of premium on bonds payable.

10 Temporary investments in marketable securities sold for cash at cost, i.e., its carrying value.

INSTRUCTIONS a List the numbers 1 to 10 on your answer sheet, and set up two columns headed "Effect on cash and cash equivalents" and "Effect on net income conversion." For each item, write the words *increase, decrease,* or *no change* in the appropriate column to indicate the effect of the item on cash and cash equivalents, and on net income conversion.

b Are any of the items listed above considered "exchange transactions," which would be listed as both a source and use of cash in a statement of changes in financial position? Explain.

PROBLEM 19A-2
Computation of Net Cash Flow from Operating Activities

The data below are taken from the income statement and balance sheets of Discount Pharmacies, Inc.:

	1996	1995
Income statement:		
Net income...	$300,000	
Depreciation expense..	140,000	
Amortization of intangible assets................................	20,000	
Gain on sale of plant assets	70,000	
Loss on sale of long-term investments	25,000	
Balance sheets:		
Accounts receivable..	$365,000	$410,000
Inventory...	513,000	585,000
Prepaid expenses	22,000	10,000
Accounts payable (to merchandise suppliers)....................	369,000	410,000
Accrued expenses..	190,000	155,000

INSTRUCTIONS Using this information, prepare a partial statement of changes in financial position for the year ended December 31, 1996, showing the determination of net cash flow from operating activities.

PROBLEM 19A-3
Prepare and Comment on a Statement of Changes in Financial Position

The information that is illustrated below is taken from the financial statements of Toro Corporation:

	1996	1995
Cash...	$ 65,000	$ 85,000
Temporary investments	35,000	20,000
Accounts receivable (net)......................................	180,000	125,000
Inventories...	220,000	250,000
Prepaid expenses	20,000	15,000
Long-term investments	110,000	130,000
Equipment	600,000	420,000
Less: Accumulated depreciation	(190,000)	(110,000)
Bank loan..	75,000	55,000
Accounts payable	140,000	165,000
Accrued expenses..	25,000	20,000
Capital stock...	300,000	255,000
Retained earnings	500,000	440,000

Depreciation for 1996 amounted to $80,000; no equipment items were sold; long-term investments were sold at a gain of $10,000; capital stock was issued for $45,000; and net income was $135,000. Cash dividends of $75,000 were declared and paid.

INSTRUCTIONS

a Compute the amount of increase or decrease in cash and cash equivalents for 1996.

b Prepare a statement of changes in financial position for 1996, without using working papers.

c Briefly comment on the company's liquidity position and cash policies on operating, financing, and investing activities for 1996.

PROBLEM 19A-4
Working Paper

Using the information provided in Problem 19A-3, prepare a working paper for a statement of changes in financial position. (If you have already worked Problem 19A-3, determine that your solutions to both problems are in agreement.)

PROBLEM 19A-5
Show How the Increase in Cash and Cash Equivalents Is Determined and Prepare a Statement of Changes in Financial Position

During the year, Montiris Limited showed the following changes in amount for the following groups of accounts. For example, cash and cash equivalents increased by $16,000 during the year, and this amount therefore appears in the Debit change column.

	Changes during the Year	
	Debit	*Credit*
Cash and cash equivalents	$ 16,000	
Accounts receivable	54,000	
Inventories		$ 10,000
Building..	200,000	
Equipment	120,000	
Accumulated depreciation		80,000
Accounts payable	120,000	
Accrued expenses..		4,000
Capital stock, no-par		320,000
Retained earnings		96,000
Totals...	$510,000	$510,000

During the year the company sold 12,800 shares of capital stock and applied the proceeds to the purchase of building and equipment. There were no retirements of building and equipment during the year. Net income was $284,000 and cash dividends declared and paid during the year amounted to $188,000.

INSTRUCTIONS

a Show how the $16,000 increase in cash and cash equivalents may be determined by using some necessary **assumed** amounts.

b Prepare a statement of changes in financial position without using working papers.

PROBLEM 19A-6
Prepare a Schedule of Cash and Cash Equivalents, and Working Paper and Statement of Changes in Financial Position

Comparative after-closing trial balances for Vancouver Limited follow:

Debits	December 31 1996	1995
Cash..	$ 82,000	$ 88,000
Marketable securities		96,000
Accounts receivable	192,000	190,000
Inventories...	152,000	200,000
Prepaid expenses	46,000	34,000
Land...	130,000	
Buildings	510,000	
Patents (net of amortization)	68,000	78,000
Totals...	$1,180,000	$686,000

Credits		
Allowance for doubtful accounts	$ 6,000	$ 12,000
Bank loans...	30,000	10,000
Accounts payable	138,000	92,000
Accrued expenses...	72,000	78,000
Long-term notes payable	300,000	60,000
Capital stock...	396,000	226,000
Retained earnings	238,000	208,000
Totals...	$1,180,000	$686,000

During 1995, the company operated in rented space. Early in 1996, it acquired suitable land and made arrangements to borrow funds on long-term notes to finance the construction of new buildings. The company also sold additional stock for $170,000 and all its marketable securities at a gain of $2,000. Construction of the buildings was not completed until the end of 1996; therefore, no depreciation expense was recorded in 1996. Net income was $88,000; cash dividends declared and paid amounted to $58,000.

INSTRUCTIONS   a   Prepare a schedule of change in cash and cash equivalents.
b   Prepare a working paper for a statement of changes in financial position.
c   Prepare a statement of changes in financial position for 1996.

PROBLEM 19A-7
Prepare Schedule of Cash and Cash Equivalents, and Working Paper and Statement of Changes in Financial Position

Comparative account balances for Caron Corporation at the end of 1996 and 1997 follow:

Debit	1997	1996
Cash...	$ 100,000	$ 180,000
Marketable securities		30,000
Accounts receivable (net).......................................	250,000	275,000
Inventory..	450,000	350,000
Land for future expansion	200,000	
Plant and equipment	1,850,000	1,725,000
Patents (net of amortization)	190,000	200,000
Other: assets of a business segment...........................		500,000
Totals...	$3,040,000	$3,260,000

Credit	1997	1996
Accumulated depreciation	$ 262,500	$ 300,000
Bank loan...	10,000	
Accounts payable	232,500	200,000
Dividends payable...	10,000	
Notes payable (long-term)	225,000	100,000
Bonds payable	1,000,000	1,500,000
Premium on bonds payable.....................................	50,000	60,000
Capital stock	1,100,000	850,000
Retained earnings	150,000	250,000
Totals...	$3,040,000	$3,260,000

ADDITIONAL DATA

1 The net loss for 1997 amounted to $40,000.

2 Cash dividends of $10,000 were declared.

3 The company incurred the following expenses, among others: depreciation, amortization of patents, and amortization of premium on bonds payable.

4 The company issued 10,000 shares of its common stock in exchange for land to be held for future expansion. The land was appraised at $200,000.

5 The abandonment of an obsolete and fully depreciated plant with an original cost of $100,000 resulted in a $25,000 cash penalty (a nonoperating loss).

6 Sold a business segment with a carrying value of $500,000 for $530,000 cash (ignore income tax effect and assume no operating income or loss).

7 Equipment was purchased for $225,000. The company paid $100,000 of this amount in cash and issued a 12%, long-term note payable for the balance.

8 Capital stock of $50,000 was issued for stock dividends.

INSTRUCTIONS

a Prepare a schedule of change in cash and cash equivalents during 1997.

b Prepare working papers for a statement of changes in financial position for 1997.

c Prepare a statement of changes in financial position for 1997.

Group B

PROBLEM 19B-1
Effect of Transactions on Cash and Cash Equivalents and on Net Income Conversion, and Identifying Exchange Transactions

A list of business transactions and adjustments follows. For each item you are to indicate the effect, first, on cash and cash equivalents, and second, on net income in its conversion to cash provided or used by operating activities. In each case, the possible effects are an increase, a decrease, or no change.

1 Empty warehouse destroyed by fire; one-half of its carrying value covered by insurance and paid by the insurance company.

2 Amortization of discount on bonds payable.

3 Premium paid for a one-year insurance policy (debit to Unexpired Insurance) at year-end date.

4 Short-term loan from bank.

5 Temporary investments sold for cash at a price below cost.

6 Payment of an account payable.

7 Depreciation recorded for the period.

8 Sale of long-term investment at a price above its carrying value, resulting in a gain.

9 Payment of last year's income tax liability, which was previously recorded in the accounting records.

10 Shares of common stock issued in exchange for convertible bonds converted by bondholders.

INSTRUCTIONS

a List the numbers 1 to 10 on your answer sheet, and set up two columns headed "Effect on cash and cash equivalents" and "Effect on net income conversion." For each item write the words *increase, decrease,* or *no change* in the appropriate column to indicate the effect of the item on cash and cash equivalents, and on net income conversion.

b Are any of the items listed above considered "exchange transactions," which would be listed as both a source and a use of cash in a statement of changes in financial position? Explain.

PROBLEM 19B-2
An Analysis of Possible Reconciling Items

An analysis of the annual financial statements of K-G Train Corporation reveals the following:

a Prepaid expenses decreased by $500,000 over the year.

b The company had a $2 million nonoperating loss from the early retirement of bonds payable.

c Depreciation for the year amounted to $8 million.

d During the year, $3 million in cash was transferred from the company's bank account into temporary investments.

e Accounts receivable from customers increased by $6 million over the year.

f Accounts payable (to suppliers of merchandise) increased by $3 million during the year.

g Dividends declared during the year, $8 million; dividends paid during the year, $6 million.

h The liability for income taxes payable amounted to $6 million at the beginning of the year and $4 million at year-end.

INSTRUCTIONS

In the reconciliation of net income to net cash flow from operating activities, explain whether each of the above items should be *added to net income, deducted from net income,* or *omitted from the reconciliation.* Briefly explain your reasons for each answer.

PROBLEM 19B-3
Prepare and Comment on a Statement of Changes in Financial Position

The following information is taken from the 1997 annual report of Just-Arrived Fashion, Inc.:

	End of 1997	End of 1996
Cash	$ 42,000	$ 20,000
Temporary investments	29,000	12,000
Accounts receivable	63,000	54,000
Inventories	95,000	109,000
Prepaid expenses	3,000	4,000
Long-term investments	50,000	62,000
Equipment	435,000	275,000
Less: Accumulated depreciation	(120,000)	(70,000)
Bank loan	27,000	10,000
Accounts payable	70,000	68,000
Accrued expenses	–0–	8,000
Bonds payable	60,000	–0–
Capital stock	150,000	150,000
Retained earnings	290,000	230,000

Depreciation for 1997 amounted to $50,000; no equipment items were sold; long-term investments were sold at a gain of $6,000; bonds were issued for $60,000 cash; and net income was $100,000. Cash dividends of $40,000 were declared and paid.

INSTRUCTIONS

a Compute the amount of increase or decrease in cash and cash equivalents for 1997.

b Prepare a statement of changes in financial position for 1997, without using working papers.

c Briefly comment on the company's liquidity position and cash policies on operating, financing, and investing activities.

PROBLEM 19B-4
Working Paper

Using the information provided in Problem 19B-3, prepare a working paper for a statement of changes in financial position. (If you have already worked Problem 19B-3, determine that your solutions to both problems are in agreement.)

PROBLEM 19B-5
Show How the Increase in Cash and Cash Equivalents Is Determined and Prepare a Statement of Changes in Financial Position

During the year Sun Publishers showed the following *changes* in amount for the following groups of accounts. For example, cash and cash equivalents increased by $24,000 during the year, and this amount therefore appears in the Debit change column.

	Changes during the Year	
	Debit	Credit
Cash and cash equivalents	$ 24,000	
Accounts receivable		$ 16,000
Inventories	140,000	
Prepaid equipment rental	12,000	
Land	200,000	
Buildings	880,000	
Accumulated depreciation		460,000
Accounts payable		212,000
Accrued salaries	20,000	
Capital stock, no-par		324,000
Retained earnings		264,000
Totals	$1,276,000	$1,276,000

During the year the company issued 18,000 shares of capital stock at a price of $18 per share. There were no retirements of land and buildings during the year. Net income was $504,000, and cash dividends declared and paid during the year amounted to $240,000.

INSTRUCTIONS

a Show how the $24,000 increase in cash and cash equivalents may be determined by using some **assumed** amounts.

b Prepare a statement of changes in financial position for the year without using working papers.

PROBLEM 19B-6
Prepare Schedule of Cash and Cash Equivalents, and Working Paper, and Statement of Changes in Financial Position

Comparative balance sheets for Sierra Hot Tub Ltd. at the end of 1996 and 1997 are shown below:

	1997	1996
Cash...	$ 55,000	$ 70,000
Marketable securities	20,000	28,000
Accounts receivable (net).......................................	190,000	205,000
Inventory...	245,000	200,000
Prepaid rent..	20,000	18,000
Land for future expansion	85,000	
Plant and equipment (see accumulated depreciation below)	520,000	395,000
Patents (net of amortization)	65,000	70,000
Totals..	$1,200,000	$986,000
Accumulated depreciation	$157,500	$120,000
Bank loan..	36,000	30,000
Accounts payable (suppliers)	161,500	145,000
Accrued salaries	24,000	26,000
Dividends payable..	16,000	
Notes payable due in 2000......................................	55,000	
Capital stock, no-par	700,000	575,000
Retained earnings	50,000	90,000
Totals..	$1,200,000	$986,000

ADDITIONAL DATA

1 The net loss for 1997 amounted to $24,000.

2 Cash dividends of $16,000 were declared.

3 The company incurred the following expenses, which did not require the use of cash: depreciation, $37,500; and amortization of patents, $5,000.

4 Land for future expansion was acquired at a cost of $85,000. This acquisition was financed by paying $30,000 cash and issuing a 10% note payable due in three years for the balance of the purchase price.

5 The company issued 12,500 shares of its capital stock for cash. The market value of the stock was $10 per share. The proceeds were used to purchase equipment.

INSTRUCTIONS

a Prepare a schedule of cash and cash equivalents for 1997.

b Prepare a working paper for a statement of changes in financial position for 1997.

c Prepare a statement of changes in financial position for 1997.

PROBLEM 19B-7
Prepare Schedule of Cash and Cash Equivalents, and Working Paper and Statement of Changes in Financial Position

Comparative after-closing trial balances for Emerging Technologies, Inc., at the ends of 1996 and 1997 follow:

Debits	1997	1996
Cash...	$ 180,000	$ 100,000
Marketable securities	190,000	160,000
Accounts receivable (net)......................................	390,000	320,000
Inventories	710,000	875,000
Prepaid expenses	30,000	45,000
Land...	700,000	850,000
Buildings & equipment	1,700,000	1,135,000
Goodwill	288,000	300,000
Other: assets of a business segment..........................		620,000
Discount on bonds payable....................................	23,000	25,000
Totals...	$4,211,000	$4,430,000

Credits		
Bank loan (short-term)...	$ 30,000	$ 175,000
Accounts payable	545,000	525,000
Accrued expenses...	28,000	40,000
Accumulated depreciation	688,000	580,000
Long-term notes payable	250,000	
Bonds payable	1,100,000	1,100,000
11% preferred stock, $100 par		800,000
Common stock, no-par	905,000	630,000
Retained earnings	665,000	580,000
Totals...	$4,211,000	$4,430,000

ADDITIONAL DATA

1 Net income for 1997 was $260,000.

2 Land with a cost of $150,000 was sold for $170,000 cash.

3 A segment of business with a book value of $620,000 was sold for $520,000 cash (ignore the income tax effect and assume no operating income or loss).

4 The company incurred, among others, the following expenses: depreciation, amortization of goodwill, and amortization of discount on bonds payable.

5 Equipment was purchased for $565,000 by paying $315,000 in cash and issuing a 12% long-term note payable for the remaining $250,000.

6 The company issued 5,000 shares of common stock at a price of $20 per share. The proceeds, along with some additional cash, were used to retire the entire issue of 11% preferred stock at its par value.

7 Stock dividends of $175,000 in common stock were issued where shareholders were given a choice of receiving cash or common stock.

INSTRUCTIONS

a Prepare a schedule of change in cash and cash equivalents during 1997.

b Prepare a working paper for a statement of changes in financial position for 1997.

c Prepare a statement of changes in financial position for 1997.

ANALYTICAL AND DECISION PROBLEMS AND CASES

A&D 19-1
Convert Income Statement from Accrual to Cash Basis, Prepare and Comment on the Statement of Changes in Financial Position

When the controller of Southern King Corporation presented the following condensed comparative financial statements to the board of directors, the reaction of the board members was very favourable.

SOUTHERN KING CORPORATION
Comparative Financial Position
As of December 31
(in thousands of dollars)

	1997	1996
Current assets	$ 410	$395
Less: Current liabilities	200	225
Working capital	$ 210	$170
Plant and equipment (net)	962	660
Patents (net of amortization)	8	10
Other—assets of a business segment	–0–	150
Total assets minus current liabilities	$1,180	$990
Long-term liabilities	$ 250	$–0–
Preferred stock (non-cumulative)	–0–	170
Common stock	500	500
Retained earnings	430	320
Total long-term debt and capital	$1,180	$990

SOUTHERN KING CORPORATION
Comparative Income Statements
(in thousands of dollars)

	1997	1996
Net sales	$1,000	$680
Cost of goods sold	590	480
Gross profit	$ 410	$200
Operating expenses, including depreciation of $80 in 1997 and $60 in 1996	(180)	(140)
Loss on sale of a business segment	(30)	–0–
Income taxes	(90)	(25)
Net income	$ 110	$ 35

Noting that net income rose from $3.50 per share of capital stock to $11 per share, one member of the board proposed that a substantial cash dividend be paid. "Our working capital is up by $40,000; we should be able to make a distribution to shareholders," he commented. The controller replied that the company's cash position was precarious and pointed out that at the end of 1997 a cash balance of only $15,000 was on hand, a decline from $145,000 at the end of 1996. The controller also reminded the board that the company bought some new equipment during 1997. When a board member asked for an explanation of the increase of $40,000 in working capital, the controller presented the following schedule (in thousands of dollars):

	EFFECT ON WORKING CAPITAL
Increase in working capital:	
Accounts receivable increased by	$ 83
Inventories increased by	72
Accounts payable reduced by	62
Accrued expenses reduced by	28
Total increases in working capital	$245
Decreases in working capital:	
Cash decreased by $130	
Prepaid expenses reduced by 10	
Income tax liability increased by 65	205
Increase in working capital during 1997	$ 40

After examining this schedule, the board member shook his head and said, "I still don't understand how our cash position can be so tight in the face of a tripling of net income and a substantial increase in working capital! Also, I am not sure what our cash policies in the operating, financing, and investing areas are. The information provided by the controller really does not help me at all."

INSTRUCTIONS

a Prepare a statement converting Southern King Corporation's income statement to a cash basis, determining the cash generated by operations during 1997.

b From the information and the comparative statement of financial position provided above, prepare a statement of changes in financial position for 1997, explaining the $130,000 decrease in the cash balance. (Check that the cash from operating activities is the same in both **a** and **b.**)

c Comment on the issues raised by the board member.

A&D 19-2
Can We Make It?

Olympic Sportswear Limited has a cash balance of $6,450,000 at the beginning of 1996. Restrictions contained in the bank loan agreement require that the cash balance not fall below $6,000,000. The following projected information is available for 1996.

1 Budgeted net income (including the gain on sale of plant assets) is $7,200,000. The following items are included in estimating net income: depreciation, $2,100,000; amortization of premium on bonds payable, $150,000. Also, accounts receivable and inventory are expected to increase by $3,200,000 and $3,600,000 respectively. Accounts payable are expected to increase by $6,800,000. The company's sales are expected to be similar to 1995.

2 Sale of plant assets with a carrying value of $1,200,000 is expected to bring in $1,500,000 cash.

3 Additional plant assets costing $15,000,000 will be acquired. Payment will be as follows: 40% cash, and 60% through issuance of capital stock.

4 Long-term investment will be sold at cost, $300,000 cash.

5 Bonds payable in the amount of $1,500,000, bearing interest at 11%, will be redeemed at 105, approximately 10 years prior to maturity in order to eliminate the high interest expense of $165,000 per year. The elimination of this interest and the gain or loss on the retirement of bonds payable were taken into account in estimating net income for 1996. These bonds had been issued at par.

6 Tentative planned cash dividend, $4,500,000.

INSTRUCTIONS

a Consider all the information that has been given and prepare a projected statement of changes in financial position in order to determine the estimated increase or decrease in cash for 1996.

b The planned cash dividend of $4,500,000 represents the same dividend per share as paid last year. The company would like to maintain dividends at this level. Does it appear likely that the past dividend policy can be maintained in 1996? What factors other than cash position should be considered in determining the level of cash dividends declared by the board of directors?

c Comment on the company's cash policy on operating activities.

A&D 19-3
On Target or Not?

Lancaster Corporation is assessing its three-year plan on plant modernization and expansion. The company is in a capital-intensive industry where plant and equipment can become obsolete in a few years. This plan is as follows:

1995 Modernization by replacing obsolete equipment.

1996 Commencing the expansion by constructing a new plant and by purchasing equipment, financed partly by selling the remaining long-term investments of $32 million.

1997 Completing the expansion and starting the operating of the new plant at the beginning of 1998. Of the total cost of $190 million incurred in 1997 ($52 million for plant and $138 million for equipment), $170 million will be financed equally by issuing bonds payable and capital stock.

To enhance the attractiveness of its capital stock issue, the company wants to continue its long-established dividend policy of about 8% on capital, which will require a cash dividend of $38 million in 1997. Also, the company will have more than half of its assets financed by debts after issuing the bonds payable in 1997. The new and old bond indentures (bonds were also issued prior to 1995) will require the company to maintain a minimum cash balance of $30 million for 1997 and subsequent years. It is expected that the net income for 1997 will be similar to that for 1996.

The comparative statements of changes in financial position for 1995 and 1996 are presented below and on page 929.

LANCASTER CORPORATION
Comparative Statements of Changes in Financial Position
For 1996 and 1995
(in millions of dollars)

	1996	1995
Operating activities:		
Net income...	$ 12	$ 16
Add: Expenses not requiring the use of cash—Depreciation	8	6
Decrease in accounts receivable...................................	5	2
Decrease in inventories	2	2
Increase in accounts payable......................................	10	3
Increase in accrued liabilities	2	1
Cash provided by operating activities	$ 39	$ 30

	1996	1995
Financing activities:		
Sale of long-term investments	$ 32	$ 62
Issuance of bonds payable	116	
Cash dividends...	(30)	(30)
Cash provided by financing activities	$ 118	$ 32
Investing activities:		
Construction of plant	$ (90)	
Purchase of equipment	(36)	$(60)
Cash used in investing activities	$(126)	$(60)
Increase in cash..	$ 31	$ 2
Cash Balance	$ 41	$ 10

INSTRUCTIONS

a Assess the company's liquidity position for 1996.

b Comment on the company's cash policies on operating, financing, and investing activities in 1996.

c Will the company be able to finance its activities in 1997 as planned? If yes, explain. If not, explain and suggest alternatives.

20 Analysis and Interpretation of Financial Statements

In preceding chapters we have explained how decision makers analyze, interpret, and use various types of accounting information, including the statement of changes in financial position presented in Chapter 19. Now we are ready to examine the balance sheet, the income statement, and the statement of retained earnings, and to see how investors and creditors may use these statements in evaluating the profitability, solvency, and future prospects of a business. Also, the importance of the information in corporate annual reports is highlighted. A major goal of this chapter is to demonstrate how different types of investors select the accounting information that is most relevant to their decisions.

Learning Objectives

After studying this chapter you should be able to:

1 Put a company's net income into perspective by relating it to sales, assets, and shareholders' equity.

2 Describe several sources of financial information about a business.

3 Explain the uses of dollar and percentage changes, trend percentages, component percentages, and ratios.

4 Discuss the "quality" of a company's earnings, assets, and working capital.

5 Analyze financial statements from the viewpoints of common shareholders, creditors, and others.

6 Compute the ratios widely used in financial statement analysis and explain the significance of each.

*F*inancial statements are the instrument panel of a business enterprise. They constitute a report on managerial performance, attesting to managerial success or failure and flashing warning signals of impending difficulties. To read a complex instrument panel, one must understand the gauges and their calibration to make sense out of the array of data they convey. Similarly, one must understand the inner workings of the accounting system and the significance of various financial relationships to interpret the data appearing in financial statements. To a reader with a knowledge of accounting, a set of financial statements tells a great deal about a business enterprise.

The financial affairs of a business may be of interest to a number of different groups: management, creditors, investors, politicians, union officials, and government agencies. Each of the groups has somewhat different needs, and accordingly each tends to concentrate on particular aspects of a company's financial picture.

What Is Your Opinion of the Level of Corporate Earnings?

OBJECTIVE 1 Put a company's net income into perspective by relating it to sales, assets, and shareholders' equity.

As a college or university student who has completed (or almost completed) a course in accounting, you have a much better understanding of corporate earnings than do people who have never studied accounting. The level of earnings of large corporations is often a controversial topic, a favourite topic in many political speeches and at cocktail parties. Some of the statements one reads or hears from these sources are emotional rather than rational, fiction rather than fact. Public opinion polls show that the public believes the average manufacturing company has an after-tax net income of about 30% of sales, when in fact such net income has been **about 5% of sales** in recent years. A widespread public belief that net income is six times the actual rate may lead to some unwise decisions.

An in-depth knowledge of accounting does not enable you to say at what level corporate earnings **should be;** however, a knowledge of accounting does enable you to read audited financial statements that show what the level of corporate earnings **actually is.** Moreover, you are aware the information in published financial statements of corporations has been audited by public accounting firms. Consequently, you know that the earnings reported in these published financial statements are reasonably reliable; they have been determined in accordance with generally accepted accounting principles and verified by independent experts.

There are many ways of appraising the adequacy of corporate earnings. Certainly, earnings should be compared with total assets and with invested capital as well as with sales. In this chapter we shall look at a number of ways of evaluating corporate earnings and solvency.

Sources of Financial Information

For the most part, our discussion will be limited to the kind of analysis that can be made by "outsiders" who do not have access to internal accounting records. Investors must rely to a considerable extent on financial statements in published annual and quarterly reports. In the case of largely publicly owned corporations, additional information is presented in their

OBJECTIVE 2
Describe several sources of financial information about a business.

annual report. For example, large corporations include in their annual reports a **discussion and analysis** by top management of the results of the company's operations and of its current financial position. (Comprehensive Problem 5 at the end of this chapter contains an example of such information.)

Many financial analysts also study the financial position and future prospects of publicly owned corporations and sell their analyses, conclusions, and investment recommendations for a fee. For example, detailed financial analyses of most large corporations are published by *The Financial Post,* Dun & Bradstreet of Canada, Canadian Business Service *(The Investment Reporter),* Moody's Investors Service, Standard & Poor's, and The Value Line Investment Survey. Anyone may subscribe to these investment advisory services.

Bankers and major creditors usually are able to obtain detailed financial information from borrowers simply by requesting it as a condition for granting a loan. Suppliers and other trade creditors may obtain some financial information about almost any business from credit-rating agencies, such as Dun & Bradstreet of Canada.

Comparative Financial Statement

Significant changes in financial data are easy to see when financial statement amounts for two or more years are placed side by side in adjacent columns. Such a statement is called a **comparative financial statement.** The amounts for the most recent year are usually placed in the left-hand money column. All financial statements are usually prepared in the form of comparative statements. A highly condensed comparative income statement covering three years is shown below.

Condensed three-year income statement

BENSON CORPORATION
Comparative Income Statement
For the Years Ended December 31, 1997, 1996, and 1995
(in thousands of dollars)

	1997	1996	1995
Net sales	$600	$500	$400
Cost of goods sold	370	300	235
Gross profit	$230	$200	$165
Expenses	194	160	115
Net income	$ 36	$ 40	$ 50

Tools of Analysis

Few figures in a financial statement are highly significant in and of themselves. It is their relationship to other quantities or the amount and direction of change that is important. Analysis is largely a matter of establishing significant relationships and identifying changes and trends. Four widely used analytical techniques are (1) dollar and percentage changes, (2) trend percentages, (3) component percentages, and (4) ratios.

OBJECTIVE 3
Explain the
uses of dol-
lar and per-
centage
changes,
trend per-
centages,
component
percentages,
and ratios.

Dollar and Percentage Changes

The dollar amount of change from year to year is significant, but express-ing the change in percentage terms adds perspective. For example, if sales this year have increased by $100,000, the fact that this is an increase of 10% over last year's sales of $1 million puts it in a different perspective than if it represented a 1% increase over sales of $10 million for the prior year.

The dollar amount of any change is the difference between the amount for a **comparison** year and for a **base** year. The percentage change is computed by dividing the amount of the change between years by the amount for the base year. This is illustrated in the tabulation below, using data from the comparative income statement on page 932.

Dollar and percentage changes

| | In Thousands | | | Increase or (Decrease) | | | |
| | | | | 1997 over 1996 | | 1996 over 1995 | |
	Year 1997	Year 1996	Year 1995	Amount	%	Amount	%
Net sales................	$600	$500	$400	$100	20%	$100	25%
Net income..............	36	40	50	(4)	(10%)	(10)	(20%)

Although net sales increased $100,000 in both 1996 and 1997, the per-centage of change differs because of the shift in the base from 1995 to 1996. These calculations present no problems when the figures for the base year are positive amounts. If a negative amount or a zero amount appears in the base year, however, a percentage change cannot be computed. Thus if Ben-son Corporation had incurred a net loss in 1996, the percentage change in net income from 1996 to 1997 could not have been calculated.

Evaluating Percentage Changes in Sales and Earnings Computing the percentage changes in sales, gross profit, and net income from one year to the next gives insight into a company's rate of growth. If a company is experiencing growth in its economic activities, sales and earnings should increase at **more than the rate of inflation.** Assume, for example, that a company's sales increase by 6% while the general price level rises by 10%. It is probable that the entire increase in the dollar amount of sales may be explained by inflation, rather than by an increase in sales volume (the number of units sold). In fact, the company may well have sold **fewer** goods than in the preceding year.

In measuring the dollar or percentage change in **quarterly** sales or earnings, it is customary to compare the results of the current quarter with those of the **same quarter in the preceding year.** Use of the same quar-ter of the preceding year as the base period prevents our analysis from being distorted by seasonal fluctuations in business activity.

Percentages Become Misleading When the Base Is Small Percentage changes may create a misleading impression when the dollar amount used as a base is unusually small. Occasionally we hear a television newscaster say that a company's net income has increased by a very large percentage, such as 900%. The initial impression created by such a statement is that the company's net income must now be excessively large. But assume, for example, that a company had net income of $100,000 in its first year; that in the second year net income drops to $10,000; and that in the third year net income returns to the $100,000 level. In this third year, net income has increased by $90,000, representing a 900% increase over the net income of the second year. What needs to be added is that this 900% increase in net income in the third year *exactly offsets* the 90% decline in net income in the second year. Few people realize that a 90% decline in earnings must be followed by a 900% increase just to get back to the starting point.

CASE IN POINT   In 1990, Maclean Hunter Limited had a net income of $15.3 million, as compared to 1989's net income of $89 million. This represented an 83% decline in net income ($89 million minus $15.3 million divided by $89 million). How much of an increase in net income would be required in 1991 in order for the net income to return to the 1989 level? The answer is 482%, as computed as follows:

Required increase to reach the 1989 net income level	
(from $15.3 million to $89 million)	***$73.7 million***
Base period earnings (1990)	***$15.3 million***
Required percentage increase ($73.7 million ÷ $15.3 million)	***482%***

Thus, even when Maclean Hunter's net income increased by 231% in 1991 over the net income in 1990, the 1991 net income was only $50.6 million. In fact, a 431% increase in net income in 1992 over the net income in 1990 resulted only in an $81.2 million net income for 1992, still short of the 1989 net income level.

Trend Percentages

The changes in financial statement items from a base year to following years are often expressed as *trend percentages* to show the extent and direction of change. Two steps are necessary to compute trend percentages. First, a base year is selected and each item in the financial statements for the base year is given a weight of 100%. The second step is to express each item in the financial statements for following years as a percentage of its base-year amount. This computation consists of dividing an item such as Sales in the years after the base year by the amount of Sales in the base year.

For example, assume that 1991 is selected as the base year and that Sales in the base year amounted to $300,000 as shown below. The trend percentages for Sales are computed by dividing the Sales amount of each following year by $300,000. Also shown in the illustration are the yearly amounts of net income. The trend percentages for net income are computed by dividing the Net Income amount for each following year by the base-year amount of $15,000.

	1996	*1995*	*1994*	*1993*	*1992*	*1991*
Sales	*$450,000*	*$360,000*	*$330,000*	*$320,000*	*$312,000*	*$300,000*
Net income	*22,950*	*14,550*	*21,450*	*19,200*	*15,600*	*15,000*

When the computations described above have been made, the trend percentages will appear as shown below.

	1996	1995	1994	1993	1992	1991
Sales	150%	120%	110%	107%	104%	100%
Net income	153%	97%	143%	128%	104%	100%

The above trend percentages indicate a very modest growth in sales in the early years and accelerated growth in 1995 and 1996. Net income also shows an increasing growth trend with the exception of the year 1995, when net income declined despite a solid increase in sales. This variation could have resulted from an unfavourable change in the gross profit margin or from unusual expenses. However, the problem was overcome in 1996 with a sharp rise in net income. Overall the trend percentages give a picture of a profitable growing enterprise.

As another example, assume that sales are increasing each year but that the cost of goods sold is increasing at a faster rate. This means that the gross profit margin is shrinking. Perhaps the increases in sales are being achieved through excessive price cutting. The company's net income may be declining even though sales are rising.

Component Percentages

Component percentages indicate the ***relative size*** of each item included in a total. For example, each item on a balance sheet could be expressed as a percentage of total assets. This shows quickly the relative importance of current and noncurrent assets as well as the relative amount of financing obtained from current creditors, long-term creditors, and shareholders. By computing component percentages for several successive balance sheets, we can see which items are increasing in importance and which are becoming less significant.

Common Size Income Statement Another application of component percentages is to express all items in an income statement as a percentage of net sales. Such a statement is called a common size income statement. A condensed income statement in dollars and in common size form is illustrated below.

Income Statement

	Dollars		Component Percentages	
	1996	1995	1996	1995
Net sales	$1,000,000	$600,000	100.0%	100.0%
Cost of goods sold	700,000	360,000	70.0	60.0
Gross profit	$ 300,000	$240,000	30.0%	40.0%
Expenses (including income taxes)	250,000	180,000	25.0	30.0
Net income	$ 50,000	$ 60,000	5.0%	10.0%

Are the year-to-year changes favourable?

Looking only at the component percentages, we see that the decline in the gross profit rate from 40% to 30% was only partially offset by the decrease in expenses as a percentage of net sales, causing net income to decrease from 10% to 5% of net sales.

Ratios

A ratio is a simple mathematical expression of the relationship of one item to another. Every percentage may be viewed as a ratio—that is, one number expressed as a percentage of another.

Ratios may be stated in several ways. To illustrate, let us consider the current ratio, which expresses the relationship between current assets and current liabilities. If current assets are $100,000 and current liabilities are $50,000, we may say either that the current ratio is 2 to 1 (which is written as 2:1) or that current assets are 200% of current liabilities. Either statement correctly summarizes the relationship—that is, that current assets are twice as large as current liabilities.

If a ratio is to be useful, the two amounts being compared must be logically related. Our interpretation of a ratio often requires investigation of the underlying data.

Comparative Data in Annual Reports of Major Corporations

The annual reports of major corporations usually contain comparative balance sheets covering two years and comparative income statements for two or three years. Supplementary schedules showing sales, net income, and other key amounts are often presented for periods of five to 10 years. Shown below are selected items from an annual report of Bombardier, Inc. showing some interesting trends for a five-year period.

BOMBARDIER, INC.
(Dollars in millions, except per share data)

	1993	1992	1991	1990	1989
Revenue	$4,448	$3,059	$2,892	$2,143	$1,426
Net income	132	108	100	92	68
Net earnings per common share	0.85	0.73	0.71	0.68	0.52
Dividends per share (class A)	0.20	0.16	0.16	0.13	0.11
Market price per share (year-end), class A	11.88	17.13	8.44	7.81	6.69
Book value per common share	6.16	5.67	4.64	3.54	2.92

Standards of Comparison

In using dollar and percentage changes, trend percentages, component percentages, and ratios, financial analysts constantly search for some standard of comparison against which to judge whether the relationships that they have found are favourable or unfavourable. Two such standards are (1) the past performance of the company and (2) the performance of other companies in the same industry.

Past Performance of the Company   Comparing analytical data for a current period with similar computations for prior years affords some basis for judging whether the condition of the business is improving or worsening. This comparison of data over time is sometimes called *horizontal* or *trend* analysis, to express the idea of reviewing data for a number of consecutive periods. It is distinguished from **vertical** or **static** analysis, which refers to the review of the financial information for only one accounting period.

In addition to determining whether the situation is improving or becoming worse, horizontal analysis may aid in making estimates of future prospects.

Because changes may reverse their direction at any time, however, projecting past trends into the future is always a somewhat risky statistical endeavour.

A weakness of horizontal analysis is that comparison with the past does not afford any basis for evaluation in absolute terms. The fact that net income was 2% of sales last year and is 3% of sales this year indicates improvement, but if there is evidence that net income **should be** 7% of sales, the record for both years is unfavourable.

Industry Standard The limitations of horizontal analysis may be overcome to some extent by finding an appropriate "yardstick" against which to measure a particular company's performance. The yardsticks most widely used by most analysts are the performance of comparable companies and the average performance of several companies in the same industry.[1]

CASE IN POINT Dun & Bradstreet Canada Limited publishes *Key Business Ratios Canada-Corporations* for many industries. The following are "industry ratios" selected from a recent issue of this publication:

Industry Group	Average Ratios			
	Gross Margin	Current Ratio	Net Income to Sales	Rate of Return on Equity
Retail trade	25.7%	1.4	2.5%	20.9%
Wholesale trade	18.2%	1.3	1.9%	14.0%
Manufacturers...........................	22.7%	1.5	4.5%	12.4%
Construction	24.5%	1.3	3.2%	23.3%
Services	79.6%	1.0	7.0%	23.5%
Transportation, Storage & Utilities (including radio and T.V.)	78.0%	0.8	6.6%	9.9%

Assume, for example, that the revenue of Alpha Airlines drops by 5% during the current year. If the revenue for the airlines industry had dropped an average of 15% during this year, Alpha's 5% decline might be viewed as a **favourable** performance. As another example, assume that Omega Limited earns a net income equal to 2% of net sales. This would be substandard if Omega were a manufacturer of commercial aircraft, but it would be satisfactory performance if it were a grocery chain.

When we compare a given company with its competitors or with industry averages, our conclusions will be valid only if the companies in question

---

[1] Industry data are available from a number of sources. For example, Robert Morris Associates publishes *Annual Statement Studies* that include data from many thousands of annual reports, grouped into several hundred industry classifications. Industry classifications are subdivided further by company size. Dun & Bradstreet annually publishes *Key Business Ratios* for several hundred lines of business.

are reasonably comparable. Because of the large number of diversified companies formed in recent years, the term **industry** is difficult to define, and companies that fall roughly within the same industry may not be comparable in many respects. For example, one company may engage only in the marketing of oil products; another may be a fully integrated producer from the well to the gas pump, yet both are said to be in the "oil industry."

Quality of Earnings

OBJECTIVE 4
Discuss the
"quality" of
a company's
earnings,
assets, and
working
capital.

Earnings are the lifeblood of a business entity. No entity can survive for long and accomplish its other goals unless it is profitable. On the other hand, continuous losses will drain assets from the business, consume owners' equity, and leave the company at the mercy of creditors. In assessing the prospects of a company, we are interested not only in the total **amount** of earnings but also in the **rate** of earnings on sales, on total assets, and on owner's equity. In addition, we must look at the **stability** and **source** of earnings. An erratic earnings performance over a period of years, for example, is less desirable than a steady level of earnings. A history of increasing earnings is preferable to a "flat" earnings record.

A breakdown of sales and earnings by **major product lines** is useful in evaluating the future performance of a company. Publicly owned companies include with their financial statements supplementary schedules showing sales and earnings by product line and by geographical area. These schedules assist financial analysts in forecasting the effect upon the company of changes in consumer demand for particular types of products.

Financial analysts often express the opinion that the earnings of one company are of higher quality than earnings of other similar companies. This concept of **quality of earnings** arises because each company management can choose from a variety of accounting principles and methods, all of which are considered generally acceptable. A company's management often is under heavy pressure to report rising earnings, and accounting policies may be tailored toward this objective. We have already pointed out the impact on current reported earnings of the choice between the LIFO and FIFO methods of inventory valuation and the choice of depreciation policies. In judging the quality of earnings, the financial analyst should consider whether the accounting principles and methods selected by management lead to a conservative measurement of earnings or tend to inflate reported earnings.

Quality of Assets and the Relative Amount of Debt

Although a satisfactory level of earnings may be a good indication of the company's long-run ability to pay its debts and dividends, we must also look at the composition of assets, their condition and liquidity, the relationship between current assets and current liabilities, the cash flows, and the total amount of debt outstanding. A company may be profitable and yet be unable to pay its liabilities on time; sales and earnings may appear satisfactory, but plant and equipment may be deteriorating because of poor maintenance policies; valuable patents may be expiring; substantial losses may be imminent due to slow-moving inventories and past-due receivables. Companies with large amounts of debt often are vulnerable to increases in interest rates and to even temporary reductions in cash inflows.

Impact of Inflation

During a period of significant inflation, financial statements prepared in terms of historical costs do not reflect fully the economic resources or the real income (in terms of purchasing power) of a business enterprise. It is desirable that companies include in their annual reports supplementary schedules showing the effects of inflation upon their financial statements. Most companies, however, do *not* include these supplementary schedules because of the high cost of developing this information.

Illustrative Analysis for Seacliff Corporation

Keep in mind the preceding discussion of analytical principles as you study the illustrative financial analysis that follows. The basic information for our analysis is contained in a set of condensed two-year comparative financial statements for Seacliff Corporation shown below and on the following page.[2] Summarized statement data, together with computations of dollar increases and decreases, and component percentages where applicable, have been compiled. For convenience in this illustration, relatively small dollar amounts have been used in the Seacliff financial statements.

Using the information in these statements, let us consider the kind of analysis that might be of particular interest to (1) common shareholders, (2) long-term creditors, (3) preferred shareholders, and (4) short-term creditors.

SEACLIFF CORPORATION
Comparative Income Statement
For the Years Ended December 31, 1996 and December 31, 1995

	1996	1995	Increase or (Decrease) Dollars	%	Percentage of Net Sales 1996	1995
Net sales	$900,000	$750,000	$150,000	20.0	100.0	100.0
Cost of goods sold	530,000	420,000	110,000	26.2	58.9	56.0
Gross profit	$370,000	$330,000	$ 40,000	12.1	41.1	44.0
Operating expenses:						
Selling expenses:	$117,000	$ 75,000	$ 42,000	56.0	13.0	10.0
General and administrative expenses	126,000	95,000	31,000	32.6	14.0	12.7
Total operating expenses	$243,000	$170,000	$ 73,000	42.9	27.0	22.7
Operating income	$127,000	$160,000	$(33,000)	(20.6)	14.1	21.3
Interest expense	24,000	30,000	(6,000)	(20.0)	2.7	4.0
Income before income taxes	$103,000	$130,000	$(27,000)	(20.8)	11.4	17.3
Income taxes	28,000	40,000	(12,000)	(30.0)	3.1	5.3
Net income	$ 75,000	$ 90,000	$(15,000)	(16.7)	8.3	12.0
Earnings per share of common stock	$13.20	$20.25	$(7.05)	(34.8)		

---

[2] Since the statement of changes in financial position was presented and analyzed in Chapter 19, it is not included here again.

SEACLIFF CORPORATION
Statement of Retained Earnings
For the Years Ended December 31, 1996 and December 31, 1995

	1996	1995	Increase or (Decrease) Dollars	%
Retained earnings, beginning of year	$176,000	$115,000	$61,000	53.0
Net income	75,000	90,000	(15,000)	(16.7)
	$251,000	$205,000	$46,000	22.4
Less: Dividends on common stock ($5.00 per share in 1995,				
$4.80 per share in 1996)...............................	$ 24,000	$ 20,000	$ 4,000	20.0
Dividends on preferred stock ($9 per share)..............	9,000	9,000		
	$ 33,000	$ 29,000	$ 4,000	13.8
Retained earnings, end of year	$218,000	$176,000	$42,000	23.9

SEACLIFF CORPORATION
Condensed Comparative Balance Sheet*
December 31, 1996 and December 31, 1995

Assets	1996	1995	Increase or (Decrease) Dollars	%	Percentage of Total Assets 1996	1995
Current assets	$390,000	$288,000	$102,000	35.4	41.1	33.5
Plant and equipment (net)	500,000	467,000	33,000	7.1	52.6	54.3
Other assets (loans to officers)..............	60,000	105,000	(45,000)	(42.9)	6.3	12.2
Total assets	$950,000	$860,000	$ 90,000	10.5	100.0	100.0
Liabilities & Shareholders' Equity						
Liabilities:						
Current liabilities	$112,000	$ 94,000	$ 18,000	19.1	11.8	10.9
12% bonds payable	200,000	250,000	(50,000)	(20.0)	21.1	29.1
Total liabilities	$312,000	$344,000	$(32,000)	(9.3)	32.9	40.0
Shareholders' equity:						
$9 preferred stock, no-par, callable						
at 105, 1,000 shares.....................	$100,000	$100,000			10.5	11.6
Common stock (1996, 5,000 shares;						
1995, 4,000 shares)	320,000	240,000	$ 80,000	33.3	33.7	27.9
Retained earnings	218,000	176,000	42,000	23.9	22.9	20.5
Total shareholders' equity	$638,000	$516,000	$122,000	23.6	67.1	60.0
Total liabilities & shareholders' equity	$950,000	$860,000	$ 90,000	10.5	100.0	100.0

* In order to focus attention on important subtotals, this statement is highly condensed and does not show individual asset and liability items. These details will be introduced as needed in the next discussion. For example, a list of Seacliff Corporation's current assets and current liabilities appears on page 949.

Analysis by Common Shareholders

Common shareholders and potential investors in common stock look first at a company's earnings record. Their investment is in shares of stock, so *earnings per share and dividends per share* are of particular interest.

OBJECTIVE 5
Analyze
financial
statements
from the
viewpoints
of common
shareholders,
creditors,
and others.

Earnings per Share of Common Stock   As indicated in Chapter 15, earnings per share of common stock are computed by dividing the income applicable to the common stock by the weighted-average number of shares of common stock outstanding during the year. Any preferred dividend requirements must be subtracted from net income to determine income applicable to common stock, as shown in the following computations for Seacliff Corporation:

Earnings per Share of Common Stock

		1996	1995
Earnings related to number of common shares outstanding	Net income..	$75,000	$90,000
	Less: Preferred dividend requirements	9,000	9,000
	Income applicable to common stock .... (a)	$66,000	$81,000
	Shares of common stock outstanding, during the year............. (b)	5,000	4,000
	Earnings per share of common stock (a ÷ b)	$13.20	$20.25

Notice that earnings per share have decreased by *$7.05* in 1996, representing a decline of nearly *35%* from their level in 1995 ($7.05 ÷ $20.25 = 34.8%). Common shareholders consider a decline in earnings per share to be an extremely unfavourable development. A decline in earnings per share generally represents a decline in the profitability of the company, and creates doubt as to the company's prospects for future growth.

With such a significant decline in earnings per share, we should expect to see a *substantial* decline in the market value of Seacliff's common stock during 1996. [For purposes of our illustration, we will assume the common stock had a market value of *$160* at December 31, 1995 and of *$132* at the end of 1996. This drop of $28 per share represents a *$17\frac{1}{2}$%* decline in the market value of every common shareholder's investment ($28 decline ÷ $160 = 17.5%).]

Price-Earnings Ratio   The relationship between the market price of common stock and earnings per share is so widely recognized that it is expressed as a ratio, called the price-earnings ratio (or *p/e* ratio). The p/e ratio is determined by dividing the market price per share by the annual earnings per share.

The p/e ratio of the 300 stocks included in the TSE 300 Composite (Toronto Stock Exchange) has varied widely in recent years. The outlook for future earnings is the major factor influencing a company's p/e ratio. Companies with track records of rapid growth may sell at p/e ratios of perhaps 20 to 1, or even higher. Companies with "flat" earnings or earnings expected to decline in future years often sell at price-earnings ratios below, say, 10 to 1.

At the end of 1995, Seacliff's p/e ratio was approximately *8 to 1* ($160 ÷ $20.25 = 7.9), suggesting that investors *were expecting* earnings to decline in 1996. At December 31, 1996, the price earnings ratio was *10 to 1*

($132 ÷ $13.20 = 10.0). A p/e ratio in this range suggests that investors expect future earnings to stabilize around the current level.

Dividend Yield   Dividends are of prime importance to some shareholders but a secondary factor to others. In other words, some shareholders invest primarily to receive regular cash income, while others invest in stocks principally with the hope of securing capital gains through rising market prices. If a corporation is profitable and retains its earnings for expansion of the business, the expanded operations should produce an increase in the net income of the company and thus tend to make each share of stock more valuable.

In comparing the merits of alternative investment opportunities, we should relate earnings and dividends per share to the ***market value*** of the stock. Dividends per share divided by market price per share determine the ***yield*** rate of a company's stock. Dividend yield is especially important to those investors whose objective is to maximize the dividend revenue from their investments.

Summary of Earnings and Dividend Data for Seacliff   The relationships of Seacliff's per-share earnings and dividends to its year-end stock prices are summarized below:

Earnings and Dividends per Share of Common Stock

Earnings and dividends related to market price of common stock

Date	Assumed Market Value per Share	Earnings per Share	Price-Earnings Ratio	Dividends per Share	Dividend Yield, %
Dec. 31, 1995............	$160	$20.25	8	$5.00	3.1
Dec. 31, 1996............	132	13.20	10	4.80	3.6

The decline in market value during 1996 presumably reflects the decreases in both earnings and dividends per share. Investors appraising this stock at December 31, 1996, should consider whether a price-earning ratio of **10** and a dividend yield of **3.6%** represent a satisfactory situation in the light of alternative investment opportunities. These investors will also place considerable weight on estimates of the company's prospective future earnings and the probable effect of such estimated earnings on the market price of the stock and on dividend payments.

Book Value per Share of Common Stock   The procedures for computing book value per share were fully described in Chapter 14 and will not be repeated here. We will, however, determine the book value per share of common stock for Seacliff:

Book Value per Share of Common Stock

Why did book value per share increase?

		1996	1995
Total shareholders' equity		$638,000	$516,000
Less: Equity of preferred shareholders (1,000 shares at call price of $105)		105,000	105,000
Equity of common shareholders	(a)	$533,000	$411,000
Shares of common stock outstanding	(b)	5,000	4,000
Book value per share of common stock (a ÷ b)		$106.60	$102.75

Book value indicates the net assets represented by each share of stock. This statistic is often helpful in estimating a reasonable price for a company's stock, especially for small corporations whose shares are not publicly traded.[3] However, if a company's future earnings prospects are unusually good or unusually poor, or the market value of the company's assets is different from their carrying (book) value, the market price of its shares may differ significantly from their book value.

CASE IN POINT A study on Canada's top 100 public corporations (in terms of the market value of their listed shares) compared the market values with book values of the common stock of these corporations and computed a "premium market/book value" statistic. For example, a premium market/ book value of plus 100% means that the market value of common stock is twice the book value. The percentages of the premium market/book value of these top 100 public corporations range from a negative 18% for a bank and a resource company to a plus 887% for a real estate developer. A recent annual report of Bombardier, Inc. showed a premium market/book value of 192.8.

Revenue and Expense Analysis The trend of earnings of Seacliff is unfavourable, and shareholders will want to know the reasons for the decline in net income. The comparative income statement shows that despite a 20% increase in net sales, net income fell from $90,000 in 1995 to $75,000 in 1996, a decline of 16.7%. As a percentage of net sales, net income fell from 12% to only 8.3%. The primary causes of this decline were the increases in selling expenses (56.0%), in general and administrative expenses (32.6%), and in the cost of goods sold (26.2%), all of which exceeded the 20% increase in net sales.

Let us assume that further investigation reveals Seacliff decided in 1996 to reduce its sales prices in an effort to generate greater sales volume. This would explain the decrease in gross profit rate from 44% to 41.1% of net sales. Since the dollar amount of gross profit increased $40,000 in 1996, the strategy of reducing sales prices to increase volume would have been successful if there had been little or no increase in operating expenses. However, operating expenses rose by $73,000, resulting in a $33,000 decrease in operating income.

The next step is to find which expenses increased and why. An investor may be handicapped here, because detailed operating expenses are not usually shown in published financial statements. Some conclusions, however, can be reached on the basis of even the condensed information available in the comparative income statement for Seacliff.

The substantial increase in selling expenses presumably reflects greater selling effort during 1996 in an attempt to improve sales volume. However, the fact that selling expenses increased $42,000 while gross profit increased only $40,000 indicates that the cost of this increased sales

---

[3] As pointed out in Chapter 14, book value per share is regularly reported in such financial news media as *The Financial Post* and *The Financial Times,* and also in the annual reports of large corporations such as Dofasco Inc., Royal Bank of Canada, and Moore Corporation Limited.

effort was not justified in terms of results. Even more disturbing is the increase in general and administrative expenses. Some growth in administrative expenses might be expected to accompany increased sales volume, but because some of the expenses are fixed, the growth generally should be **less than proportional** to any increase in sales. The increase in general and administrative expenses from 12.7 to 14% of sales would be of serious concern to informed investors.

Management generally has greater control over operating expenses than over revenue. The **operating expense ratio** is often used as a measure of management's ability to control its operating expenses. The unfavourable trend in this ratio for Seacliff is shown below:

Operating Expense Ratio

Does a higher operating expense ratio indicate higher net income?

		1996	1995
Operating expenses	(a)	$243,000	$170,000
Net sales..	(b)	$900,000	$750,000
Operating expense ratio (a ÷ b)		27.0%	22.7%

If management were able to increase the sales volume while at the same time increasing the gross profit rate and decreasing the operating expense ratio, the effect on net income could be quite dramatic. For example, if in 1997 Seacliff can increase its sales by 11% to $1,000,000, increase its gross profit rate from 41.1 to 44%, and reduce the operating expense ratio from 27 to 24%, its operating income will increase from $127,000 to $200,000 ($1,000,000 − $560,000 − $240,000), an increase of over 57%.

Return on Investment (ROI)

The rate of return on investment (often called ROI) is a measure of management's efficiency in using available resources. Regardless of the size of the organization, capital is a scarce resource and must be used efficiently. In judging the performance of branch managers or of companywide management, it is reasonable to raise the question: What rate of return have you earned on the resources under your control? The concept of return on investment can be applied to a number of situations: for example, evaluating a branch, a total business, a product line, or an individual investment. A number of different ratios have been developed for the ROI concept, each well suited to a particular situation. We shall consider the **return on assets** and the **return on common shareholders' equity** as examples of the return on investment concept.

Return on Assets   An important test of management's ability to earn a return on funds supplied from all sources is the rate of return on total assets.

The income figure used in computing this ratio should be **operating income,** since interest expense and income taxes are determined by factors other than the efficient use of resources. Operating income is earned throughout the year and therefore should be related to the **average** investment in assets during the year. The computation of this ratio of Seacliff is as follows (assuming the 1995 beginning balance of total assets is $820,000):

Percentage Return on Assets

		1996	1995
Operating income	(a)	$127,000	$160,000
Total assets, beginning of year	(b)	$860,000	$820,000
Total assets, end of year	(c)	$950,000	$860,000
Average investment in assets [(b + c) ÷ 2]	(d)	$905,000	$840,000
Return on assets (a ÷ d)		14%	19%

Earnings related to investment in assets

This ratio shows that the rate of return earned on the company's assets has fallen off in 1996. Before drawing conclusions as to the effectiveness of Seacliff's management, however, we should consider the trend in the return on assets earned by other companies of similar kind and size.

Return on Common Shareholders' Equity   Because interest and dividends paid to creditors and preferred shareholders are fixed in amount, a company may earn a greater or smaller return on the common shareholders' equity than on its total assets. The computation of return on shareholders' equity for Seacliff is shown below:

Return on Common Shareholders' Equity

		1996	1995
Net income		$ 75,000	$ 90,000
Less: Preferred dividend requirements		9,000	9,000
Net income applicable to common stock	(a)	$ 66,000	$ 81,000
Common shareholders' equity, beginning of year	(b)	$416,000	$355,000*
Common shareholders' equity, end of year	(c)	$538,000	$416,000
Average common shareholders' equity [(b + c) ÷ 2]	(d)	$477,000	$385,500
Return on common shareholders' equity (a ÷ d)		13.8%	21.0%

Does the use of leverage benefit common shareholders?

*Assumed

In both years, the rate of return on common shareholders' equity was higher than the 12% rate of interest paid to long-term creditors or the 9% dividend rate paid to preferred shareholders. This result was achieved through the favourable use of leverage.

Leverage

The term ***leverage*** means operating a business with borrowed money. If the borrowed capital can be used in the business to earn a return ***greater*** than the cost of borrowing, then the net income and the return on common shareholders' equity will ***increase.*** In other words, if you can borrow money at 12% and use it to earn 20%, you will benefit by doing so. However, leverage can act as a "double-edged sword"; the effects may be favourable or unfavourable to the holders of common stock.

If the rate of return on total assets should fall ***below*** the average rate of interest on borrowed capital, leverage will ***reduce*** net income and the return on common shareholders' equity. In this situation, paying off the loans that carry high interest rates would appear to be a logical move. However, most companies do not have enough cash to retire long-term debt on short notice. Therefore, the common shareholders may become "locked in" to the unfavourable effects of leverage.

In deciding how much leverage is appropriate, the common shareholders should consider the *stability* of the company's return on assets as well as the relationship of this return to the average cost of borrowed capital. If a business incurs so much debt that it becomes unable to meet the required interest and principal payments, the creditors may force liquidation or reorganization of the business.

CASE IN POINT   After two mega acquisitions in the United States for a total price tag of over $13 billion, most of which was financed by debt, Campeau Corporation was highly leveraged. With more than $11 billion in debt and only slightly over $110 million in equity, Campeau's equity ratio was exceedingly low. The rising interest rate, coupled with poor operating results, led to serious financial trouble for Campeau. In a span of six months, Campeau's stock plummeted from a high of $22 per share to less than $2. Consequently, the company had to be restructured, reorganized, and drastically "downsized."

Equity Ratio   One indicator of the amount of leverage used by a business is the equity ratio. This ratio measures the proportion of the total assets financed by shareholders, as distinguished from creditors. It is computed by dividing total shareholders' equity by total assets. A *low* equity ratio indicates an extensive use of leverage, that is, a large proportion of financing provided by creditors. A high equity ratio, on the other hand, indicates that the business is making little use of leverage.

The equity ratio at year-end for Seacliff is determined as follows:

Equity Ratio

		1996	1995
Proportion of assets financed by shareholders	Total shareholders' equity	(a) $638,000	$516,000
	Total assets (or total liabilities & shareholders' equity)	(b) $950,000	$860,000
	Equity ratio (a ÷ b)	67.2%	60.0%

Seacliff has a higher equity ratio in 1996 than in 1995. Is this favourable or unfavourable?

From the viewpoint of the common shareholder, a low equity ratio will produce maximum benefits if management is able to earn a rate of return on assets greater than the rate of interest paid to creditors. However, a low equity ratio can be very *unfavourable* if the return on assets falls *below* the rate of interest paid to creditors. Since the return on total assets earned by Seacliff has declined from 19% in 1995 to a relatively low 14% in 1996, the common shareholders probably would *not* want to risk a low equity ratio. The action by management in 1996 of retiring $50,000 in long-term liabilities will help to protect the common shareholders from the unfavourable effects of leverage if the rate of return on assets continues to decline.

Analysis by Long-Term Creditors

Bondholders and other long-term creditors are primarily interested in three factors: (1) the rate of return on their investment, (2) the firm's ability to meet its interest requirements, and (3) the firm's ability to repay the principal of the debt when it falls due.

Yield Rate on Bonds The yield rate on bonds or other long-term indebtedness cannot be computed in the same manner as the yield rate on shares of stock, because bonds, unlike stocks, have a definite maturity date and amount. The ownership of a 12%, 10-year, $1,000 bond represents the right to receive $120 each year for 10 years plus the right to receive $1,000 at the end of 10 years. If the market price of this bond is $950, the yield rate on an investment in the bond is the rate of interest that will make the present value of these two contractual rights equal to $950. When bonds sell at maturity value, the yield rate is equal to the bond interest rate. ***The yield rate varies inversely with changes in the market price of the bond.*** If interest rates rise, the market price of existing bonds will fall; if interest rates decline, the price of bonds will rise. If the price of a bond is above maturity value, the yield rate is less than the bond interest rate; if the price of a bond is below maturity value, the yield rate is higher than the bond interest rate.

Interest Coverage Ratio Bondholders feel that their investments are relatively safe if the issuing company earns enough income to cover its annual interest obligations by a wide margin.

A common measure of creditors' safety is the ratio of operating income available to cover the annual interest expense, called the ***interest coverage ratio.*** This computation for Seacliff would be:

Interest Coverage Ratio

	1996	1995
Operating income (before interest and income taxes)	(a) $127,000	$160,000
Annual interest expense	(b) $ 24,000	$ 30,000
Interest coverage (a ÷ b)..	5.3 times	5.3 times

Long-term creditors watch this ratio

The ratio remained unchanged at a satisfactory level during 1996. A ratio of 5.3 times interest earned would be considered strong in many industries. In the electric utilities industry, for example, the interest coverage ratio for the leading companies generally averages about 3, with the ratios of individual companies varying from 2 to 6.

Debt Ratio Long-term creditors are interested in the percentage of total assets financed by debt, as distinguished from the percentage financed by shareholders. The percentage of total assets financed by debt is measured by the debt ratio. This ratio is computed by dividing total liabilities by total assets, shown below for Seacliff.

Debt Ratio

	1996	1995
Total liabilities...	(a) $312,000	$344,000
Total assets (or total liabilities & shareholders' equity)...........	(b) $950,000	$860,000
Debt ratio (a ÷ b)...	32.8%	40.0%

What portion of total assets is financed by creditors?

From a creditor's viewpoint, the lower the debt ratio (or the higher the equity ratio) the better, since this means that shareholders have contributed the bulk of the funds to the business, and therefore the margin of protection to creditors against a shrinkage of the assets is high.

Analysis by Preferred Shareholders

Some preferred stocks are convertible into common stock at the option of the holder. However, many preferred stocks do not have the conversion privilege. If a preferred stock is convertible, the interests of the preferred shareholders are similar to those of common shareholders. If a preferred stock is not convertible, the interests of the preferred shareholders are more like those of long-term creditors.

Preferred shareholders are interested in the yield on their investment. The yield is computed by dividing the dividend per share by the market value per share. The dividend per share of Seacliff preferred stock is $9. If we assume that the market value at December 31, 1996, is $75 per share, the yield rate at that time would be 12% ($9 ÷ $75).

The primary measurement of the safety of an investment in preferred stock is the ability of the firm to meet its preferred dividend requirements. The best test of this ability is the ratio of the net income to the amount of the annual preferred dividends, as follows:

Preferred Dividends Coverage Ratio

		1996	1995
Is the preferred dividend safe? Net income..	(a)	$75,000	$90,000
Annual preferred dividend requirements	(b)	$ 9,000	$ 9,000
Preferred dividend coverage (a ÷ b)		8.3 times	10 times

Although the margin of protection declined in 1996, the annual preferred dividend requirement still appears well protected.

As previously discussed in Chapter 14 the market price of a preferred stock tends to *vary inversely* with interest rates. When interest rates are moving up, preferred stock prices tend to decline, when interest rates are dropping, preferred stock prices rise.

Analysis by Short-Term Creditors

Bankers and other short-term creditors share the interest of shareholders and bondholders in the profitability and long-run stability of a business. Their primary interest, however, is in the current position of the firm—its ability to generate sufficient funds (working capital) to meet current operating needs and to pay current debts promptly. Thus the analysis of financial statements by a banker considering a short-term loan, or by a trade creditor investigating the credit status of a customer, is likely to centre on the working capital position of the prospective debtor.

Amount of Working Capital The details of the working capital of Seacliff are as follows:

SEACLIFF CORPORATION
Comparative Schedule of Working Capital
As of December 31, 1996 and December 31, 1995

	1996	1995	Increase or (Decrease)		Percentage of Total Current Items	
			Dollars	%	1996	1995
Current assets:						
Cash	$ 38,000	$ 40,000	$ (2,000)	(5.0)	9.7	13.9
Receivables (net)	117,000	86,000	31,000	36.0	30.0	29.9
Inventories	180,000	120,000	60,000	50.0	46.2	41.6
Prepaid expenses	55,000	42,000	13,000	31.0	14.1	14.6
Total current assets	$390,000	$288,000	$102,000	35.4	100.0	100.0
Current liabilities:						
Notes payable to creditors	$ 14,600	$ 10,000	$ 4,600	46.0	13.1	10.7
Accounts payable	66,000	30,000	36,000	120.0	58.9	31.9
Accrued liabilities	31,400	54,000	(22,600)	(41.9)	28.0	57.4
Total current liabilities	$112,000	$ 94,000	$ 18,000	19.1	100.0	100.0
Working capital	$278,000	$194,000	$84,000	43.3		

The amount of working capital is measured by the ***excess of current assets over current liabilities.*** Thus, working capital represents the amount of cash, near-cash items, and cash substitutes (prepayments) on hand after providing for payment of all current liabilities.

This schedule shows that current assets increased $102,000, while current liabilities rose by only $18,000, with the result that working capital increased $84,000.

Quality of Working Capital In evaluating the debt-paying ability of a business, short-term creditors should consider the quality of working capital as well as the total dollar amount. The principal factors affecting the quality of working capital are (1) the nature of the current assets and (2) the length of time required to convert these assets into cash.

The preceding schedule shows an unfavourable shift in the composition of Seacliff's working capital during 1996; cash decreased from 13.9% to 9.7% of current assets, while inventory rose from 41.6% to 46.2%. Inventory is a less liquid resource than cash. Therefore, the quality of working capital is not as liquid as in 1995. ***Turnover rates*** (or ***ratios***) may be used to assist short-term creditors in estimating the time required to turn assets such as receivables and inventory into cash.

Accounts Receivable Turnover Rate As explained in Chapter 8, the accounts receivable turnover rate indicates how quickly a company converts its accounts receivable into cash. The accounts receivable turnover ***rate*** is determined by dividing net sales by the average balance of accounts receivable.[4] The number of **days** required (on average) to collect accounts receivable then may be determined by dividing the number of days in a year (365) by the turnover rate. These computations are shown below using the data in our Seacliff example:

Accounts Receivable Turnover

<table>
<tr><td></td><td></td><td>1996</td><td>1995</td></tr>
<tr><td>Net sales...</td><td>(a)</td><td>$900,000</td><td>$750,000</td></tr>
<tr><td>Receivables, beginning of year...............................</td><td></td><td>$ 86,000</td><td>$ 80,000*</td></tr>
<tr><td>Receivables, end of year......................................</td><td></td><td>$117,000</td><td>$ 86,000</td></tr>
<tr><td>Average receivables ....</td><td>(b)</td><td>$101,500</td><td>$ 83,000</td></tr>
<tr><td>Receivable turnover per year (a ÷ b) ....</td><td></td><td>8.9 times</td><td>9.0 times</td></tr>
<tr><td>Average number of days to collect receivables (divide
   365 days by receivable turnover)............................</td><td></td><td>41 days</td><td>41 days</td></tr>
</table>

*Assumed

Are customers paying promptly?

There has been no significant change in the average time required to collect receivables. The interpretation of the average age of receivables depends upon the company's credit terms and the seasonal activity immediately before year-end. For example, if the company grants 30-day credit terms to its customers, the above analysis indicates that accounts receivable collections are lagging. If the terms are for 60 days, however, collections are being made ahead of schedule.

Inventory Turnover Rate   The inventory turnover rate indicates how many times during the year the company is able to sell a quantity of goods equal to its average inventory. Mechanically, this rate is determined by dividing the cost of goods sold for the year by the average amount of inventory on hand during the year. The number of days required to sell this amount of inventory may be determined by dividing 365 days by the turnover rate. These computations were explained in Chapter 9, and are demonstrated below using the data of Seacliff:

Inventory Turnover

<table>
<tr><td></td><td></td><td>1996</td><td>1995</td></tr>
<tr><td>Cost of goods sold...</td><td>(a)</td><td>$530,000</td><td>$420,000</td></tr>
<tr><td>Inventory, beginning of year ....</td><td></td><td>$120,000</td><td>$100,000*</td></tr>
<tr><td>Inventory, end of year ....</td><td></td><td>$180,000</td><td>$120,000</td></tr>
<tr><td>Average inventory ....</td><td>(b)</td><td>$150,000</td><td>$110,000</td></tr>
<tr><td>Average inventory turnover per year (a ÷ b) ....</td><td></td><td>3.5 times</td><td>3.8 times</td></tr>
<tr><td>Average number of days to sell inventory (divide 365
   days by inventory turnover)..................................</td><td></td><td>104 days</td><td>96 days</td></tr>
</table>

*Assumed

The trend indicated by this analysis is unfavourable, since the length of time required for Seacliff to turn over (sell) its inventory is increasing.

---

[4]   Ideally, the accounts receivable turnover is computed by dividing net **credit** sales by the **monthly** average of receivables. Such detailed information, however, generally is not provided in annual financial statements.

Companies that have low gross profit rates often need high inventory turnover rates in order to operate profitably. This is merely another way of saying that if the gross profit rate is low, a high volume of transactions is necessary to produce a satisfactory amount of profits. Companies that sell "high markup" items, such as jewellery stores and art galleries, can operate successfully with much lower inventory turnover rates.

Operating Cycle   In Chapter 5 we defined the term ***operating cycle*** as the average time period between the purchase of merchandise and the conversion of this merchandise back into cash. In other words, the merchandise acquired for inventory is gradually converted into accounts receivable by selling goods to customers on credit, and these receivables are converted into cash through the process of collection. The word ***cycle*** refers to the circular flow of assets from cash to inventory to receivables and back into cash.

Seacliff's operating cycle in 1996 was approximately 145 days, computed by adding the 104 days required to turn over inventory and the average 41 days required to collect receivables. This compares to an operating cycle of only 137 days in 1995, computed as 96 days to dispose of the inventory plus 41 days to collect the resulting receivables. From the viewpoint of short-term creditors, the shorter the operating cycle, the better the quality of the borrower's working capital. Therefore, these creditors would regard the lengthening of Seacliff's operating cycle as an unfavourable trend.

Current Ratio   The current ratio (current assets divided by current liabilities) expresses the relationship between current assets and current liabilities. As debts come due, they must be paid out of current assets. Therefore, short-term creditors frequently compare the amount of current assets with the amount of current liabilities. The current ratio indicates a company's short-run, debt-paying ability. It is a measure of liquidity and of solvency. A strong current ratio provides considerable assurance that a company will be able to meet its obligations coming due in the near future. The current ratio for Seacliff is computed as follows:

Current Ratio

	1996	1995
Total current assets	(a) $390,000	$288,000
Total current liabilities	(b) $112,000	$ 94,000
Current ratio (a ÷ b)	3.5	3.1

Does this indicate satisfactory debt-paying ability?

A general rule is that a current ratio of 2 to 1 or better is satisfactory. By this standard, Seacliff's current ratio appears quite strong. Creditors tend to feel that the higher the current ratio the better. From a managerial point of view, however, there is an upper limit. Too high a current ratio may indicate that capital is not being used productively in the business as the amount of cash, accounts receivable, and inventories may be excessive.

Use of both the current ratio and the amount of working capital helps to place debt-paying ability in its proper perspective. For example, if Company X has current assets of $200,000 and current liabilities of $100,000 and Company Y has current assets of $2,000,000 and current liabilities of $1,900,000, each company has $100,000 of working capital, but the current position of Company X is clearly superior to that of Company Y. The current ratio for Company X is quite satisfactory at 2 to 1, but Company Y's current ratio is very low—only slightly above 1 to 1.

As another example, assume that Company A and Company B both have current ratios of 3 to 1. However, Company A has working capital of $50,000 and Company B has working capital of $500,000. Although both companies appear to be good credit risks, Company B would no doubt be able to qualify for a much *larger* bank loan than would Company A.

Quick Ratio   Because inventories and prepaid expenses are further removed from conversion into cash than other current assets, a statistic known as the ***quick ratio*** is sometimes computed as a supplement to the current ratio. The quick ratio compares the highly liquid current assets (cash, marketable securities, and receivables) with current liabilities. Seacliff has no marketable securities; its quick ratio is computed as follows:

Quick Ratio

		1996	1995
A measure of liquidity	*Quick assets (cash and receivables)*	*(a) $155,000*	*$126,000*
	Current liabilities	*(b) $112,000*	*$ 94,000*
	Quick ratio (a ÷ b)	*1.4*	*1.3*

Here again the analysis reveals a favourable trend and a strong position. If the credit periods extended to customers and granted by creditors are roughly equal, a quick ratio of 1.0 or better is considered satisfactory.

Unused Lines of Credit   From the viewpoint of a short-term creditor, a company's unused lines of credit represent a "resource" almost as liquid as cash. An unused line of credit means that a bank has agreed in advance to lend the company any amount, up to the specified limit. As long as this line of credit remains available, creditors know that the business can borrow cash quickly and easily for any purpose, including payments of creditors' claims.

Existing unused lines of credit are ***disclosed*** in notes accompanying the financial statements and in the management's discussion and analysis section of the annual report.

CASE IN POINT   The unused lines of credit can be substantial in amount. The recent annual reports of the following corporations provide a glimpse of such a picture: NOVA Corporation of Alberta, unutilized lines of credit of $1.2 billion; Canadian Pacific Limited, unused commitments for long-term financing in excess of $1.1 billion and unused lines of credit for short-term financing of $738.9 million; Maclean Hunter Limited, unused credit lines of approximately $340 million; Univa Inc., unused lines of credit of $307 million; Bow Valley Industries Ltd., unused long- and short-term lines of credit of approximately $265 million and $18 million, respectively; and Hayes-Dana Inc., unused lines of credit of approximately $100 million. Of course, there is a cost for such unused lines of credit. For one of the corporations, the annual commitment fees on the unused long-term credit lines were $\frac{1}{10}$ to $\frac{1}{8}$ of one percent of the unused amount.

Usefulness of the Notes to Financial Statements

A set of financial statements normally is accompanied by several pages of *notes*, disclosing information useful in interpretation of the statements. Users should view these notes as an *integral part* of the financial statements.

In our preceding chapters, we have identified many items that are disclosed in notes to the financial statements. Among the most useful disclosures are (a) a summary of the accounting methods in use, (b) material contingent losses, (c) current market value of financial instruments, (d) identification of the assets pledged to secure specific liabilities, (e) maturity dates of significant liabilities, (f) unused lines of credit, and (g) preferred stock dividends in arrears. The notes also supplement the financial statements by providing further explanation of such items as extraordinary gains and losses, changes in accounting principle, and significant financial events occurring after the balance sheet date.

In summary, the notes often contain information *essential* to a proper interpretation of the company's financial position, operating results, and future prospects.

OBJECTIVE 6
Compute the
ratios widely
used in finan-
cial statement
analysis and
explain the
significance
of each.

Summary of Analytical Measurements

The basic ratios and other measurements discussed in this chapter and their significance are summarized below.

The student should keep in mind the fact that the full significance of any of these ratios or other measurements depends on the *direction of its trend* and its *relationship to some predetermined standard* or industry average.

Ratio or Other Measurement	Method of Computation	Significance
1 Earnings per share of common stock	$\dfrac{\textit{Net income} - \textit{preferred dividends}}{\textit{Shares of common outstanding}}$	Indicates the amount of earnings applicable to a share of common stock.
2 Price-earnings ratio	$\dfrac{\textit{Market price per share}}{\textit{Earnings per share}}$	Indicates if price of stock is in line with earnings.
3 Dividend yield	$\dfrac{\textit{Dividend per share}}{\textit{Market price per share}}$	Shows the rate of return earned by shareholders based on current price for a share of stock.
4 Book value per share of common stock	$\dfrac{\textit{Common shareholders' equity}}{\textit{Shares of common outstanding}}$	Measures the recorded value of net assets behind each share of common stock.
5 Operating expense ratio	$\dfrac{\textit{Operating expenses}}{\textit{Net sales}}$	Indicates management's ability to control expenses.

6 Return on assets	$\dfrac{\text{Operating income}}{\text{Average total assets}}$	Measures the productivity of assets regardless of capital structure.
7 Return on common shareholders' equity	$\dfrac{\text{Net income} - \text{preferred dividends}}{\text{Average common shareholders' equity}}$	Indicates the earning power of common stock equity.
8 Equity ratio	$\dfrac{\text{Total shareholders' equity}}{\text{Total assets}}$	Shows the protection to creditors and the extent of leverage being used.
9 Debt ratio	$\dfrac{\text{Total liabilities}}{\text{Total assets}}$	Indicates the percentage of assets financed through borrowing; it shows the extent of leverage being used.
10 Interest coverage ratio	$\dfrac{\text{Operating income}}{\text{Annual interest expense}}$	Measures the coverage of interest requirements, particularly on long-term debt.
11 Preferred dividends coverage ratio	$\dfrac{\text{Net income}}{\text{Annual preferred dividends}}$	Shows the adequacy of current earnings to cover dividends on preferred stocks.
12 Working capital	Current assets − current liabilities	Measures short-run debt-paying ability.
13 Accounts receivable turnover rate	$\dfrac{\text{Net sales}}{\text{Average receivables}}$	Indicates reasonableness of accounts receivable balance and effectiveness of collections.
14 Inventory turnover rate	$\dfrac{\text{Cost of goods sold}}{\text{Average inventory}}$	Indicates marketability of inventory and reasonableness of quantity on hand.
15 Current ratio	$\dfrac{\text{Current assets}}{\text{Current liabilities}}$	Measures short-run debt-paying ability.
16 Quick ratio	$\dfrac{\text{Quick assets}}{\text{Current liabilities}}$	Measures the short-term liquidity of a firm.

Annual Reports

Annual reports of corporations contain a plethora of information. In addition to the audited financial statements and the auditors' reports, these corporate annual reports include such information as: financial or operating highlights; message to shareholders from the chief executive and chief operating officers on the current operations and future outlook of the company; profile of the company, focusing on the nature of operations, products, and personnel; management's discussion and analysis on the financial statements regarding liquidity, capital resources, and results of operations; statistical reports such as five- or ten-year summary; stock market prices, book value per share, and dividends; list of directors and officers; shareholder information; and a host of other items. This information takes up between twenty and fifty pages in an annual report.

Much of this material complements the information in the financial statements and is useful in assessing the present and future prospects of a company. Consequently, investors, creditors, and other interested parties should review and analyze this information in the corporate annual report in order to get a more complete picture of the company.

The following excerpts, selected from the 1992 annual report of Maclean Hunter Limited, provide a glimpse of such information. (Additional information in the annual report is presented in Comprehensive Problem 5 at the end of this chapter.)

CORPORATE HIGHLIGHTS

Revenue
(in millions)

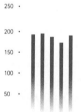

Operating income
before amortization
(in millions)

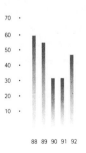

Earnings
per share before
unusual items
(in cents)

(millions of dollars except per share data)	1992	1991	1990
Operating Summary			
Revenue	$ 1,635	$ 1,535	$ 1,536
Operating income before amortization	194	171	189
Income before unusual items	81	51	49
Unusual items	—	—	(34)
Consolidated net income	81	51	15
Cash Flow			
Earnings before interest, taxes, depreciation and amortization	302	276	287
Cash flow from operations	200	170	161
Dividends	45	42	40
Purchase of property, plant and equipment	99	105	128
Per Share Data			
Income before unusual items	47¢	32¢	32¢
Unusual items	—	—	(21)
Consolidated earnings per share	47¢	32¢	11¢
Earnings before interest, taxes, depreciation and amortization	$ 1.71	$ 1.70	$ 1.79
Cash flow from operations	$ 1.14	$ 1.05	$ 1.01
Dividends	25¢	25¢	25¢
Financial Position at Year-End			
Working capital (excluding current indebtedness)	183	77	141
Total assets	1,872	1,754	1,831
Total debt	468	616	725
Shareholders' equity plus convertible debentures	887	667	655
Ratios			
Operating return on revenue	12%	11%	12%
Operating return on assets employed	13%	11%	13%
Return on average shareholders' equity plus convertible debentures	10%	8%	8%*
Total debt to capital employed	29%	40%	45%
Employees			
Number of employees	12,432	11,850	12,425
Share Prices			
Year-end closing	$ 12.13	$ 11.50	$ 9.63
Current (March 12, 1993)	$ 11.75		

*Before unusual items.

LETTER TO
SHAREHOLDERS

An interview with Ron Osborne

Q *How would you characterize the year 1992 for Maclean Hunter?*
It's been a very good year for us in many respects. We're by no means back where we should be in terms of operating results and profitability, but clearly we are heading in the right direction. It's been first-rate for cable, but disappointing from an advertising recovery point of view. Given that the economy is not yet "firing on eight cylinders", we are pleased to report a 7% increase in revenue to $1.6 billion, a 14% increase in operating income before amortization to $194 million for 1992, and a 47% increase in earnings per share.

Q *What factors had the greatest bearing on results?*
Four major factors. First, we have the stability of our cable television operations, which, even in relatively tough economic times, have found ways to be creative in providing relevant services to customers and generating additional revenue.

Second, the significant drop in interest rates has had a beneficial effect on financing costs and our Treasury Department has taken full advantage of that decline with an aggressive but appropriate policy on our rate and debt structure, maximizing the use of short-term money market instruments.

Third, our cyclical operations, which are more dependent on economic conditions, have yet to benefit from major fixed cost reductions implemented over the past two to three years.

Fourth, partly as a reflection of the cyclical nature of our publishing business, we have benefited from significant paper price discounts.

Q *What were the areas of strength and weakness, beginning with the strengths?*
Clearly cable had another excellent year in both the United States and Canada. Our commercial printing division has recovered nicely from 1991, and the Aurora web operation and Yorkville group continued to outperform their markets. Davis + Henderson, our specialty printing group, also had another fine year.

In television, our Calgary CTV-affiliate, CFCN, performed extremely well, and the CTV network also saw significantly improved results. CHCH-TV in Hamilton turned in excellent results

after a successful turnaround, and has now been sold to WIC Western International Communications.

I would say the improvement in The Financial Post should be characterized as an area of strength, although in absolute terms it continues to incur significant operating losses over a period that's extended beyond what anybody anticipated as a result of the recession. These losses have declined substantially in 1992 and should continue to do so in 1993. That has to be counted as a major plus.

Q *And the weaknesses?*
On the negative side of the ledger, our business forms operations, both in Canada and in the U.S., have softened due to weak demand and excess capacity in that industry. Our radio operations have had a rougher time, reflecting the weakness in the retail sector in the Maritimes and in Ontario.

Business publishing in Canada has been a mixed bag with a few notable exceptions such as medical publishing. Our U.S. publishing operations have done very well, not only in the medical field, but also in a number of industrial fields and in training and development. Britain had a very difficult year due to the economic climate, and despite the strength of our construc-

tion industry publications in Germany, we're starting to see signs of a slowdown in Europe. However, overall, our European operations are performing quite respectably.

The Toronto Sun's financial results were down compared to its peak of two or three years ago – essentially a function of the soft retail and employment market. This was somewhat offset by reductions in newsprint costs, which are a major factor in the performance of our newspapers. The Ottawa Sun continues to gain ground and it's only a matter of time before it's a significant contributor to the Sun group. The Calgary Sun had an excellent year with Edmonton somewhat weaker.

Q *What plans are in place to minimize weaknesses and build on strengths?*
I would refer the reader to the Review of Operations for details, as I will only list the main points here.
• Radio – Our format switch in Kitchener will enable us to repatriate significant listenership. The new broadcast centre we're building in Toronto will bring operating synergies and we're completely revamping the sound and operating style of CFNY.
• Television – The restructuring of CTV has been finalized and will enable the network to complete its financial turnaround. Maclean

Hunter will continue to play a role and have an increased share in future profits.

• Cable – We've successfully introduced the Full Cable Service tier in Ontario and are developing additional revenue streams in the area of "alternate access" in Canada and the U.S., allowing customers to choose how they wish to interconnect with telephone services.

• Consumer Magazines – In conjunction with the Sun newspapers, we've launched Modern Woman to extend the audience for our women's magazines and to offer customers a broader advertising base.

• Business Publishing – Having rationalized some of our non-performing assets, we will concentrate on developing our existing areas of strength and extending our expertise in these areas into new markets in the form of international, even global, publishing networks. We continue to invest in electronic publishing, which is still something of a "Holy Grail", but we have a number of initiatives in this area in our international directory operations.

• Business Forms – We doubled our volumes at a very favourable cost with the acquisition of Southam Business Forms. ...

Q *What is your number one priority for 1993?*
If I had to choose one, it would be to maintain our earnings growth without sacrificing product quality. We will continue looking for new revenue streams, controlling our costs, capitalizing on existing products, and turning those around that need to be turned around without turning a blind eye to potential acquisitions that offer a fair return for our shareholders over the short to medium term. We've made some major longer-term investments in recent years and launched some major new products, so our focus, as in 1992, will be on maximizing those.

Q *What is the outlook for 1993?*
We expect to show growth in earnings per share throughout 1993. The worst of the recession appears to be over in the U.S. and that can only be good for Canada. The first quarter is not necessarily much of an indication, because the first and third quarters are always softer in our advertising-based products, which tend to lag behind economic recovery. Any significant improvement in earnings would require a strong and sustained upturn in these more cyclical products.

. . . .

COMMUNITY
INVOLVEMENT

Maclean Hunter has been designated "a caring company" by the Canadian Centre for Philanthropy for its practice of contributing a portion of its pre-tax earnings and providing in-house services to worthy organizations in the various communities we serve. Our cash and non-cash contribution to hospitals and cultural and community organizations was approximately $15 million in 1992. Much of this consisted of contributed advertising space and broadcast airtime.

We make additional cultural contributions through The Maclean Hunter Television Fund, established as part of the Selkirk acquisition in 1989. In 1992, the Fund invested over $3 million in the production of Canadian dramatic television series. In education, we fund six chairs in journalism and business at academic institutions across Canada. This $3 million endowment made in 1987 was our way of investing in the future of Canada and giving something back to the communities we serve. ...

On behalf of the Board

Donald G. Campbell
Chairman

Ronald W. Osborne
President and Chief Executive Officer

CHAPTER REVIEW

KEY TERMS INTRODUCED OR EMPHASIZED IN CHAPTER 20

Comparative financial statements   Financial statement data for two or more successive years placed side by side in adjacent columns to facilitate study of changes.

Component percentage   The percentage relationship of any financial statement item to a total including that item. For example, each type of asset as a percentage of total assets.

Horizontal analysis   Comparison of the change in a financial statement item such as inventories during two or more accounting periods.

Leverage   Refers to the practice of financing assets with borrowed capital. Extensive leverage creates the possibility for the rate of return on common shareholders' equity to be substantially above or below the rate of return on total assets. When the rate of return on total assets exceeds the average cost of borrowed capital, leverage increases net income and the return on common shareholders' equity. However, when the return on total assets is less than the average cost of borrowed capital, leverage reduces net income and the return on common shareholders' equity.

Quality of assets   The concept that some companies have assets of better quality than others, such as well-balanced composition of assets, well-maintained plant and equipment, and receivables that are all current. A lower quality of assets might be indicated by poor maintenance of plant and equipment, slow-moving inventories with high danger of obsolescence, past-due receivables, and patents approaching an expiration date.

Quality of earnings   Earnings are said to be of high quality if they are stable, the source seems assured, and the methods used in measuring income are conservative. The existence of this concept suggests that the range of alternative but acceptable accounting principles may still be too wide to produce financial statements that are comparable.

Rate of return on investment (ROI)   A measure of management's ability to earn a satisfactory return on the assets under its control. Numerous variations of the ROI concept are used, such as return on total assets, return on total shareholders' equity, and return on common shareholders' equity.

Ratios   See pages 953–954 for list of ratios, methods of computation, and significance.

Trend percentages   The purpose of computing trend percentages is to measure the increase or decrease in financial items (such as sales, net income, cash, etc.) from a selected base year to a series of following years. For example, the dollar amount of net income each year is divided by the base year net income to determine the trend percentage.

Vertical analysis   Comparison of a particular financial statement item to a total including that item, such as inventories as a percentage of current assets, or operating expenses in relation to net sales.

DEMONSTRATION PROBLEM FOR YOUR REVIEW

The accounting records of King Corporation showed the following balances at the end of 1995 and 1996:

	1996	1995
Cash...	$ 35,000	$ 25,000
Accounts receivable (net)......................................	91,000	90,000
Inventory..	160,000	140,000
Short-term prepayments	4,000	5,000
Investment in land...	90,000	100,000
Equipment	880,000	640,000
Less: Accumulated depreciation	(260,000)	(200,000)
Total assets	$1,000,000	$ 800,000
Accounts payable	$ 105,000	$ 46,000
Income taxes payable and other accrued liabilities.............	40,000	25,000
Bonds payable—8%	280,000	280,000
Premium on bonds payable....................................	3,600	4,000
Capital stock (33,000 shares in 1996; 22,000 shares in 1995) ...	165,000	110,000
Retained earnings	406,400	335,000
Total liabilities and shareholders' equity.......................	$1,000,000	$ 800,000
Sales (net of discounts and allowances).......................	$2,200,000	$1,600,000
Cost of goods sold	1,606,000	1,120,000
Gross profit	$ 594,000	$ 480,000
Expenses (including $22,400 interest expense).................	(336,600)	(352,000)
Income taxes..	(91,000)	(48,000)
Net income..	$ 166,400	$ 80,000

Cash dividends of $40,000 were paid and a 50% stock dividend was distributed early in 1996. All sales were made on credit at a relatively uniform rate during the year. Inventory and receivables did not fluctuate materially. The market price of the company's stock on December 31, 1996, was $86 per share; on December 31, 1995, it was $43.50 (before the 50% stock dividend distributed in 1996).

INSTRUCTIONS Compute the following for 1996 and 1995:

1 Quick ratio.

2 Current ratio.

3 Equity ratio.

4 Debt ratio.

5 Book value per share of capital stock (based on shares outstanding after 50% stock dividend in 1996).

6 Earnings per share of capital stock.

7 Price-earnings ratio.

8 Gross profit percentage.

9 Operating expense ratio.

10 Net income as a percentage of net sales.

11 Inventory turnover. (Assume an average inventory of $150,000 for both years.)

12 Accounts receivable turnover. (Assume average accounts receivable for $90,000 for 1995.)

13 Interest coverage ratio.

SOLUTION TO DEMONSTRATION PROBLEM

	1996	*1995*
(1) Quick ratio:		
$126,000 ÷ $145,000	*.9 to 1*	
$115,000 ÷ $71,000		*1.6 to 1*
(2) Current ratio:		
$290,000 ÷ $145,000	*2 to 1*	
$260,000 ÷ $71,000		*3.7 to 1*
(3) Equity ratio:		
$571,400 ÷ $1,000,000	*57%*	
$445,000 ÷ $800,000		*56%*
(4) Debt ratio:		
$428,600 ÷ $1,000,000	*43%*	
$355,000 ÷ $800,000		*44%*
(5) Book value per share of capital stock:		
$571,400 ÷ 33,000 shares	*$17.32*	
$445,000 ÷ 33,000* shares		*$13.48*
(6) Earnings per share of capital stock:		
$166,400 ÷ 33,000 shares	*$5.04*	
$80,000 ÷ 33,000* shares		*$2.42*
(7) Price-earnings ratio:		
$86 ÷ $5.04	*17 times*	
$43.50 ÷ 1.5* = $29, adjusted market price;		
$29 ÷ $2.42		*12 times*
(8) Gross profit percentage:		
$594,000 ÷ $2,200,000	*27%*	
$480,000 ÷ $1,600,000		*30%*
(9) Operating expense ratio:		
($336,600 − $22,400) ÷ $2,200,000	*14%*	
($352,000 − $22,400) ÷ $1,600,000		*20.6%*
(10) Net income as a percentage of net sales:		
$166,400 ÷ $2,200,000	*7.6%*	
$80,000 ÷ $1,600,000		*5%*
(11) Inventory turnover:		
$1,606,000 ÷ $150,000	*10.7 times*	
$1,120,000 ÷ $150,000		*7.5 times*
(12) Accounts receivable turnover:		
$2,200,000 ÷ $90,500	*24.3 times*	
$1,600,000 ÷ $90,000		*17.8 times*
(13) Interest coverage ratio:		
($166,400 + $22,400 + $91,000) ÷ $22,400	*12.5 times*	
($80,000 + $22,400 + $48,000) ÷ $22,400		*6.7 times*

*Adjusted retroactively for 50% stock dividend.

ASSIGNMENT MATERIAL

DISCUSSION QUESTIONS

1 a What groups are interested in the financial affairs of publicly owned corporations?

b List some of the more important sources of financial information for investors.

2 In financial statement analysis, what is the basic objective of observing trends in data and ratios? Suggest some other standards of comparison.

3 Distinguish between ***trend percentages*** and ***component percentages.*** Which would be better suited to analyzing the change in sales over a term of several years?

4 In financial statement analysis, what information is produced by computing a ratio that is not available in a simple observation of the underlying data?

5 "Although net income declined this year as compared with last year, it increased from 3% to 5% of net sales." Are sales increasing or decreasing?

6 Differentiate between ***horizontal*** and ***vertical*** analysis.

7 Assume that Chemco Corporation is engaged in the manufacture and distribution of a variety of chemicals. In analyzing the financial statements of this corporation, why would you want to refer to the ratios and other measurements of companies in the chemical industry? In comparing the financial results of Chemco Corporation with another chemical company, why would you be interested in the accounting practices used by the two companies?

8 Explain how the following accounting practices will tend to raise or lower the quality of a company's earnings. (Assume the continuance of inflation.)

a Adoption of an accelerated depreciation method rather than straight-line depreciation.

b Adoption of FIFO rather than LIFO for the valuation of inventories.

c Adoption of a 7-year life rather than a 10-year life for the depreciation of equipment.

9 What single ratio do you think should be of greatest interest to:

a A banker considering a short-term loan?

b A common shareholder?

c An insurance company considering a long-term mortgage loan?

10 Modern Corporation earned a 16% return on its total assets. Current liabilities are 10% of total assets. Long-term bonds carrying a 13% interest rate are equal to 30% of total assets. There is no preferred stock. Is this application of leverage favourable or unfavourable from the viewpoint of Modern's shareholders?

11 In deciding whether a company's equity ratio is favourable or unfavourable, creditors and shareholders may have different views. Why?

12 Ahi Ltd. has a current ratio of 3 to 1. Ono Corp. has a current ratio of 2 to 1. Does this mean that Ahi's operating cycle is longer than Ono's? Why?

13 An investor states, "I bought this stock for $50 several years ago and it now sells for $100. It paid $5 per share in dividends last year so I'm earning 10% on my investment." Criticize this statement.

14 Alpine Products experiences a considerable seasonal variation in its business. The high point in the year's activity comes in November, the low point in July. During which month would you expect the company's current ratio to be higher? If the company were choosing a fiscal year for accounting purposes, how would you advise them?

15 Auto Parts' inventory turnover and accounts receivable turnover both increased from 1995 to 1996, but net income decreased. Can you offer some possible reasons for this?

16 Is the rate of return on investment (ROI) intended primarily to measure liquidity, solvency, or some other aspect of business operations? Explain.

17 Mention three financial amounts to which corporate earnings can logically be compared in judging their adequacy or reasonableness.

18 Under what circumstances would you consider a corporate net income of $1 million for the year as being unreasonably low? Under what circumstances would you consider a corporate net income of $1 million as being unreasonably high?

MULTIPLE CHOICE QUESTIONS

1 Which of the following is **not** an accurate statement?

   a Expressing the various items in the income statement as a percentage of net sales illustrates the use of component percentages.

   b An increase in the market price of bonds causes the yield rate to decline.

   c A high debt ratio is viewed favourably by long-term creditors as long as the number of times interest earned is at least 1.

   d In measuring the dollar or percentage change in quarterly sales or earnings, it is appropriate to compare the results of the current quarter with those of the same quarter in the preceding year.

2 Which of the following actions will improve the "quality" of earnings, even though the total dollar amount of earnings may not increase?

   a Increasing the uncollectible accounts expense from 1% to 2% of net credit sales to reflect current conditions.

   b Switching from an accelerated method to the straight-line method for depreciating assets.

   c Changing from LIFO to the FIFO method of inventory valuation during a period of rising prices.

   d Lengthening the estimated useful lives of depreciable assets.

3 Hunter Corporation's net income was $400,000 in 1995 and $160,000 in 1996. What percentage increase in net income must Hunter achieve in 1997 to offset the decline in profits in 1996?

   a 60%   b 150%   c 600%   d 67%

4 Of the following situations, which would be considered the most favourable for the common shareholders?

   a The company stops paying dividends on its cumulative preferred stock; the price-earnings ratio of common stock is low.

   b Equity ratio is high; return on assets exceeds the cost of borrowing.

   c Book value per share of common stock is substantially higher than market value per share; return on common shareholders' equity is less than the rate of interest paid to creditors.

   d Equity ratio is low; return on assets exceeds the cost of borrowing.

5   During 1996, Ganey Corporation had sales of $4,000,000, all on credit. Accounts receivable averaged $400,000 and inventory levels averaged $250,000 throughout the year. If Ganey's gross profit rate during 1996 was 25% of net sales, which of the following statements are correct? (More than one statement may be correct. Assume 360 days in a year.)

   a   Ganey "turns over" its accounts receivable more times per year than it turns over its average inventory.

   b   Ganey collects the amount of its average accounts receivable in about 36 to 37 days.

   c   Ganey's operating cycle is 66 days.

   d   The quality of Ganey's working capital would improve if the company could reduce its inventory and receivables turnover rates.

EXERCISES

EXERCISE 20-1
Accounting Terminology

Listed below are nine technical accounting terms introduced or emphasized in this chapter.

Inventory turnover	*Trend percentages*	*Leverage*
Operating cycle	*Vertical analysis*	*Yield*
Price-earning ratio	*Return on assets*	*Quick ratio*

Each of the following statements may (or may not) describe one of these technical terms. For each statement, indicate the accounting term described, or answer "None" if the statement does not correctly describe any of the terms.

   a   The proportion of total assets financed by shareholders, as distinguished from creditors.

   b   Market price per common share divided by earnings per common share.

   c   Changes in financial statement items from a base year to following years expressed as a percentage of the base year amount and designed to show the extent and direction of change.

   d   Dividends per share divided by market price per share.

   e   Average time period between the purchase of merchandise and the conversion of this merchandise back into cash.

   f   Study of relationships among the data of a single accounting period.

   g   Net sales divided by average inventory.

   h   Comparison of highly liquid current assets (cash, marketable securities, and receivables) with current liabilities.

   i   Buying assets with money raised by borrowing.

EXERCISE 20-2
Percentage Changes

Selected information taken from financial statements of Kowloon Corporation for two successive years follows. You are to compute the percentage change from 1995 to 1996 whenever possible.

	1996	*1995*
a Accounts receivable	*$126,000*	*$150,000*
b Marketable securities	*–0–*	*250,000*
c Retained earnings	*80,000*	*(80,000)*
d Notes receivable	*120,000*	*–0–*
e Notes payable	*860,000*	*800,000*
f Cash	*82,400*	*80,000*
g Sales	*990,000*	*900,000*

EXERCISE 20-3
Intuition versus Calculation

Tait Corporation had net income of $4 million in its first year. In the second year, net income decreased by 75%. In the third year, due to an improved business environment, net income increased by 250%.

INSTRUCTIONS

a Prior to making any computations, do you think Tait's net income was higher or lower in the third year than in the first year?

b Compute Tait's net income for the second year and for the third year. Do your computations support your initial response in part **a**?

EXERCISE 20-4
Trend Percentages

Compute **trend percentages** for the following items taken from the financial statements of Water-Wise Plumbing Fixtures over a five-year period. Treat 1992 as the base year. State whether the trends are favourable or unfavourable. (Dollar amounts are stated in thousands.)

	1996	*1995*	*1994*	*1993*	*1992*
Sales	*$85,000*	*$74,000*	*$61,500*	*$59,000*	*$50,000*
Cost of goods sold	*$58,500*	*$48,000*	*$40,500*	*$36,000*	*$30,000*

EXERCISE 20-5
Common Size Income Statements

Prepare **common size** income statements for Toyoda Company, a sole proprietorship, for the two years shown below by converting the dollar amounts into percentages. For each year, sales will appear as 100% and other items will be expressed as a percentage of sales. (Income taxes are not involved as the business is not incorporated.) Comment on whether the changes from 1995 to 1996 are favourable or unfavourable.

	1996	*1995*
Sales	*$500,000*	*$400,000*
Cost of goods sold	*330,000*	*268,000*
Gross profit	*$170,000*	*$132,000*
Operating expenses	*140,000*	*116,000*
Net income	*$ 30,000*	*$ 16,000*

EXERCISE 20-6
Ratios for a Retail Store

Selected financial data for Vashon's, a retail store, appear below. Since monthly figures are not available, the average amounts for inventories and for accounts receivable should be based on the amounts shown for the beginning and end of 1996.

	1996	*1995*
Sales (terms 2/10, n/30)	*$750,000*	*$600,000*
Cost of goods sold	*495,000*	*408,000*
Inventory at end of year	*85,500*	*94,500*
Accounts receivable at end of year	*87,500*	*100,000*

INSTRUCTIONS

Compute the following for 1996:

a Gross profit percentage

b Inventory turnover

c Accounts receivable turnover

EXERCISE 20-7
Computing Ratios

A condensed balance sheet for Durham Corporation prepared at the end of the year appears below.

Assets		Liabilities & Shareholders' Equity	
Cash........................	$ 55,000	Notes payable (due in 6 months).......................	$ 40,000
Accounts receivable	155,000	Accounts payable	110,000
Inventory...................	270,000	Long-term liabilities	330,000
Prepaid expenses	60,000	Capital stock (60,000 shares).....	300,000
Plant & equipment (net).....	570,000	Retained earnings	420,000
Other assets	90,000		
Total	$1,200,000	Total	$1,200,000

During the year the company earned a gross profit of $1,116,000 on sales of $2,790,000. Accounts receivable, inventory, and plant assets remained almost constant in amount throughout the year.

INSTRUCTIONS   Compute the following:

a   Current ratio

b   Quick ratio

c   Working capital

d   Equity ratio

e   Accounts receivable turnover (all sales were on credit)

f   Inventory turnover

g   Book value per share of capital stock

EXERCISE 20-8
Current Ratio, Debt Ratio, and Earnings per Share

Selected items from successive annual reports of Hastings, Inc., appear below.

	1996	1995
Total assets (40% of which are current)	$400,000	$325,000
Current liabilities	$ 80,000	$100,000
Bonds payable, 12%..	100,000	50,000
Capital stock (20,000 shares).....................................	100,000	100,000
Retained earnings	120,000	75,000
Total liabilities & shareholders' equity	$400,000	$325,000

Dividends of $26,000 were declared and paid in 1996.

INSTRUCTIONS   Compute the following:

a   Current ratio for 1996 and 1995

b   Debt ratio for 1996 and 1995

c   Earnings per share for 1996

EXERCISE 20-9
Ratio Analysis for Two Similar Companies

Selected data from the financial statements of Italian Marble Ltd. and Toro Stone Products for the year just ended follow. Assume that for both companies dividends declared were equal in amount to net earnings during the year and therefore shareholders' equity did not change. The two companies are in the same line of business.

	Italian Marble Ltd.	Toro Stone Products
Total liabilities..	$ 200,000	$ 100,000
Total assets	800,000	400,000
Sales (all on credit)...	1,800,000	1,200,000
Average inventory	240,000	140,000
Average receivables	200,000	100,000
Gross profit as a percentage of sales	40%	30%
Operating expenses as a percentage of sales..................	36%	25%
Net income as a percentage of sales	4%	5%

INSTRUCTIONS   Compute the following for each company:

a Net income

b Net income as a percentage of shareholders' equity

c Accounts receivable turnover

d Inventory turnover

PROBLEMS

Note: In this chapter, we provide an unusually wide variety of problem assignments. In order to make the full range of these assignments available to all users of the text, we present them in one consecutive series, rather than splitting them into A and B groups. This entire series is supported in both the Group A and Group B accounting work sheets.

PROBLEM 20-1
Analysis to Identify Favourable and Unfavourable Trends

The following information was developed from the December 31, year-end financial statements of Custom Logos, Inc. At the beginning of 1996, the company's former supplier went bankrupt, and the company began buying merchandise from another supplier.

	1996	1995
Gross profit	$1,008,000	$1,134,000
Income before income taxes	230,400	252,000
Net income...	172,800	189,000
Net income as a percentage of net sales	6.0%	7.5%

INSTRUCTIONS

a Compute the net sales for each year.

b Compute the cost of goods sold in dollars and as a percentage of net sales for each year.

c Compute operating expenses in dollars and as a percentage of net sales for each year. (Income taxes expense is not an operating expense.)

d Prepare a condensed comparative income statement for 1995 and 1996. Include the following items: net sales, cost of goods sold, gross profit, operating expenses, income before income taxes, income taxes expense, and net income. Omit earnings per share statistics.

e Identify the significant favourable trends and unfavourable trends in the performance of Custom Logos, Inc. Comment on any unusual changes.

PROBLEM 20-2
Comparing Operating Results with Average Performance in the Industry

Sub Zero, Inc., manufactures camping equipment. Shown below for the current year are the income statement for the company and a common size summary for the industry in which the company operates. (Notice that the percentages in the right-hand column are *not* for Sub Zero, Inc., but are average percentages for the industry.)

	Sub Zero, Inc.	Industry Average
Sales (net)	$20,000,000	100%
Cost of goods sold	9,800,000	57
Gross profit	$10,200,000	43%
Operating expenses:		
Selling	$ 4,200,000	16%
General and administrative	3,400,000	20
Total operating expenses	$ 7,600,000	36%
Operating income	$ 2,600,000	7%
Income taxes...	1,200,000	3
Net income...	$ 1,400,000	4%
Return on assets	18%	9%

INSTRUCTIONS

a Prepare a two-column common size income statement. The first column should show for Sub Zero, Inc., all items expressed as a percentage of net sales. The second column should show as an industry average the percentage data given in the problem. The purpose of this common size statement is to compare the operating results of Sub Zero, Inc., with the average for the industry.

b Comment specifically on differences between Sub Zero, Inc., and the industry average with respect to gross profit, selling expenses, general and administrative expenses, operating income, net income, and return on assets. Suggest possible reasons for the more important disparities.

PROBLEM 20-3
Ratios Based on Balance Sheet and Income Statement Data

Barnum Corporation has issued common stock only. The company has been successful and has a gross profit rate of 25%. The information shown below was derived from the company's financial statements.

Beginning inventory	$ 700,000
Ending inventory	800,000
Average accounts receivable...	250,000
Average common shareholders' equity	1,800,000
Sales (80% on credit)...	4,000,000
Net income..	225,000

INSTRUCTIONS

On the basis of the above information, compute the following:

a Accounts receivable turnover and the average number of days required to collect the accounts receivable

b The inventory turnover and the average number of days required to turn over the inventory

c Length of Barnum Corporation's operating cycle

d Return on common shareholders' equity

PROBLEM 20-4
Ratios;
Consider
Advisability of
Incurring Long-
Term Debt

At the end of the year, the following information was obtained from the accounting records of Carleton Office Products:

Sales (all on credit)	$2,700,000
Cost of goods sold	1,755,000
Average inventory	351,000
Average accounts receivable	300,000
Interest expense	45,000
Income taxes	84,000
Net income	159,000
Average investment in assets	1,800,000
Average shareholders' equity	795,000

INSTRUCTIONS   **a** From the information given, compute the following:

    1 Inventory turnover

    2 Accounts receivable turnover

    3 Total operating expenses

    4 Gross profit percentage

    5 Return on average shareholders' equity

    6 Return on average assets

  b Carleton has an opportunity to obtain a long-term loan at an annual interest rate of 12% and could use this additional capital at the same rate of profitability as indicated above. Would obtaining the loan be desirable from the viewpoint of the shareholders? Explain.

PROBLEM 20-5
Ratios;
Consider
Advisability of
Incurring Long-
Term Debt—
A Second
Problem

At the end of the year, the following information was obtained from the accounting records of Santa Fe Boot Limited.

Sales (all on credit)	$800,000
Cost of goods sold	480,000
Average inventory	120,000
Average accounts receivable	80,000
Interest expense	6,000
Income taxes	8,000
Net income for the year	36,000
Average investment in assets	500,000
Average shareholders' equity	400,000

    The company declared no dividends of any kind during the year and did not issue or retire any capital stock.

INSTRUCTIONS   **a** From the information given, compute the following for the year:

    1 Inventory turnover

    2 Accounts receivable turnover

    3 Total operating expenses

    4 Gross profit percentage

    5 Return on average shareholders' equity

    6 Return on average assets

b Santa Fe Boot Limited has an opportunity to obtain a long-term loan at an annual interest rate of 12% and could use this additional capital at the same rate of profitability as indicated in **a.** Would obtaining the loan be desirable from the viewpoint of the shareholders? Explain.

PROBLEM 20-6
Analysis and Interpretation from Viewpoint of Short-Term Creditor

Shown below are selected financial data for Mondo Corporation and Global, Inc., at the end of the current year.

	Mondo Corporation	*Global, Inc.*
Net sales (all on credit)	*$1,440,000*	*$1,190,000*
Cost of goods sold	*1,260,000*	*825,000*
Cash	*36,000*	*70,000*
Accounts receivable (net)	*180,000*	*140,000*
Inventory	*504,000*	*165,000*
Current liabilities	*240,000*	*150,000*

Assume that the year-end balances shown for accounts receivable and for inventory also represent the average balances of these accounts throughout the year.

INSTRUCTIONS

a For each company, compute the following:

1 Working capital.

2 Current ratio.

3 Quick ratio.

4 Number of times inventory turned over during the year and the average number of days required to turn over inventory.

5 Number of times accounts receivable turned over during the year and the average number of days required to collect accounts receivable. (Round to the nearest day.)

6 Operating cycle.

b From the viewpoint of a short-term creditor, comment upon the *quality* of each company's working capital. To which company would you prefer to sell $50,000 in merchandise on a 30-day open account?

PROBLEM 20-7
Ratios: Evaluation of Two Companies

Shown below are selected financial data for Another World and Imports, Inc., at the end of the current year:

	Another World	*Imports, Inc.*
Net credit sales	*$675,000*	*$560,000*
Cost of goods sold	*504,000*	*480,000*
Cash	*51,000*	*20,000*
Accounts receivable (net)	*75,000*	*70,000*
Inventory	*84,000*	*160,000*
Current liabilities	*105,000*	*100,000*

Assume that the year-end balances shown for accounts receivable and for inventory also represent the average balances of these items throughout the year.

INSTRUCTIONS

a For each of the two companies, compute the following:

1 Working capital.

2 Current ratio.

    3 Quick ratio.

    4 Number of times inventory turned over during the year and the average number of days required to turn over inventory. (Round computation to the nearest day.)

    5 Number of times accounts receivable turned over during the year and the average number of days required to collect accounts receivable. (Round computation to the nearest day.)

    6 Operating cycle.

b From the viewpoint of a short-term creditor, comment upon the *quality* of each company's working capital. To which company would you prefer to sell $30,000 in merchandise on a 30-day open account?

PROBLEM 20-8
Evaluating
Short-Term
Debt-Paying
Ability

Listed below is the working capital information for Imperial Products, Inc., at the beginning of the year.

Cash	*$405,000*
Temporary investments in marketable securities	*216,000*
Notes receivable—current	*324,000*
Accounts receivable	*540,000*
Allowance for doubtful accounts	*27,000*
Inventory	*432,000*
Prepaid expenses	*54,000*
Notes payable within one year	*162,000*
Accounts payable	*445,500*
Accrued liabilities	*40,500*

The following transactions are completed during the year:

  0 Sold on account inventory costing $72,000 for $65,000.

  1 Issued additional shares of capital stock for cash, $800,000.

  2 Sold temporary investments costing $60,000 for $54,000 cash.

  3 Acquired temporary investments, $105,000. Paid cash.

  4 Wrote off uncollectible accounts, $18,000.

  5 Sold on account inventory costing $75,000 for $90,000.

  6 Acquired plant and equipment for cash, $480,000.

  7 Declared a cash dividend, $240,000.

  8 Declared a 10% stock dividend.

  9 Paid accounts payable, $120,000.

10 Purchased goods on account, $90,000.

11 Collected cash on accounts receivable, $180,000.

12 Borrowed cash from a bank by issuing a short-term note, $250,000.

INSTRUCTIONS

a Compute the amount of quick assets, current assets, and current liabilities at the beginning of the year as shown by the above account balances.

b Use the data compiled in part **a** to compute: (1) current ratio; (2) quick ratio; and (3) working capital.

c Indicate the effect (Increase, Decrease, and No Effect) of each independent transaction listed above on the current ratio, quick ratio, and working capital. Use the following four-column format (item **0** is given as an example):

	Effect on		
Item	Current Ratio	Quick Ratio	Working Capital
0	Decrease	Increase	Decrease

PROBLEM 20-9
Effects of Transactions on Various Ratios

Listed in the left-hand column below is a series of 12 business transactions and events relating to the activities of Wabash Industries. Opposite each transaction is listed a particular ratio used in financial analysis.

Transaction	Ratio
(1) Purchased inventory on open account.	Quick ratio
(2) A larger physical volume of goods was sold at smaller unit prices.	Gross profit percentage
(3) Corporation declared a cash dividend.	Current ratio
(4) An uncollectible account receivable was written off against the allowance account.	Current ratio
(5) Issued additional shares of common stock and used proceeds to retire long-term debt.	Debt ratio
(6) Paid stock dividend on common stock, in common stock.	Earnings per share
(7) Conversion of a portion of bonds payable into common stock. (Ignore income taxes.)	Interest coverage ratio
(8) Appropriated retained earnings.	Rate of return on shareholders' equity
(9) During period of rising prices, company changed from FIFO to LIFO method of inventory pricing.	Inventory turnover
(10) Paid a previously declared cash dividend.	Debt ratio
(11) Purchased factory supplies on open account.	Current ratio (assume that ratio is greater than 1:1)
(12) Issued shares of capital stock in exchange for patents.	Equity ratio

INSTRUCTIONS

What effect would each transaction or event have on the ratio listed opposite to it; that is, as a result of this event would the ratio increase, decrease, or remain unchanged? Your answer for each of the 12 transactions should include a brief explanation.

PROBLEM 20-10
Building Financial Statements from Limited Information, Including Ratios

Pete Mitchell, the accountant for Hercules Construction, prepared the year-end financial statements, including all ratios, and was invited to bring them along on a wilderness retreat with the executives of the corporation. To his embarrassment, he found that only certain fragmentary information had been placed in his briefcase and the completed statements had been left in his office. One hour before Mitchell was to present the financial statements to the executives, he was able to come up with the following information:

HERCULES CONSTRUCTION
Balance Sheet
December 31, 19__
(in thousands of dollars)

Assets			Liabilities & Shareholders' Equity		
Current assets:			Current liabilities		$?
Cash...........................		?	Long-term debt, 8% interest........		?
Accounts receivable (net)........		?	Total liabilities...............		$?
Inventory......................		?	Shareholders' equity:		
Total current assets		$?	Capital stock	$300	
Plant assets:			Retained earnings	100	
Machinery and			Total shareholders' equity		400
equipment	$580				
Less: Accumulated					
depreciation............	80	500	Total liabilities & shareholders'		
Total assets		$?	equity..........................		$?

HERCULES CONSTRUCTION
Income Statement
For the Year Ended December 31, 19__
(in thousands of dollars)

Net sales..	$?
Cost of goods sold	?
Gross profit (25% of net sales)..	$?
Operating expenses	?
Operating income (10% of net sales)	$?
Interest expense...	28
Income before income taxes	$?
Income taxes—40% of income before income taxes............................	?
Net income...	$60

ADDITIONAL
INFORMATION

1 The equity ratio was 40%; the debt ratio was 60%.

2 The only interest expense was on the long-term debt.

3 The beginning inventory was $150,000; the inventory turnover was 4.8 times.

4 The current ratio was 2 to 1; the quick ratio was 1 to 1.

5 The beginning balance in accounts receivable was $80,000; the accounts receivable turnover for the year was 12.8 times. All sales were made on account.

INSTRUCTIONS The accountant asks you to help complete the financial statements for Hercules Construction, using only the information available. Present supporting computations and explanations for all amounts appearing in the balance sheet and the income statement.

PROBLEM 20-11
Analysis and Interpretation from Viewpoint of Common Shareholders and of Bond-holders

The following financial information for Continental Transfer and Canadian Van Lines (except market price per share of stock) is stated in ***thousands of dollars.*** The figures are as of the end of the current year. The two companies are in the same industry and are quite similar as to operations, facilities, and accounting methods. Assume that both companies pay income taxes equal to 50% of income before income taxes.

Assets	*Continental Transfer*	*Canadian Van Lines*
Current assets	$ 97,500	$132,320
Plant and equipment	397,500	495,680
Less: Accumulated depreciation	(55,000)	(78,000)
Total assets	$440,000	$550,000

Liabilities & Shareholders' Equity		
Current liabilities	$ 34,000	$ 65,000
Bonds payable, 12%, due in 15 years.........................	120,000	100,000
Capital stock, no par	150,000	200,000
Retained earnings	136,000	185,000
Total liabilities & shareholders' equity	$440,000	$550,000

Analysis of retained earnings:		
Balance, beginning of year..................................	$125,200	$167,200
Net income for the year.....................................	19,800	37,400
Dividends	(9,000)	(19,600)
Balance, end of year..	$136,000	$185,000
Market price of capital stock, per share	$30	$61
Number of shares of capital stock outstanding	6 million	8 million

INSTRUCTIONS   **a** Compute for each company:

    1 The interest coverage ratio (number of times bond interest was earned during the current year).

    2 The debt ratio.

  b In light of the information developed in **a** above, write a paragraph indicating which company's bonds you think would trade in the market at the higher price. Which would probably provide the higher yield? Explain how the ratios developed influence your answer. (It may be assumed that the bonds were issued several years ago and are traded on an organized securities exchange.)

  c For each company compute the dividend yield, earnings per share, the price-earnings ratio, and the book value per share. (Show supporting computations. Remember that dollar amounts in the problem are in thousands of dollars, that is, three zeros omitted.)

  d Assume that you expect both companies to grow at the same rate. Express an opinion, based solely on the data developed in **c** above, as to which company's stock is a better investment at the present market price.

PROBLEM 20-12
A Financial Taste Test

Selected data from recent annual reports of *The Coca-Cola Company* and *PepsiCo, Inc.* (and subsidiaries) are shown below. (Dollar amounts are stated in millions.)

	Coca-Cola	PepsiCo*
Balance sheet statistics:		
At year-end:		
Quick assets	$2,002	$ 2,774
Current assets	3,604	3,551
Total assets	8,283	15,127
Current liabilities	3,658	3,692
Total liabilities	4,798	11,236
Total shareholders' equity	3,485	3,891
Average throughout the year:		
Accounts receivable	802	1,110
Inventory	784	494
Total assets	7,867	13,131
Total shareholders' equity	3,415	3,526
Income statement statistics:		
Net sales	8,966	15,242
Cost of goods sold	3,892	7,468
Interest expense	308	610
Operating income	1,726	1,783
Net income	1,724	901

* More than one-half of PepsiCo's revenue and profits stem from its snack food and restaurant operations, rather than from soft drink sales.

INSTRUCTIONS

a Compute the following for each company:

1 Net income as a percentage of sales

2 Return on assets

3 Return on equity

4 Working capital

5 Accounts receivable turnover rate

6 Inventory turnover rate

7 Quick ratio

8 Debt ratio

9 Interest coverage ratio

b Both Coca-Cola and PepsiCo are highly successful companies with excellent credit ratings. Based on your analysis in part **a**, however, indicate which of these companies you believe:

1 Provides the greatest degree of safety for its ***short-term*** creditors.

2 Provides the greatest degree of safety for its ***long-term*** creditors.

3 Would have the higher p/e ratio (that is, the stock would sell at the greater market value relative to the current earnings per share).

In each case, ***explain your reasoning.***

ANALYTICAL AND DECISION PROBLEMS AND CASES

A&D 20-1
Season's
Greetings

Holiday Greeting Cards is a local company organized late in July of 1995. The company's net income for each of its first six calendar quarters of operations is summarized below. The amounts are stated in thousands of dollars.

	1996	1995
First quarter (January through March)	$ 253	—
Second quarter (April through June)	308	—
Third quarter (July through September)	100	$ 50
Fourth quarter (October through December)	450	500
Total for the calendar year	$1,111	$550

Glen Wallace reports the business and economic news for a local radio station. On the day that Holiday Greeting Cards released the above financial information, you heard Wallace make the following statement during his broadcast: "Holiday Greeting Cards enjoyed a 350% increase in its net income for the fourth quarter, and net income for the entire year was up by over 100%."

INSTRUCTIONS
a Show the computations that Wallace probably made in arriving at his statistics.

b Do you believe that Wallace's percentage changes present a realistic impression of Holiday Greeting Cards' rate of growth in 1996? Explain.

c What figure would you use to express the percentage change in Holiday's fourth quarter net income in 1996? Explain why you would compute the change in this manner.

A&D 20-2
Limit on
Dividends

During each of the last 10 years, Reese Corporation has increased the common stock dividend per share by about 10%. Total dividends now amount to $9 million per year, consisting of $2 million paid to preferred shareholders and $7 million paid to common shareholders. The preferred stock is cumulative but not convertible. Annual net income had been rising steadily until two years ago, when it peaked at $44 million. Last year, increased competition caused net income to decline to $37 million. Management expects net income to stabilize around this level for several years. This year, Reese Corporation issued bonds payable. The contract with bondholders requires Reese Corporation to limit total dividends to not more than 25% of net income.

INSTRUCTIONS
Evaluate this situation from the perspective of:

a Common shareholders

b Preferred shareholders

A&D 20-3
Improving
Cash Flow

Reynolds Labs develops and manufactures pharmaceutical products. The company has been growing rapidly during the past 10 years, due primarily to having discovered, patented, and successfully marketed dozens of new products. Net income has increased annually by 30% or more. The company pays no dividend but has a very high price-earnings ratio. Due to its rapid growth and large expenditures for research and development, the company has experienced occasional cash shortages. To solve this problem, Reynolds has decided to improve its cash position by (1) requiring customers to pay for products purchased on account from the company in 30 days instead of 60 days and (2) reducing expenditures for research and development by 20%.

INSTRUCTIONS Evaluate this situation from the perspective of:

a Short-term creditors.

b Common shareholders.

A&D 20-4
Declining
Interest Rate

Metro Utilities has outstanding 16 issues of bonds payable, with interest rates ranging from 5½% to 14%. The company's rate of return on assets consistently averages 12%. Almost every year, the company issues additional bonds to finance growth, to pay maturing bonds, or to call outstanding bonds when advantageous. During the current year, long-term interest rates have fallen dramatically. At the beginning of the year, these rates were between 12% and 13%; now, however, they are down to between 8% and 9%. Management currently is planning a large 8% bond issue.

INSTRUCTIONS Evaluate this situation from the perspective of:

a Holders of 5½% bonds, maturing in 11 years but redeemable now at 103.

b Holders of 14% bonds, maturing in 23 years but redeemable now at 103.

c Common shareholders.

A&D 20-5
Which One Is
Better?

The following presents certain financial information relating to two companies, London Toyland and Nathan Toymart as of the end of the current year. All figures (except market price per share of stock) are in ***thousands of dollars.***

Assets	London Toyland	Nathan Toymart
Cash...	$ 252	$ 360
Marketable securities, at lower of cost and market....................	258	906
Accounts receivable, net..	290	334
Inventories, at lower of cost and market............................	1,510	770
Prepaid expenses	50	30
Plant and equipment, net	3,360	3,140
Intangibles and other assets	280	60
Total assets	$6,000	$5,600

Liabilities & Shareholders' Equity		
Accounts payable	$ 690	$ 608
Accrued liabilities, including income taxes	310	192
Bonds payable, 8%, due in 10 years...............................	400	1,000
Capital stock (London, 150,000 shares; Nathan, 120,000 shares)......	2,780	2,700
Retained earnings	1,820	1,100
Total liabilities & shareholders' equity	$6,000	$5,600

Analysis of retained earnings:		
Balance, beginning of year...	$1,424	$ 860
Add: Net income	690	480
Less: Dividends	(294)	(240)
Balance, end of year..	$1,820	$1,100
Market price per share of stock, end of year........................	46	40
Net sales...	$6,900	$6,000

INSTRUCTIONS   London Toyland and Nathan Toymart are generally comparable in the nature of their operations, products, and accounting procedures used. Use whatever analytical computations you feel will best support each of the following evaluations.

a   Evaluate these two companies from the perspective of short-term creditors and explain which company you feel is more credit worthy.

b   Evaluate these two companies from the perspective of common shareholders and explain which company you feel is a better investment.

COMPREHENSIVE PROBLEM 5

MACLEAN HUNTER LIMITED

ANALYSIS OF THE FINANCIAL STATEMENTS OF A PUBLICLY OWNED CORPORATION

The purpose of this Comprehensive Problem is to acquaint you with the financial statements of a publicly owned company. The financial statements included in the 1992 annual report of **Maclean Hunter Limited** (the company) were selected because they illustrate many of the financial reporting issues discussed in this textbook. Notice that several pages of explanatory notes are included with the basic statements. These explanatory notes supplement the condensed information in the financial statements and are intended to carry out the generally accepted accounting principle of adequate disclosure. Also, selected information in the annual report is included.

This Comprehensive Problem is subdivided into three parts. **Part 1** is designed to familiarize you with the content of these financial statements and other information in the annual report. **Part 2** requires analysis from the viewpoint of a short-term creditor, and **Part 3,** from the perspective of a shareholder.

PART 1
An Overview of the Statements and the Related Notes, Reports, and Other Information

A corporate annual report includes not only the financial statements, but also notes, auditors' reports, corporate profile, corporate plan, management's discussion and analysis, management's responsibility for financial reporting, consolidated financial statement—summary of accounting policies, an 11-year financial summary. Our purpose in Part 1 of this comprehensive problem is to acquaint you with the form and content of these materials.

INSTRUCTIONS   Answer each of the following questions and briefly explain where in the statements, notes, reports by the auditors, other information in the annual report (presented in this problem) you located the information used in your answer.

a   What is the nature and scope of Maclean Hunter's operations?

b   What is Maclean Hunter's corporate plan?

c   The comparative financial statements include the statements of income, retained earnings, changes in cash position, and financial position. Were all of these statements audited by a firm of public accountants? Name the firm that audited these statements. What were the auditors' conclusions?

d   Who is responsible for the content of these statements—management, the company's board of directors, or the auditors? In general terms, what measures have been undertaken by ***management*** to ensure the reliability of these statements?

(Continued on page 994.)

CORPORATE PROFILE

Maclean Hunter is a diversified communications company operating across Canada and in the United States and Europe, with 12,000 employees and 1992 revenue of $1.6 billion. Almost half of our 1992 operating income was earned in the United States.

With more than 1.2 million subscribers, our cable television operations in Canada and the United States have been a sustaining force in our growth accounting for 72% of our operating income before amortization of $194 million in 1992.

We began in periodical publishing in 1887, and are best known in Canada for Maclean's, L'actualité, Chatelaine and Flare. In total, we publish more than 200 consumer and business periodicals in 10 countries.

We produce business forms and specialty printing items in both Canada and the United States and are major commercial printers in Canada.

We have a 62% interest in The Toronto Sun Publishing Corporation, which publishes Sun newspapers in four Canadian cities, The Financial Post, and 62 community newspapers in Canada and the U.S.

Our broadcasting interests include a CTV-affiliated television station in Calgary and 21 radio stations in Ontario and the Maritimes.

Related communication services include radio paging, trade and consumer shows, co-op advertising and media monitoring, and post-production services.

CORPORATE PLAN

We will stay exclusively within the communications business, primarily in North America and Europe.

All investments that fall into the normal-risk category will achieve a minimum after-tax return on net assets employed of 15%. In lower-risk investments (e.g. in most cable TV operations), a minimum after-tax return of 12% may be more appropriate.

All properties that do not measure up to the corporate plan's objectives will require approval for continuance.

We will own, if not a majority interest, at least effective control of all activities.

The Company has a target of paying 40% of the previous year's after-tax earnings in dividends.

We will manage our growth so that any new venture or acquisition will not jeopardize the future stability of the Company.

MANAGEMENT'S DISCUSSION AND ANALYSIS

This analysis is supplemental to the Consolidated Financial Statements . . . and is intended to provide investors with additional information on the recent performance of the Company, its current financial situation, and its future prospects. For a more complete understanding of the Company's operations, readers should refer to the Letter to Shareholders and the Review of Operations sections of this annual report, which include other detailed information which has not been duplicated in this analysis.

OPERATING RESULTS

OVERVIEW

Revenue
Revenue for the year increased by $100 million or 7% compared to 1991. Approximately $29 million or 2% of this growth was due to acquisitions completed during the last two years, the largest being the acquisition in the fourth quarter of 1992 of the Southam business forms operations. Offsetting this, revenue declined by approximately $11 million due to dispositions. An additional $22 million of the increase was due to the weakening of the Canadian dollar compared to the U.S. dollar during 1992.

(millions)	1992		1991	
Cable television	$ 398	24%	$ 358	23%
Periodicals	366	22	354	23
Business forms and commercial printing	409	25	354	23˙
Newspapers	329	20	322	21
Broadcasting	74	5	77	5
Communication services	59	4	70	5
	1,635	100	1,535	100
Canada	1,094	67	1,046	68
United States and Europe	541	33	489	32
Total revenue	$1,635	100%	$1,535	100%

The above breakdown of revenue by industry and geographic segments shows that the growth occurred mainly in cable television and business forms and commercial printing, and there were slight declines in revenue from the broadcasting and communication services segments. These developments did not, however, significantly change the proportion of revenue generated by each segment, and the proportion of revenue generated outside Canada has also remained stable relative to 1991.

The Company's objective over the long term is to maintain a balance between advertising and non-advertising revenue. As a result of growth and investment in cable television, together with depressed advertising markets during the last three years, revenue from non-advertising sources was a greater percentage of the total in 1992 than it has been for many years. A sustained economic recovery should result in faster growth of advertising revenues compared to non-advertising revenues, and may therefore slow or reverse this trend.

LIQUIDITY AND CAPITAL RESOURCES

CASH FLOW

(millions)	1992	1991
Cash flow from operations	$200	$170
Dividends	(45)	(42)
Purchase of property, plant and equipment	(99)	(105)
Business acquisitions	(56)	(13)
Business divestitures	9	22
Receipt of mortgage	–	43
Other	59	25
Surplus cash	68	100
Issue of common shares	173	–
Net repayment of debt	(190)	(105)
Increase (decrease) in cash	$ 51	$ (5)

Cash flow from operations (defined as operating income plus depreciation and amortization and other items, less net interest expense and current income taxes) increased from $170 million in 1991 to $200 million in 1992. Cash flow from operations per share increased from $1.05 per share in 1991 to $1.14 per share in 1992. The increase in operating cash flow is due to higher operating income and lower interest expense.

In the publishing and cable television industries, subscribers prepay for services to be rendered. As a result of this deferred revenue, together with the minimal current assets of cable television operations, the Company does not have a large investment in non-cash working capital.

1992 dividends amounted to $45 million and dividends declared per common share were 25¢ per share in 1992 and 1991. It is the Company's target to pay 40% of the previous year's after-tax earnings in dividends with the dividend rate being reviewed beginning with the second quarter dividend payable in August. The Company has an Automatic Dividend Reinvestment Plan whereby cash dividends may be automatically reinvested in new shares at 95% of the current stock price. Cash dividends reinvested amounted to $6 million in 1992 and $3 million in 1991.

1992 additions to property, plant and equipment totalled $99 million including $60 million in cable television and $13 million at The Toronto Sun. Business acquisitions amounted to $56 million in 1992, including $24 million for working capital and $21 million for property, plant and equipment.

The remaining surplus cash, together with the proceeds of the common share issue, enabled $190 million of debt to be repaid and cash balances were $51 million higher at the end of the year.

CAPITAL EXPENDITURES

An analysis of capital expenditures and depreciation by business segment is provided in note 1 to the Consolidated Financial Statements. Major individual projects were to complete construction and refurbishment of new premises for our New Jersey cable operations ($5 million), and to rebuild and upgrade channel capacity of the Florida cable system ($12 million).

The Company has planned capital expenditures for 1993 amounting to approximately $100 million, $49 million of which is for cable television in Ontario and the United States.

DEBT

Details of the Company's debt position are included in note 9 to the Consolidated Financial Statements.

One important source of debt financing for the Company continues to be short-term notes in its commercial paper program. At December 31, 1992, notes outstanding totalled $285 million, comprised of 19 separate issues with terms mostly from 30-90 days and representing an average maturing amount to be "rolled over" on any one day of approximately $15 million. Notes are generally issued at interest rates related to LIBOR in U.S. dollars or Banker's Acceptances in Canadian dollars; at December 31, 1992, all commercial paper was either denominated in U.S. dollars, or converted thereto using currency exchanges, at interest rates ranging from 3.3% to 4.1%.

While these notes are classified as current liabilities in the Consolidated Statement of Financial Position since the terms of the individual notes are for periods under one year, it is the Company's intention that the commercial paper program will represent an ongoing source of financing. Although the Company to date always has been able to roll over maturing notes, there are approximately $340 million of unused bank credit lines available for general corporate purposes, $150 million of which is dedicated as back-up for the commercial paper program.

The proceeds received on the sale of CHCH-TV in January 1993 were used to repay commercial paper by approximately $53 million.

MANAGEMENT'S RESPONSIBILITY FOR FINANCIAL REPORTING

The preparation of the Consolidated Financial Statements accompanying this annual report and the presentation of all other information in the report are the responsibilities of management. The Consolidated Financial Statements have been prepared in accordance with appropriate and generally accepted accounting principles, and reflect management's estimates and judgements in situations where a precise determination of the value of certain assets and liabilities is dependent on future events. Management has also ensured that the financial information presented elsewhere in this annual report is consistent with the Consolidated Financial Statements.

Management is also responsible for a system of internal control which is designed to provide reasonable assurance that assets are safeguarded and accounting systems provide timely, accurate financial reports.

The Board of Directors is responsible for ensuring that management fulfils its responsibilities for financial reporting and internal control and is ultimately responsible for reviewing and approving the Consolidated Financial Statements. The Board is assisted in exercising its responsibilities through its Audit Committee, which is composed of outside Directors. The Committee meets periodically with management, as well as the internal and external auditors, to discuss internal controls, auditing matters and financial reporting issues, to satisfy itself that each party is properly discharging its responsibilities, and to review the interim and annual Consolidated Financial Statements. The Committee also considers, for review by the Board and approval by the shareholders, the engagement or re-appointment of the external auditors.

Ernst & Young, the external auditors appointed by the shareholders of the Company, have audited the Consolidated Financial Statements and their report follows. The external auditors have full and unrestricted access to the Audit Committee to discuss their audit and their related findings as to the Company's financial reporting and the system of internal controls.

February 12, 1993

Ronald W. Osborne
President and Chief Executive Officer

J. Robert Furse
Vice President, Finance and Chief Financial Officer

AUDITORS' REPORT

TO THE SHAREHOLDERS OF MACLEAN HUNTER LIMITED:

We have audited the consolidated statements of financial position of Maclean Hunter Limited as at December 31, 1992 and 1991 and the consolidated statements of income, retained earnings and changes in cash position for the years then ended. The preparation of these financial statements is the responsibility of the Company's management. Our responsibility is to express an opinion on these financial statements based on our audits.

We conducted our audits in accordance with generally accepted auditing standards. Those standards require that we plan and perform an audit to obtain reasonable assurance whether the financial statements are free of material misstatement. An audit includes examining, on a test basis, evidence supporting the amounts and disclosures in the financial statements. An audit also includes assessing the accounting principles used and estimates made by management, as well as evaluating the overall financial statement presentation.

In our opinion, these consolidated financial statements present fairly, in all material respects, the financial position of the Company as at December 31, 1992 and 1991 and the results of its operations and the changes in its financial position for the years then ended in accordance with generally accepted accounting principles.

Chartered Accountants
Toronto, Canada
February 12, 1993

CONSOLIDATED FINANCIAL STATEMENTS
SUMMARY OF ACCOUNTING POLICIES

CONSOLIDATION AND INVESTMENTS

The accounts of subsidiaries are consolidated with those of the Company. Certain subsidiary companies hold a non-controlling interest in Maclean Hunter Holdings Limited which owns shares of the Company. The Company's proportionate interest in the cost of such shares is deducted from shareholders' equity. Earnings and cash flow per share are calculated after eliminating the Company's indirect interest in its own shares. Similarly, the dividends deducted from retained earnings exclude that portion which relates to the Company's indirect interest in its own shares.

Investments in entities where the Company exercises significant influence but does not have voting control are accounted for using the equity method whereby the Company includes its proportionate share of their net income or loss in consolidated net income. Investments held for resale are valued at the lower of cost and estimated net realizable value.

TRANSLATION OF FOREIGN CURRENCIES

Foreign currency amounts and the financial statements of foreign subsidiaries are translated into Canadian dollars on the following basis:

- assets and liabilities at the year-end rate of exchange (1992 – $1 U.S. = $1.271 Cdn.; 1991 – $1 U.S. = $1.156 Cdn.)
- revenue and expenses at the average rate calculated monthly (1992 – $1 U.S. = $1.210 Cdn.; 1991 – $1 U.S. = $1.149 Cdn.)

Exchange gains or losses arising from the translation of the Company's net investment in self-sustaining foreign operations, net of the Company's U.S. dollar denominated debt, are accumulated in the foreign currency translation adjustment account in shareholders' equity and included in income if realized through sale of the investment or distribution of foreign assets.

UNEARNED REVENUE

Prepaid subscriptions for business magazines that are substantially dependent on subscription revenue, for cable television and for newspapers are deferred and taken into income as the services are provided to the subscribers. These deferred amounts are included in accounts payable.

Net revenue pertaining to prepaid subscriptions from consumer magazines is also deferred and taken into income over the terms of the various subscriptions. These magazines derive a substantial majority of their net revenue from advertising and, since current assets will not be used to discharge any obligations to subscribers, no portion of such unearned revenue is included in current liabilities.

INCOME TAXES

The deferral method is used in accounting for income taxes whereby timing differences between income reported in the financial statements and taxable income result in deferred income taxes. Such timing differences occur when revenue or expenses are recognized in the accounts in one year and are included in taxable income in another year.

INVENTORIES

Inventories, principally materials for printing and business forms, are valued at the lower of cost, calculated using the first-in, first-out method, and replacement cost.

CAPITAL ASSETS

Property, plant and equipment are recorded at cost less related investment tax credits. Interest on borrowings is capitalized during the construction of new plant and equipment.

For newly licensed areas within a cable television system, all costs are capitalized prior to the prematurity period. During the prematurity period, a portion of the fixed system costs attributable to future operations is capitalized. Prematurity begins with the first subscriber hook-up and ends when construction is planned to be substantially complete.

Capital leases, which transfer substantially all the benefits and risks of ownership, are recorded as the acquisition of an asset and the incurrence of an obligation based on the present value of future rental payments.

Property, plant and equipment, including capital leases, is depreciated in a rational and systematic manner appropriate to the nature of the assets using straight-line or diminishing balance methods over the estimated life of the assets as follows:

	Amortization Period
Buildings	20 to 40 years
Leasehold improvements	Lease term
Cable television equipment	5 to 15 years
Presses and printing equipment	5 to 15 years
Broadcasting equipment	5 to 20 years
Office furniture and fixtures	5 to 10 years
Vehicles	3 to 5 years
Pagers and paging equipment	5 to 10 years
Computer hardware and software	2 to 7 years
Other equipment	3 to 15 years

The excess of the cost of acquiring businesses over the value assigned to identifiable net tangible assets acquired is allocated first to intangible assets and the residual is allocated to goodwill.

Intangible assets which include broadcast licences, circulation bases, subscriber lists, radio paging frequencies, favourable contracts and non-compete agreements are amortized on a straight-line basis over their estimated economic life up to a maximum of forty years. Cable television franchises are amortized using the sinking fund method with an interest rate of 4% over periods not exceeding forty years.

Goodwill is amortized on a straight-line basis over ten years for trade and consumer shows and over periods not exceeding forty years for other operations.

Periodically, management re-evaluates the remaining useful life of all capital assets, and extends or shortens the amortization periods accordingly. Management also periodically reviews the carrying amount of all capital assets, and writes them down when the long-term expectation is that the net carrying amount will not be recovered.

PENSION COSTS AND OBLIGATIONS

For defined benefit plans, pension costs are actuarially determined on the basis of management's estimates using the projected benefit method prorated over the service lives of the employees. Actuarial surpluses or deficiencies are amortized to income over the expected average remaining service life of pension plan members. Pension fund assets are valued using market prices averaged over a five year period.

CONSOLIDATED STATEMENT OF INCOME

		December 31	
(millions)	*Notes*	**1992**	1991
Revenue			
Cable television		$ **398.3**	$ 357.6
Periodicals		**365.4**	353.5
Business forms and commercial printing		**408.9**	353.7
Newspapers		**329.4**	322.5
Broadcasting		**73.6**	76.9
Communication services		**59.0**	70.4
Total revenue		**1,634.6**	1,534.6
Operating income			
Cable television		**139.0**	120.3
Periodicals		**16.1**	10.1
Business forms and commercial printing		**31.2**	31.6
Newspapers		**4.3**	3.5
Broadcasting		**6.3**	6.0
Communication services		**(2.8)**	(0.8)
Operating income before amortization		**194.1**	170.7
Amortization of intangible assets and goodwill	*1(b)*	**(17.0)**	(16.2)
Total operating income		**177.1**	154.5
Other income, net	*5(b)*	**10.8**	3.8
Interest expense	*9 and 10*	**(31.0)**	(59.2)
Minority interest		**—**	2.2
Income taxes	*3*	**(75.7)**	(50.7)
Consolidated net income		$ **81.2**	$ 50.6
Earnings per share	*2*	**47¢**	32¢

CONSOLIDATED STATEMENT OF RETAINED EARNINGS

		December 31	
(millions)	*Notes*	**1992**	1991
Retained earnings, beginning of year		$ **438.4**	$ 429.3
Consolidated net income		**81.2**	50.6
Dividends declared	*11(b)*	**(45.4)**	(41.5)
Cost of common share issue (net of tax)	*11(e)*	**(4.5)**	—
Retained earnings, end of year		$ **469.7**	$ 438.4

CONSOLIDATED STATEMENT OF CHANGES IN CASH POSITION

(millions)	*Notes*	December 31 1992	1991
Operating activities			
Operating income before amortization		$ 194.1	$ 170.7
Depreciation	*1(b)*	100.6	96.1
Other items, net		7.1	9.1
Earnings before interest, taxes, depreciation and amortization		301.8	275.9
Interest expense		(31.0)	(59.2)
Current income taxes	*3*	(70.9)	(46.4)
Cash flow from operations		199.9	170.3
Decrease in non-cash working capital		33.9	12.4
Total cash provided by operating activities		233.8	182.7
Investment activities			
Purchase of property, plant and equipment	*1(d)*	(99.4)	(105.4)
Business acquisitions	*1(d) and 5(a)*	(56.1)	(13.2)
Business divestitures	*5(b)*	8.6	22.2
Other		2.4	(1.3)
Total cash used in investment activities		(144.5)	(97.7)
Financing activities			
Issue of common shares	*11*	179.3	3.1
Repayment of notes and other indebtedness	*9*	(189.6)	(105.2)
Dividends declared	*11(b)*	(45.4)	(41.5)
Received from minority shareholders		6.2	10.4
Distribution from Barden Cablevision, Partnership	*8*	11.2	—
Receipt of mortgage		—	43.0
Total cash used in financing activities		(38.3)	(90.2)
Increase (decrease) in cash		51.0	(5.2)
Cash and short-term investments, beginning of year		36.7	41.9
Cash and short-term investments, end of year		$ 87.7	$ 36.7
Cash flow per share	*2*		
Earnings before interest, taxes, depreciation and amortization		$ 1.71	$ 1.70
Cash flow from operations		$ 1.14	$ 1.05

CONSOLIDATED STATEMENT OF FINANCIAL POSITION

Maclean Hunter Limited
(Incorporated
under the laws of Ontario)

		December 31	
(millions)	*Notes*	**1992**	1991
Assets			
Current assets			
Cash and short-term investments		$ **87.7**	$ 36.7
Accounts receivable		**195.4**	179.2
Inventories		**66.2**	50.6
Prepaids and other receivables	*5(b)*	**89.0**	35.7
Total current assets		**438.3**	302.2
Property, plant and equipment	*6*	**658.8**	632.4
Intangible assets	*7*	**383.5**	377.2
Goodwill		**293.8**	295.2
Investments and other assets	*8*	**97.5**	146.6
Total Assets		**$1,871.9**	$1,753.6
Liabilities and Shareholders' Equity			
Current liabilities			
Accounts payable		$ **222.2**	$ 201.5
Income and other taxes payable		**32.8**	24.1
		255.0	225.6
Indebtedness due within one year	*9*	**301.2**	449.7
Total current liabilities		**556.2**	675.3
Long-term debt	*9*	**166.7**	166.5
Unearned revenue		**36.6**	37.7
Deferred income taxes		**119.4**	102.0
Minority interest		**106.3**	105.5
Convertible debentures	*10*	**21.4**	23.0
Shareholders' equity			
Share capital	*11*	**490.1**	292.2
Retained earnings		**469.7**	438.4
Foreign currency translation adjustment	*12*	**(17.3)**	(18.6)
		942.5	712.0
Less the Company's indirect interest in its own shares	*13*	**(77.2)**	(68.4)
Total shareholders' equity		**865.3**	643.6
Total Liabilities and Shareholders' Equity		**$1,871.9**	$1,753.6

On behalf of the Board:

Radcliffe R. Latimer
Director

Ronald W. Osborne
Director

NOTES TO CONSOLIDATED FINANCIAL STATEMENTS

I. INDUSTRY AND GEOGRAPHIC SEGMENT INFORMATION

(a) Revenue and operating income before amortization

(millions)	1992	1991
Revenue		
Canada	$1,093.9	$1,045.5
United States and Europe	540.7	489.1
	1,634.6	1,534.6
Operating income before amortization		
Canada	99.6	86.4
United States and Europe	94.5	84.3
	$ 194.1	$ 170.7

(b) Depreciation and amortization

	Depreciation		Amortization of intangible assets and goodwill	
(millions)	1992	1991	1992	1991
Industry				
Cable television	$ 46.4	$44.0	$ 6.0	$ 5.5
Periodicals	7.4	7.4	3.5	3.3
Business forms and commercial printing	20.1	17.6	2.2	2.1
Newspapers	16.3	15.8	2.7	2.4
Broadcasting	3.1	3.2	1.1	1.1
Communication services	7.3	8.1	1.5	1.8
	100.6	96.1	17.0	16.2
Geographic				
Canada	64.4	63.0	10.2	10.2
United States and Europe	36.2	33.1	6.8	6.0
	$100.6	$96.1	$17.0	$16.2

6. PROPERTY, PLANT AND EQUIPMENT

(millions)	Cost	1992 Accumulated depreciation	Net	1991 Net
Land	$ 36.4	$ —	$ 36.4	$ 34.6
Buildings	165.8	40.0	125.8	120.2
Leasehold improvements	28.3	17.3	11.0	13.8
Cable television systems				
– equipment	464.0	219.2	244.8	230.1
– deferred prematurity costs	24.1	15.4	8.7	10.5
Presses and printing equipment	280.1	152.1	128.0	119.6
Broadcasting equipment	53.6	37.8	15.8	20.2
Office furniture and fixtures	53.3	33.8	19.5	11.3
Vehicles	16.6	10.1	6.5	5.6
Pagers and paging equipment	28.8	14.0	14.8	17.1
Computer hardware and software	64.9	39.8	25.1	20.8
Other equipment	84.9	63.6	21.3	27.7
Construction in progress	1.1	—	1.1	0.9
Total 1992	**$1,301.9**	**$643.1**	**$658.8**	**$632.4**
Total 1991	$ 1,185.4	$ 553.0	$ 632.4	

The above amounts include net property, plant and equipment of $2.9 million (1991 – $8.1 million) under capital leases.

The Company has planned capital expenditures for 1993 amounting to approximately $100 million, $49 million of which is for cable television in Ontario and the United States.

9. DEBT

(millions)	1992	1991
Short-term notes	$285.4	$374.2
Medium-term notes	2.0	50.9
Debentures, due July 1995	164.2	150.8
Bank loans, revolving credit lines, capital leases and other	16.3	40.3
Total	467.9	616.2
Classified as:		
Indebtedness due within one year	301.2	449.7
Long-term debt	166.7	166.5
Total	467.9	616.2
Total debt is denominated in, or converted using forward currency and interest rate swap agreements into, currencies as follows:		
Canadian dollars	3.1	207.6
United States dollars	458.4	403.3
European currencies	6.4	5.3
	$467.9	$616.2

(a) Short-term notes

The Company issues short-term notes in the form of commercial paper in both Canadian and U.S. dollars. At December 31, 1992, the notes bear interest at rates ranging from 3.3% to 4.1% (1991 – 4.5% to 8.5%), with a weighted average interest rate at December 31, 1992 of 3.8% (1991 – 6.0%). From time to time, the Company purchases future rate agreements to fix the future interest cost with respect to these short-term notes. While the notes are classified as a current liability on the Consolidated Statement of Financial Position as the terms of the individual notes are less than one year, it is the Company's intention that the commercial paper program will represent an ongoing source of financing.

Interest expense on commercial paper amounted to $11.7 million in 1992 ($31.2 million in 1991).

(b) Medium-term notes

The medium-term notes outstanding are due in 1993 and bear interest at 11.8%.

Interest expense on the medium-term notes amounted to $4.4 million in 1992 ($5.3 million in 1991).

(c) Debentures, due July 1995

The debentures bear interest at 12.2%, are unsecured and are due on July 19, 1995. Interest is payable in equal semi-annual instalments on January 19 and July 19 in each year. At December 31, 1992, the original debentures had all been swapped into three month U.S. floating rates for which the effective interest rate was 6.2%. The interest rate has been fixed until July 19, 1993 using future rate agreements at 6.4%.

Interest expense on the debentures amounted to $11.0 million in 1992 ($16.2 million in 1991).

(d) Bank loans, revolving credit lines, capital leases and other

Interest rates on bank revolving credits lines are based on various options including bank prime, banker's acceptances for Canadian funds and London Interbank Offered Rate (LIBOR) for U.S. funds.

Interest expense on these other financial instruments amounted to $2.0 million in 1992 ($4.5 million in 1991).

The Company has approximately $340 million of unused bank credit lines available for general corporate purposes, $150 million of which is dedicated as back-up for the commercial paper program.

(e) Principal repayments of indebtedness other than short-term notes are as follows:

	(millions)
1993	$ 15.8
1994	1.1
1995	165.3
1996	0.3
Total	$182.5

ELEVEN-YEAR FINANCIAL SUMMARY

Maclean Hunter
Limited

(dollar amounts in millions)	1992	1991	1990
OPERATING RESULTS			
Revenue			
Cable television	$ 398.3	$ 357.6	$ 326.1
Periodicals	365.4	353.5	372.0
Business forms and commercial printing	408.9	353.7	351.7
Newspapers	329.4	322.5	323.3
Broadcasting	73.6	76.9	82.8
Communication services	59.0	70.4	80.1
Total revenue	1,634.6	1,534.6	1,536.0
Operating Income			
Cable television	139.0	120.3	106.0
Periodicals	16.1	10.1	23.3
Business forms and commercial printing	31.2	31.6	38.3
Newspapers	4.3	3.5	5.1
Broadcasting	6.3	6.0	12.4
Communication services	(2.8)	(0.8)	3.7
Operating income before amortization	194.1	170.7	188.8
Net Income			
Income before unusual items	81.2	50.6	49.5
Unusual items	—	—	(34.2)
Consolidated net income	$ 81.2	$ 50.6	$ 15.3
PER SHARE DATA			
Income before unusual items	47¢	32¢	32¢
Unusual items	—	—	(21)
Consolidated earnings per share	47¢	32¢	11¢
Cash flow from operations	$ 1.14	$ 1.05	$ 1.01
Dividends	25.0¢	25.0¢	25.0¢
Number of shares less indirect interest (thousands)			
Year end	171,616	155,713	154,803
Weighted average (fully diluted)	176,219	162,579	160,514
CASH FLOW			
Cash flow from operations	$ 199.9	$ 170.3	$ 160.9
Capital expenditures			
Business acquisitions	56.1	13.2	44.7
Purchase of property, plant and equipment	99.4	105.4	128.1
Dividends declared	45.4	41.5	39.5
YEAR-END FINANCIAL POSITION			
Working capital (excluding current indebtedness)	$ 183.3	$ 76.6	$ 140.8
Property, plant and equipment	658.8	632.4	628.7
Intangible assets and goodwill	677.3	672.4	682.3
Assets and capital employed	1,616.9	1,528.0	1,619.5
Total debt	467.9	616.2	724.9
Minority interest	106.3	105.5	102.5
Convertible debentures	21.4	23.0	24.9
Shareholders' equity	865.3	643.6	630.5
RATIOS			
Operating return on revenue	12%	11%	12%
Return on average shareholders' equity			
plus convertible debentures	10%	8%	8%
ANNUAL STOCK PRICES			
High	$ 13.00	$ 11.75	$ 12.38
Low	11.00	9.13	7.88
Close	12.13	11.50	9.63

	1989	1988	1987	1986	1985	1984	1983	1982
	$ 255.9	$ 219.7	$ 199.5	$ 177.8	$ 162.1	$ 137.1	$ 115.1	$ 92.6
	355.7	336.0	316.8	292.4	238.8	212.4	184.0	168.4
	353.6	337.6	293.6	237.7	134.9	125.9	100.2	95.6
	312.2	278.2	213.3	183.8	166.0	153.7	140.5	94.1
	77.8	72.2	69.0	53.3	51.1	52.1	51.5	51.4
	71.0	58.4	32.8	28.9	32.1	28.0	26.5	22.8
	1,426.2	1,302.1	1,125.0	973.9	785.0	709.2	617.8	524.9
	87.4	75.6	70.2	60.3	53.0	39.2	31.4	24.1
	29.2	32.7	34.1	32.9	27.5	24.4	14.4	10.3
	41.2	38.7	33.5	31.5	18.7	18.0	11.7	10.0
	15.7	26.3	35.0	26.7	23.4	20.8	19.9	8.2
	14.6	13.3	14.7	9.0	11.3	12.3	13.2	15.3
	9.0	9.4	7.2	6.1	6.8	5.6	4.8	3.7
	197.1	196.0	194.7	166.5	140.7	120.3	95.4	71.6
	87.1	93.6	82.8	69.5	59.7	49.5	31.0	21.8
	1.9	1.3	50.5	–	5.2	–	16.9	2.9
	$ 89.0	$ 94.9	$ 133.3	$ 69.5	$ 64.9	$ 49.5	$ 47.9	$ 24.7
	56¢	60¢	53¢	45¢	40¢	34¢	22¢	17¢
	1	1	32	–	3	–	12	2
	57¢	61¢	85¢	45¢	43¢	34¢	34¢	19¢
	$ 1.28	$ 1.10	$ 1.10	98¢	86¢	81¢	59¢	48¢
	24.3¢	21.0¢	17.5¢	15.4¢	12.6¢	9.6¢	8.5¢	8.3¢
	153,937	151,512	147,514	148,716	146,697	143,972	142,777	118,585
	159,492	159,016	160,073	158,229	155,331	150,797	142,412	141,244
	$ 202.0	$ 173.3	$ 174.2	$ 151.9	$ 131.6	$ 120.7	$ 82.3	$ 65.7
	62.0	723.7	58.8	96.2	35.2	7.5	122.5	71.7
	167.2	124.5	97.4	72.2	48.0	51.1	58.9	71.5
	37.8	32.5	26.9	23.0	18.6	14.2	11.6	10.1
	$ 78.0	$ 99.7	$ 140.9	$ 97.0	$ 127.4	$ 80.7	$ 27.1	$ 36.7
	589.7	446.0	370.4	338.7	303.0	298.6	288.4	268.7
	601.8	282.3	213.6	197.5	140.4	110.6	104.5	93.5
	1,545.4	1,604.1	884.2	821.0	733.2	657.9	548.5	415.6
	655.4	771.7	105.9	175.8	187.3	216.8	269.6	168.0
	110.5	107.5	106.8	82.2	71.3	61.3	36.4	31.7
	27.7	33.1	52.3	54.3	55.0	55.0	–	45.0
	607.1	551.5	479.6	392.6	318.3	247.9	203.9	119.5
	14%	15%	17%	17%	18%	17%	15%	14%
	15%	17%	17%	18%	18%	20%	18%	15%
	$ 14.25	$ 14.88	$ 12.88	$ 10.75	$ 7.82	$ 5.91	$ 4.66	$ 3.06
	11.50	9.88	8.25	7.32	5.50	4.10	2.63	2.00
	12.13	13.25	9.81	9.50	7.44	5.69	4.25	2.69

e   Are these financial statements prepared for a single legal entity or for a parent corporation and its subsidiaries?

f   What are the company's four major sources of revenue and which of these sources provides the largest operating income?

g   What are the company's accounting policies on unearned revenue?

h   What valuation method was used for inventories in 1992?

i   How much cash did the company spend during 1992 on additions to property, plant, and equipment and on business acquisitions?

j   How much are the expected capital expenditures for 1993?

k   What are the rates of return on average shareholders' equity plus convertible debentures for 1990, 1991, 1992? Are these rates increasing or decreasing?

l   Has the company maintained a stable dividend policy over the years 1990 to 1992? What is its dividend policy?

m   Indicate for the years 1992 and 1988 the following per share amount: (1) earnings, (2) cash dividends, and (3) stock price range (high and low).

**PART 2
Evaluation of
Credit Worthi-
ness**

Assume that in early 1993 you are the credit manager of a potential supplier of Maclean Hunter Limited. Maclean Hunter wants to make credit purchases from your company of between $5 million and $10 million per month, with payment due in 60 days.

INSTRUCTIONS   a   As part of your credit investigation, compute the following for the years ended December 31, 1992 and 1991. (Follow the company's policy of stating dollar amounts in millions.)

1 Current ratio.

2 Quick ratio.

3 Working capital.

4 Percentage of current assets comprised of cash and cash equivalents.

5 The increase (or decrease) in cash and cash equivalents in 1991 and 1992.

6 Accounts receivable turnover rate and the average number of days required to collect accounts receivable. (Assume that the 1990 accounts receivable amounted to $179.4 million.)

b   Does the company have lines of credit that could assist it in meeting its short-term obligations for cash payments?

c   Based upon your above analyses, has this company's liquidity *increased* or *decreased* during 1992? Explain. If you indicated that liquidity has decreased, explain whether you consider this a serious problem.

d   Your company assigns each customer one of the four credit ratings listed below. Assign a credit rating to Maclean Hunter and write a memorandum explaining your decision. (In your memorandum, you may use any of your computations in parts **a** or **b**, and may refer to other information in the financial statements and in the annual report.)

*POSSIBLE
CREDIT
RATINGS*

A   **Outstanding.**   Little or no risk of inability to pay. For customers in this category, we fill any reasonable order, without imposing a credit limit. The customer's credit is reevaluated annually.

B   **Good.**   Customer has good debt-paying ability, but is assigned a credit limit that is reviewed every six months. Orders above the established credit limit are accepted only on a cash basis.

C **Marginal.** Customer appears sound, but credit should be extended only on a 30-day basis with a relatively low credit limit. Credit status and credit limit are reevaluated every 90 days.

D **Unacceptable.** Customer does not qualify for credit.

PART 3
Analysis of
Common Stock

Assume that you are an investment advisor who publishes a monthly newsletter with recommendations to your clients as to whether to buy, hold, or sell specific stocks. One of the common stocks that you will evaluate this month is Maclean Hunter. It is now almost mid 1993, and the price of the company's common stock is *$12* per share.

INSTRUCTIONS a As a starting point, compute the following for the years ended December 31, 1992 and 1991. (Follow the company's policy of stating dollar amounts in millions, except for per share amounts. Round percentage computations to $\frac{1}{10}$ of 1%.)

1 Price-earnings ratio. (For 1992, use the current stock price of $12 per share; for 1991, use the high stock price for the year.)

2 Dividend yield. (Use the stock prices indicated in item **1**.)

3 Return on average total assets. Assume that the total assets for 1990 amounted to $1,844.2 (in millions).

4 Return on average shareholders' equity. Assume that the shareholders' equity for 1990 amounted to $630.5 (in millions).

5 Equity ratio.

b Prepare trend analyses of (1) total revenue, (2) net income, (3) dividends per share, and (4) highest market price per share for the three years from 1990 through 1992. (Use 1990 as the base year, which will be stated at 100% in each trend analysis. Round to the nearest percent.)

c Maclean Hunter has a target of paying 40% of the previous year's after-tax earnings as dividends. Write a memorandum indicating whether this target has been met in the past 3 years and evaluating the company's ability to meet this target in the near future without reducing its dividend of 25 cents per share.

d Write a brief memorandum on the topic of leverage as it relates to Maclean Hunter. Does the company make extensive use of long-term debt financing? Assuming that long-term interest rates are about 9%, would the use of long-term debt as a means of financing future growth be desirable from the viewpoint of common shareholders?

e Write a brief memorandum on the "quality" of the company's earnings. As a basis for this memorandum, review trends in the comparative income statements and in the 11-year summary. Also consider management's discussion and analysis of the company's operations results.

f Write a statement for your newsletter in which you recommend that your clients take one of the following actions with respect to Maclean Hunter's common stock:

Buy (Your positive recommendation; you think the market price of the stock will go up.)

Sell (Your negative recommendation; you feel that the stock is overpriced and will fall in value.)

Hold (A relatively neutral position: you feel that the stock is priced at a fair value with good but not exceptional prospects.)

Explain the reasoning behind your recommendation.

In addition to the information developed in other parts of this problem, your recommendation should consider the following facts about the economic environment in early and mid 1993.

The country had recently entered a recession. Corporate earnings were declining in many industries. Interest rates remained low. Many economists were forecasting a period of slow recovery and modest economic growth.

Dividend yields for growth-oriented companies ranged from zero to about 3%; for slow-growth companies, yields were from 5% to 7%.

g   Look up the current market price of Maclean Hunter's common stock in the financial pages of a newspaper. (The stock trades on the Toronto Stock Exchange.) How did your recommendation work out in the long run?

Index

‐ ‐ ‐ ‐ ‐ ‐ ‐ ‐ ‐ ‐ *cut here* ‐ ‐ ‐ ‐ ‐ ‐ ‐ ‐ ‐ ‐ ‐

STUDENT REPLY CARD

In order to improve future editions, we are seeking your comments on
ACCOUNTING: The Basis for Business Decisions, Seventh Canadian Edition,
Volume 2, by Meigs, Meigs, and Lam.
Please answer the following questions and return this form via Business Reply
Mail. Your opinions matter. Thank you in advance for sharing them with us!

Name of your college or university: _____

Major program of study: _____

Course title: _____

Were you required to buy this book? _____ yes _____ no

Did you buy this book new or used? _____ new _____ used ($_____)

Do you plan to keep or sell this book? _____ keep _____ sell

Is the order of topic coverage consistent with what was taught in your course?

‐ ‐ ‐ ‐ ‐ ‐ ‐ ‐ ‐ ‐ *fold here* ‐ ‐ ‐ ‐ ‐ ‐ ‐ ‐ ‐ ‐ ‐

Are there chapters or sections of this text that were not assigned for your course?
Please specify:

Were there topics covered in your course that are not included in the text?
Please specify:

What did you like most about this text?

What did you like least?

If you would like to say more, we would appreciate hearing from you. Please write
to us at the address shown on the reverse of this page.

- - - - - - - - - - - - - - - - *cut here* - - - - - - - - - - - - - - - ⌐
                                                                          ¦
                                                                          ¦
                                                                          ¦
                                                                          ¦
                                                                          ¦
                                                                          ¦
                                                                          ¦
                                                                          ¦
                                                                          ¦ *cut here*
- - - - - - - - - - - - - *fold here* - - - - - - - - - - - - - - - - - -

Postage will be paid by

MC
Graw
Hill

‖‖‖

<table>
<tr><td colspan="2">MAIL ⟫POSTE</td></tr>
<tr><td colspan="2">Canada Post Corporation / Société canadienne des postes</td></tr>
<tr><td>Postage paid
if mailed in Canada</td><td>Port payé
si posté au Canada</td></tr>
<tr><td>Business
Reply</td><td>Réponse
d'affaires</td></tr>
<tr><td>0183560299</td><td>01</td></tr>
</table>

⟫
⟫

‖‖‖‖‖‖‖‖‖‖‖‖‖‖‖‖‖‖‖‖‖‖‖‖‖‖‖‖‖‖‖‖‖‖‖

0183560299-L1N9B6-BR01

Attn.: Sponsoring Editor
College Division

MCGRAW-HILL RYERSON LIMITED
300 WATER ST
WHITBY ON   L1N 9Z9

tape shut

(continued from inside front cover)

15 A-3	(b) Retained earnings, $7,230,000
15 A-4	(a) Net income, $420,000
15 A-5	(1) Total shareholders' equity, $743,600
15 A-6	(b) Total shareholders' equity, $8,792,800
15 A-7	(a) Total contributed capital, $4,990,000; (b) retained earnings, $874,000
15 B-1	(a) Income before extraordinary items, $11,820,000
15 B-2	(a) Retained earnings, $606,800
15 B-3	(b) Retained earnings, $8,220,000
15 B-4	(a) Net income, $190,000
15 B-5	(1) Total shareholders' equity, $4,578,000
15 B-6	(b) Total shareholders' equity, $9,318,000
15 B-7	(b) Retained earnings, $469,800
16-1	(c) Bond interest expense, $1,500,000
16-2	(b) Long-term liabilities, $58,880,000
16-3	(b) Carrying value of bond liability, bonds issued at 101, $60,560,000
16-4	(c) (1) Long-term liabilities, $29,570,000
16-5	(c) (1) Long-term liabilities, $80,800,000
16-6	(b) Gain on retirement of bonds, $8,800
16-7	(b) Loss on early retirement of bonds, $76,480
16-8	(a) (2) Amortization of discount, $5,400
16-9	(c) Long-term liabilities, $9,473,818
16-10	(c) Long-term liabilities, $10,189,225
16-11	(c) Liability, bonds issued at discount, $8,706,000
16-12	No key figure
16-13	(d) Lease payment obligation, $23,870
16-14	(a) Total liabilities, $1,088,620
CP-4	(c) (1) Net income, $383,710; (c) (3) total assets, $32,067,410

Appendix A

1	(d) Present value, $96,120
2	(a) Issuance price, $9,428,500
3	(c) Liability, Dec. 31, $23,197
4	(a) Present value of payments, 10-year lease, $8,032,300
5	(d) Lease payment obligation, Dec. 31, $40,184
6	(b) (2) Discount on Notes Receivable, $259,920
17 A-1	(b) (2) Gain on sale, $3,700
17 A-2	No key figure
17 A-3	(b) Market value, $305,000
17 A-4	(b) (3) Carrying value, Dec. 31, 1996, $4,995,000
17 A-5	(c) Consolidated total assets, $7,525,000
17 A-6	Consolidated total assets, $3,928,000
17 A-7	Consolidated total assets, $1,204,000
17 B-1	(b) (2) Loss on sale, $5,600
17 B-2	No key figure

17 B-3	(b) Market value, $224,000
17 B-4	(b) (3) Carrying value, Dec. 31, 1997, $1,710,000
17 B-5	(c) Consolidated total assets, $10,670,000
17 B-6	Consolidated total assets, $7,760,000
17 B-7	Consolidated total assets, $1,326,000
18 A-1	No key figure
18 A-2	No key figure
18 A-3	Taxable income, $79,920
18 A-4	(a) Capital cost allowance, $225,000
18 A-5	(a) Accounting income, $969,000
18 B-1	No key figure
18 B-2	No key figure
18 B-3	Taxable income, $75,470
18 B-4	(a) Capital cost allowance, $160,000
18 B-5	(a) Accounting income, $150,000
19 A-1	No key figure
19 A-2	Cash provided by operating activities, $514,000
19 A-3	(b) Cash provided by operating activities, $155,000
19 A-4	Cash provided by operating activities, $155,000
19 A-5	(b) Cash provided by operating activities, $204,000
19 A-6	(c) Cash provided by operating activities, $166,000
19 A-7	(c) Cash used in investing activities, $80,000
19 B-1	No key figure
19 B-2	No key figure
19 B-3	(b) Cash provided by operating activities, $144,000
19 B-4	Cash provided by operating activities, $144,000
19 B-5	(b) Cash provided by operating activities, $1,020,000
19 B-6	(c) Cash provided by operating activities, $1,000
19 B-7	(c) Cash provided by operating activities, $580,000
20-1	(a) Net sales, 1995, $2,520,000
20-2	(a) Net income, Sub Zero, 7%
20-3	(c) Operating cycle, 119.8 days
20-4	(a) (6) Return on average assets, 16%
20-5	(a) (3) Operating expenses, $270,000
20-6	(a) (6) Operating cycle, Mondo, 192 days
20-7	(a) (6) Operating cycle, Imports, 168 days
20-8	(b) (3) Working capital, $1,296,000
20-9	No key figure
20-10	Total assets, $1,000; net sales, $1,280
20-11	(c) Price-earnings ratio, Continental, 9.1 times
20-12	(a) (9) Interest coverage ratio, PepsiCo, 2.9 times
CP-5	Part 1: No key figure
	Part 2: (a) (6) Accounts receivable turnover rate, 1992, 42 days